DECOLONISATION, ANTI-RACISM, AND LEGAL PEDAGOGY

This book offers an international breadth of historical and theoretical insights into recent efforts to "decolonise" legal education across the world.

With a specific focus on post- and decolonial thought and anti-racist methods in pedagogy, this edited collection provides an accessible illustration of pedagogical innovation in teaching and learning law. Chapters cover civil and common law legal systems, incorporate cases from non-state Indigenous legal systems, and critically examine key topics such as decolonisation and anti-racism in criminology, colonialism and the British Empire, and court process and Indigenous justice. The book demonstrates how teaching can be modified and adapted to address long-standing injustice in the curriculum.

Offering a systematic collection of theoretical and practical examples of anti-racist and decolonial legal pedagogy, this volume will appeal to curriculum designers and law educators as well as to undergraduate and post-graduate level law teachers and researchers.

Foluke I Adebisi is an Associate Professor in Law at the University of Bristol, UK.

Suhraiya Jivraj is a Reader in Law and Social Justice at the University of Kent, UK.

Ntina Tzouvala is an Associate Professor at the Australian National University College of Law and a Global Fellow at the Centre for International Law of the National University of Singapore.

Legal Pedagogy

Series Editor

Kris Gledhill, *Auckland University of Technology, New Zealand*

This series consists of high-quality monographs, each of which explores best practice in an aspect of the law school curriculum. Books cover teaching methods and curriculum design in the main areas of law, how to integrate themes and areas of jurisprudential thought, and wider questions about legal education more generally. With contributions from around the world, this series explores innovative thinking and practice within the context of a generally conservative branch of academia, with the aim of promoting discussion as to how best to teach the various aspects of the law degree and ensure the ongoing validity of the law degree as a whole. Typical topics addressed include the value of variety in teaching methods and curriculum design, how best to incorporate educational research, the role for more practical courses, and the need to ensure that law schools provide degrees of relevance to the needs of students and of society.

The books in this series will be of great interest to academics, researchers and postgraduates in the fields of law and education, as well as teachers of law who may be interested in revising curricula and need guidance in doing so. In addition, the legal profession, and in particular those who regulate entry into the profession, will find much to interest them within the series.

Books in this series:

Teaching Family Law
Reflections on Pedagogy and Practice
Edited by Henry Kha and Mark Henaghan

Decolonisation, Anti-Racism, and Legal Pedagogy
Strategies, Successes, and Challenges
Edited by Foluke I Adebisi, Suhraiya Jivraj, and Ntina Tzouvala

For more information about books in this series, please visit https://www.routledge.com/Legal-Pedagogy/book-series/LEGPED

DECOLONISATION, ANTI-RACISM, AND LEGAL PEDAGOGY

Strategies, Successes, and Challenges

Edited by Foluke I Adebisi, Suhraiya Jivraj, and Ntina Tzouvala

Routledge
Taylor & Francis Group
LONDON AND NEW YORK

Designed cover image: © Getty Images

First published 2024
by Routledge
4 Park Square, Milton Park, Abingdon, Oxon OX14 4RN

and by Routledge
605 Third Avenue, New York, NY 10158

Routledge is an imprint of the Taylor & Francis Group, an informa business

British Library Cataloguing-in-Publication Data
A catalogue record for this book is available from the British Library

Library of Congress Cataloging-in-Publication Data
Names: Adébísí, Folúké, editor. | Jivraj, Suhraiya, editor. |
Tzouvala, Ntina, editor.
Title: Decolonisation, anti-racism, and legal pedagogy : strategies, successes, and challenges / edited by Foluke Adebisi, Suhraiya Jivraj, and Ntina Tzouvala.
Description: Abingdon, Oxon [UK] ; New York, NY : Routledge, 2024. |
Series: Legal pedagogy | Includes bibliographical references and index.
Identifiers: LCCN 2023034381 (print) | LCCN 2023034382 (ebook) | ISBN 9781032503097 (hardback) | ISBN 9781032498249 (paperback) | ISBN 9781003397885 (ebook)
Subjects: LCSH: Law--Study and teaching--Social aspects |
Decolonization--Philosophy. | Postcolonialism--Philosophy. |
Anti-racism.
Classification: LCC K100 .D43 2024 (print) | LCC K100 (ebook) | DDC 340.071--dc23/eng/20231002
LC record available at https://lccn.loc.gov/2023034381
LC ebook record available at https://lccn.loc.gov/2023034382

ISBN: 978-1-032-50309-7 (hbk)
ISBN: 978-1-032-49824-9 (pbk)
ISBN: 978-1-003-39788-5 (ebk)

DOI: 10.4324/9781003397885

Typeset in Times New Roman
by SPi Technologies India Pvt Ltd (Straive)

CONTENTS

ILLUSTRATIONS

Figures

Table

EDITORS

Foluke I Adebisi is a Professor in Law at the University of Bristol, UK. Her scholarship focuses mainly on the relationship between theories of decolonisation and how they do and can interact with legal knowledge. She writes widely in this area, including editing a special issue for the *Law Teacher* journal on decolonisation in 2019. She founded and runs Forever Africa Conference and Events (FACE), a Pan-African inter-disciplinary conference. She blogs about her scholarship and pedagogy on her website "Foluke's African Skies" at https://FolukeAfrica.com. Her monograph *Decolonisation and Legal Knowledge: Reflections on Power and Possibility* was published in March 2023.

Suhraiya Jivraj is a Reader in Law and Social Justice at the University of Kent, UK. She is Co-Director of the Centre for Sexuality, Race & Gender Justice and previous founding Co-ordinator of the Decolonizing Sexualities Network until 2021. Her publications include *Decolonizing Sexualities: Transnational Perspectives, Critical Interventions* (2016) and co-authored collection with her students of colour: *Towards Decolonising the University: A Kaleidoscope for Empowered Action* (2020). She is also author of the SLSA-funded resource for law school teachers: *Towards an Anti-racist Legal Pedagogy* (2020).

Ntina Tzouvala is an Associate Professor at the Australian National University College of Law and a Global Fellow at the Centre for International Law of the National University of Singapore. Her work focuses on the history, theory, and political economy of international law. Her first monograph, *Capitalism as Civilisation: A History of International Law*, was published in 2020, and it was awarded the 2022 ASIL Certificate of Merit for a preeminent contribution to creative scholarship and the Australian Legal Research Award (ALRA) in the book category.

CONTRIBUTORS

Sahar Ahmed is an Assistant Professor of Law at University College Dublin's Sutherland School of Law. Sahar holds a PhD on the intersection of law, religion, and human rights; she places a lot of importance on public-facing scholarship and routinely publishes her research in widely accessible blogs and journals. Sahar is a barrister member of the Honourable Society of Gray's Inn and has practised as a commercial and corporate barrister in Lahore, appearing before the courts as an Advocate of the High Courts of Pakistan.

Fady Aoun is a Senior Lecturer at the University of Sydney Law School and is admitted to practice law in New South Wales. His research and teaching interests are mainly in intellectual property, legal history, and corporations law. He has a strong commitment to legal education and teaches across a range of undergraduate and post-graduate students. Fady completed his doctoral thesis on the law, theory, and policy relating to stigmatising trade marks.

Phoebe Boateng is an LLB Law graduate from Keele University. During her undergraduate degree, she became interested in the growing Decolonise Keele Network (DKN). Her involvement in this network informed the optional modules that she chose in her penultimate and final year of study and pushed her to reflect on how and what she is taught within the law school and her approach to critical thinking. The work that Phoebe did as part of DKN led her to put together a case study on Boohoo and modern slavery in the UK for her dissertation with a focus on post-colonialism and feminism.

Louise Boon-Kuo works as a Senior Lecturer at the University of Sydney Law School. Louise's research focuses on the interplay between criminal and immigration law systems, and the impacts of law and policing on racialised communities. Louise is committed to teaching compulsory law subjects in part because of their potential to transform student thinking on core legal issues and established an elective to enable students to delve further into the relation between race and the law.

Cristy Clark was raised in Ngunnawal Country. She is an Associate Professor of Law in the Faculty of Business, Government and Law at the University of Canberra, Australia. Her research focuses on legal geography, the commons, and the intersection of human rights, activism, and the environment.

Bridget Fa'amatuainu is a Lecturer in Law at the Auckland University of Technology School of Law, New Zealand (Aotearoa). Bridget is finalising a PhD by publication exploring the Talanoa approach to law reform and recognition of fa'atama in Samoa. Bridget's research interests are law reform, legal pluralism, private law in the Pacific; Samoa critical legal theory and gender methodology; socioeconomic justice and meaningful access to justice; self-represented litigation; critical legal education and Pasifika decolonial pedagogies in law teaching. Bridget is also working on the second edition of *Commercial Law in the South Pacific* with Professor Mohammed Ahmadu (forthcoming, Routledge 2024).

Chaumtoli Huq is an Associate Professor of Law at City University New York (CUNY) School of Law and the Founder/Editor of an innovative non-profit focused on law and social justice called Law@theMargins. Her expertise lies in labour and employment, and human rights. Her professional career is devoted to public service focusing on issues impacting low-income New Yorkers. In 2014, she was appointed as the General Counsel for Litigation for the New York City Office of the Public Advocate, becoming then the highest-ranking Bangladeshi-American in New York City government, for which she received a New American Heroes award from the New American Leaders Project. Along with holding leadership roles at Legal Services of NYC and MFY Legal Services, she also served as Director of the first South Asian Workers' Rights Project at the Asian American Legal Defense and Education Fund, the first staff attorney to the New York Taxi Workers Alliance, and has served Community Board 7 for the Upper West Side.

Sarah Keenan was raised on Giabal and Jarowair land in Toowoomba, "Australia," and now works at Birkbeck Law School, where she co-founded the Centre for Research on Race and Law. Her work sits at the intersection of legal and political thought, geography, feminist theory, and postcolonial studies. Sarah is particularly interested in the malleability of property and how it might be reshaped for a better world.

Amanda Kramer is a Lecturer in Law at Queen's University Belfast. Her research focuses mainly on two areas: the consequences of Brexit and critical perspectives on international law (with a particular concentration on postcolonial and decolonial theory).

Helene Love is an Assistant Professor at Simon Fraser University, Canada. She teaches and conducts research in the areas of criminal law, criminal procedure, and the rules of evidence.

C. P. McGrath is a Senior Lecturer in Tort Law at the Dickson Poon School of Law, King's College London, and an Academic Fellow of the Middle Temple. His research focuses on comparative private law and professional liability in both the common law and civilian legal traditions. He is joint General Editor of the *Journal of Professional Negligence* in the UK and a Fellow and Member of the European Centre of Tort and Insurance Law in Vienna.

Sumayyah Malna is a pro bono lawyer and lecturer of law at the University of Bristol, UK. As a practising solicitor, she runs cases with students through the University of Bristol Law Clinic. Her practice expertise is in inquests, family law, and medical law. She has a particular interest in how race and racism impact the construction and experience of the law.

Aysha Mazhar is a PhD candidate based at Keele University, UK. Her doctoral research explores the manifestations of compassion in legal academia in the jurisdiction of England and Wales. Her further work outside of her PhD covers doctoral education and on decolonising legal education. Additionally, Aysha's works have appeared in journals such as *The Law Teacher* and the *British Journal of Educational Studies*. Aysha holds a BA (Hons) in History, a Graduate Diploma in Law (Common Professional Examination), and a Master of Laws.

Tanya Mitchell is a Senior Lecturer at the University of Sydney Law School, where she specialises in criminal law and procedure. She wrote her PhD thesis on the transformation of the summary criminal jurisdiction into a mechanism of social control. She has also taught the elective subject Indigenous Peoples and the Law. Before moving into academia, Tanya was a senior solicitor-advocate at the New South Wales Aboriginal Legal Service.

Tamara O'Doherty is a Senior Lecturer in the School of Criminology at Simon Fraser University in British Columbia, Canada. In addition to nearly two decades of teaching in higher education and conducting related pedagogical inquiry, Tamara maintains a strong research and publication portfolio related to human rights, criminalisation, human trafficking, and participatory and legal research methods.

Kate Ogg is an Associate Professor and Associate Dean (Higher Degree Research) at the ANU College of Law, Australian National University. Her areas of research are refugee law, human rights, litigation, and feminist legal theory and method. Kate is the author of *Protection from Refuge: From Refugee Rights to Migration Management* (2022). The monograph is the first global and comparative examination of the role courts play in refugee journeys. In 2021, Kate was part of a team that was awarded an Australian Research Council Discovery Project Grant to conduct a study on private refugee sponsorship.

John Page is a Professor in the School of Private and Commercial Law in the Faculty of Law & Justice at the University of New South Wales. John is a scholar of critical property law and theory, and the legal geography of property diversity.

Alice Panepinto is a Senior Lecturer in Law at Queen's University Belfast. Her research mainly explores international law and human rights, with a regional interest in the Middle East.

Gulika Reddy is an Assistant Professor and the Director of the International Human Rights and Conflict Resolution Clinic at Stanford Law School. Reddy has conducted human rights advocacy around the world, including in India, Kashmir, Yemen, the Central African Republic, Jamaica, and Papua New Guinea. Her work has focused on inequality, discrimination, armed conflict, peacebuilding, and the role of education in unlearning bias and fostering inclusion. Her academic research interests include critical perspectives on human rights, decolonial and anti-racist pedagogy, and the intersection between human rights and peacebuilding.

Yvette Russell is an Associate Professor in Law and Feminist Theory at the University of Bristol Law School, UK. She has published widely on law, sexual violence, and feminist philosophy and is the author (with Joanne Conaghan) of *Sexual History Evidence and the Rape Trial* (2023).

Ntando Sindane is a Lecturer at the Department of Private Law in the University of the Free State, South Africa. Currently, he is interested in, and is thinking about, the fatuous relationship between capitalism and the global intellectual property rights regime. He holds LLB and LLM degrees from the University of South Africa and is a PhD candidate in Intellectual Property Law (University of Cape Town). His ongoing PhD thesis is titled "Abezimu/Badimo (ancestors) and Copyright Law: From the *Decolonial Turn* to the Pluriversal Author." He is an ardent follower of Test Cricket and an undying supporter of Kaizer Chiefs Football club, #Amakhosi4Life!

Sophia Hayat Taha is a PhD candidate at Keele University. Her PhD uses an inter-disciplinary approach combining Law and International Relations to allow for a different understanding of how the state interacts with migrant women, moving away from a Eurocentric interpretation of law. The project combines postcolonial legal methodology with empirical research in local partner agency, Staffordshire North and Stoke-on-Trent Citizens Advice (SNSCA). She also works on projects covering digital exclusion, international students' learning environments during lockdown and decolonising the curriculum. Sophia holds a BSc (Hons) in Physics, a PGDip in International Relations and Security Studies, an MA in International Relations, and an MRes in Social Science Research Methods.

Marsha-Ann Scott is a PhD candidate at Simon Fraser University's School of Criminology and a social justice advocate. She critically assesses systems/programmes/policies to identify colonial and/or racist underpinnings with a view to making change. Her research interests include post-colonialism and anti-colonialism, decolonisation, critical criminology, comparative criminal justice, particularly informal justice systems of the Global South, and garrison communities and their effect on Jamaican society.

Asmi Wood is a Professor of Law at the Australian National University, Principal Fellow of the Higher Education Academy (UK), and a barrister and solicitor. He supports the ANU College of Law Indigenous Programme and works closely with the Tjabal Centre. His areas of research and teaching interest include legal ethics, constitutional law, international law, and the treatment of Indigenous peoples within legal frameworks other than their own normative systems. He serves on the Attorney-General's Constitutional Expert Group on an Indigenous Voice to the Parliament.

FOREWORD

Towards Decolonising Legal Pedagogy: Multijurisdictional Methods, Actions, and Perspectives

How to decolonise the law? This question has been raised and answered in myriad ways by an impressive group of scholars, particularly those from the Global South, including Antony Anghie, Makau Mutua, Sylvia Tamale, and others. The issue concerning decolonisation of law emanates from and is inextricably linked to the wider question of decolonisation, which, as we know, has been confronted, contested, and challenged since the end of colonialism. Such contestations play out in the writings of Franz Fanon, Amilcar Cabral, and others, as well as in the literature examining the colonial period and its aftermath in the postcolonial era.

Decolonisation, in its original iteration, signalled the end of the formal structures of colonial rule. In addition to ending formal rule by the imperial powers, decolonisation entailed the transfer of political power, various modes of reparations including return of land and control of commodities, and an erasure of the colonial order. But the end of colonial rule inevitably spawned contesting theoretical perspectives resulting in the term itself sometimes defying meaning. Still a contested concept and embodying several definitions, decolonisation has been described by Achille Mbembe as a project of "re-centering."[1]

But was there an end to colonialism? The attempts to construct a defining moment between colonisation and decolonisation seem futile in the face of the continuities embedded in the transition from the colonial project. Within these continuities, there existed a certain vision of society that mapped hierarchies of power in the political, legal, and social spheres, with the privileging of an economic order that was predicated on production and extraction. The intellectual tools necessary to confront these deep and vast inherited problems following the formal end of colonialism and disrupt the hierarchies of power were entwined with methodologies and epistemologies, a by-product of colonialism, from which decolonial advocates and scholars were seeking liberation. According to Mahmood Mamdani, decolonisation "has moved from one limited to political independence" and external domination "to a broader transformation of institutions," especially those institutions that were "critical to the reproduction of racial and ethnic subjectivities legally enforced under colonialism," as universities arguably were.[2]

In the past few decades, decolonisation and anti-racist discourses have provided discursive spaces in law schools across the globe to engage in a range of questions regarding the seminal questions of legal education more generally, and legal pedagogy, specifically. Traditional methodologies and trusted epistemologies of legal knowledge have encountered the imperative of transformative legal education models that are mandated in the conditions of what Achille Mbembe refers to as the postcolony.[3] In the past three years, the conditions of the post-pandemic have also contributed to the transformative impulse. This transformation seeks a reimagining of the structural underpinnings of legal pedagogy, including its hierarchical edifice, modes of knowledge production, and its relationship to the wider community in which it operates. It calls for the embrace of more plural forms of knowledge and warns against cynical attempts to decolonise the university through rhetoric and not substance, resulting in what Boateng, Mazhar, and Hayat Taha refer to as the "colonisation of decolonising."[4]

The chapters in this volume stimulate a range of piercing questions, some original and others not novel but worthy of constant evaluation. The editors and contributors, a talented and thoughtful array of inter-disciplinary scholars, explore the possibilities and limitations to the decolonial and anti-racist turn in legal pedagogy. Indeed, the editors are thought leaders in the decolonial and anti-racist space in the legal academy. Combining theory and practice, the individual chapters examine the philosophical, historical, and political debates within the various initiatives to decolonise legal pedagogy, while also offering practical strategies to accompany the transformative project in pursuit of decolonising legal pedagogies.

The contributions in this volume represent a range of legal pedagogy traditions and jurisdictions from both the common and civil law systems. They incorporate perspectives from the Global South and elsewhere, as well as from Indigenous and non-state jurisdictions. Their perspectives embrace a range of public and private law areas, offering a comprehensive examination of legal education that is provocative and thoughtful. Their struggle with the complexity and contradictions inherent in research and scholarship on this topic is transparent and candid.

This volume intersects with some of the most compelling and significant theoretical insights of the past few decades, drawing from critical race theory, feminist legal theory, third-world approaches to international law (TWAIL), and decolonial theory. Utilising the insights of critical race and feminist theory, for example, the volume offers personal narrative and exploration of the personal experiences of protagonists – either as agent or subject.

The sweep of the global and local renders the volume particularly rich. The remnants of the United Kingdom's imperial legacies in legal education are distributed globally and not just in the Global South, but in places like Northern Ireland, where scholars are engaged in decolonial projects to develop a legal culture and legal pedagogies bereft of their colonial inheritances. We also observe the impact of the #FeesMustFall movement on South African universities and the missed opportunities on the part of the legal academy to engage in a purposive project of decolonising legal pedagogy. The impediments to the incorporation of Pasifika pedagogies to transform Indigenous private law, as well as the dearth of legal scholarship written by Indigenous scholars in New Zealand, are highlighted, "bound by the structural and institutional coloniality of a Eurocentric and western, as well as the death of university system."[5] Similarly, the myths and destruction of *terra nullius* are exploded to highlight the continuous subordination of and discrimination against Indigenous peoples and their ongoing quest for self-determination. Indeed, the entire edifice of international law, including human rights law, and its role as the handmaiden of colonisation and exploitation are rigorously examined. Through their critiques, they provide us with the tools to reimagine moral approaches to the international legal order in the hope of its transformation.

Like an archaeological dig, uncovering the issues layer by layer, the discrete areas of the law are uncovered and exposed in all their colonial trappings. This exposure is an essential step to creating the conditions for a decolonised legal education committed to social justice and anti-racist goals. So, the prevalence of the "ordinary person" standard in Australia in both public and private law is subjected to a decolonial reorientation through an examination of criminal and trade mark law. So too the reasonable person standard in contract law in the United States is subjected to a decolonial redirection. The field of criminology too comes under the spotlight. The structural and substantive challenges to teaching tort law in a decolonised and anti-racist way in Canada are highlighted. Decolonisation attempts at alternative pedagogies are also pursued through a reimagining of civil procedure in Australia, exposing its structure and content as more than legal technicalities but in fact conducive to continuing colonisation.

Clinical legal pedagogy, seemingly the most promising corner of the law school curriculum for disrupting hegemonic approaches and practices, is considered as a powerful site for decoloniality in the legal academy. It is in this space that contestations around identity and pedagogy may be pursued through an anti-racist, decolonial, and intersectional lens.

The research produced in this volume is impactful and of significant scholarly merit. The focus and objectives of each chapter, its local, comparative, and global strategy and research approach demonstrate innovative and creative thought. The volume will no doubt make a huge contribution to the research and literature in the field of critical and decolonial pedagogies. Each contributor has articulated an inspired and reimagined way of considering the transformative possibilities of a decolonised approach to legal pedagogy and its enormous potential to contribute to social justice. The volume will comprehensively engage the profound issues that have been and continue to be raised by historical and contemporary debates around decolonising the law school curricula and their attendant pedagogies. The contributions to this volume sharpen our sense of what is at stake in the transformation of the legal academy at this pivotal historical moment. At local and global levels, the volume also has the potential to contribute to law reform and legal culture more generally.

Professor Penelope (Penny) Andrews
John Marshall Harlan II Professor
Director, Racial Justice Project
New York Law School

Notes

1 Mbembe, Achille. Decolonizing Knowledge and the Question of the Archive, at: http://wiser.wits.ac.za/system/files/Achille%20Mbembe%20-%20Decolonizing%20Knowledge%20and%20the%20Question%20of%20the%20Archive.pdf
2 Mahmood Mamdani, Between the Public Intellectual and the Scholar: Decolonization and Some Post-Independence Initiatives in African Higher Education, at: http://www.tandfonline.com/doi/full/10.1080/14649373.2016.1140260
3 Achille Mbebme, on the Postcolony (2001).
4 Phoebe Boateng, Aysha Mazhar and Sophia Hayat Taha, *Abolish the Law School: To Decolonise is Disingenous* (in this volume).
5 Bridget Fa'amatuainu, *Pasifika decolonial pedagogies in Indigenous Private Law teaching* (in this volume).

EDITORS' ACKNOWLEDGEMENTS

To say that this was an enjoyable and meaningful project for all three of us is not the same as saying that it was an easy one. Punctuated by pandemics, industrial action, and personal disasters (and triumphs), this project was eventually possible due to the dedication, generosity, and good humour of this volume's contributors. Their willingness to discuss their teaching experiments including at online workshops in July 2022, to theorise out of practice, and – above all – their patience with "one more round of comments" are the beating heart of this volume. We thank each and every one of them, and we are looking forward to staying engaged with their thoughtful work. Professor Penelope Andrews and Dr Tshepo Madlingozi read this book and wrote generous and generative comments about it. We are grateful for their time and for their own indispensable work on legal pedagogy.

When we first embarked on this project in 2021, we decided to rely on an open call for papers, rather than on individualised invitations. What we did not expect was the volume of responses that this public call would elicit. As a result, we had to make tough choices about whose work would be eventually included in this volume. Nevertheless, we are grateful to everyone who has shown interest in this project. They are comrades and fellow travellers in a project that far exceeds the bounds of this, or any, book.

Allow us to come back to this book, though, which would not have existed without the invitation, encouragement, patience, and work of the series editor, Professor Kris Gledhill. Kris showed remarkable faith in this project since its inception and has been generous with his time and insights ever since. We are also thankful to Routledge for its commitment to quality publications on legal pedagogy and, in particular, to AnnaMary Goodall for all her work on this book. We also acknowledge with gratitude the work and dedication of typesetters, copy-editors, and printers who transformed our manuscript into a book – properly – so-called.

This volume was very much inspired by the challenges and breakthroughs of our own teaching practices, and none of us embarks on teaching alone. Discussions with our colleagues and students over the years have shaped on thinking and practice in regard to the possibility of an anti-racist, decolonised law classroom. These interlocutors are too many to thank by name, but their influence on this book has been profound.

Finally, we want to thank our families and friends for their patience and support while we were working on this project. This book is dedicated to them.

INTRODUCTION

Decolonisation, Anti-Racism, and Legal Pedagogy

Introduction

To talk about "decolonisation" in relation to the law school is to enter a perilous terrain. Few terms have gained prominence so fast, while triggering seemingly never-ending debates about their meaning, agents, goals, and preconditions. The demand to build broad alliances that will facilitate change has to be balanced against theoretical and political clarity and a dedication to the radical origins and aims of decolonisation as a pedagogical endeavour with broader aspirations for social transformation. Trying to strike this balance in the context of a law school is even more complicated: it requires reflecting on the role of law in society and, in particular, its complicity in the construction of capitalist modernity and its ideological justifications (Tzouvala 2020) and on whether and to what extent it can nevertheless be used to promote the interests of the oppressed (Matsuda 1991). It also demands that we reflect on the purposes of the law school as an institution and to what extent they can be reconciled with each other and with decolonisation, especially if the latter is understood as entailing (much) more than "diversity" (Adebisi 2022). It is not lost on us that law schools have not historically been bastions of radicalism (at least not in the Global North) and that this is both due to the demographics of teachers and students, as well as because of the nature of the subject matter. Hierarchy, deference to authority, rationalisation of power and violence, and mystification of both poverty and wealth seem to be at the core of legal education. Even scholars with radical research agendas often struggle to teach in ways that go against these tendencies (Kennedy 2004; Thornton 1998: 337). This is partly due to constraints posed by the law school environment, an issue that we will address shortly. At the same time, we cannot ignore systematic

DOI: 10.4324/9781003397885-1

undervaluing of both teaching and research concerning pedagogy within the modern law school. As teaching loads become unsustainable and pedagogical work remains feminised and undervalued, engaging in a scholarly and self-reflexive manner with our teaching may be seen as a distraction from "real" research. We, obviously, disagree with this approach. In fact, we are convinced that work on legal teaching can bring together different methods: "traditional" theory and storytelling, quantitative methods and personal narrative, doctrine and law-in-context work. The chapters of this volume evidence that pedagogical research can be methodologically innovative and rigorous and that taking teaching seriously can change our understanding of our own subject.

At the same time, and despite institutional commitments to "decolonise," the structure, demographics, and goals of the law school pose challenges for those who want to implement radical reforms. Broadening access to higher education has led to relative diversification of both staff and students, but law schools, especially in elite universities, remain disproportionately rich and white in the Global North (or over-representative of other dominant social groups in non-white majority contexts). This means that many of our students and colleagues will be indifferent or even hostile towards efforts to remake our curricula and classroom practices insofar as the legal system protects their material interests and reproduces their worldview. Additionally, the fact that law remains a form of vocational training means that the political economy, practices, and ethos of the legal profession exert unique influence over our teaching, not least because of mounting pressures to ensure that graduates are "job ready." This means that reform and change in the law school remain – to an extent – captive of reform and change in the legal profession. For example, feminist scholars, such as Thornton, have argued that in many jurisdictions the number of female law students has increased rapidly, but the predominance of masculine values remains largely unchallenged (Thornton 2013). Feminists have attributed this contradiction to the fact that most (elite) law schools still operate as conveyor belts for commercial legal practice, where aggression, overwork, and an amoral approach to one's profession continue to predominate.

When we find, then, ourselves in such perilous terrains, it is worth remembering that we are not the first ones to have attempted this journey. This is a matter of both intellectual honesty and self-preservation. It is widely known that the asymmetries of power, material resources, and prestige that characterise legal academia worldwide lead systematically to the erasure of the work and insights of racialised people, especially women of colour, and to that of scholars based in the Global South or historically racialised and less privileged institutions in the Global North (Naqvi et al. 2019; Tan 2021). At the same time, the current historical moment may be unique, but this does not mean that it bears no resemblance to earlier historical instances or that the current push towards decolonising the university is without its own history and genealogy. The most immediate trigger was, of course, the demand that

#RhodesMustFall, which emerged at the University of Cape Town (UCT) in early 2015 and quickly spread across South Africa and beyond. The movement quickly broadened its focus demanding that #FeesMustFall and raising broader issues about higher education in post-Apartheid South Africa, where racial inequality remains a central feature of social organisation, despite the end of legalised white supremacy (Ndlovu-Gatsheni 2018; 37). South African students and scholars, then, have led contemporary debates about decolonising higher education, and this is because its history and present circumstances might be unique, but they are by no means unparalleled (Mamdani 2018). White-majority settler colonies have also been struggling with the ongoing reality of Indigenous legal orders and with the well-documented complicity of settler law with both physical and cultural genocide against Indigenous peoples (Behrendt 2001; Starblanket 2018; Mutu 2019). These struggles have not culminated in a wholesale questioning of settler legal education, even as limited reforms have been carried out to at least reflect the (partial and delayed) recognition of Indigenous legal systems by settler courts (Watson 2005; Williams 2021; Xavier et al. 2021).

All this is to say that a top-down or Western-centric understanding of efforts to decolonise legal pedagogy would be both historically inaccurate and politically misguided. The same applies to an understanding of decolonisation as confined to 21st-century "identity politics" and to the recent push for "diversity and inclusion." This is an accusation frequently articulated by the political Right, which sees such initiatives as a threat to its escalating embrace of white identity politics and colonial apology. It is also a concern articulated by parts of the political Left, who raise concerns about the (purported) over-emphasis of the movement on representation and ideas instead of material structures. This concern correctly identifies the shortcomings of the liberal and neoliberal visions of "decolonisation" (we are using the inverted commas advisedly). These at best reduce "decolonisation" to diversification of the existing structures of legal education and at worst turn "decolonisation" into a motor for further marketisation of higher education and for the extraction of even more unpaid labour by staff and students (Bhambra et al. 2020: 4). However, reducing the movement to some of its contemporary (neo)liberal iterations obscures its deep roots in a move that – paradoxically – shows undue deference to its most conservative representatives. Rather, there is both intellectual and political value in situating current initiatives within a broader lineage of thinking deeply about the role of legal education and attempting to reform the law school away from its colonial roots.

In the aftermath of formal decolonisation, post-colonial leaders, scholars, students, and lawyers as well as their Western counterparts were keenly aware that the shape of legal education would be consequential far beyond law faculties. The establishment of law schools was particularly important in post-colonial African states, where colonisers had decided against establishing local law schools due to what they perceived as the dangerous precedent of India, where law schools turned out to be fertile grounds for nationalist mobilisation (Ghai 1987: 751). However, the emergence of new law schools in the continent was anything but seamless. The relevant struggles are often recounted as clashes between foreigners and Africanisers or between Britain and the United States in order to export their legal pedagogy paradigms (Ross 1973; Harrington & Manji 2019). There is undeniable truth to these divisions, but the debates and divergences went much deeper as did the influence of these experiments. The famously radical law faculty of Dar-es-Salaam became a centre of experimentation and genuine intellectual innovation in ways that radiated well beyond Tanzania (at the time Tanganyika) and Africa. Both the more conservative and the more radical members of the faculty rejected legal formalism in both their teaching and their research. Instead, a distinctive tradition of "law in context" was developed with a view of educating students about the distinct legal challenges faced by East African states and peoples (Harrington & Manji 2017: 703). Some drew inspiration from the US "law and development" movement, while others relied on dependency theory and Marxism. Importantly, neither wing simply imported these insights nor applied them mechanically to their local circumstances. Radical legal scholars such as Issa Shivji developed elaborate accounts of both East African society and its laws in ways that highlighted both the ongoing constraints posed by imperialism and the limitations of post-colonial nationalism as a vehicle for emancipation (Shivji 1986, 1995). In terms of pedagogy, Shivji emphasised the importance of showing rather than telling, especially when adopting a radical approach to law. In recounting his efforts to teach a radical and Africanised version of labour law, he emphasises how both practical legal work and class discussions about the possibility of legal reform organically led the students to reflect on broader questions about the nature of law and its role in society (Shivji 1993: 98–102).

In addition to such subversive engagements with traditional legal fields, both radical and moderate scholars made efforts to overcome the state-centrism of traditional legal education by highlighting (without romanticising) the ongoing importance of customary law in their local context (Ghai 1987: 762–766). This challenge to state-centrism was anything but comprehensive, as the sympathy of radical scholars towards left-wing governments often anchored their teaching and research to the state. Nevertheless, this tentative acknowledgement of legal pluralism opened the door for further scholarly developments. The circulation of scholars (Africans as well as foreigners) between Dar-es-Salaam and Warwick Law School contributed to the development of a uniquely British version of the "law in context" movement, which was arguably much more radical than its US counterpart precisely because of its roots in struggles for decolonisation. Much contemporary work on law and gender as well as on land law acknowledges the foundational legal pluralism of both and traces its origins to early jurisprudential experiments in post-colonial Africa (Harrington & Manji 2017: 706–708). Indeed, any effort to decolonise legal pedagogy demands that we acknowledge that state law plays a crucial role in the government of humans and the distribution of resources, but it does not command uncontested or final authority over the entirety of social affairs. Socio-legal studies, Indigenous legal studies, legal pluralism, and other currents have developed sophisticated versions of this argument. However, these insights are not always translated into pedagogical approaches. Even in the realm of state law, adjudication, especially in front of appellate courts, continues to be at the heart of common law legal education, while in civil law jurisdictions learning revolves around the supposed completeness and coherence of legal codes. This approach ignores both the importance of non-statist legal systems for billions (Manji 1999; Pasternak 2017; Monson 2023) and the fact that within state legal systems, racialised and other marginalised populations tend to encounter the executive–administrative branch of the state (in the form of police encounters, fines, planning regulations, welfare bureaucracies, etc.) much more often than they do the (appellate) judiciary (Spade 2018). It is for this reason that legal clinics can then offer invaluable insights into the everyday workings (and traps) of legality and potentially (but not automatically) enable students to work with grassroots movements and disenfranchised clients (Ashar 2008; Shah 2017). At the same time, there is no doubt that contextualisation and critical analysis of case law and codified legislation is a valuable tool that enables us to combine doctrinal rigour with critical analysis. The volume at hand offers examples of both orientations: it shows both how to utilise and subvert traditional modes of legal teaching while documenting the importance of moving beyond them, especially in regard to clinical legal education.

At the same time, we turn to the past in order to gain a realistic understanding of the limitations and challenges that we face. The precedent of post-colonial experimentation with legal teaching is also important because the aporias and defeats of these initiatives are instructive for us today. In Ghana, tensions arose between the Pan-Africanist, left-wing government of Kwame Nkrumah, and the law faculty about the purpose of legal education in the newly established and fast-changing state. The former, including Nkrumah himself, insisted that legal education should be practical and directed towards the immediate material needs of the people and the developmental aspirations of the state (Harrington & Manji 2019). Contrastingly, part of the faculty, led by its American dean, insisted that legal education should offer a broader, humanistic outlook that cannot be reduced to political calculations. This struggle is often recast as one between an increasingly authoritarian government and academic freedom or, on the other end of the spectrum, as a clash between bourgeois detractors and a vision of law(yers) as a decolonised profession in the service of the people. Both versions of the story carry more than one kernel of truth.

Our purpose here is not to re-litigate the past but to flag the ongoing significance of this dilemma even as the circumstances have changed dramatically. Legal educators have to make almost impossible choices between the technicalities of legal education, especially when these technicalities might enable the oppressed to game a system that has been stacked against them, and an inter-disciplinary, critical engagement with the law that does not aim at thinking along with the "rules" but through and against them. Even though there is reason to believe that the two aims are not inherently contradictory, they may well become so in concrete contexts where overwork, time constraints, accreditation requirements, and assessment pressures require tough choices to be made. One of the principal aims of this volume is, then, to offer educators and students concrete examples of how to balance these competing requirements of legal education. We do not believe that these examples can eliminate these tensions or contradictions, which are inherent both in law as a social phenomenon and in the university as an institution. However, we hope to show that the room for manoeuvre is greater than professional conformism and the innate conservatism of institutions would have us assume. Chapters featuring in this volume offer guidance to pedagogues and students on different stages of their journeys. Incorporating different "proportions" of theory, personal reflection, and practical advice, our contributors do not offer one coherent blueprint but many possible solutions to the devilish problem of trying to do radical work within an inherently conservative context. Some chapters will be particularly useful to those who are taking their first steps towards an anti-racist and decolonised legal pedagogy, while other pieces will be of interest to scholars and activists who already have years of engagement with the subject behind them. Despite these differences, most chapters share the conviction that one need not be ready to radically remake the content and mode of their teaching in order to implement small but influential changes as soon as possible.

Many contributors remain sceptical about whether a full "decolonisation" of the law school is ever possible. Nevertheless, the same contributions also show that assigning "unconventional" materials at times, highlighting the direct involvement of "founding fathers" of a field with dispossession or enslavement even in passing, engaging properly with the factual background of case law to show how colonialism, imperialism, and enslavement were the direct sources of supposedly "neutral" doctrines, or event adopting a conversational format that questions rule-centrism and professorial authority can lead to significant shifts. This is partly thanks to the interest and enthusiasm of many of our own students, who will be able to use these fissures and openings creatively to advance their understanding of the subject.

With this optimistic note in mind, a second lesson to be drawn from this longer history of decolonisation efforts concerns the limitations presented by material resources (and their withdrawal) and the overall political and social context. Prominent figures of Dar-es-Salaam, such as Issa Shivji and Yash

Ghai, and more recent accounts alike confirm that the decline of the faculty was not related to the quality of its pedagogy or research. Rather, it was caused by devastating funding cuts, which were brought about by neoliberal structural adjustment spearheaded by the international financial institutions (Ghai 1987: 774–776; Paliwala 2017: 59). Systematic underinvestment worsened the ratios between students and teachers, led to declining salaries and social standing, and impoverished university libraries and access to other intellectual resources undermining the quality of research. As a result, many prominent and emerging scholars (both Africans and others) moved overseas, and they continue to do so. This one-way mobility was also caused by hostile political developments as the first generation of radical post-colonial leaders were voted out or, more frequently, removed from power through violent and unconstitutional means. This emphasis on material factors and broader political developments does not imply fatalism. It does though reflect a conviction that the success of even the most modest versions of decolonisation depends on broader struggles about the fate of the public university both in the Global North and in the Global South. So far, marketisation has created a contradictory environment: on the one hand, "innovation" is welcomed or at least tolerated provided that it is translated into the language of managerial goals, student satisfaction, and personal achievement. On the other, it is exactly the same dedication to market logic that makes any gain vulnerable to reversal as university bureaucracies become answerable to donors and creditors more than their own students and staff (Tzouvala 2019). As the idea of the university as a public good and a public space comes under attack, private security, "anti-radicalisation" programmes, and immigration checks erode the preconditions for vibrant student movements that challenge the university to its core. Fee increases place disproportionate burdens on racialised, poor students and shift perceptions of higher education as (exclusively) an accreditation mechanism rather than a space of political and intellectual inquiry. Finally, the deterioration of academic working conditions also has disproportionate effects on women and racialised people and discourages creative engagement with our jobs, including with our teaching. All this is to say that although challenging the epistemological and theoretical underpinnings of the modern law school is indispensable, the success or failure of such classroom experiments hinges on broader political struggles and considerations.

To highlight this broader context is not, however, to abdicate our own responsibility by reference to "structural problems" and "structural solutions." This is not to say that this is not an accurate diagnosis of the situation. However, it is also the case that such diagnoses are often used as excuses for inaction or, worse, as justifications for poor behaviour. Equally, epistemological and political modesty and self-awareness are important virtues but do not justify inaction. This is a familiar scenario: colleagues refuse to address racism, coloniality, and other oppressive structures in their teaching not because they think that these do not exist or that they are of no relevance to law, but because they belong to a dominant social group and they feel that they do not know enough about the topic and/or it is insensitive or otherwise improper for them to comment of such issues. These concerns are not unwarranted: it has been observed time and again that activists, scholars, or teachers who belong to dominant groups (white people, settlers, scholars based in the Global North) can exert disproportionate intellectual and material influence on how racism and/or coloniality are conceptualised and confronted. This dominance reproduces the same structures that it seeks to undo, and, often, it results in overly narrow understandings of the problem and unambitious programmes for transformation. One typical example is what Derrick Bell, one of the founding figures of critical race theory in the United States, identified as the predominance of white, liberal civil rights lawyers in academic discussions about law and race between the 1950s and the 1980s. Bell lamented the fact that this group adopted an overly narrow understanding of law and racism, and, in turn, placed too much faith into the rulings of the US Supreme Court that questioned legalised segregation but on grounds narrow enough that allowed its survival in subtler forms (Bell 1992: 375–377). In fact, critical race theory's main contribution has been to highlight the shortsightedness of this optimistic approach and to uncover the structuring effects of white supremacy (and of anti-Black racism, in particular) for the US legal system as a whole (Peller et al. 1995).

The problem, then, is a serious one. However, the fact that colleagues or students from dominant social groups might not know how a specific form of oppression feels, it does not mean that they cannot gain insight on how it works or that they are unaffected by it (Adebisi 2022). In fact, allyship as deference and inaction carries its own risks. It perpetuates the idea that racism and coloniality are supposedly niche concerns of a particularistic (as opposed to universal) nature rather than frameworks of thought and material/institutional structures that shape law in a fundamental way. Relatedly, insofar as scholars from dominant groups are over-represented in legal academia, such an attitude objectively impedes change. It is one thing to acknowledge the limitations of pedagogical reforms that are not led by the oppressed themselves and, consequently, to advocate for more hires, promotions, and scholarships for people of colour, and it is another thing to defer all change to an unspecified point in the future when institutional parity has been achieved. In addition, even the most robust versions of standpoint epistemology do not collapse understanding of oppressive social structures to identity alone. This subtle distinction works both ways: on the one hand, belonging to an oppressed social group does not automatically guarantee critical awareness of oppression or the adoption of emancipatory politics. On the other, belonging to a dominant social group does not operate as a permanent and inescapable epistemological barrier against comprehending, deconstructing, and resisting oppression (Tilton 2023). What follows is that law teachers and students of both dominant and subordinated groups will have to engage in the work of decolonisation without guarantees of praise or success but rather in a spirit of comradely solidarity, curiosity, and responsibility.

However, this process of coming together will be anything but straightforward. A final lesson from the formal process of decolonisation concerns the precarious exercise of building broad alliances without diluting one's theoretical commitments and political goals. Frantz Fanon issued this warning early in the process of formal decolonisation when he warned against the double danger of (our words) liberalism and parochialism. *The Wretched of the Earth* is a salient warning about the danger of nationalist ruling classes hijacking the process of decolonisation and undermining it from within (Fanon 1963). Fanon warned about two things that are of immediate interest to our efforts. First, he was concerned about the danger of maintaining the economic, political, and social structures of colonialism and simply replacing the people in charge of these structures with local elites (Ibid. 100–102). In this respect, we appreciate that the meaning of "decolonisation" in the university context is a contested one, but in the context of this volume it emphatically cannot be reduced to "diversity and inclusion." Both diversity and inclusion can be commendable goals, but they do not question the structures, epistemologies, and methods that underlie our teaching and research. As decolonial, post-colonial, Marxist, and other radical thinkers have argued (albeit with substantial differences amongst them), formal processes of imperialism and colonialism where accompanied by and justified through processes of epistemic imperialism and epistemicide, as historically contingent and imperfect ways of understanding the world positioned themselves as universal (Quijano 2020; Amin 2009; Said 1985). Albeit these thinkers do not always agree about the relationship between material and epistemic injustice, they emphasise that these cognitive frames survived the process of formal decolonisation and remain relevant to this day. The ongoing allure of metropolitan models of legal education in the post-colonial world exemplifies this persistence. The language of instruction, the flow of students and textbooks, the diffusion of teaching methods, and assessment standards all replicate patterns of formal colonialism (Roberts 2017). Colonial legacies, then, do not only shape the substantive legal systems of post-colonial states but also how students learn about them and how practitioners implement them. To emphasise this persistence of colonial patterns of knowledge transmission does not necessarily imply a rejection of legal modernity, even though some might choose to do exactly that. However, it involves acknowledging the fact that even if (legal) modernity was indeed co-created by the colonised and the coloniser, as some opponents of "decolonisation" movements argue (Táíwò 2022), this co-creation did not happen through rational dialogue and exploration but rather through violent means. Therefore, questioning the outcomes of these processes need not lead to their wholesale rejection but to a sober (some would say, distinctly rational) evaluation of their foundations and consequences.

This takes us to the second major concern of Fanon, namely the adoption of regressive practices and ideologies under the mantle of "decolonisation." Fanon predicted that when post-colonial leaders would fail to deliver substantive decolonisation and better the lives of their citizens, they would turn to reactionary practices and ideologies to rationalise their rule (Fanon 1963: 104–106). Unfortunately, his warnings turned out to be correct. The utilisation of the language of "decolonisation" by far-right, Islamophobic thinkers and politicians in India and the carelessness toward such experiments by some decolonial scholars point at the ongoing relevance of Fanon's warnings. In resisting the mobilisation of the frame of "decolonisation" by Hindu nationalists, Gopal urges us to remember that "part of the work of decolonisation is to excavate these lines of influence and dialogue, often obscured by cultural triumphalism or exceptionalism" (2021: 892). When it comes to law, introducing into the classroom concepts of legal pluralism should not lead to the calcification of each of these legal systems or the presentation of any of them as the "authentic" and stable expression of a people's "essence." Rather, we can and should emphasise the plasticity and contested character of all legal systems. Showing, for example, how Muslim feminists have been able to articulate arguments from within Islamic law to promote the interests of women within and beyond the courtroom shows Islamic law to be a living, breathing legal system in opposition to the rigid set of rules imagined by both Islamophobes and conservative adherents (Ibrahim 2013). In addition, feminist and queer thinkers and activists, such as Sylvia Tamale or members of the Decolonial Sexualities Network, have articulated arguments against efforts of post-colonial ruling classes to position misogyny or queer-phobia as "decolonial" ideologies (Tamale 2014; Tamale 2020). These arguments strike a delicate balance between emphasising human diversity before and after colonialism without romanticising the pre-colonial past and can offer useful guidance on how to navigate "decolonisation" in legal education in ways that actively resist politically reactionary and parochial iterations of such efforts.

Following in the footsteps of this diverse global lineage, the authors in this volume demonstrate the rich ways in which decolonial and anti-racist thinking, activism, and methodologies can inform, inflect, and elevate our pedagogical praxis in different contexts and jurisdictions. They highlight what has emerged and is important in our transnational discussions from different corners of critical theory to "decolonising the curriculum" initiatives during our workshops (held in July 2022) and through our various forms of knowledge sharing and exchange. The aim of the book is to assist fellow travellers, both new to this journey and those who consider themselves more experienced to navigate and draw on the contributions to push at the institutional and epistemological containers of what is pedagogically possible.

An Outline of the Chapters in This Volume

The core of the book is divided into four main parts. Each of the chapters, in each of the parts, proceeds from a spatially context-dependent positional understanding of what it means to decolonise or adopt an anti-racist pedagogy. Some of the chapters consider both approaches. In Part I, we have writers from the UK, South Africa, and Samoa. These writers use both their contexts and their positionalities to reflect on the pitfalls and possibilities of engaging with decolonising and anti-racist pedagogy in law schools. They reflect on how being racialised as non-white/Indigenous and gendered female make the absences within the law school more stark. Sindane, in particular, writing from the South African context troubles the possibility of Euro-modern law being completely anti-racist or decolonial. Overall, they all make insightful observations about what can be brought into law schools, but also on institutional reluctance and imperviousness to engage with decolonisation in honest and effective ways. These reflections place the sections that follow into clearer context.

In Part II, scholars explain how they have engaged with anti-racist/decolonising pedagogy in their teaching of private law subjects. These subjects include contract, tort, trademark law, and tort. While these writers are teaching in a wide range of jurisdictions – the UK, Northern Ireland, Australia, India, and the United States, their analyses are heavily influenced by the colonial spread of the common law. This informs the focus of three of the chapters in Part II on the ordinary/reasonable person standard. All three chapters that focus on this standard are from different jurisdictions and the authors explain from these different perspectives how the "man" at the centre of private law casts out many humans from being seen by the law. Thus, the authors demonstrate how this "ordinary/reasonable man" is fashioned through unacknowledged processes that racialise and construct hierarchies through this racialisation. They suggest ways to unpack this history and present it to students in the classroom. The chapters on property law, written from Australia and Northern Ireland, explain the imperatives of including brutal colonial histories of Indigenous dispossession to convey a fuller understanding of the origins of rules of property. The writers in Part II are acutely aware of the limits placed on their work by having to work within the confines of state and disciplinary rules. For example, Colm McGrath, in discussing anti-racist approaches to tort law teaching, examines how the regulatory requirements of tort often prevent tort teachers from adopting more disruptive design and content that seek to unsettle the foundations of tort law to make it more anti-racist in its aims.

Part III turns to a variety of subjects within public law; there are two chapters on human rights, two on international law, and one on civil procedure. The chapters on human rights are written from intersecting and divergent contexts as the authors travel through India and Pakistan through to Europe and the United States. Both Gulika Reddy and Sahar Ahmed describe how the experience of law's power changes on either side of the abyssal line. They also note the hope that human rights hold out as an escape from this power and how they have tried to communicate this duality to their students. Similarly, both Ntina Tzouvala and Asmi Wood note the limitations of international law in their chapters. For both of them, it is imperative to consider within the study of international law the possibilities for communicating understanding of the impacts of colonial encounters. They both caution us about the limits of this study. Tzouvala hesitates to label her teaching "decolonised." Wood, in turn, distinguishes between the leeway available to settler and Indigenous teachers in a context where courts remain committed to preserving the "skeleton" of settler law.

Part IV takes a socio-legal approach to anti-racist/decolonising pedagogy. The authors in this part take a deliberate view of how law school pedagogy can uncover the law's complicity with power. Using critical race theory as a pedagogical tool, Sumayyah Malna's writing from the UK suggests ways in which law clinics can educate students about anti-racism as a praxis. The second set of authors writing from Canada – O'Doherty, Love, and Scott – use a survey to test the efficiency of anti-racist and decolonial approaches to teaching the entanglements between criminology and colonial power in a settler colonial. Finally, Adebisi and Russell examine the importance of a longitudinal and structural examination of the relationship between racism, colonialism, and the law. The writers in Part IV are acutely aware of the limitations of their work, both as a corrective to the system and as actors within these systems.

Ultimately, while the contributors write from different jurisdictions and there are some differences in how they have proceeded in their work, they all recognise their work as fitting into a longer history of anti-racism and anti-colonialism that operates both within and outside the university. A key question for many of our contributors is how the law helps people beyond the law school. Thus, the contributors are, in the tradition of the anti-colonial and anti-racist campaigners that have come before them, using the tools they must to do work that can be done. Building in this way recognises that the limitations that we work within are cracks in hard rock. The patient seed planted is watered by those who come behind. This is ongoing work. The contributors are watering what may one day become a mighty oak of liberation.

References

Adebisi, F., 'Are we Allies in the Struggle or Just Struggling with the Idea of Allyship?' *African Skies* (4 July 2022), available at: https://folukeafrica.com/are-we-allies-in-the-struggle-or-just-struggling-with-the-idea-of-allyship/

Adebisi, F. and Jivraj, S., (2021) 'Racism as Legal Pandemic: Thoughts on Critical Legal Pedagogies', in Cowan, D. and Mumford, A. (eds) *Pandemic Legalities: Legal Responses to COVID-19 – Justice and Social Responsibility*. Bristol University Press, pp. 65–78.

Amin, S., (2009) *Eurocentrism: Modernity, Religion and Democracy; A Critique of Eurocentrism and Culturalism*. Monthly Review Press.
Ashar, S.M., 'Law Clinics and Collective Mobilization' *Clinical Law Review* 14 (2008): 355–414.
Behrendt, L., 'Genocide: The Distance between Law and Life' *Aboriginal History* 25 (2001): 132–147.
Bell, D., 'Racial Realism' *Connecticut Law Review* 24, no. 2 (1992): 363–380.
Bhambra, G.K., Nisanscioglu, K., Gebrial, D., 'Decolonising the University in 2020', *Identities: Global Studies in Culture and Power* 27, no. 4 (2020): 509–516.
Fanon, F., (1963) *The Wretched of the Earth*. New York: Grove Press.
Ghai, Y., 'Law, Development and African Scholarship', *Modern Law Review* 50, no. 6 (1987): 750–776.
Gopal, P., 'On Decolonisation and the University' *Textual Practice* 35, no. 2 (2021): 873–899.
Harrington, J., Manji, A. 'The Limits of Socio-Legal Radicalism: Social and Legal Studies and Third Word Scholarship', *Social & Legal Studies* 26, no. 6 (2017): 700–715.
Harrington, J., Manji, A., '"Africa Needs Many Lawyers Trained for the Need of their Peoples": Struggles over Legal Education in Kwame Nkrumah's Ghana', *American Journal of Legal History* 59, no. 2 (2019): 149–177.
Ibrahim, H., (2013) *Practicing Shariah Law: Seven Strategies for Achieving Justice in Shariah Courts*. American Bar Association.
Jivraj, S. (2020a) Towards Anti-racist Legal Pedagogy: A Resource for law school teachers.
Jivraj, S., 'Decolonizing the Academy – Between a Rock and a Hard Place', *Interventions: The International Journal of Postcolonial Studies* 22, no. 4 (2020b): 552–573.
Kennedy, D., (2004) *Legal Education and the Reproduction of Hierarchy: A Polemic Against the System*. NYU Press.
Mamdani, M., (2018) *Citizen and Subject: Contemporary Africa and the Legacy of Late Colonialism*. Princeton University Press.
Manji, A.S., 'Imagining Women's "Legal World": Towards a Feminist Theory of Legal Pluralism in Africa', *Social & Legal Studies* 8, no. 4 (1999): 435–455.
Matsuda, M.J., 'Beside My Sister, Facing the Enemy: Legal Theory out of Coalition', *Stanford Law Review* 43, no. 3 (1991): 1183–1192.
Monson, R., (2023) *Gender, Property and Politics in the Pacific: Who Speaks for the Land?* Cambridge University Press.
Mutu, M., 'The Treaty Claims Settlement Process in New Zealand and Its Impact on Māori', *Land* 8, no. 10 (2019): 152–170.
Naqvi, Z. B., Fletcher, R., Ashiagbor, D., Cruz, K., Russell, Y., 'Back at the Kitchen Table: Reflections on Decolonising and Internationalising with the Global South Socio-legal Writing Workshops', *Feminist Legal Studies* 27 (2019): 123–137.
Ndlovu-Gatsheni, S. J., ed. (2018) *Epistemic Freedom in Africa: Deprovincialization and Decolonization*. Taylor & Francis. https://doi.org/10.4324/9780429492204
Paliwala, A., (2017) 'Context, Political Economy and Good Governance: Avatars for Dar Legal Education' in Zartaloudis, T. (ed.), *Land Law and Urban Policy in Context: Essays on the Contributions of Patrick McAuslan*. Birkbeck Law Press, pp. 56–78.
Pasternak, S., (2017) *Grounded Authority: The Algonquins of Barriere Lake against the State*. Minnesota University Press.

Peller, G., Crenshaw, K., Gotanda, N. (eds.) (1995) *Critical Race Theory: The Key Writings that Formed the Movement*. New Press.

Quijano, A., 'Coloniality of Power and Eurocentrism in Latin America'. *International Sociology* 15, no. 2 (2020): 215–232.

Roberts, A., (2017) *Is International Law International?* Oxford University Press.

Ross, S.D., 'A Comparative Study of the Legal Profession in East Africa', *Journal of African Law* 17, no. 3 (1973): 279–299.

Said, E.W., 'Orientalism Reconsidered', *Race and Class* 27, no. 2 (1985): 1–15.

Shah, J. 'Rebellious Lawyering in Big Case Clinics', *Clinical Law Review* 23, no. 2 (2017): 775–815.

Shivji, I.G., (1986) *Law, State and the Working Class in Tanzania*, N.H. Heinemann.

Shivji, I.G., (1993) *Intellectuals at the Hill: Essays and Talks 1969–1993*. Dares Salaam University Press.

Shivji, I.G., 'The Rule of Law and Ujamaa in the Ideological Formation of Tasmania', *Social & Legal Studies* 4, no 2 (1995): 147–174.

Spade, D., (2018) *Normal Life: Administrative Violence, Critical Trans Politics, and the Limits of the Law*. Duke University Press.

Starblanket, T., (2018) *Suffer the Little Children: Genocide, Indigenous Nations and the Canadian State*. Clarity Press.

Táíwò, O., (2022) *Against Decolonisation: Taking African Agency Seriously*. Oxford University Press.

Tamale, S., 'Exploring the Contours of African Sexualities: Religion, Law and Power', *African Human Rights Law Journal* 14, no. 1 (2014): 150–177.

Tamale, S., (2020) *Decolonisation and Afro-Feminism*. Ottawa: Daraja Press.

Tan, J.M., 'The Many Layers of Invisible Labour Decolonising the Academy' *TWAIL Review* (2021), available at: https://twailr.com/the-many-layers-of-invisible-labour-decolonising-the-academy/

Thornton, M., 'Technocentrism in the Law School: Why the Gender and Colour of Law Remain the Same' *Osgoode Hall Law Journal* 36, no. 2 (1998): 369–398.

Thornton, M., 'The Changing Gender Regime in the Neoliberal Legal Academy' *Zeitschrift für Rechtssoziologie* 33, no. 2 (2013): 235–252.

Tilton, E.C.R., '"That's Above my Paygrade": Woke Excuses for Ignorance' *Philosopher's Imprint* (2023) (forthcoming).

Tzouvala, N., (2019) 'The future of feminist international legal scholarship in a neoliberal university: doing law differently?' in Harris-Rimmer, S., Ogg, K., *Research Handbook on Feminist Engagement with International Law*. Edward Elgar, pp. 269–285.

Tzouvala, N., (2020) *Capitalism as Civilisation: A History of International Law*. Cambridge University Press.

Watson, N., (2005) 'Racism in Legal Education Special – Indigenous People in Legal Education: Staring into a Mirror without Reflection', *Indigenous Law Bulletin 6*, vol. 8 (2005): 4–7.

Williams, J., 'Decolonising the Law in Aotearoa; Can We Start with the Law Schools?', *Otago Law Review* 17, no. 1 (2021): 1–30.

Xavier, S. et al. (2021) *Decolonizing Law: Indigenous, Third World and Settler Perspectives*. Routledge.

PART I

Questioning the Decolonising Project in Law Schools

Limitations and Critique

1

ABOLISH THE LAW SCHOOL

To Decolonise Is Disingenuous

Phoebe Boateng, Aysha Mazhar, and Sophia Hayat Taha

Introduction: The Abolitionist/Decolonial Nexus

This chapter uses the scholarly personal narrative method as a means to call for the abolition of the (colonial) law school as it stands. It draws upon the lived experiences of three early career legal scholars based in the jurisdiction of England and Wales. Our provocative title speaks to the necessity to strive towards more plural forms of knowledge within the legal curriculum (Adébísí, 2021, p. 440; Mason, 2021) and how an understanding of abolition in relation to decolonising the legal curriculum can help in this endeavour. The subtitle of our chapter highlights how managers in higher education have diluted the meanings of decolonising and have co-opted this into the university's mission, resulting in the colonisation of decolonising. We therefore argue that when law schools attempt to decolonise, it stems from a place of disingenuity.

We define decolonising legal education as a set of structural changes, enacted by individuals removing hierarchy, questioning knowledge production, and arguing against "core" parts of legal education that are engaged with uncritically. This process requires creativity and action, and to sit in discomfort, and reflect upon questions, as suggested by Adébísí (2021, p. 471), "how law is taught, what law is taught, who the law works for, and who the law does not work for." This chapter discusses burnout and co-option within the colonial law school, the impact of parasitic spaces, and illuminates our response via the creation of spaces that are beyond the law school. Abolition opposes the current iteration of higher education institutions, where critical thinking is exalted, "while critical action must be crushed" (Eve, 2021, p. 4). We show that reclaiming the hidden curriculum is part of our resistance and that our experience of teaching ourselves is our living embodiment of abolition. We conclude

DOI: 10.4324/9781003397885-3

by arguing that the current structures of the law school need to be abolished and that without abolition, the call to decolonise is a disingenuous draining of labour.

To understand this further, we begin with a general understanding of abolition. Day and McBean define it as moving towards a "future run by people, for people, and not by profit" (2022, p. 17). Abolition as a movement is recognised as having its origins in the ending of slavery, which has been inextricably connected to colonialism (Day and McBean, 2022, p. 4; Eve, 2021, p. 3; Rodríguez, 2019, p. 1576). Currently, there is a wealth of literature that focuses on abolition in the prison industrial complex, policing, and borders (Bradley and de Noronha, 2022, pp. 148–149). With this acknowledged, Gilich and Boardman (2022, p. 110) note a hesitancy by abolitionists in including the university on the list of institutions referenced in abolitionist theory/praxis. This is illustrated in the following list quoted from Day and McBean (2022, p. 4): "institutions of state coercion such as police, prisons, detention centres, borders, arms and the military." A justification as to why this may be the case is that to abolish the university "might feel intimidating or appear ludicrous" (Gilich and Boardman, 2022, p. 110). Furthermore, the extent of abolition when applied to the law school may be a question that the readers of this chapter may have. Responding to this, we argue that to abolish the law school is not synonymous with a complete eradication of legal learning but rather for appreciation of legal knowledge that is outside of, or even outright excluded from, the prescribed legal curriculum.

Considering the broader context, if legal education is the result of its "social, economic and political" factors (Morgan and Thorpe, 2022, p. 427), this would indicate that both law students and legal educators are invariably social, economic, and political actors. This is an imperative in understanding abolition in relation to the law school. The importance of educators and students needing to work together when adopting an abolitionist framework is underscored in Rodríguez's question "how can a teacher expect her/his students to undertake the courageous and difficult work of inhabiting an abolitionist positionality – even if only as an 'academic' exercise – unless the teacher herself/himself embodies, performs and oozes that very same political desire?" (2010, p. 14). This demonstrates that to understand abolition solely as a theory would result in an overlooking of "abolition as cultural, political, educational, community-building, and decolonial praxis" (Zembylas, 2021a, p. 125). This chapter demonstrates a possibility in how this can be reached, but more importantly, where abolition begins. Harney and Moten's description of abolition supports the understanding of it being an embodied phenomenon between, and with each other, by arguing that it "starts with the self, so we may lose our individuated selves in favor of a blurred, irreducible sociality of the senses" (2021, p. 172). Via the visceral process of writing together, we exercise another manifestation of abolitionist and decolonial thinking: that multiple voices are vital.

There is a growing appreciation for the relaying of the "stories about the law school," which has been achieved by methods such as autoethnography (Gregersen, 2022) and counter-storytelling (Jivraj, 2022). Where this chapter diverges is through the deliberate use of the scholarly personal narrative (Nash and Viray, 2013), which at the crux is a pedagogic method. Abolitionist approaches to higher (and legal) education pedagogy demand a "creative destruction and creativity of thought-in-destruction" (Rodríguez, 2019, p. 1611), which is foundational to our use of the scholarly personal narrative method. Through this, we creatively disentangle illusions of the managerial attempts to decolonise. Additionally, the method grounds us as writers and requires that our narrative is central to the themes drawn upon in the piece (Nash and Viray, 2013, p. 53). In doing so, our writing reinforces the impossibility of the separation of the theoretical from the practical (hooks, 1994, p. 61).

This method includes giving ourselves permission to express ourselves, by diligently "listening to the sound" of our own voices (Nash and Viray, 2013, p. 16). We construct and tell our stories, via the use of poetry and pithy reflections based on our experiences in decolonising, thereby situating ourselves as knowledge reclaimers. We recognise that different forms of knowledge co-exist and that our cultural identities are also sites of knowledge (Wane, 2013, p. 102). Locating ourselves as co-authors, our legal education traverses undergraduate level, postgraduate taught and postgraduate research, in the varied capacities of student, teacher, and researcher. Our identities weave together multiple complex experiences including but not limited to being Queer and/or Black and/or PoC Women existing in direct opposition to Het-White normative spaces. Our multi-national, multi-ethnic, multi-lingual selves lie in juxtaposition to the expectations of the colonial law school.

When we define abolition in the context of our chapter, we assert that it is an embodied way of knowing. Similarly to Coles, Ohito, Green, and Lyiscott (2021), citing Rodríguez (2019, p. 1576), we contend that abolition is not just rooted in a complete destruction of a system but also entails a striving for the hopeful. Our call for abolition is a hopeful one, shown through this chapter and our ongoing relationship as co-authors, co-conspirators, and co-learners/teachers. We show that there are already spaces for decolonised ways of learning and being. Our call aims to surpass the spaces we have created for ourselves and ask for the community of legal educators to join us in our abolitionist approach to the law school. As shown by Mayorga, Leidecker, and Orr de Gutiérrez (2019), we developed similar survival strategies due to our educational experiences. It is interesting to see these approaches organically develop in different contexts but as a response to the violence of a colonial educational system. While they write from the settler colony, we write from the heartlands of the coloniser, though our experiences of unease within the institutions and our resistances are mirrored. This abolitionist reclaiming of educational spaces is seen also in the undercommons. Placing ourselves as disruptors of the colonial institution, we "steal what one can" (Harney and Moten, 2013, p. 26). The rationale for our stealing is twofold: we steal ourselves away from management, and we steal back ourselves to counter the depletion of our time and energy. This is not done to reject the law school but as protective means to distance ourselves from management's artificial attempt to decolonise it.

Burnout and Co-option

To understand the impact of burnout and co-option, first, we must understand that the law school is a site of colonial knowledge. We must therefore speak of the reductive nature of legal knowledge that is currently conveyed in legal curricula. There has been an appreciation that there are multiple ways of knowing the law (Adébísí, 2021, p. 440; Mason 2021). However, considering the elements of what needs to be studied to gain a qualifying law degree (The Law Society and the General Council of the Bar, 1999), we notice that there is no space to understand how colonisation feeds directly into the foundations of law. Optional modules present potential avenues for the undergraduate student to explore decolonial legal concepts, for instance within international law (al Attar and Abdelkarim, 2023), or human rights (Rigney, 2020). Whilst a masters or a doctorate could be pathways to explore the colonial dimensions of law, not every undergraduate law student will go on to do this.

Reflection 1: During my undergraduate experience, discourse surrounding decolonisation, or 'well known' topics such as feminism, were only included in the reading lists of non-core modules. Social and critical theories were never woven into our core curriculum. Any discussion surrounding decolonisation, feminism, or anything outside the 'mainstream' is not recognised in the standard undergraduate offering.

Law teachers inadvertently replicate colonial forms of knowing due to their own experiences. The continuation of this cycle results in a loss of legal learning. This is because, with an absence of legal scholars who centre the decolonial, a cycle continues where new lawyers, unquestioning of the colonial systems in the legal profession, become unconscious agents of colonialism (Tan, 2021). Nonetheless, there is progress, countering this phenomenon. The creation of resources that focus on decolonising the legal curriculum and anti-racist pedagogy demonstrates this (Jivraj, 2020; see the rest of this volume). It is in situating the law school as a place that spawns colonial knowledge, and silences via absence of space or time to critically engage with the law, that we can understand the impact of burnout and co-option as we try to decolonise.

In our experiences, we encountered institutional betrayal and parasitic spaces and had to weather the impact of our work being co-opted. Unfortunately, whilst not a unique experience, it led to our collective burnout, a consequence perhaps common to all social justice work (Gorski and Chen, 2015). Decolonising the curriculum is not a new call to action; this work has been occurring for decades. Like most liberation movements, action occurs in waves, with key moments including the "great Nairobi literature debate" incident in 1968/69, where it was argued a diversified syllabus would be "less British" leading to three lecturers at the university to call for the abolition of the English department (wa Thiong'o, 1986, p. 89). Our wave of action came after the 2015 student protests in Cape Town, which began, following actions by Chumani Maxwele, a student who surrounded a statue of colonialist Cecil Rhodes with human faeces. The demand that "Rhodes must Fall" led to a wider call to decolonise curricula across the world (Le Grange, 2016; van Jaarsveldt, de Vries and Kroukamp, 2018). By 2017, Keele University had its own critical friend, a student–staff decolonising network (Keele Student Union, Keele Postgraduate Association and Keele University College Union, 2018).

Like many decolonial student movements, we were supported by staff in our efforts. We had a student–staff network which extended into the law school space. However, these spaces were squeezed, and the collaborator staff were pressured to work within existing structures and often had to shield individual student names from those less enamoured by the decolonising agendas. Institutional backlash again is not unique, an empirical investigation illuminated the responses across nine universities in England over the period 2014–2021, which depicted institutional-level reactions to decolonising the curriculum as "rejection, reluctant acceptance, and strategic advancement" (Shain, Yıldız, Poku and Gokay, 2021, p. 920). So, when colonial law schools call to decolonise, they drain PoC and Black labour, using the parasitic nature of white middle-class leaders to recreate and reproduce the very structures they claim to want to reform. The co-option of decolonising by the law school, often apparent with buzzwording of the word exposes the systemic "problem." When "invited" to decolonise, you are "invited" within the "masters house" (Lorde, 2007, p. 112). A hierarchical imposition demands you join them at their table, where your work is delegitimised but you can do their work for them.

Decolonisation of the curriculum has become a "buzzword" (Doharty, Madriaga, and Joseph-Salisbury, 2021, p. 234), and we argue it is disingenuous when universities lay claim to the word and the work. In our experience, the use of the law student to "represent" the law school's culture has meant that engagement is tokenistic. When "management" go to decolonise using established hierarchical systems, they leech on Black and PoC staff and student labour, and so this will always be disingenuous. This is because any movement to change is already marketised before the change has really begun. When a university declares its progress before systematic change has occurred, then it becomes a tool to draw in more students. This is illusionary due to the stark contrast between the prospectus and what actually occurs in the law school classroom. So, by co-opting, marketising, and sanitising the work, the colonial law school and the wider university also colonise the decolonising process. The work to decolonise is conflated with equality, diversity, and inclusion (EDI), and the same Black and PoC students and staff are called upon to give their labour, under-accounting for their emotional energy and time (Memon and Jivraj, 2020, p. 485). From wa Thiong'o to 2015 in Cape Town, to the work in the UK, we see actions arising but being co-opted or exhausted. Therefore, we join others in saying that these spaces do not work; they cannot be reformed or slightly amended. Instead, we call for abolition. We call for the abolition of the *British* law school.

Teaching [ourselves] to Transgress

We now reflect upon our everyday resistance to the colonial law school and how we recreated the law school to encompass our needs. We saw/see the current law school as unfit for purpose; therefore, we are "Teaching [ourselves] to Transgress" (hooks, 1994) through exploring beyond the law school curricula and guiding our own learning. By reclaiming and reimagining our education, we engage with the hopeful and creative side of abolition. We identify and place ourselves as the antithesis of the "unmarked scholar" (Dennis, 2018, pp. 192–196) because unlike for him, where colonisation is an inconsequential thing of the past, we know that Britain is a "contemporary colonial space" (El-Enany, 2020, pp. 27–28). Our call to abolish the law school is derived from an abolitionist reimagining. Present in the call for university abolition, a new possibility is imagined and drawn upon (Luke and Heynen, 2021, p. 414). As Bhambra, Nişancıoğlu, and Gebrial (2020) argue:

> [A]bolition provides a way of reframing 'decolonising the university' as a position against (rather than for) the university … [which] might also better attune us to the possibilities of solidarity with the university's Others and other disloyal subjects that sneak in and out of higher education.
>
> *(p. 513)*

As "disloyal subjects" we are calling for liberation. Yet, given the nature of university-level legal education in England, we are stuck in a neoliberal business model, which manufactures law graduates who may be oblivious to the colonial dimensions of the law. Perhaps we are calling for abolition in both senses of the term: an ending of the colonial law school and, in its place, one that benefits all. Through discussion, we note our conclusions have been echoed in the growing literature on decolonising the legal curriculum. We acknowledge that the writing of this chapter is a demonstration of our collective learning. The abolition of the university (and consequently the law school) is framed as the destination, which can be achieved by refusing to adhere to the colonial customs of the university (Zembylas, 2021b, p. 954).

Our work to decolonise the law school pushes back, by refusing to recognise the law school's demand for authority. This was evident in our refusal to attend meetings when we felt uncomfortable. We consider a formative set of incidents between our working group and management that we refer to as "the email battle." The email battle occurred when we asked the law school to meet us in spaces we had already created, on our terms. However, the response was to demand/ "invite" us into their spaces, their table, on their terms. The result was that meetings with us, those already doing the work, never occurred. We withdrew our labour and engagement. Limited sessions continued without us, using student voice representatives to meet the criteria of student engagement. Applying Dennis' ten significant "pedagogic action" points (2018, p. 202), and recommendations of declining the most "easily available" spaces, we argue our "email battle" demonstrates the law school's failure to engage in pedagogic action. To date, decolonising work has stalled and has not yet become a meaningful engagement process. When we considered what spaces to work in, we would constantly reflect and discuss what the implications of our being in those spaces meant. This is an approach often lacking, where management would want space and engagement at their convenience. Staff who were part of the grassroots decolonising work would work hard to reclaim spaces for grassroots work, but the result would often be the silencing and exhausting of them.

The dissatisfaction (from the university) that a "to-do" list cannot be created, ticked off, and then decolonisation has occurred neatly in a once-a-term meeting needs to be recognised. When we ask ourselves: what we must do to decolonise? We reply: listen, share power, and accept that this will never be done instantaneously. However, the actions and inactions of the institution demonstrate that we are considered to be obtuse, unengaged, or unrealistic in our response. The reality is this is part of the "pedagogy of refusal" (Zembylas, 2021b, pp. 962–965). We know that this work will never be done, in this current environment. We know that we could look back and disagree with ourselves. This stands in stark opposition to the majority of disciplines that start with sacrosanct texts by a "pale, male and stale" (Qureshi, 2019, p. 205) academic. It would be hypocritical if we did not accept that what we say can always be dismantled and rebuilt, whilst we critique canonised sources of knowledge. By acknowledging this, we recognise the beauty and privilege of learning and unlearning. Locating "unheard, silenced" voices (Dennis, 2018, p. 202) we argue that to unsilence other voices, the very sources of knowledge need to be diversified. We ask why the written academic source is held in higher esteem above the social media post, the video, the artwork, the podcast, and the undergraduate.

Going beyond the physical law school, we offer resistance by practising abolition of the colonial law school. To practice abolition is to imagine and manifest an alternative learning space: to work together in a flattened space without hierarchy; to listen to each other and learn from each other; to centre lived experience; and to learn from readings, art, music, hobbies, and alternative knowledge that exists "outside" of academia. Here, we offer three reflections on why we do this work. We highlight how we learned from each other and our comrades and how we learned *outside* of the law school.

Reflection 2: Decolonising the university entails going beyond the co-opted catchphrases of EDI, by the answering of serious questions on the nature of teaching and research. We need to consider: Who is producing this knowledge? Why are they producing this knowledge? And who exactly benefits in this? In doing this work, there is the acceptance that the sole act of inserting materials authored or edited by BIPoC academics into a reading list – a shallow '"solution"' – is insufficient. Instead, a deeper understanding of how knowledge has disadvantaged others is required.

Reflection 3: Decol work is important to me as it looks beyond the performative aspects of diversity and "BAME attainment" quotas. It is a way to reimagine a system that has existed for hundreds of years and radically change how and what we learn.

In reflection, working with the decol movement (Decolonise Keele Network) has been the best network that I have been involved in at uni. Working collaboratively with students and staff without hierarchy has been unlike any networks I have been part of previously.

Reflection 4: Through peer-supported spaces with my co-authors and others who did grassroots decolonise Keele work I constantly learn in spaces of mutual trust, respect and understanding. I have spaces where, contrary to the hierarchy academia tries to embed within us we are all treated as equal knowers. We use group WhatsApp messages, emails, video calls, shared drive spaces to share knowledge. If someone has a book or talk or paper to recommend it is worth looking at not because they are dictating as a teacher but because they found it interesting or relevant. We have spaces to discuss the everyday and the theoretical. These spaces are not there for an exam or qualification but for a love of education and discussion. It is often what I think the university *should* be as a space. The work we do to "Decolonise the Curriculum" is important because so much is missing from the curricula we are presented with. There is so little time and resource given to critical thinking, the "mainstream" theories presented are so lacking. From a purely academic point of view, it allows us to demand a curriculum that pushes us. From a social justice point of view, it lets us question whose knowledge is hidden, suppressed and undervalued. Grassroots work has given me inspirational peers, respite in toxic spaces, confidence and comradery.

As part of the time to educate ourselves beyond the offered curriculum, we attended numerous events and discussed as a collective. Through attending events that unpack the enduring facets of empire, such as the applicability of equalities and who benefits from such notions (Connected Sociologies, 2020) or online lectures, film Q&A panels, discussions, and book launches, we shared our learning and enthusiasm. Examples include attending an "in conversation with" Pravini Baboeram exploring *The Uprising*, a music documentary exploring resistance against racism in Europe (Baboeram, 2020), and an engaging panel discussion from hosts of *Literature Must Fall*. Notable discussion points included defining the mainstream and its accessibility, who controls it and whether it co-opts how we see ourselves, and whether EDI is a handmaiden for racial capitalism (Literature Must Fall, 2021). By educating ourselves in our own time, away from the formal curriculum, and the demands of the neoliberal university, we rebel: through regular messages on a group chat, scheduled weekend video calls, sharing of PDFs, reading lists, recommending a book, a Twitter thread, a voice hitherto absent from our reading lists meant that we refashioned and created new tools of knowledge production and knowledge sharing. Our WhatsApp group chat for working to decolonise the law school began in November 2020. Whilst we had already communicated and worked together before this, the group chat created became pivotal to our learning. This became a space where joy and frustrations were shared, amidst our organising efforts. We talk to each other throughout the week, most weeks. We discuss decolonisation theory, papers, talks, conferences, and work in general. This work continues past graduations and through Covid-19's lockdowns and releases. We share articles and memes and talk about mental health, life, and job opportunities. Through this we create our own space where our knowledge of the law far outstrips what we were offered in the law school, thus changing our methods of legal learning.

Abolition and Hope: Vision(s) of the Law School

As US-based activist network Critical Resistance argues, an abolitionist vision involves building the structures today, by taking practical steps, to enable us to have hope and change in the future (Critical Resistance, n.d.). Ergo, the abolitionist clarion, demands for a reimagination of an alternative law school. As Olufemi says, "We must rise to the challenge with a revolutionary and collective sense of determination" (2020, p. 9). We imagine a law school, abolished, with legal education transformed into something revolutionary but also within reach. As scholarly personal narratives allow for a multitude of methods to centre voices, we lead this section with a poem. The poem below, our manifesto, and thoughts on healing are reflexive slivers that imagine and focus on what exactly we are working towards. We use these approaches to envisage an alternative law school.

The Law School

An institution created by those who hold power that continues to validate and uphold archaic structures.

To that, we say no.

Our vision of the Law School is founded on principles deemed more 'informal' in practice and structure,
Allowing those within, to be their own instructor.
Students and their experiences shape the curriculum,
Widening the material provided and pushing discussion further, in particular.
Giving students space and resources to exchange knowledge,
To see more independent thought, enabling them to flourish.

Our Law School is reflective of those who study and teach within,
It is a vision that goes beyond diversity, inclusion and quotas that are tactically used, as it always has been.

Visions of this future Law School appear almost utopian in nature.
'To abolish' is deemed too radical by this institution's creator.
But we know to strive for this in our future.

The Hopeful Manifesto

A hope for the law school on undergraduate and postgraduate taught level? To genuinely move away from insidious phrases about the competitiveness in the law school that encourage unscrupulous behaviour that is a hindrance to legal learning. As for learning the law? To be provided the readings for the seminar in advance so one can have that time and the space to really engage with the materials. To really think deeply about the framings of the law. Time in the seminar room that is dedicated to really understanding the points of law that are presented to us. Going beyond the law teacher just talking aloud the rules or the theories but that space for the student to have a go at understanding them (whether aloud or quietly). A hope for doctoral legal education and for legal academia? No more precarity. No more of this sense of urgency to secure competitive funds for legal research. No more legal knowledge being locked behind outrageously priced academic publications. Accessible – in all forms of the word – legal education for all. To approach all facets of the legal (and the wider) academy with genuine care. The extra facets that keep a law school running, that is often unacknowledged? Reimbursement for the academic's engagement in "academic citizenship" (Davids, 2022, pp. 1–3).

Healing Time

In our vision for a law school, we see more time to pause. We dream and have more time to read, to heal and hold space for each other. We imagine time for staff to reflect upon their pedagogical approach and continuously learn. We foresee time for students to grasp the impact of the present laws they must work with and to learn how to challenge injustice. We demand more time to understand restorative justice and access to justice. In abolition we rebuild and revalue and give students choices on how they show learning. When we transform our relationships with time, we stop competing, the currency of the neoliberal law school is inconsequential and we are never productive again.

In the spirit of Tuck and Yang's argument that decolonisation is "not a metaphor" (2012, p. 1), we expand and assert that decolonising the curriculum is not a gimmick. We argue this to admonish the speed at which the term has been co-opted by upper-level management in higher education institutions. When we use the word "gimmick," we lean into the word both as the idea of a cheap showy ornamental figure and as a trick or device used to attract attention or market an institution. As a response to this, we offer the below advice to those who wish to decolonise.

Authors' Advice

1. ***Engage with Your Ego****. If engaged in decolonial work at the law school, explicitly credit your colleagues. Do credit your students for that privilege of developing a perspective of legal pedagogy. If someone's conversations have influenced your philosophy on legal pedagogy, acknowledge them explicitly. If you mention the work of others in your conference paper who have clearly influenced your course of thought, mention them, aloud and directly by name. Cite them in your publications (Ahmed, 2017, p. 14).*
2. ***Engage with Your Humanity****. Learn how to pronounce the names of your students and colleagues properly. This applies to the academics that you cite in your writings. This takes time; it is uncomfortable; everyone is vulnerable, but the power of taking the time to recognise and humanise each other is important.*
3. ***Engage with Your Resources****. PAY YOUR LABOUR COSTS. You cannot ask for volunteers, whether they are staff or students and draw on their free labour. Some of the basic needs for more genuine engagement can be met if the law school pays for the labour they demand, if they do not seek to control the process and they understand that it is labour intensive.*
4. ***Engage with Your Spaces****. Understand inclusive spaces, physical and digital spaces. You cannot hold a few meetings and then declare that the university is active in such work. Do not isolate the work from the person who is doing the work. Understand that these spaces may already exist; do not assume someone will want to work in the space you create if they already work in their own space.*
5. ***Engage with Your Perspectives****. To effectively decolonise the legal curriculum, you need to consider the whole law school and legal academia. Colonialism is*

a multi-institutional ongoing operation and so, you must be able to make individual interventions and system interventions. You must reflect upon every personal interaction, as well as the systems that interact with yourself, colleagues, and students. Decolonising the legal curriculum has to surpass the singular seminar, a sole module, or a university law school. It is a multi-institutional effort, requiring collective input. These things are important, not just for work that pertains to explicitly decolonising the legal curriculum but also work that is regarded as falling outside of that scope. It is not external or peripheral to the university; it should be part of the whole.

Conclusion

Ultimately, there is a limit to what could be decolonised, even if there is appetite, because it is the foundations of the law school that require transformation. It is important to note that our experiences of failure to decolonise our law school are echoed elsewhere. We argue that to decolonise there must be equal room for multiple voices, that you cannot decolonise alone, and, finally, that you cannot decolonise within the unchanging hierarchies of a university department. We contend that Queer, Black, and PoC women have spaces where they survive but do not thrive and so we, invoking Lorde's "masters tools," argue that you cannot decolonise a colonised system of knowledge; you can only transiently "beat him at his own game" (Lorde, 2007, p. 112). Perhaps, our mere existence is the embodiment of abolishing the law school. Our bodies, names, thoughts, and emotions are framed as unapologetic to the colonialist's eye and are interpreted as a threat to the status quo of legal education. The act of writing this chapter is a subversion of the "institutional legacy" (Ahmed, 2021, p. 158) and instead actively honours the legacy of the laborious efforts made by the Decolonise Keele Network, which has faded (Keele Student Union, Keele Postgraduate Association and Keele University College Union, 2018).

Additionally, we promise to return to these printed words with care (Coopmans, 2022) and to reflect further on what it means to decolonise legal education. We understand that the decolonial processes do not occur instantaneously but require approaches that are contrary to the neoliberal university. Resisting the allure of expertise, we are participants in a conversation, always learning, changing our minds, hearing others, and rebuilding constantly with our collective efforts. We promise to be humbled, to be corrected, and to enjoy the privilege to return to these words. We therefore conclude by demanding an end to the law school as it stands. As co-authors, we demand structural changes. Whilst we know our individual and collective existence, self-education, and conversation with one another threaten the status quo, we still take up space and embody resistance. However, until the time is valued, and space is made for dissent and thought to thrive, when the colonial law school calls to decolonise, it will always be disingenuous.

Acknowledgements

We would like to thank our comrades, S.A Bákàrè, Fides Dagongdong, Raveena Francis and Monique Sang, who have graduated and did so much of the initial grassroots work at Keele University. We want to appreciate the often-ignored space of Academic Instagram and Academic Twitter, where frequently a thread can change perspective, or recommend something new to read. We would like to acknowledge the collaborator staff, who work so hard to decolonise.

Many thanks are in order for the participants at the "Decolonisation, Anti-racism and Legal Pedagogy: Theory in Action" workshop, who took the time to listen to an earlier version of this chapter and for their insightful comments.

We would also like to give special thanks to the editors of the collection, Foluke Adebisi, Suhraiya Jivraj and Ntina Tzouvala for the space to host our words, and for providing generous feedback.

References

Adébísí, F. (2021) "Should We Rethink the Purposes of the Law School? A Case for Decolonial Thought In Legal Pedagogy", *Amicus Curiae*, 2(3), 428–449.

Ahmed, S. (2017) *Living a Feminist Life*, Durham, Duke University Press.

Ahmed, S. (2021) *Complaint!*, Durham, Duke University Press.

al Attar, M. and Abdelkarim, S. "Decolonising the Curriculum in International Law: Entrapments in Praxis and Critical Thought", *Law and Critique*, https://doi.org/10.1007/s10978-021-09313-y (accessed 2 January 2023).

Baboeram, P. (2020) *The Uprising*, https://www.youtube.com/watch?v=8GjRMQrJ2ig (accessed on 2 January 2023).

Bhambra, G. K., Nişancıoğlu, K. and Gebrial, D. (2020) "Decolonising the university in 2020", *Identities: Global Studies in Culture and Power*, 27(4), 509–516.

Bradley, G. M. and de Noronha, L. (2022) *Against Borders: The Case for Abolition*, London, Verso.

Coles, J. A., Ohito, E.O., Green, K. L. and Lyiscott, J. (2021) "Fugitivity and Abolition in Educational Research and Practice: An Offering", *Excellence in Education*, 54(2), 103–111.

Connected Sociologies (2020) *Equality and Rights in 21st Century Britain: From Trojan Horse to Grenfell*, https://www.connectedsociologies.org/events/equality_and_rights/ (accessed 2 January 2023).

Coopmans, C. (2022) "Recovering care for past publications: An exercise in vocation", in Lemon, N. (ed), *Healthy Relationships in Higher Education: Promoting Wellbeing Across Academia*, Abingdon, Routledge, 185–196.

Critical Resistance (n.d.) *What is Abolition?*, https://criticalresistance.org/mission-vision/not-so-common-language/ (accessed 2 January 2023).

Davids, N. (2022) "Professing the vulnerabilities of academic citizenship", *Ethics and Education*, 17(1), 1–13.

Day, A. S. and McBean, S. O. (2022) *Abolition Revolution*, London, Pluto Press.

Dennis, C. A. (2018) "Decolonising Education: A Pedagogic Intervention", in Bhambra, G. K., Gebrial, D. and Nişancıoğlu K. (eds), *Decolonising the University*, London, Pluto Press, 190–207.

Doharty, N., Madriaga, M. and Joseph-Salisbury, R. (2021) "The university went to 'decolonise' and all they brought back was lousy diversity double-speak! Critical race counter-stories from faculty of colour in 'decolonial' times", *Educational Philosophy and Theory*, 53(3), 233–244.

Eve, M. P. (2021) "The Abolition of the University", *Open Library of Humanities*, 7(1) 1–6.

El-Enany, N. (2020) *(B)ordering Britain: Law, Race and Empire*, Manchester, Manchester University Press.

Gilich, Y. and Boardman, T. (2022) "Wildcat Imaginaries: From Abolition University to University Abolition", *Critical Times* 5(1), 109–120.

Gorski, P. C. and Chen, C. (2015) " "Frayed All Over": The Causes and Consequences of Activist Burnout Among Social Justice Education Activists", *Educational Studies*, 51(5) 385–405.

Gregersen, E. (2022) "Telling stories about the law school: autoethnography and legal education", *The Law Teacher*, 56(2) 241–256.

Harney, S. and Moten, F. (2021) *All Incomplete*, New York, Minor Compositions.

Harney, S. and Moten F. (2013) *The Undercommons: Fugitive Planning & Black Study*, New York, Minor Compositions.

hooks, b. (1994) *Teaching to Transgress: Education as the Practice of Freedom*, London, Routledge.

Jivraj, S. (2022) "Researching Racialised Bodies in Higher Education: From Statistics to Storytelling", in Herman, D. and Parsley, C. (eds), *Interdisciplinarities: Research Process, Method, and the Body of Law*, Cham, Springer, 37–52.

Jivraj, S. (2020) *Towards Anti-Racist Legal Pedagogy: A Resource*, https://research.kent.ac.uk/decolonising-law-schools/wp-content/uploads/sites/866/2020/09/Towards-Anti-racist-Legal-Pedagogy-A-Resource.pdf (accessed 2 January 2023).

Keele Student Union, Keele Postgraduate Association and Keele University College Union. (2018) *Keele Decolonising the Curriculum Network: Why is My Curriculum So White?*, https://www.keele.ac.uk/equalitydiversity/equalityframeworksandactivities/equalityawardsandreports/equalityawards/raceequalitycharter/keeledecolonisingthecurriculumnetwork/ (accessed 2 January 2023).

Le Grange, L. (2016) "Decolonising the University Curriculum", *South African Journal of Higher Education*, 30(2), 1–12.

Literature Must Fall (2021) *Where Are All The White Voices – Panel Discussion*, https://www.instagram.com/p/CWJEORpMbo0/ (accessed 2 January 2023).

Lorde, A. (2007) *Sister Outsider: Essays & Speeches*, Berkley, Ten Speed Press.

Luke, N. and Heynen, N. (2021) "Abolishing the frontier: (De)colonizing 'public' education", *Social & Cultural Geography*, 22(3), 403–424.

Mason, L. (2021) *Decolonisation, Law and Legal Education: A Multimodal View*, https://africanlegalstudies.blog/2021/07/30/decolonisation-law-and-legal-education-a-multimodal-view/ (accessed 2 January 2023).

Mayorga, E., Leidecker, L. and Orr de Gutiérrez, D. (2019) "Burn it Down: The Incommensurability of the University and Decolonization", *Journal of Critical Thought and Praxis*, 8(1), 87–106.

Memon, A. R. and Jivraj, S. (2020) "Trust, courage and silence: carving out decolonial spaces in higher education through student-staff partnerships", *The Law Teacher*, 54(4), 475–488.

Morgan, B. and Thorpe, A. (2022) "Place-based pedagogies of hope", *International Journal of Law in Context* 18(4), 427–439.

Nash, R. J. and Viray, S. (2013) *Our Stories Matter: Liberating the Voices of Marginalized Students Through Scholarly Personal Narrative Writing*, New York, Peter Lang.
Olufemi, L. (2020) *Feminism, Interrupted: Disrupting Power*, London, Pluto Press.
Qureshi, S. (2019) "A Manifesto for Survival", in Emejulu, A. and Sobande, F. (eds), *To Exist is to Resist: Black Feminism in Europe*, London, Pluto Press, 205–218.
Rigney, S. (2020) "Creating the law school as a meeting place for epistemologies: decolonising the teaching of jurisprudence and human rights", *The Law Teacher*, 54(4), 503–516.
Rodríguez, D. (2019) "Abolition as Praxis of Human Being: A Foreword", *Harvard Law Review*, 132(6), 1575–1612.
Rodríguez, D. (2010) "The Disorientation of the Teaching Act: Abolition as Pedagogical Position", *The Radical Teacher* 88, 7–19.
The Law Society and the General Council of the Bar. (1999) *Joint statement on the academic stage of training*, https://www.sra.org.uk/students/academic-stage/academic-stage-joint-statement-bsb-law-society/ (accessed 2 January 2023).
Shain, F., Yıldız, Ü. K., Poku, V. and Gokay, B. (2021) "From silence to 'strategic advancement': institutional responses to 'decolonising' in higher education in England", *Teaching in Higher Education: Critical Perspectives*, 26(7–8), 920–936.
Tan, J. M. (2021) *The Many Layers of Invisible Labour Decolonising the Academy*, https://twailr.com/the-many-layers-of-invisible-labour-decolonising-the-academy/ (accessed 2 January 2023).
Tuck, E. and Yang, K. W. (2012) "Decolonization is not a metaphor", *Decolonization: Indigeneity, Education & Society*, 1(1), 1–40.
van Jaarsveldt, L. C., de Vries, M. S. and Kroukamp, H. J. (2018) "South African students call to decolonize science: Implications for international standards, curriculum development and Public Administration education", *Teaching Public Administration*, 37(1), 12–30.
wa Thiong'o, N. (1986) *Decolonising the Mind: The Politics of Language in African Literature*, Harare, Zimbabwe Publishing House.
Wane, N. N. (2013) "[Re]claiming Indigenous Knowledge: Challenges, Resistance, and Opportunities", *Decolonization: Indigeneity, Education & Society*, 2(1), 93–107.
Zembylas, M. (2021a) "Affective Strategies of Abolition Pedagogies in Higher Education: Dismantling the Affective Governmentality of Colonial University", *Equity & Excellence in Education* 54(2), 121–135.
Zembylas, M. (2021b) "Refusal as affective and pedagogical practice in higher education decolonization: a modest proposal", *Teaching in Higher Education: Critical Perspectives*, 26(7–8), 953–968.

2

THE PEDAGOGY OF MEMORY AND FORGETFULNESS

A Critical Review of Selected Aspects of the LLB Curriculum in ~~South~~ Africa

Ntando Sindane

Introduction

In his sermon about the consequences of forgetfulness, Barret J. Miller paraphrases Milan Kundera's iconic adage "The struggle of man against power is the struggle of memory against forgetting"; he explains that whenever the people of God forget who they are and their role in society, the church becomes embroiled in activities that are inimical to *the kingdom of God* (Miller 1984:279). Miller explains that in the task of confronting the empire and the powers of this world, there exists an omnipresent struggle between memory and forgetfulness.

In the context of ~~South~~ Africa, nobody unpacks this phenomenon better than artist/musician Thandiswa Mazwai. Thandiswa opens her song *Nizalwa Ngobani?* with the sentence "The world changes, revolutionaries die, and the children forget." Later in the song, she continues to lament: "We don't even cry, we don't even cry about it no more. Are the beautiful ones really dead?"[1] Only the first part of the song and the chorus are in English; the rest is in isiXhosa – the song's title *Nizalwa Ngobani* can be loosely translated to mean "Who has given birth to you?" She responds to this poignant question in the isiXhosa part of the song where she interludes: *Nizilibel'uba nizalwa ngobani*, which means "you have forgotten the people who gave birth to you." The struggle against memory and forgetting is encapsulated in Thandiswa's stern rebuke to Black ~~South~~ Africans whose conduct appears to be that of people who have forgotten that the fight to end apartheid and colonialism is ongoing and requires a memory of resistance and revolutionary vigilance. Prevailing forgetfulness is caused by the post-1994 culture of uncritical thinking and the ideologically porous politics of the mythical rainbow nation that neglect a holistic

DOI: 10.4324/9781003397885-4

analysis of the prevailing colonially structured polity. To be sure, after the attainment of political freedom, ~~South~~ Africans forgot to remember: thus failing to understand that the struggle between memory and forgetfulness means that they should continuously study the ontological granularities that define the 1994 moment.

~~South~~ Africa's Council on Higher Education (CHE) reviewed the LLB degree between 2013 and 2018, and it recommended that critical thinking skills should be the cornerstone of the LLB curriculum (Mokgatle 2018). The report is largely obscure on how exactly law teachers should include the aspect of critical thinking in the curriculum. This lack of definitional clarity as regards critical thinking skills stems from the fact that the review panel appreciates that "critical thinking" means that law teachers must, among other things, tell students to question and be critical of every prescribed reading, including the constitution.[2] Of course, the constitution enjoys "bible status" in post-1994 law academy, so it would be anomalous for CHE to boldly encourage an LLB curriculum that says to students, "Question this Eurocentric document that arrogantly claims legal/political/ideological supremacy." Indeed, this would go against the very culture of deifying the constitution that persists in ~~South~~ African law schools. The idea of decolonisation and decolonial approaches to the LLB curriculum appears to be an afterthought in the CHE report. The report does not apply itself sufficiently to the concept – as a result, it does not emerge in large portions of the text.

The argument in this chapter will be propounded in five segments, following this introduction, the second segment provides a theoretical basis for the claim that the #MustFall moment presented a *Decolonial Turn* in ~~South~~ Africa. The third segment illustratively studies two LLB curriculum study guides from two ~~South~~ African law faculties. The segment demonstrates the spectre of constitutional deification in ~~South~~ African law faculties and argues that this reality inevitably gives birth to a value-neutral enunciation of justice, freedom, and related topics and that this is an enactment of the lack of memory and the presence of forgetfulness because it broaches decolonisation using approaches that are inimical to it. The fourth segment notes the strides that have been made in seeking to decolonise the content of law that is taught in law faculties and argues that these should be seen as a launching pad for the more work that still needs to be done. The fifth and final segment concludes this chapter.

Theorising #MustFall Movements and the *Decolonial Turn*

Sabelo Ndlovu-Gatsheni historicises decolonial efforts into three epochal moments. The first two are the political decolonisation moment, as understood by the Kwame Nkrumah Generation, under the slogan: "seek first the political kingdom, and the rest shall follow." The second is known as the Bandung moment, which focused its energies on economic decolonisation. The third is the #FeesMustFall and #RhodesMustFall moment, which Ndlovu-Gatsheni describes as follows:

> The third is the current epistemological decolonisation represented by the Rhodes Must Fall (RMF) and Fees Must Fall (FMF) movements in ~~South~~ Africa, and which demand decommissioning of colonial/apartheid iconographies, changing the very idea of the university, its curriculum, scholarship, institutional cultures, and pedagogies.
>
> *(Ndlovu-Gatsheni 2021:16)*

From the third epochal moment, we are able to think and reflect on the meaning of the *Decolonial Turn*. The praxis, and contextual relevance, of the *Decolonial Turn* is such that it presents an invitation, particularly to law teachers and academics, to begin (and continue) thinking about the meanings of concepts such as freedom and justice in ~~South~~ Africa after the 1994 [democratic] breakthrough. Closely studied, #MustFall's call for free education goes beyond fees and translates to an education system that is free from everything that maintains and replicates all known forms of oppression, these include racism, sexism, coloniality, homophobia, xenophobia, Afrophobia, Westernisation, Eurocentricism, dis-memberment, othering, and so forth.

The *Decolonial Turn* places a positive duty on law academics and thinkers to reflect on what #FeesMustFall means for their respective areas of discipline. The intellectual epoch insists that the academy should engage in an inquiry to ascertain the opportunities that the *Decolonial Turn* presents to the epistemic foundations/compositions of the LLB curriculum.

Mignolo's *Local Histories/Global Designs: Coloniality, Subaltern Knowledges, and Border Thinking* serves as an appropriate starting point when historicising discussions about the *Decolonial Turn* – he explains that in the 16th-century Spanish missionaries came into contact with people from the Global South and declared that people shall be judged (engaged with) on the basis of their (in)ability to read/write and use the European alphabet (Mignolo 2012:3). Mignolo figures that this was the beginning of the colonial difference and the Atlantic imaginary – he defines colonial difference to mean "the classification of the planet in the modern/colonial imaginary by enacting coloniality of power to transform differences into values" (Mignolo 2012:13).

Towards the 18th century and the beginning of the 19th century, the yardstick was no longer the ability to read/write in alphabet but rather "history" – the resultant effect of this was that those who could read/write in alphabet were said to have had a history, and those who could not read/write in alphabet had no history (Mignolo 2012:3). The function of relegating to "sub-human," people who could not read/write in alphabet, and declaring that their inability to read/write in alphabet to mean that they do not have a history, is at the centre of the coloniality of knowledge, and it is what Mignolo refers to as the "subalternization of knowledge" (Mignolo 2012:12–13).

A fundamental understanding of the essence of the *Decolonial Turn* can be drawn from another of Walter Mignolo's works, "Epistemic Disobedience and the Decolonial Option: A Manifesto,":

> The decolonial turn is the opening and the freedom from the thinking and the forms of living (economies-other, political theories-other), the cleansing of the coloniality of being and of knowledge; the de-linking from the spell of the rhetoric of modernity, from its imperial imaginary articulated in the rhetoric of democracy.
>
> *(Mignolo 2011:48)*

The *Decolonial Turn* is thus a fundamental rupture that happens when a specific colonial society undergoes a notable action that seeks and calls for radical change. This rupture may be evidenced in different epochs of history – for example, the youth uprising of June 1976 could legitimately be understood as a form of a *Decolonial Turn* because the uprisings brought about a precise rupture that had the impact of changing ~~South~~ Africa's course of history. To be sure, the June 16 generation of students precipitated a rupture that had the ~~South~~ African society questioning (with the intention to de-link), the colonial modes of control that insisted that a colonial and regressive Afrikaans language should become the medium of instruction in ~~South~~ African schools. This *Decolonial Turn* presented the academy with an opportunity to extensively engage with the epistemic toxicity of language in colonies – wherein the oppressor used language as a weapon to replicate and reinscribe his image in the imaginations of the colonised, and thus deepen their colonial malady.

~~South~~ Africa is currently undergoing a *Decolonial Turn* – this reality comes in the aftermath of the 2015/2016 #MustFall student protests in Technical and Vocational Education and Training colleges (TVETs) and Universities. Having firmly made the resounding calls for ~~South~~ Africa's epistemic systems to be decolonised, #MustFall places a duty on critical academics to read, think, and investigate the conceptual possibilities that decoloniality would/could present to prospects of transforming the LLB curriculum.

Grosfoguel (2007) puts forth three suppositions to crystalise his critique of "one world" fundamentalisms: (1) that a decolonial epistemic perspective requires a broader canon of thought than simply the Western canon, (2) that a truly universal decolonial perspective cannot be based on an abstract universal (one particular that raises itself as universal global design) but would have to be the result of the critical dialogue between diverse critical epistemic/ethical/political projects towards a pluriversal as opposed to a universal world, and (3) that decolonisation of knowledge would require to take seriously the epistemic perspective/cosmologies/insights of critical thinkers from the Global South thinking from and with subalternised racial/ethnic/sexual spaces and bodies.

The Two Study Guides – Selected Aspects of the LLB Curriculum

The general teaching practice in South African law faculties entails the use of study guides. These are book-presented pamphlets wherein lecturers carefully take students through the most important aspects of the module. Although the study guide is usually accompanied by other teaching material (such as prescribed textbooks, articles, and case law), it is the most comprehensive teaching tool, because it embodies all aspects of the module content.

To illustrate the essence of the pedagogy of memory and forgetfulness in the LLB curriculum in the era after the #MustFall moment, this chapter samples two LLB study guides from two of ~~South~~ Africa's law faculties; the first is Historical Foundations of South African Law – HFL1501 (compiled by A Bauling & L Wildenboer) – and the second is Private International Law – LPIL4814 (compiled by A September van Huffel). The latter is a final-year module presented at the University of the Free State's Faculty of Law, whilst the former is a first-year module presented at the University of South Africa's College of Law. Both study guides are compiled in the aftermath of the #MustFall moment and in law faculties that have publicly claimed to embrace the calls for the LLB curriculum to be decolonised.

I have been an academic at both universities where these modules are taught and am currently engaged in the teaching of the latter. Although the critique presented in this chapter may largely appear as a critique of the teaching methods of others, it is actually constitutive of self-critique and reflection. Decolonially speaking, this chapter's critique presents an inward-looking attempt to respond to the pitfalls of the pedagogy of memory and forgetfulness.

HFL1501 is an introductory module that sets itself to the task of unpacking the historical foundations of ~~South~~ African law. The study guide is divided into three parts and 15 units (learning areas): the first part deals with the origins of *South* African law, the second part deals with the historical foundations and development of the law of property and obligations, and the third part deals with the role of the Constitution in ~~South~~ African legal development.

LPIL4814 is a final-year elective that aims to equip students with the skills to apply international legal principles to private conflicts. The purpose of this module is to introduce students to the operation of private international law in the ~~South~~ African legal system and its origins, theories, roles, and functions. The module is organised into 17 units (learning areas) that range from discussing the scope, place, and choice of law rules within the legal system, the Roman Empire and Roman-Dutch contribution to private international law, the Statutists theories up to the early 20th century in private international law: 12th to 15th centuries, the French 16th century, the 19th and 20th centuries, the Incidental Question, Renvoi, and others.

The LPIL4814 module deserves further comment: although private international law is mainly focused on the conflict of laws (or instances where local courts have to adjudicate over matters that are governed by foreign legal prescripts) rather than international law per se, it is prudent to assert that the international law element is reasonably subject to decolonial and critical scrutiny by international scholars from the Global South, notably known as Third World Approaches to International Law (TWAIL).[3] TWAIL mostly sets its sights and critique on the public law aspects of international law. Arguably, TWAIL's methodological problematisation of (public) international law is applicable to private international law. Indeed, this is because TWAIL *inter alia* insists that the problematic in the setting of international law is that it continues to mirror the intellectual/legalistic sensitivities of the Global North, thus deepening the undoing and othering the pluriversal epistemic traditions of the Global South and the rest of the colonised world. As shown below, the LPIL4814 module is guilty of the very habit of the problematic illustrated by TWAIL; it recounts the idea of conflict of laws from the prism of Europe (most notably Roman-Dutch histories and traditions), whilst neglecting to concern itself with how Africans and all colonised societies contended/grappled with the idea of conflict of laws at an international level.

Synoptically, these two modules are good examples of the prevailing lack of memory and presence of forgetfulness in ~~South~~ African law faculties as regards how the law must be taught in the aftermath of the #MustFall call for the curriculum to be decolonised. Although many issues can be raised, I shall zone in on four aspects of these study guides to illustrate the pedagogy of memory and forgetfulness:

First, there appears to be a constitutional deification in both study guides. Notwithstanding that ~~South~~ Africa is a constitutional democracy that espouses a supreme constitution, the guides tend not to be attentive to the decolonial critique of the South African constitution – the guides fail to demonstrate #MustFall's clear rejection of the constitution, and its accompanied critique that the constitution is an embodiment of the politics, sensitivities, and aspirations of colonial worldmaking, and a racist structural design that continues to cement white privilege and supremacy. HFL1501 dedicates four of its 15 units to this exercise, it further argues that the constitution is the most viable tool to transform ~~South~~ Africa, failing to appreciate the memory of #MustFall's contrary approach to the same question.

Second, both study guides have a singular and universalistic reading of the history of ~~South~~ Africa and the world. To be sure, this means that both study guides tend to be absent of the fact that history is an exercise of power and that the decolonial project calls for a pluriversal reading and conception of history; an understanding that many worlds exist in one world, and that history does not begin and end with Europe, Rome, British, and Roman-Dutch traditions. LPIL4814 is most guilty of this habit; it begins the history of private international law in Roman Empire and Roman-Dutch contribution to private international law, completely ignoring to canvass how Africa and the Global South dealt with questions of private law conflicts at an international level.

Third, there is a glaring absence of race, culture, and socio-political analysis in how both study guides approach their teaching of the origins of ~~South~~ African law. This is emblematic of pre #MustFall legal pedagogical patterns that wrongly insisted that the law is a science that is insulated from political and social currents of the day.

Fourth, both study guides completely avoid/ignore the #MustFall moment and the *Decolonial Turn* it presented to the academy. None of the two study guides even attempt to grapple with the idea of decolonisation, let alone Africanisation and related critical approaches to the law. From reading the two guides, you wouldn't be faulted for thinking that the #MustFall moment did not happen, because the teaching of law has maintained a "business as usual" approach.

Cumulatively, these examples of the pedagogy of memory and forgetfulness are at the heart of ongoing debates and critiques in the ~~South~~ African academy. For example, in a different text, I address the question of constitutional deification, summarily making a threefold argument: (1) that there is a very real difference between decolonisation/Africanisation and transformative constitutionalism; (2) decolonial theory and ~~South~~ Africa's *Decolonial Turn* precisely rejects and criticises the post-1994 constitutional arrangement, therefore, making transformative constitutionalism a misfit in the quest to decolonise and Africanise the LLB curriculum; and (3) that the commitment to decolonisation means to embrace a comprehensive rethink of ~~South~~ Africa, including its foundational chassis, the constitution (Sindane 2021:238).

The thesis of my argument is that in the intervening period between #MustFall protests and 2022, law teachers have sought to use a liberal constitutionalist language to articulate the goals of decolonisation and that this stifles the very essence of decolonisation. This liberal constitutionalist habit appears to be not unique to ~~South~~ Africa, especially when considering that Tuck and Yang note the same sort of attitude in the United States of America, where the academy tends to speak about decolonisation in the metaphorical:

> One trend we have noticed, with growing apprehension, is the ease with which the language of decolonization has been superficially adopted into education and other social sciences, supplanting prior ways of talking about social justice, critical methodologies, or approaches which decenter settler perspectives. Decolonization, which we assert is a distinct project from other civil and human rights-based social justice projects, is far too often subsumed into the directives of these projects, with no regard for how decolonization wants something different than those forms of justice.
>
> *(Tuck & Yang 2012:12)*

Decolonial and constitutional lexicography are inherently contradictory to each other because their ontological starting points are different; the constitution assumes that the 1994 moment sufficiently humanised the dehumanised colonial bodies (Sindane 2020:23), whereas decolonial theory lends a definition of peoples in accordance to the prevailing colonially structured setting, which asserts that there can never be equality between humans residing in the zone of being and those residing in the zone of non-being (Sindane 2021:243).

Albertyn contrarily contends that the constitution should be construed as non-static and forward-looking document, instead of it being cast in stone – she insists that it has a role in addressing inequalities in ~~South~~ Africa and precisely wants to bring about the envisaged, yet highly elusive equality (Albertyn 2019:753). Albertyn's framing of the debate about equality is not hinged on the analysis of the prevailing colonially structured setting, neither does it stick to the zone of being and zone of non-being markers; she instead insists that the debate is between a dominant, liberal egalitarian/social democratic view based on social inclusion and sufficiency, and a more transformative/democratic socialist approach based on greater material and social equality (Albertyn 2019:756).

The images "zone of being" and "zone of non-being" are drawn from Frantz Fanon's conceptualisation of the colonial reality that others, dismembers, and dehumanises colonised people, thus relegating them to the zone of dehumanised bodies, also known as the zone of non-being – he posits that

> [t]he effective disalienation of the black man entails an immediate recognition of social and economic realities. If there is an inferiority complex, it is the outcome of a double process: primarily economic; subsequently, the internalization – or, better, the epidermalization of this inferiority.
>
> *(Fanon 1952:4)*

Although Fanon was observing the particular colonial situation of his time, this specificity is not lost to the argument advanced in this chapter because the present-day situation differs very little, and as a result, there still exists a zone of being and a zone of non-being because coloniality is the vestigial force of colonialism (Maldonado-Torres 2007:4).

Tuck and Yang insist that decolonisation is not a metaphor, arguing that prevailing decolonial discourse has had the habit of assuming a value-neutral lexicon in articulating its intended goals and objectives. In this instance, decolonisation loses its original meaning, instead taking a metaphorical enunciation where it is used to advance social justice, human rights, and other struggles, whilst neglecting the core demands of decolonisation (Tuck & Yang 2012:3).

Heyns does not reject transformative constitutionalism and transformative legal education; she instead notes the paradox between change and stability, arguing that transformation requires change whereas constitutionalism assumes stability – ideologically contradictory ideals which may lead to varying outcomes (Heyns 2014:85).

The two study guides used in this chapter fail to appreciate that the constitutional demands of ~~South~~ Africa are set up to protect private property in the strongest terms, thus making it impossible to "seize imperial wealth" either through a mass-led revolutionary programme or by means of state-led expropriation without compensation. This chapter's critique exposes that the equality expectations of the constitutional polity tend to muddy the waters in terms of specifically identifying victims and perpetrators, preferring instead to focus on peace, stability of democratic institutions, and the highly elusive rainbow nation reconciliation project.

Decolonial theory, according to Tuck and Yang, specifically understands that white people enjoy an undeserved white privilege in the post-colony and that their insistence on the metaphor is a deliberate ploy to maintain and (re) produce white privilege in self-defined anti-racist settings and organisations (Tuck & Yang 2012:9). This phenomenon is what they refer to as a "settler move to innocence," which encapsulates the metaphor as a sanitisation of white people from their racism, the sins of their ancestors, and their subsequent benefits therein – they succeed through "framework of excuses, distractions, and diversions from decolonization."

Another trick of the metaphor exists in the implicit appropriation of the pain of colonised peoples. This cannot be truer in the constitutionalist notion of "we the people" and the "injustices of our past," which somewhat seek to suggest that settlers and colonised peoples can have a shared history.[4] Modiri coins this as the disavowal of colonial horrors by a constitutional project that claims unity of a people in the absence of justice, reparation, and restoration (Modiri 2018:308). The homogenising of various experiences of oppression as colonisation, calling different groups "colonized" without describing their relationship to settler colonialism is an equivocation, which again begs the point to be made about how the constitution jumps the hurdle of expressly recognising the status of colonised people, as worthy of redress and indeed reparations.

Tuck, Yang, Madlingozi, Modiri, and Zitzke are just a few of the many examples that could be drawn from critical legal scholarship that bemoan the post-#MustFall constitutional deification, the continued triumph of liberal conceptions of constitutionalism, and the stifling of decolonial articulations.

Decolonial Directions for the LLB Curriculum

Although there are a handful of scholars who have wrestled with the question of how to approach decolonising the LLB curriculum, this segment studies the contributions of three law academics who come from the leftist critical legal school, and these are Dlamini, Zitzke, and Madlingozi.

Notwithstanding that the thesis of this chapter's argument is that the #MustFall protest amounts to a *Decolonial Turn*, it is crucial to assert that the discussions problematising ~~South~~ Africa's legal education predate the CHE LLB report and indeed the #MustFall uprisings. Various scholars have grappled with this topic since the dawn of democracy, and Dlamini is said to be the most prominent among them. Dlamini acknowledges that the fundamental question in the LLB curriculum lies in honestly grappling with the purpose of legal education. He insists that law teachers should always look towards the end goal – he argues that beyond the expectation that law graduates should be able to think logically and critically, legal education should engender a strong sense of social justice in a student (Dlamini 1992:596). Dlamini argues that colonial and apartheid legal education is not able to realise this ideal, especially for Black students (Dlamini 1992:597). Dlamini digs even deeper, to the extent that he problematises the medium of instruction in law faculties – his critique reminds us that the question of language remains unresolved in the post-1994 polity (Dlamini 1992:604).

Zitzke launches his critique of the LLB curriculum by illustrating that it has reached what he calls a "code red" status (Zitzke 2014:53); this is exemplified by how South Africa's legal education is still steeped in conservative legal traditions in terms of which teachers train students to become docile bodies fit to serve at the behest of capitalist interests (Zitzke 2014:64). This type of legal education embraces positivist ideals and urges students to be indifferent towards South Africa's apartheid and colonial reality – indeed, it is a curriculum that is committed to race denialism and forgetfulness. The emphasis of the LLB curriculum is not to produce intellectually astute law graduates, with adequate critical legal skills but instead law faculties focus on crafting a curricular framework that is linked to profit and the marketability of law graduates (Modiri 2014:2). Zitzke's critique is launched in 2014, just a year before the outbreak of the #MustFall protests – in 2018, two years after the #MustFall protests, he follows through with an even stronger critique of the law itself, in a treatise entitled: "A decolonial critique of private law and human rights" (Zitzke 2018:492–516). Zitzke's 2018 critique is hedged in his fundamental belief that an uncritical acceptance of a transformative constitutionalist reading of human rights is not the solution to the epistemic challenges that face private law (Zitzke 2018:494).

Thinking beyond transformation lends itself to more critical approaches to the law and inevitably teases out the authenticity of the calls to decolonise legal education. The assertion that transformative constitutionalist methods may not be helpful should not be misconstrued as a rejection of constitutionalism per se. Instead, Zitzke notes that constitutionalist rejection has its roots in conservative and purist traditions and histories of South Africa's apartheid jurisprudence. In the wake of the growing calls for the release of Nelson Mandela, and for apartheid to end, the South African judiciary saw classic common law purism transmute into a different form; instead of boasting overly Roman-Dutch Law and English law normative legalist systems, this new wave of purism could be evidenced by its avoidance of constitutionalism and human rights discourses post-1994 (Zitzke 2018:495). As a result, Zitzke does not pit himself in the same hymn sheet as common law purists (Zitzke 2017:202) of the 1980s by proposing a complete rejection of the constitution; instead, he opines that for the current epistemic challenges, there is a need to look beyond liberal constitutionalist suppositions (Zitzke 2018:502).

The 2018 critique is relevant to this chapter because it echoes the Tuck and Yang sentiment that the transformative articulations of law and justice in pursuit of re-ordering society in the aftermath/afterlife of colonial apartheid do not have the same ideational thrust as decolonial suppositions; instead, it evades serious questions of redress and reparations, preferring not to disturb prevailing social order and thus create a false sense of comfort and complacency.

Madlingozi authors a PhD thesis titled "Mayibuye iAfrika?: Disjunctive inclusions and black strivings for constitution and belonging in '~~South~~ Africa.'" In this thesis, Madlingozi analyses the strivings for constitution and belonging from the perspective of an African (Madlingozi 2018:1–225). He sharply criticises ~~South~~ Africa's constitutional polity, arguing that it is founded on elitist pacts that do not reflect the material and spiritual aspirations of the people on whose behalf it claims its genesis.

The central thesis of Madlingozi's argument is twofold: (1) that the perennial protest by marginalised communities is impelled by the fact that the constitution does not rise to the demand of decolonisation and (2) that the constitution's failure to live up to decolonial demands can be understood from studying the ambivalent racial melancholia and the double-consciousness of ~~South~~ Africa's political elite. Madlingozi accordingly labels these ANC (cohort of leaders between 1984 and 1996) political elites as *exceptional natives* and *amakholwa* (Madlingozi 2018:68). This labelling is a testament, and with reference, to their mostly Western-educated and Christiancentric conditioning. The constitution that is agreed upon between colonisers and their collaborating Black elites is thus not a product of a people coming together but rather a pact between colonisers and native elites who assimilated and were co-opted into whiteness and the white-dominated world.

In a subsequent intervention, Madlingozi argues that the post-1994 reality should be understood as a subtler form of apartheid; he accordingly labels this as "neo-apartheid constitutionalism," he accordingly posits:

> Neo-apartheid constitutionalism is the name I propose to call this political and legal system that reiterates the constitutive ontological Manichaeism at the heart of the founding of South Africa in 1910. I borrow and expand

> upon the concept of "neo-apartheid" from Leonard Gentle who defines it as a socioeconomic system where "capitalist accumulation has been filtered through and sustained by social relations inherited from colonialism …" I expand on this concept and propose to introduce it into the lexicon of constitutional discourse to call attention to the fact that post-1994 constitutional re-arrangements are transforming society in ways that do not instantiate a fundamental rupture with the inherited, sedimented and bifurcated social configuration.
>
> *(Madlingozi 2017:125)*

The image "bifurcated social configuration" speaks to the very lived ~~South~~ African reality of a socio-economic gap that continues to widen between rich people and poor people. The meanings of rich and poor still carry the same race/class divide that it did prior to the democratic breakthrough, and indeed the promulgation of the constitution. The absence of a fundamental rupture means that the constitution does very little to constitute a new polity; instead, it reconstitutes the old political society but now with a newer post-1994 language of optimism and rainbow nation, whilst maintaining the racist colonial patterns of power and control.

By Way of Conclusion

Towards the end of *Nizalwa Ngobani*, Thandiswa Mazwai interludes in isiXhosa: *Ntlungu zobawo belwel'inguquko – Ntlungu zonina belilela wena – Int'oyaziyo kuzigqib'iindab'eGoli. – Ntlungu zobawo befel'inguquko – Ntlungu zonina belilela wena – Int'oyaziyo kuzigqib'iindab'eGoli.* Loosely translated:

> The struggles of your fathers fighting for freedom – The struggles of your mother's tears – The struggles of your fathers dying for freedom – The struggles of your mother's tears – What you know is to be a gossip monger in eGoli (the city).

In this part of the song, Thandiswa appears to be rebuking and reprimanding forgetfulness, loss of memory, and the lack of critical introspection by the children of freedom.

The struggle between memory and forgetfulness is a theme on which this chapter's argument is based. The chapter demonstrated that the #MustFall moment presented a *Decolonial Turn* to ~~South~~ Africa's polity. The thesis of the chapter's argument is that the most intellectually candid way to respond to the struggle between memory and forgetfulness is to engage in the continuous task of critically assessing the strides/losses that have been made/suffered in between epochs of worldmaking. The chapter's critical assessment was located on the articulation of decolonisation in the LLB curriculum in ~~South~~ African universities in the period in the aftermath of the #MustFall moment. It found that ~~South~~ African law faculties have the liberal habit of ascribing to decolonisation a language of reform and constitutionalism. ~~South~~ African law faculties must be wary of the pedagogy of memory and forgetfulness because it presents a reactionary danger to the strides that have been made in the quest to transform the LLB curriculum specifically, and the academy in general.

Acknowledgments

I wish to thank Thabile Ntiwane for the generous donations towards buying some of the books that I use for my postgraduate studies and research. I am mightily thankful to Keslyn Swartz for sharing some of her Unisa LLB study material with me in the course of putting this chapter together. I co-teach African Customary Law with Caroline Müller van der Westhuizen. I wish to thank her for taking the leading role in the teaching and administration of our module; this has afforded me ample time to focus on research. This chapter is a product of numerous debates with colleagues and comrades at the University of the Free State (UFS) and the University of South Africa (Unisa). The acknowledgement of my UFS and Unisa colleagues is particularly crucial because this work is critical of some of their teaching methods and approaches. I thank all of them for their contribution. The usual disclaimers are applicable.

Notes

1 Mazwai T, Nizalwa Ngobani? YouTube – https://youtu.be/AfT6qk0--H (Accessed at 27 November 2021)

2 For purposes of this exposition, "constitution" will be intentionally written with a small letter "c" instead of caps. This complements the chapter's approach that hedges a decolonial critique against the deification of the constitution of the Republic of South Africa. Decolonial legal critical scholarship appreciates that one of the weaknesses of ~~South~~ Africa's intellectual traditions is that it unduly places the constitution at the zenith of epistemic suppositions, falsely claiming that this is so merely because of its supremacy. Because of the reality of coloniality, and the need for ~~South~~ Africa to still undergo substantive decolonisation, it is prudent to revisit all institutions of power and control, and this includes the constitution. This approach/reasoning is drawn from a similar practice in Mogobe Ramose, "Towards a Post-conquest South Africa: Beyond the Constitution of 1996" (Ramose 2018: 326–341).

3 Some prominent TWAIL scholars include Mohammed Bedjaoui, Antony Anghie, Makau Mutua, Sylvia Tamale, Mohsen Al Attar, Tendayi Achiume, Babatunde Fagbayibo, Khaled Al-Kassimi, Thomas Gathii, and others.

4 The preamble of the ~~South~~ African constitution 1996 reads: "We, the people of South Africa, Recognise the injustices of our past; Honour those who suffered for justice and freedom in our land; Respect those who have worked to build and develop our country."

References

Albertyn C, '(In)Equality and the South African Constitution' (2019) *Development Southern Africa* 36 751.

Dladla N, 'The Liberation of History and the End of South Africa: Some Notes towards an Azanian Historiography in Africa, South' (2018) *South African Journal on Human Rights* 34 415.

Dlamini CRM, 'The Law Teacher, The Law Student and Legal Education in South Africa' (1992) *South African Law Journal* 109 595.

Fanon F, *Black Skin White Masks* (Pluto Press 1952).

Grosfoguel R, 'The Epistemic Decolonial Turn' (2007) *Cultural Studies* 21 211.

Heyns A, 'The Inoperative Community of Law Students: Rethinking the Foundations of Legal Culture' (2014) *Acta Academica* 46 77.

Madlingozi T, 'Social Justice in a Time of Neo-Apartheid Constitutionalism: Critiquing the Anti-Black Economy of Recognition, Incorporation and Distribution' (2017) *Stellenbosch Law Review* 28 123.

Madlingozi T, *Mayibuye IAfrika?: Disjunctive Inclusions and Black Strivings for Constitution and Belonging in "South Africa"* (Birkbeck, University of London 2018).

Maldonado-Torres N, 'On the Coloniality of Being: Contributions to the Development of a Concept' (2007) *Cultural Studies* 21 240.

Mignolo W, 'Epistemic Disobedience and the Decolonial Option: A Manifesto' (2011) *Transmodernity* 44 66.

Mignolo W, *Local Histories/Global Designs* (Princeton University Press 2012).

Miller JB, 'The Struggle of Memory Against Forgetting' (1984) *Historical Magazine of the Protestant Episcopal Church* 53 279.

Modiri JM, 'The Crises in Legal Education' (2014) *Acta Academica* 46 1.

Modiri JM, 'Conquest and Constitutionalism: First Thoughts on an Alternative Jurisprudence' (2018) *South African Journal on Human Rights* 34 300.

Mokgatle O and others, 'The State of the Provision of the Bachelor of Laws (LLB) Qualification in South Africa' (2018) *De Rebus Magazine.*

Ndlovu-Gatsheni SJ, 'The Cognitive Empire, Politics of Knowledge and African Intellectual Productions: Reflections on Struggles for Epistemic Freedom and Resurgence of Decolonisation in the Twenty-First Century' (2021) *Third World Quarterly* 42 882.

Nizalwa Ngobani - Thandiswa Mazwai (2004).

Ramose MB, 'Towards a Post-Conquest South Africa: Beyond the Constitution of 1996' (2018) *South African Journal on Human Rights* 34 326.

Sindane N, 'The Call to Decolonise Higher Education: Copyright Law through an African Lens' (University of South Africa 2020).

Sindane N, 'Why Decolonisation and Not Transformative Constitutionalism' (2021) *Pretoria Student Law Review* 15 236.

Tuck E and Yang W, 'Decolonization Is Not a Metaphor' (2012) *Decolonization: Indigeneity, Education & Society* 1 1.

Zitzke E, 'Stop the Illusory Nonsense! Teaching Transformative Delict' (2014) *Acta Academica* 46 52.

Zitzke E, 'The History and Politics of Contemporary Common-Law Purism' (2017) *Fundamina Journal of Legal History* 23 185.

Zitzke E, 'A Decolonial Critique of Private Law and Human Rights' (2018) *South African Journal on Human Rights* 34 492.

The Study Guides Used

Historical Foundations of South African Law – HFL1501 (compiled by A Bauling & L Wildenboer), University of South Africa, 2022.
Private International Law – LPIL4814 (compiled by A September van Huffel), University of the Free State, 2020.

3

THE RECOGNITION OF PASIFIKA DECOLONIAL PEDAGOGIES AS INCLUSIVE PRACTICE IN LAW SCHOOLS AND CRITICAL LEGAL SCHOLARSHIP

Bridget Fa'amatuainu

Part I: Introduction

This chapter explores structural challenges to using Pasifika decolonial pedagogies in legal education in Aotearoa (New Zealand). I adopt the *Cartography of Decolonization* conceptual framework of analysis (Andreotti et al. 2015) to critically draw out the experience of Pasifika Early Career Academics (PECA) in the legal academy and to enable discussion and reflection on whether the pedagogical practices adopted are in fact decolonising. This conceptual framework further enables the critique of inclusivity and representational diversity schemes that – ironically – reproduce the harms of coloniality through hierarchised inequalities without adequately addressing the deeply entrenched coloniality and racialisation of legal education. And herein lies the problem: the entanglement with unequal power relations that elevate the status of those claiming benefits of coloniality at the expense of "othered" populations evidently reproduce the very epistemic injustices, inequalities, and traditional teaching pedagogies in legal education that are reflective of coloniality (Adebisi 2021). The law is a double-edged sword in Māori and Pasifika communities: on the one hand, it was a mechanism for colonial governance, exclusion, and assimilation, resulting in ongoing intergenerational legal, political, and economic marginalisation and disenfranchisement; on the other hand, it contributes to emancipation, inclusion, and protection. I argue that more legal academics should commit to building decolonial knowledge production, in practice, theory, research, and teaching, not to tick boxes but to equip all legal academics (not just PECA) to engage in decolonial legal and plural epistemologies that seek to embrace new ways of thinking, new ways of teaching, new

DOI: 10.4324/9781003397885-5

ways of inclusive diverse representation, in the "beyond reform" space to disrupt the racial disparities embedded in structural and institutional practices.

In this chapter, "Pasifika" encompasses the different ethnic population groups from Melanesia, Micronesia, and Polynesia residing in Aotearoa. I emphasise Samoa because I identify as Samoan by descent, although I am recognised as a diasporic Samoan by local Samoan as I was born, raised, and educated in Aotearoa. Samoa is known to be hierarchical and ordered according to customs and traditions reflected in chiefly village and family status. Samoa carries a colonial legacy of introduced common law from its former colonial administrators (Care 1997), England and Aotearoa. The establishment of institutions and legal systems that reflected patriarchal and Christian ideals of their own societies no doubt impacted political and legal thought on democracy, justice, and human rights in Samoa and other colonised nations across the commonwealth (Huffer 2006).

Samoa gained political independence from New Zealand in 1962 becoming the first Pacific nation to achieve this status and was the first Pacific nation with a written constitution which enumerates fundamental human rights. This resulted in an overriding bi-jural system in Samoa (i.e. customary legal system and state legal system) which operates alongside village councils, either governed under separate legal orders or in conflict with or complementary to the overriding bi-jural system (Merry 1988). This legacy remains after the end of formal colonialism, a reality shared across countries with a similar post-colonial legacy (Merry 1988). In *FAST Party v Attorney General* [2021] WSSC 24 at 91, the Supreme Court of Samoa noted: "The whole raison d'etre of Independence was for Samoa to free itself from its colonial shackles retaining only those institutions and practices it considered worthwhile." Reflecting this, a decolonial approach is foregrounded in "the praxis of living and in the idea of theory-and-as-praxis and praxis-and-as-theory, and in the interdependence and continuous flow of movement of both" (Mignolo 2007; Mignolo and Walsh 2018: 7p; Monson et al. 2022). Its starting point is to undo the oppressive frameworks and Western tools of colonisation embedded in laws and institutions while privileging critical and multidimensional approaches to legal scholarship as a form of anti-subordination (Kabutaulaka 2015; Thaman 2003).

Aotearoa is not only a bi-jural country where common law and Māori law co-exist together (Mikaere 2005, 2007) but also a diverse country with a variety of different ethnic population groups. Of the main population groups, the largest ethnic group is European (70.2%), followed by Māori (16.5%), the indigenous people of Aotearoa, Asian people (15.5%), Pacific (Pasifika) peoples (8.3%), and a small percentage of other ethnicities. The main Pasifika populations are Sāmoan (47.9%), Tongan (21.6%), Cook Islands Māori (21.1%), Niuean (8.1%), Fijian (5.2%), and Tokelauan (2.3%) (Statistics New Zealand 2019, 2020). Each island nation has its own unique cultures and traditions, and there are diasporic people born and raised in Aotearoa, some of whom may not affiliate with their culture. Many people in Aotearoa identify with multiple ethnicities or cultural backgrounds (which is why the percentages above add up to more than 100) (Ministry for Pacific Peoples 2021).

With the background set, this chapter proceeds as follows: Part II outlines the growth of Māori pedagogy in Aotearoa, both generally and in law, and its acceptance by the legal profession and law schools, identifying the gaps that existed and the need for change. Part III outlines the growth of Pasifika decolonial pedagogy and what it entails, with commentary as to any overlaps, differences, or similarities with Māori pedagogy. Finally, Part IV provides concluding commentary on progress and recommendations for the future.

Part II: The growth of Māori pedagogy in Aotearoa

Since the 1970s, and in partial response to the Māori Land Rights advocacy work of Whina Cooper and Te Roopu o Matakite (O'Malley, Stirling and Penetito 2010), there has been a growing recognition of the importance of biculturalism and of the traditional teaching and learning practices of Māori people in the education system and a push to incorporate them into mainstream teaching practices. Critical to this was the revitalisation of te reo Māori (the Māori language) in the 1970s and 1980s (Kāretu 1993, King 2018, Tawhiwhirangi 2014, Te Huia 2015). As more Māori language immersion schools were established, Māori pedagogy became more widely recognised and valued (King 2018, Muller and Kire 2014). The Crown's commitment to this was marked by the launch of the Maihi Karauna Māori Language Revitalisation Strategy 2019–2023 (Te Puni Kōkiri 2019) in response to the increasing use of te reo Māori as a "living language" (Te Puni Kōkiri 2019, 9) foregrounded in the Treaty of Waitangi (Te Tiriti o Waitangi), signed in 1840 between Māori chiefs (Rangatira) and the British Crown, which guaranteed Māori tino rangatiratanga (sovereignty and self-determination) over their lands and resources (King 2018; Waitangi Tribunal 2011).

The Treaty of Waitangi has been a significant factor in these initiatives: it has been interpreted as a commitment to partnership, participation, and protection, which has influenced the way that law schools approach the teaching of Māori law and legal issues affecting Māori, and the use of te reo Māori in courts and Parliament. Māori tauira (students) have expressed a growing preference towards te reo Māori, Māori legal academics, and Māori pedagogies in law schools across Aotearoa (Ruru et al. 2020). These developments are vital in order to honour and fully realise Te Tiriti o Waitangi principles (Durie 1996, Jones 2016), the growing Māori population and resurgence of intergenerational transmission or adoption of te reo Māori as a first language (Ruru et al. 2020), alongside potential movements towards co-governance and tri-juralism in Aotearoa as the situation in Canada has indicated (Borrows 2005, 2010).

Some statutory developments reflect this. The Education Act 1989 required schools to recognise the importance of te reo Māori and Māori culture in the education system (King 2018). The Māori Language Act 1986 recognises te reo Māori as an official language of Aotearoa and requires government agencies to promote its use (King 2018), and Te Ture mō te reo Māori 2016 (Māori Language Act 2016) entitles any person to speak in te reo Māori, irrespective of whether the person appearing may also speak in English, including any witness, member of the court, and counsel: the Court must provide an interpreter.

The Kohanga Reo movement, established in the 1980s and involving Māori language immersion early childhood centres that provide a culturally responsive learning environment for young Māori children, has also been significant (Benton 1986, 1991, Kāretu 1993, King 2018). Supporting this movement, Te Mātauranga o Aotearoa was developed in 2008 as the national curriculum framework for Māori-medium education (Ministry of Education 2008), using national standards (Ministry of Education 2010) based on mātauranga Māori (cultural values, knowledge, practices, worldviews) integrated in teaching and learning. This emphasises the importance of a culturally responsive approach to education and now legal education and judicial education also (Joseph 2009, Stewart, Trinick and Dale 2017).

More generally, Whānau Ora was established as the government policy that promotes a holistic approach to health and wellbeing for Māori families (Turia 2011, Whānau Ora Commissioning Agency 2020). It recognises the importance of Māori cultural practices and values in achieving positive outcomes for Māori communities.

The growth of Māori pedagogy in Aotearoa Law Schools

The relatively recent growth of Māori pedagogy in Aotearoa's six law schools has gained momentum. The issue is not so much whether institutional structures exist to teach tikanga (Māori law and values) in the LLB but more how to have Aotearoa recognise itself as a bi-jural country with tikanga as a legal system coexisting with the common law and having a status that warrants it being taught as a core subject in LLB curricula. To do so would be to follow the path laid out by retired Justice Durie, who referred to the development of a single jurisprudence from "two streams," in Aotearoa's journey of "cultural conciliation" (Durie 1996, 449; Benton, Frame and Meredith 2013), or by Justice Heath, who in *R v Mason* (2012, 48), referred to an "evolutionary rebuilding."

Academics from each law school have been involved in a three-phase project, "Inspiring National Indigenous Legal Education for Aotearoa New Zealand's Bachelor of Laws Degree" (the "Tikanga Project"), which complements a growing body of scholarship. In the "Introduction" to the "Phase One" report, they highlight "Ten Key Messages" (Ruru et al. 2020, 8–9), provide "A Starter

Reading List: Ten Readings to Begin to Understand Māori Law" (Ruru et al. 2020, 9), and conclude that "[t]here can be no systemic change to how we understand law in contemporary Aotearoa New Zealand if we do not teach it differently in our law schools" (Ruru et al. 2020, 46). This will involve bicultural and bilingual teaching and learning for all law students, to train them to practise in a bi-jural, bicultural, and bilingual legal system (Ruru et al. 2020, 37). Bi-juralism would mean the equitable treatment of both tikanga and the common law as legitimate sources of legal rights and obligations, such that tikanga becomes a foundational component of the curriculum delivered in a manner consistent with "Māori transmission methods of knowledge" (Ruru et al. 2020, 8). Bilingualism will be improved through using te reo Māori in teaching and privileging Māori legal concepts. Perhaps the most important of these are the "core values" listed by Williams (2013, 3):

- *whanaungatanga* or the source of the rights and obligations of kinship;
- *mana* or the source of rights and obligations of leadership;
- *tapu* as both a social control on behaviour and evidence of the indivisibility of divine and profane;
- *utu* or the obligation to give and the right (and sometimes obligation) to receive constant reciprocity; and
- *kaitiakitanga* or the obligation to care for one's own.

This project faces barriers, including the under-representation of full-time legal academics of Māori descent; capacity to develop, design, assess and implement te ao Māori (Māori worldview); and the logistics and funding of cooperation and negotiation with iwi (tribes) local to each law school, given that tikanga has regional variations. The mana and tapu (both core values are defined above) of te ao Māori knowledge and material pose more challenges to how and where the incorporation into an accredited LLB degree programme is undertaken (Kerr and Averill 2021, Markham-Nicklin and Wharehoka 2021). If the view is that "only Māori can teach tikanga Māori," non-Māori staff will require considerable specialist professional development training to upskill and indigenise material and assessments into core and elective courses by the 2024/2025 academic year (AUT Law School 2022, 5).

Aotearoa has institutional and regulatory mechanisms in place to address the ongoing disparities and inequities faced by vulnerable communities. This echoes the work of Penn (2010) and Matapo (2021), to name a few, calling on universities to adopt pedagogies and practices that are more culturally responsive to the interests of indigenous communities. This aligns with indigenous cultural competency (ICC) principles adopted across law schools in Australia and Canada (Burns et al. 2019; Coyle 2017; Fa'amatuainu 2023). The growth of indigenous legal education internationally has also provided a framework for the development of Māori pedagogy in New Zealand law schools

(Burns 2013, Burns, Lee Hong and Asmi 2019, Coyle 2017, Maguire and Young 2015, Saul 2009). The recognition of the importance of indigenous legal systems, practices, and values in legal education has led to the development of courses and programmes that incorporate Māori legal perspectives in law schools (Ruru et al. 2020). The growth of Māori legal scholarship has also played a key role in the development of Māori pedagogy in law schools (Durie 1996, Jones 2016, Mikaere 2005, 2007, Williams 2013). Initiatives to incorporate Māori pedagogy into teaching practices include the development of courses that focus on Māori legal issues, the incorporation of Māori legal perspectives into mainstream courses, and the provision of support for Māori law (Ruru et al. 2020). Support has come from the increasing number of Māori legal professionals, who have worked to raise awareness of the importance of Māori legal perspectives and have advocated for the inclusion of Māori legal issues in legal education (Ruru et al. 2020).

These developments reflect a growing recognition of the importance of Māori legal perspectives in legal education and a commitment to honouring the Treaty partnership between Māori and the Crown. It is important to note that Māori pedagogies are unique and specific to mātauranga Māori and should not be misinterpreted as Pasifika or equated with Pasifika pedagogy or teaching material, given the distinct historical and contemporary experiences with colonisation (for reasons discussed further in Part III).

Part III: Pasifika decolonial pedagogies

From the late 1990s to the early 2000s, more Pasifika academics advocated for the creation of new knowledge in education to move beyond the limitations entrenched in Western pedagogical norms. This reflected the ongoing failure of the Aotearoa education system to create culturally informed learning environments, namely student-centric, pastoral care, respectful cultural lecturer–student relationships premised on the collective relational nature of Pasifika people (Asafo and Tuiburelevu 2021; Chu, Abella, and Paurini 2013). Pasifika academics united "to collectively critique, engage with, and reimagine equitably transformative futures" (Asafo and Tuiburelevu 2021: 64) for Pasifika students, where the solution is to include Pasifika worldviews, narratives and privilege Pasifika knowledge and voices in teaching pedagogies to enable Pasifika student success and high achievement (Airini et al. 2010). This led to the development of innovative Pasifika decolonial pedagogies in education, though they are in their early stages in legal academia.

There are systemic barriers for Pasifika law students and Pasifika legal academics to achieve the above goals. The most common pedagogy adopted at university is inadequate, especially when coupled with the attitude demonstrated by many lecturers, including voicing personal opinions against equitable student support; lacking cultural competence; tokenising Pasifika students with some even singling out one Pasifika student to represent all Pasifika groups; expressing subtle micro-aggressions and racism in the lecture which negatively impact perceptions towards Māori and Pasifika law students. In addition, many lecturers adopt a rigid style of English communication, which effectively leads to students internalising racism (Fa'amatuainu 2023; Hosoda 2015; Penn 2010). Since 2014, more research on the experience of Pasifika law students has led to noticeable changes with more equity programmes and pastoral support for Pasifika law students, and law schools offering Pasifika law courses, organising Pasifika law-focused seminars and guest lectures (Mara 2006; Taylor et al. 2017).

I now turn to Samoan teaching pedagogies, noting of course that the cultures from other islands will produce different pedagogies.

Samoan pedagogy

The essence of fa'asamoa (the samoan way) teaching methods is underpinned by core values which guide social action: *usitai* (obedience), *faaaloalo* (respect), *alofa* (love), and *tautua* (service) (Anae et al. 2001; Meleisea 1987). When framed within the ICC paradigm, *teu le vā* is a Samoan Pasifika-specific holistic model (Anae 2010). Anae's *teu le vā* paradigm governs the expression of fa'asamoa values and beliefs in practice and "in any context, [whereby] respectful and polite communication is adhered to by all" (Ponton 2018). I explored the application of this to private law teaching in "Indigenising Private Law: Lessons from Samoa" (Fa'amatuainu 2023).

On this view, I adapted Anae et al's education research guideline principles as Pasifika pedagogies in law teaching (Fa'amatuainu 2021). First, introductory protocols are important. In a Māori context, a pepeha outlines one's connection to iwi, hapū (sub-tribes, clan), whānau (family), whakapapa (ancestral affiliations), and kinship ties to marae (sacred communal complex used every day in Māori life), rivers, mountains, and waka (canoes reflecting journeys). Similarly, a breakdown of my Pasifika genealogy helps to reaffirm the spirit of Pasifika values such as respect, reciprocity, and service, though one does not need to be of Pasifika descent or affiliate with a Pasifika ethnic group in order to teach law focused on the Pacific region or teach law to Pasifika students, as genuine respect towards Pasifika and Pasifika-specific and ICC values is of paramount consideration (Fa'amatuainu 2023). Second, teaching boundaries must be sensitive to the cultural and personal contexts of all learners. For example, the language used should not be culturally offensive, be it Samoan, Tongan, or even English (bi-lingual learning being common in Pasifika education contexts). Third, we ought to build rapport with learners, through humour or sharing common experiences. And lastly, we should choose suitable teaching instruments, for example, more Pasifika focused material, collaborative assessment processes, or grade key competencies required for advocacy and legal practice (such as people skills, networks in the community, natural oratory). We should also be open to asking learners about what they prefer – more visual content, more class exercises, and so on.

Challenges faced by Pasifika legal academics

As the global COVID-19 pandemic exacerbated vulnerability and structural problems resulting in extreme levels of poverty and inequality, law schools in Aotearoa were called on to add systemic racial diversity in course content and implement representational diversity schemes in early career academic programmes targeting Māori and Pasifika academics, mentoring programmes, diversification in assigned course reading lists, and inclusive recruitment practices (Naepi 2019; McAllister et al. 2020). This spurred academic outputs on how to approach diversity and inclusion within academia, the legal profession, and also politics (Baice et al. 2021; Thomsen et al. 2021). But inclusivity should not be confused with decoloniality: diversity measures that amount to an "add on" without fully confronting racialisation in legal epistemologies and the epistemic injustices and inequalities only affirm that "structural and representational changes operate in vain" (Adebisi 2021: 440).

The "Fofola na ibe – Improving Pasifika Legal Education in Aotearoa" Report was published in 2022 (Tupou-Vaitohi and Gucake 2022), and I was on its academic advisory panel. It was developed to understand the appalling statistics of Pasifika under-representation as law students, practitioners, and academics. It adopted a qualitative *Talanoa* (i.e. depending on the context, to hold an inclusive, participatory, and transparent dialogue, to have a meaningful conversation or to tell stories) approach to understand the experiences and journeys of Pasifika law students and professionals, finding that Pasifika students did not feel supported, and, at times, felt oppressed by the existing teaching and learning settings. The Report strongly recommended that law schools develop cultural competency to ensure that "staff understand the rigour and resilience required of Pasifika students to survive law school and the cultural identity that underpins them" (Tupou-Vaitohi and Gucake 2022: 10), that "law schools and universities diversify their curricula and pedagogical practices to include Pasifika views and values" (Tupou-Vaitohi and Gucake 2022: 78), that they continue to respond to racism and discrimination experienced by Pasifika law students through educational activities such as workshops on cultural awareness and racism, and that law schools and universities actively support Pasifika legal academics by diversifying teaching staff and to develop foundational programmes such as *Susuga Faiako* (Teaching Fellow) positions.

The problem with diversity measures, however, is the lack of consensus on their goal. There is often an incorrect presumption that inclusivity will yield transformation and social justice. Ironically, diversity continues to reproduce inequalities because it ignores the fundamental starting point: part of the "epistemological task" is to persistently interrogate the very norms of our institutional practices, our legal discipline, and areas of our legal profession which are complicit in the social reproduction of structural injustices (Adebisi 2021). Diversity measures fail to adequately address why legal academia continues to reproduce inequalities, with very little contemplation on the socio-political impacts or how the presumption of neutrality in legal education impedes the ability of the law school curriculum to transform society while assisting in the reproduction of gender, racial, and other disparities (Adebisi 2021: 440). Evidently, racial disparities persist across the spectrum in employment and promotions. Instead, inclusivity must directly engage in meaningful ways to promote the re-examination and therefore reconstruction of the legal discipline from within – the history, ontology, and epistemology of law and legal education. I agree, then, with Adebisi that this "will bring about more organic diversity and inclusion" (2021: 433).

Conceptual framework of analysis: Relevance to decolonisation and pedagogy

As mentioned earlier, Andreotti et al.'s *Cartography of Decolonization* (2015) is the conceptual framework of analysis used to explore legal pedagogies and to prompt critical discussions among PECA about whether the legal pedagogies adopted are decolonising. Following the *talanoa* framing and the adoption of Adreotti et al.'s three reform spaces by PECA in non-legal academic disciplines (Leenen-Young et al. 2021), I follow this very framework in the context of decolonising legal pedagogies. We now examine these in turn.

Soft reform space

Soft reform space is the inclusion (or, arguably, the superficial inclusion) of academically robust Pasifika decolonial pedagogies in law teaching without deconstructing and challenging the colonial foundations that have often served to exclude the voice of Pasifika people (Naepi et al. 2017). The non-traditional approaches have been adopted in law teaching to disrupt entanglements with colonial power. The increased inclusivity of critical legal and socio-legal approaches in legal education is one example of this approach.

Evaluation of successes and failures

In my experience of enacting Pasifika decolonial pedagogies, embedding *talanoa* and *teu le vā* in the indigenous private law course and south-pacific law course teaching (Fa'amatuainu 2023: 6; Thomsen et al. 2021), I often questioned whether such efforts would make any meaningful impact to decolonising the university at an institutional (macro) level. As a Pasifika legal academic of Samoan descent, a product of the system and institutional training, I consciously choose to resist the temptations of colonial reproduction by proactively asserting the culturally informed training of decolonial praxis in the design and delivery of law courses. For example, the first assessment for my course was a critical self-reflective opinion, privileging indigenous and Pasifika notions of knowledge transmission alongside Western or traditional modes of transmitting knowledge in legal academia (Fa'amatuainu 2023; Matapo 2021; Siilata, Samu, and Siteine 2017). It caused many students to reflect deeply, beyond the law school curriculum, on the structural and institutional design of the law, justice, and education system as a whole.

In articulating the metaphor of a canoe to rationalise how cooperative learning is a voyage of exploration (process of learning) rather than a means to discover the end product (the destination), the late Dr Teresia Teaiwa (2005), i-Kiribati/African American and Pacific scholar herself, has recognised the value of colonial Western education, while inspiring countless PECA to utilise the tools a colonial university offers for liberation, as it attempts to dominate us. This begins by indigenising the colonial classroom (canoe) and fostering cooperative learning between students and lecturers. To disrupt the common classroom dynamics and expectations embedded in the traditional static "performer-spectator" approach to learning (Lowman 1984), interactive learning is encouraged to unravel and inspire both learner and lecturer to be transformative. In this context, the lecture theatre could be likened to large canoes, and tutorials/workshops would be likened to smaller outrigger canoes. The coxswain could be likened to the lecturer or teaching assistant/workshop leader who steers the canoe with the students as the crew (Teaiwa 2005). The lecturer–student, coxswain–crew relationship is essentially a symbiotic relationship. It entails a level of trust, mutual commitment, cooperation, and communication, for without it, exploration is unsustainable.

The inclusion of soft reform spaces in Indigenous Private law and South Pacific law teaching, whilst capable of decolonising teaching pedagogies in two law courses within the boundaries of the colonial university, has not led to transformational change on a much wider scale across all law course offerings. This echoes the experience of other PECA (Leenen-Young et al. 2021; Thomsen et al. 2021) and Pasifika legal academics in Aotearoa (Asafo and Tuiburelevu 2021).

Radical reform space

Radical reform space, the second reform space, addresses the shortcomings of soft reform. It is transformative and involves Pasifika students actively disrupting the system by enabling other expressions of knowing (pluriversities) (Grosfoguel 2013). This is evidenced in explicit naming aspects of colonialism and racism (Naepi et al. 2017) to enforce Pasifika decolonial pedagogy in the education space, whilst asserting the voice of "marginalised subjects" (Andreotti et al. 2015).

Evaluation of successes and failures

During lectures, it was encouraging to observe students of non-Pasifika descent volunteer their personal opinions against colonial aspects of the law. The difficulty in translating or reframing Pasifika decolonial pedagogies in Western colonial institutions is a common experience of PECA (Leenen-Young et al. 2021; Thomsen et al. 2021). This was further affirmed by my students who questioned the patriarchal foundations of the law, which aligns with disrupting patriarchal ideals of hierarchy entrenched in the law. Moreso, law students felt a sense of ease in critiquing the negative impact of colonisation whilst others delved deeper into their cultural identity or discovered specific aspects to their inherited and cultural knowledge of their ancestors. These factors contributed to students feeling more engaged and connected as a class and to overall student success. This was unsurprising due to the adoption of Pasifika decolonial pedagogies (Allen, Taleni, and Robertson 2009; Manuel et al. 2014) in the form of culturally informed learning – student-centric, embedding pastoral care, and respectful connections of relationality between lecturer–student and peers.

Facilitating smaller outrigger canoe-type discussions or tutorials, comprised of less than five students, is another effective way for students to critically discuss a question assigned to one of the readings. The ground rules set for the talanoa enable shared responsibility and accountability for enforcement – assigning a talanoa facilitator and another person to report back to the large canoe, may lead to innovative forms of cooperative learning. In 2021, the students of the South Pacific law course joined in singing to wrap up the "reflections" part of the course, while other students took ownership of their learning and the learning of their children, some of whom sat and listened to the lecture as part of the shared responsibility of intergenerational learning.

While student presentations are not always part of the course assessment in law schools, I adopted presentations, critical reflective writing, and essays, to enable both oral and written forms of communication. Essentially, this diversity of assessment resonates well with Pasifika learning and as most of the law elective courses I teach are relatively small, it impresses upon the students the value of active listening, active participation, and the value of honouring your peer by remembering their identity – their name.

To ensure that the students are committed to the exploratory process of learning, I regularly update the course readings and texts so that it is relatable to local, national, and global events. The periodical assessment of course materials and pedagogical strategies is meant to reflect the ongoing changes to student demographics, technology, and critical legal scholarship.

As demonstrated by other Pasifika legal academics in Aotearoa (Asafo and Tuiburelevu 2021), I institute an indigenous and Pasifika-first policy in my assigned readings for the course that validates indigenous holders of knowledge

(Thomsen et al., 2021). This is a powerful catalyst in inclusivity to achieving decolonisation, but it is subject to limitations at the macro level. Unfortunately, critical legal scholarship produced by legal academics of Pasifika descent is still in the early stages. Some of the Pasifika legal academics whom I respect are white European, Asian, or African by descent, and teach law focused on the South Pacific region. My learned friend, Professor Rebecca Monson, a leading Pacific legal scholar, first drew my attention to the works of the late Dr Teresia Teaiwa, and Professor Mohammed L. Ahmadu first inspired my interest in commercial law in the South Pacific. I am indeed grateful for their contributions to Pacific law, some of which are listed as assigned readings for my courses. To exclude their contributions would ironically serve as a reproduction of the harms of coloniality through hierarchised inequalities.

In all topics for both law electives I teach, Pasifika law materials are used. For the introduction lecture to Indigenous Private Law, I assigned a reading by well-known Pacific law Scholar, Professor Jennifer Corrin (2015) "'A Disfunctional Spouse': The Relevance of the Public or Private Dichotomy for Indigenous Customary Laws in Solomon Islands and Vanuatu." This reading allows students to critically engage with the work of leading Private law scholar, Professor Ernest Weinrib, in exploring the categorisation of law into public or private in the context of indigenous customary laws in two Melanesian countries. I weave similar readings throughout the course: Epeli Hau'ofa's (1994) "Our Sea of Islands" always sets the tone for the comparative legal framework I embed in the course and resonates extremely well with students, while Andrew Hutchison and Sibanda Nkanyiso's (2017) "A living customary law of commercial contradicting in South Africa: some law-related hypotheses" challenges students to recognise that contracts existed in customary law and to consider other theories of contracts including the relational contract theory, where contracting is analysed in relational terms based on status, where consideration is not an essential feature.

The impact of the global COVID-19 pandemic helped us reimagine how teaching is conducted (Thomsen et al. 2021). It created meaningful online teaching *talanoa* forums enacting Pasifika decolonial pedagogies privileging relationality and maintenance of the vā (relational space) – vital to Pasifika student success). This is because the physical space of lecture theatres and seminar-style classrooms are often critiqued as symbol of settler colonialism likened to a "knowledge prison" (Smith, Funaki and MacDonald 2021).

Interdependence in cooperative learning is where guest lecturers are invited to share their expertise. For South Pacific Law, I designed a wraparound guest lecturer seminar series, focussed on exploring Contemporary Issues (Gender in the law), Family law, and Constitutional law. For Indigenous Private Law, I invited a guest lecturer to cover the topic of fiduciary duties. All guest lectures were open to staff, students, and the public. During the COVID pandemic, it inspired more students and interested learners to join the online sessions and interact as part of a community of learners. The invitation to guest lecturers did not undermine the authority of the regular lecturer: rather, the enrichment modelled to students the significance of collaboration, networking, and diverse ontologies required in charting the course of the voyage, to ensure its sustainability. It also highlights why professional jealousy or putting potential rivals at bay is not a sustainable practice in the long term. However, despite these great strides, recent developments did not eventuate in dismantling the colonial structures embedded in university institutions. Such an undertaking most certainly calls for a long-term project.

Beyond-reform space

The beyond-reform space addresses shortcomings prevalent in the radical reform space which effectively enables engagement in alternative ontologies within the existing system. This third reform space, whilst it asserts that ontological (ways of being) understandings can engage with other ontologies (pluriversities), cannot be enacted when still operating within the existing system. It involves three common responses: (1) system walk-out, where you opt out of the system; (2) hacking, which entails using the current system against itself; and (3) hospicing, which involves enabling the current system to die.

Evaluation of successes and failures

Thomsen et al. (2021) assert that the epistemological tension, uncertainty, and frustrations experienced during teaching, compounded by the tensions between positionality, cultural identity, and formal training in their academic discipline are all too common amongst PECA who often feel frustrated when enacting Pasifika decolonial pedagogies in teaching or in expressing different Pasifika philosophies which may not always be supported by the colonial university. In this regard, the most immediate concern is the impact on Pasifika law students, more specifically, the indigenous private law and south-pacific law students in the course I teach, due to the neo-liberal imposition of (Kidman and Chu 2017; Kidman 2020) the institutional, physical, and intellectual limitations on PECA (Smith, Funaki and MacDonald 2021). Personal acts of decolonisation through attempts to practice Pasifika decolonial pedagogies law teaching, while worth documenting, are not enough to penetrate the foundational Eurocentric tenets that uphold settler colonialism at the University.

Part IV: Conclusion

The emerging themes in this chapter illustrate the shared perception among PECA and Pasifika legal academics in Aotearoa that privileging Pasifika decolonial pedagogies is still an undervalued inclusive practice by universities across

Aotearoa. Crucially, what this chapter also highlights are the key lessons inspired by the growth of Māori pedagogies in education and law, which demonstrate the significance of positionality with respect to Pasifika legal academics, as potential allies through which Pasifika knowledge systems informing decolonial pedagogical praxis may be used to disrupt and deconstruct the foundational whiteness entrenched in colonial university systems. By looking at some of the fruitful ways of reimagining the teaching of law in Aotearoa, this chapter outlines some of the key challenges and successes I experienced in adopting decolonial thinking, practice, and theory in Aotearoa. It also closely examines the three different reform spaces through which Pasifika decolonial pedagogies are enacted as a benefit to both Pasifika and non-Pasifika students. It further highlights the need for more Pasifika legal academics as well as related pastoral care and support for PECA to better facilitate the foundational shift privileging Pasifika knowledge in decolonial pedagogical praxis whilst dismantling the colonial structures of the University on a macro sustainable level. In this regard, I leave you with the enduring words from postcolonial Pasifika scholar, Professor Albert Wendt (1976: 206, 215):

> Our quest should not be for a revival of our past cultures, but for the creation of new cultures, which are free of the taint of colonialism and based firmly on our own pasts. The quest should be for a new Oceania.

References

Adebisi, Foluke. (2021). "Should We Rethink the Purposes of the Law School? A Case for Decolonial Thought in Legal Pedagogy." *Amicus Curiae* 2(3): 428–449. https://doi.org/10.14296/ac.v2i3.5309

Airini, Deidre Brown, Curtis, Elana, Johnson, Odie, Luatua, Fred, O'Shea, Mona, Rakena, Te Oti, Reynolds, Gillian, et al. (2010). *Success for all: Improving Māori and Pasifika Student Success in Degree-Level Studies.* Wellington: Teaching and Learning Research Initiative, University of Auckland. http://www.tlri.org.nz/tlri-research/

Allen, Peter, Taleni, Leali'ie'e Tufulasi and Robertson, Jane. (2009). "'In Order to Teach you, I Must Know you.' The Pasifika Initiative: A Professional Development Project for Teachers." *New Zealand Journal of Educational Studies* 44(2): 47–62.

Anae, Melani, et al. (2001). *Pasifika Education Research Guidelines: Final Report* (for the Ministry of Education) (*Education Counts*) https://www.educationcounts.govt.nz/__data/assets/pdf_file/0010/7669/pacrsrch--guide.pdf accessed 16 February 2021.

Anae, Melani. (2010). "Research for Better Pacific Schooling in New Zealand: *Teu Le Va*—A Samoan Perspective." *MAI Review* 1: 1–24.

Andreotti, Vanessa de Oliveira, Stein, Sharon, Ahenakew, Cash and Dallas, Hunt. (2015). "Mapping Interpretations of Decolonization in the Context of Higher Education." *Decolonization: Indigeneity, Education & Society* 4(1): 21–40.

Asafo, Dylan and Tuiburelevu, Litia. (2021). "Finding Our Way to the Island: Critical Reflections from Two Emerging Pacific Legal Academics in Aotearoa." *Journal of New Zealand Studies* NS33: 55–69. https://doi.org/10.26686/jnzs.iNS33.7382

AUT School of Law (2022). "LLB Curriculum Review: Part One. (Draft for Consultation)" Auckland: Working Group, AUT School of Law.

Baice, Tim, Lealaiauloto, Betty, Meiklejohn-Whiu, Selena, Fonua, Sonia M., Allen, Jean M., Matapo, Jacoba, Iosefo, Fetaui and Fa'avae, David. (2021). "Responding to the Call: Talanoa, va-vā, Early Career Network and Enabling Academic Pathways at a University in New Zealand." *Higher Education Research & Development* 40(1): 75–89. https://doi.org/10.1080/07294360.2020.1852187

Benton, Richard A. (1986). "Schools as Agents for Language Revival in Ireland and New Zealand." In *Language and Education in Multilingual Settings*, edited by Bernard Spolsky, 53–76. Clevedon, UK: Multilingual Matters.

Benton, Richard A. (1991). *The Maori Language: Dying or Reviving?* Honolulu: East West Center. (Reprinted by New Zealand Council for Educational Research 1997.)

Benton, Richard, Frame, Alex and Meredith, Paul. (2013). *Te Mātāpunenga: A Compendium of References to the Concepts and Institutions of Māori Customary Law.* Wellington: Victoria University Press, 429.

Borrows, John. (2005). "Creating an Indigenous Legal Community." *McGill Law Journal* 50: 153.

Borrows, John. (2010). *Canada's Indigenous Constitution.* Toronto: University of Toronto Press, 6.

Burns, Marcelle. (2013). "Towards Growing Indigenous Culturally Competent Legal Professionals in Australia." *International Education Journal* 12(1): 226–248.

Burns, Marcelle, Hong, Anita Lee and Wood, Asmi. (2019) Indigenous Cultural Competency for Legal Academics Program: Final Report. Australia, Department of Education and Training.

Care, Jennifer Corrin. (1997). "Colonial legacies?" *Journal of Pacific Studies* 21: 33–59.

Chu, Cherie, Abella, Ivy Samala and Paurini, Seann. (2013). *Educational Practices That Benefit Pacific Students in Tertiary Education.* Wellington, NZ: Ako Aotearoa.

Corrin, Jennifer. (2015). "'A Disfunctional Spouse': The Relevance of the Public or Private Dichotomy for Indigenous Customary Laws in Solomon Islands and Vanuatu" *Comparative Law Journal of the Pacific* 21: 69–91.

Coyle, Michael. (2017). "Indigenous Legal Orders in Canada—A Literature Review" Western Law Publications 92 http://ir.lib.uwo.ca/lawpub/92 accessed 21 March 2022.

Durie, Edward. (1996). "Will the Settlers Settle—Cultural Conciliation Law" *Otago Law Review* 8: 449.

Fa'amatuainu, Bridget. (2021, August 24). *Critical reflections on teaching pedagogies adopted in law teaching in Aotearoa: Case for Pacific pedagogies in law teaching.* (Online Research presentation). *New Zealand Law Librarians Association (NZLLA) Conference*, 23–27 August 2021 Waiho i te toipoto, kaua i te toiroa – Stronger together, Tuesday Day 2.

Fa'amatuainu, Bridget. (2023). "Indigenising Private Law: Lessons from Samoa." *Journal of Commonwealth Law* 4: 101–126.

FAST Party v Attorney General [2021] WSSC 24 at 91.

Grosfoguel, Ramón. (2013). "The Structure of Knowledge in Westernised Universities: Epistemic Racism/Sexism and the Four Genocides/Epistemicides." *Human Architecture: Journal of the Sociology of Self-Knowledge* 11(1): 73–90.

Hau'ofa, Epeili. (1994). "Our Sea of Islands." *The Contemporary Pacific* 6(1): 148–161.

Hosoda, Mara Kawehiwehi. (2015). "Optimising the New Zealand School Experience for Pacific Lawyers." PhD Thesis, University of Otago.

Huffer, Elise. (2006). "Desk Review of the Factors which Enable and Constrain the Advancement of Women's Political Representation in Forum Island Countries." In *A Woman's Place is in the House – the House of Parliament; Research to Advance Women's Political Representation in Forum Island Countries*. Suva: Pacific Islands Forum Secretariat.

Hutchison, Andrew and Nkanyiso, Sibanda. (2017). "A living customary law of commercial contradicting in South Africa: some law-related hypotheses" *South African Journal on Human Rights* 33(3): 380–405.

Jones, Carwyn. (2016). *New Treaty, New Tradition: Reconciling New Zealand and Māori Law*. University of British Columbia Press.

Joseph, Robert. (2009). "Re-creating Space for the First Law of Aotearoa-New Zealand" 17 *Wai L Rev* 74.

Kabutaulaka, Tarcisius. (2015). "Re-Presenting Melanesia: Ignoble Savages and Melanesian Alter-Natives." *The Contemporary Pacific* 27(1): 110–145.

Kāretu, Timoti. (1993). "Toku reo, toku mana." In *Te ao marama 2. He whakaatanga o te ao: The Reality*, edited by Witi T. Ihimaera with Haare Williams, Irihapeti Ramsden, and Don S. Long, 222–229. Auckland: Reed.

Kerr, Brigit G., and Averill, Robin M. (2021). Contextualising assessment within Aotearoa New Zealand: drawing from mātauranga Māori. *AlterNative: An International Journal of Indigenous Peoples* 17(2), 236–245. https://doi.org/10.1177/11771801211016450

Kidman, Joanna. (2020). "Whither Decolonisation? Indigenous Scholars and the Problem of Inclusion in the Neoliberal University." *Journal of Sociology* 56(2): 247–262. https://doi.org/10.1177% 2F1440783319835958

Kidman, Joanna, and Chu, Cherie. (2017). "Scholar Outsiders in the Neoliberal University: Transgressive Academic Labour in the Whitestream." *New Zealand Journal of Educational Studies* 52(1): 7–19.

King, Jeanette. (2018). "Māori: Revitalization of an Endangered Language." In *The Oxford Handbook of Endangered Languages*, edited by Kenneth L. Rehg and Lyle Campbell, 592–612. Oxford: Oxford University Press. https://doi.org/10.1093/oxfordhb/9780190610029.013.28

Leenen-Young, Marcia, Naepi, Sereana, Thomsen, Patrick Saulmatino, Fa'avae, David, Taufui Mikato, Keil, Moeata and Matapo, Jacoba. (2021). "'Pillars of the colonial institution are like a knowledge prison': the significance of decolonizing knowledge and pedagogical practice for Pacific early." *Teaching in Higher Education*. https://doi.org/10.1080/13562517.2021.1928062

Lowman, Joseph. (1984). *Mastering the Techniques of Teaching*. San Francisco: Jossey-Bass.

Maguire, Amy and Young, Tamara. (2015). "Indigenisation of Curricula: Current Teaching Practices in Law" *Legal Education Review* 5.

Manuel, Theo, Lefono, Tainafi, Lagolago Wesley, Zaveri, Vedant, Smith, Naumai and Nanai, Juliet. (2014). "Peer-Based Pasifika Pedagogies: Gift of knowledge." Presented at *Samoa Conference III: Opportunities and Challenges for a Sustainable Cultural and Natural Environment*. National University of Samoa: Apia, Samoa.

Māori Language Act 1986, repealed (New Zealand).

Māori Language Act 2016 (New Zealand).

Mara, Diane Lysette. (2006). "Theories and Narratives: Pacific Women in Tertiary Education and the Social Construction of Ethnic Identities in Aotearoa New Zealand." PhD Thesis, Victoria University of Wellington.

Markham-Nicklin, Hinemoana and Wharehoka, Toni. (2021). "Legal education – reflecting on a bijural, bilingual and bicultural law degree". *Māori Law Review*. https://maorilawreview.co.nz/2021/07/legal-education-reflecting-on-a-bijural-bilingual-and-bicultural-law-degree/

Matapo, Jacoba. (2021). "Tangata o le Moana – The people of Moana: Traversing Pacific Indigenous philosophy in Pasifika education research." PhD thesis, Auckland University of Technology.

McAllister, Tara, Kokaua, Jesse, Naepi, Sereana, Kidman, Joanna and Theodore, Reremoana. (2020). "Glass Ceilings in New Zealand Universities." *MAI Journal* 9(3): 272–285.

Meleisea, Malama. (1987). *Lagaga: A Short History of Samoa* Institute of Pacific Studies and the Western Samoa Extension Centre of the University of the South Pacific.

Merry, Sally Engle. (1988). "Legal pluralism." *Law Society* 22(5): 869–896.

Mignolo, Walter D. (2007). "Introduction: Coloniality of Power and De-colonial Thinking." *Cultural Studies* 21(2–3): 155–167.

Mignolo, Walter D. and Walsh, Catherine E. (2018). *On Decoloniality: Concepts, Analytics, Praxis*. Durham, NC and London: Duke University Press.

Mikaere, Ani. (2005). "The Treaty of Waitangi and Recognition of Tikanga Māori." In *Waitangi Revisited: Perspectives on the Treaty of Waitangi*, edited by Michael Belgrave, Merata Kawharu and David Williams, 330, Oxford: Oxford University Press.

Mikaere, Ani. (2007). "Tikanga as the First Law of Aotearoa" *Yearbook of New Zealand Jurisprudence* 10: 24 at 25.

Ministry for Pacific Peoples. (2021). Pacific Aotearoa status report: A Snapshot 2020. https://www.mpp.govt.nz/assets/Reports/Pacific-Peoples-in-Aotearoa-Report.pdf

Ministry of Education. (2008). *Te Marautanga o Aotearoa*. Wellington: Ministry of Education.

Ministry of Education. (2010). *Ngā Whanaketanga Rumaki Māori*. [draft] Wellington: Learning Media.

Monson, Rebecca, Camacho, Keith, Foukona, Joseph. (2022). "Re-Storying Law and Development in Oceania." In *Oxford Handbook of International Law and Development*, edited by Sundhya Pahuja, Luis Eslava and Ruth Buchanan, Oxford: Oxford University Press.

Muller, Maureen and Kire, Andrea. (2014). "Kotahi Kapua i te Rangi he Marangai ki te Whenua: The Philosophy and Pedagogy of Te Ataarangi." In *Te Hua o Te Rea Maori: The Value of the Maori Language*, edited by Rawinia Higgins, Poia Rewi, and Vincent OlsenReeder, 291–303. Wellington, NZ: Huia Publishers.

Naepi, Sereana. (2019). "Why Isn't my Professor Pasifika? A Snapshot of the Academic Workforce in New Zealand Universities." *MAI Journal* 8(2): 219–234.

Naepi, Sereana, Stein, Sharon, Ahenakew, Cash and Andreotti, Vanessa de Oliveira. (2017). "A Cartography of Higher Education: Attempts at Inclusion and Insights from Pasifika Scholarship in Aotearoa New Zealand." In *Global Teaching: Southern Perspectives on Teachers Working with Diversity*, edited by Carol Reid and Jae Major, 81–99. New York, NY: Palgrave Macmillan. https://doi.org/10.1057/978-1-137-52526-0_5

O'Malley, Vincent, Stirling, Bruce and Penetito, Wally (eds). (2010). "Te Roopu o te Matakite 1975." In *The Treaty of Waitangi Companion Māori and Pākehā from Tasman to Today*. Auckland: Auckland University Press, 313.

Penn, Rosemarie. (2010). "Manumalo: A Study of Factors which facilitate success for New Zealand-born Samoan students at University." Med thesis, Auckland University of Technology.

Ponton, Vaoiva. (2018). "Utilizing Pacific Methodologies as Inclusive Practice." *SAGE Open* 1, 3.

R v Mason [2012] NZHC 1361, [2012] 2 NZLR 695 [48].

Ruru, Jacinta, Turei, Metiria, Jones, Carwyn and Quince, Khylee. (2020). *Inspiring National Indigenous Legal Education for Aotearoa New Zealand's Bachelor of Laws Degree: Phase One* (*University of Otago*). https://www.otago.ac.nz/law/otago742878.pdf accessed 15 March 2022.

Saul, Ben, Indigenous Issues in the Teaching of International Law (October 7, 2009). *Legal Education Review*, 2009, Sydney Law School Research Paper No. 09/108, Available at SSRN: https://ssrn.com/abstract=1485210

Siilata, Raewynn, Wendt Samu, Tanya and Siteine, Alexis. (2017). "The Va 'Atele Framework: Redefining and Transforming Pasifika Education." In *Handbook of Indigenous Education*, edited by Elizabeth McKinley and Linda Tuhiwai Smith, 1–30. Singapore: Springer.

Smith, Avery, Funaki, Hine and MacDonald, Liana. (2021). "Living, Breathing Settler-Colonialism: the Reification of Settler Norms in a Common University Space." *Higher Education Research & Development* 40(1): 132–145. https://doi.org/10.1080/07294360.2020.1852190

Statistics New Zealand. (2019, September 23). 2018 Census Population and Dwelling Counts, Census Usually Resident Population Count by Ethnic Group (Grouped Total Responses). https://www.stats.govt.nz/information-releases/2018-census-population-and-dwelling-counts

Statistics New Zealand. (2020, September 3). 2018 Census Ethnic Group summaries: Pacific Peoples Ethnic Group. https://www.stats.govt.nz/tools/2018-census-ethnic-groupsummaries/pacific-peoples

Stewart, Georgina, Tony Trinick and Darrell Dale. (2017). "Te Marautanga o Aotearoa: History of a national Māori curriculum." *Curriculum Matters* 13: 8–20. https://doi.org/10.18296/cm.0018

Tawhiwhirangi, Iritana. (2014). "Kua Tu Tangata El-Moving a Critical Mass." In *Te Hua o Te Reo Māori: The Value of the Maori Language*, edited by Rawinia Higgins, Poia Rewi, and Vincent Olsen-Reeder, 33–52. Wellington, NZ: Huia Publishers.

Taylor, Lynne, Brogt, Erik, Cheer, Ursula, Baird, Natalie, Caldwell, John and Wilson, Debra. (2017) "Ethnicity and engagement in first-year New Zealand law programmes" *Higher Education Research & Development* 36(5): 1047.

Te Huia, Awanui. (2015). "Exploring Goals and Motivations of Māori Heritage Language Learners" *Studies in Second Language Learning and Teaching* 5(4): 609–635.

Te Puni Kōkiri. (2019). Maihi Karauna. "The Crown's Strategy for Māori Language Revitalisation 2019–2023" https://www.tpk.govt.nz/en/a-matou-kaupapa/maihi-karauna

Teaiwa, Teresia. (2005). 'The Classroom as a Metaphorical Canoe: Co-operative Learning in Pacific Studies' *World Indigenous Nations Higher Education Consortium Journal* 1: 38–48.

Thaman, Konai Helu. (2003). "Decolonizing Pacific Studies: Indigenous Perspectives, Knowledge, and Wisdom in Higher Education." *The Contemporary Pacific* 15(1): 1–17.

Thomsen, Patrick, Leenen-Young, Marcia, Naepi, Sereana, Müller, Karamia, Manuela, Sam, Sisifa, Sisikula and Baice, Tim. (2021). "In our own Words: Pacific Early Career Academics (PECA) and Pacific Knowledges in Higher Education Pedagogical Praxis." *Higher Education Research & Development* 40(1): 49–62. https://doi.org/10.1080/07294360.2020.1852188

Tupou-Vaitohi, Mele and Gucake, Wiliame. (2022). *Fofola na ibe – Improving Pasifika Legal Education in Aotearoa Report on Talanoa Research Findings and Recommendations. A Report for the Equity, Belonging, Power/Authority – How can law, policy and practice support Pasifika law students – Improving Pasifika Legal Education Project.* https://www.wgtn.ac.nz/pasifika-legal/research-themes/documents/fofola-na-ibe-improving-pasifika-legal-education-full-report.pdf accessed 9 January 2023.

Turia, Tariana. (2011). "Whānau Ora: The theory and the practice." *Best Practice Journal* 37: 1–8.

Waitangi Tribunal. (2011). *Ko Aotearoa Tenei: Te Taumata Tuarua.* Wellington, NZ: Legislation Direct.

Wendt, Albert. (1976). "Towards a New Oceania" in *Writers in East-West Encounter, New Cultural Bearings*, edited by Guy Amirthanayagam. London, Macmillan, 1982, 206, 215.

Whānau Ora Commissioning Agency. (2020, November 22). How We Commission. Whānau Ora: https://whanauora.nz/what-we-do/commission/

Williams, Joseph. (2013). "Lex Aotearoa: An Heroic Attempt to Map the Māori Dimension in Modern New Zealand Law." *Waikato Law Review* 21: 1, 3.

PART II

Private Law

Teaching Obligations and Property

4

DECOLONIZING OBJECTIVE THEORY

Race and Coloniality in US Contract Law[1]

Chaumtoli Huq

Contract law emerged as a distinct legal field in the US toward the end of the nineteenth century. American legal scholars and courts adopted the objective theory to interpret contracts using the reasonable person standard, which imagines a fictional legal person with no racial, cultural, gendered, political, or class characteristics. Contract scholars and legal educators at that time looked toward English common law decisions to construct the objective theory and the reasonable person doctrine. This period was marked by US colonization of Indigenous populations through Westward expansion and a continuation of British colonialism of other countries. Thus, this fictive legal "reasonable person" through which objective theory is operationalized normalizes the Western cis-heterosexual propertied man as the reasonable person. It embeds the imperialist frame of universalizing the experiences of colonizer into the doctrine and discounts the experiences of colonized persons and other historically marginalized persons. It also legitimizes the stated civilizing mission of colonialism, which viewed colonialists as rational and modern, and the subjugated as uncivilized, intellectually inferior, and as the Other or non-being. Law, specifically contract law, provided the juridical vehicle through which this colonial ideology could be extended to justify imperial expansion and capitalism. Even after formerly colonized nations gained political independence, logics of coloniality remain in the doctrine through the continued application of "reasonable person" doctrine in contract law and other legal subjects. Decolonizing a cornerstone doctrine such as the reasonable person in contract law is crucial for the present educational project of creating an equitable, inclusive, decolonial, and anti-racist legal education.

Decoloniality seeks to untangle this construction of the doctrine and production of knowledge from a Eurocentric colonial framework and dismantle

DOI: 10.4324/9781003397885-7

structures of oppression that continue to work to justify the subjugation of historically marginalized communities. Decoloniality as a theoretical framework while distinct in its origins complements the existing critical race theory (CRT) framework and other critical legal frameworks within legal education to provide law students with a more robust understanding of the law. While much has been written on the racist, patriarchal underpinning of objective theory and reasonable person standard, this chapter focuses on how legal educators committed to an emancipatory and anti-racist pedagogy should add a decolonial framework to their teaching. More specifically, this chapter focuses on how law professors can employ a decolonial pedagogy to the reasonable person standard in a first-year contract class.

The chapter provides a brief overview of the objective theory and reasonable person standard and its link to coloniality, and then, as the main focus of this chapter, discusses three methods to incorporate a decolonial perspective into contracts. The first method introduces first-year law students to decolonial and CRT theories. It integrates these theories with the case method of teaching contracts to demonstrate how coloniality is present in the cases and to disrupt the case method of teaching prevalent in law schools. The second method concretizes this theoretical exploration through a reflection and writing assignment I name Praxis Post. The third method highlights the importance of contextualizing and deconstructing contract cases and does so with the popular contract case *Raffles v. Wichelhaus* ("Peerless ships") (1864), which is promoted as the case that exemplified the law's shift from a subjectivist approach to the objective theory. Finally, through contemporary cases, this method shows how explicitly and implicitly Eurocentrism and coloniality are extended in the doctrine to the present day.

> For the colonized subject, objectivity is always directed against him.
>
> *(Fanon, Wretched of the Earth, 2004, 37)*

Overview of the Objective Theory and the Reasonable Person Standard and Links to Coloniality

All first-year law students in the US learn that contractual disputes are analyzed using the objective theory of interpretation, which is operationalized through the "reasonable person" standard. Originally called the "reasonable man" standard, it is now referred to in gender-neutral terms as the "reasonable person" standard. US common law shifted from a subjective to an objective theory of contract interpretation as the "decisional axis" to resolve questions of law and fact in the late nineteenth century and early twentieth century (DiMatteo 1997, p. 295; Perillo 2000). Contract law, as a distinct legal field, emerged at this time of imperialism, capitalist expansion, and racism, and adopted the objective theory and reasonableness standard, which was instrumental in facilitating the expansion of colonialism. The ideological link between colonialism and the objective theory can be found in the political and philosophical influences of early contract law adherents of the objective theory (O'Gorman 2019, p. 75). Rationalism and subjugation were not inconsistent with European thinkers, who saw their society as advanced and therefore domination of non-Western societies justified for their benefit. In the US, objective theory allowed dominant norms to be integrated into contracts, which appealed to the white male propertied elite, who were threatened by social changes including abolition of slavery and immigration. Through the doctrine of objectivity, jurists and lawyers were able to "control difference" while maintaining white supremacy (Kastely 1994, p. 304). US legal educators and jurists like Christopher Columbus Langdell and Oliver Wendell Holmes Jr. saw contracts as the juridical vehicle through which European notions of modernity, rationality, and objectivity can be embedded into the law. Langdell, Dean of Harvard Law School and founder of the case method to legal education, made contract law the subject of his legal education experimentation (Simpson 1989, p. 327; O'Gorman 2019, p. 76), making it suitable for a decolonial pedagogy.

Legal scholar Grant Gilmore describes objective theory as the great "metaphysical solvent – the critical test for distinguishing between the false and the true" (1974, p. 47). Scholar Larry DiMatteo describes the reasonable person as "contractual mystic" and "all knowing arbiter of reasonableness" (DiMatteo 2017, p. 295). Under the objective theory, the court inquires and exercises conjecture as what a reasonable person would do or think in the context of a contract dispute (Barnes 2008). Whereas under the older subjective approach, courts ascertained the actual intention of the parties and conducted a full factual inquiry, an objective approach relies on external facts on what is said or done. Objectivity, thus, seeks to suppress alternative values by "discounting the relevance of any *particular* perspective in legal analysis and by positing an analytical stance that has no specific cultural, political or class characteristics" (Crenshaw 1998, p. 2). It functions to supplant actual subjects, their intentions, and lived experiences (Astrada and Astrada 2017, p. 204). Objective theory is presented as a universal and broader theory of interpretation, when in fact it operates to narrow the set of facts and experiences that become legally cognizable and credible to assess a contract claim.

Under the objective theory, the intent of the parties is mediated through a fictional reasonable person thereby allowing for the infusion of an "externally imposed substantive moral judgment" (DiMatteo 1997, p. 298). In US contracts doctrine, the fictive reasonable person has come to signify the white, upper-class, heterosexual male and embody the universalization of the Eurocentric values, which is viewed as the objective position (Astrada and Astrada 2017, p. 200; Hernandez-Truyol 1994, p. 372; Kastely 1994). Eurocentrism defines non-European communities in relation to whiteness, with European values as modern/rational and subjugated communities as inferior/uncivilized

(Munshi 2017, p. 226). Notions of "objectivity" and reasonable person then become ideological constructs that constitute the boundaries of who is human, superior (mainly European), and who is othered, sub-human or non-human (Maldonado-Torres 2016, p. 14; Lugones 2010, p. 751) These categorizations are not only racialized but gendered and classed. This conception of objectivity/reasonable person views anyone else that does not align with European values as not being reasonable or reliable, thereby maintaining hierarchies of race, class, and gender (Kastely 1994). Thus, objective theory has the effect of legitimizing the "imposition of dominant [European] norms of human obligation on subordinate groups, under the guise of normalcy, and simultaneously defining those groups and individuals who would assert an alternative meaning as deficient: lacking in education, sophistication, ability, or credibility" (Kastely 1994, p. 304). Such a separation between modern/rational/objective/colonizer and uncivilized/inferior/colonized was critical for the colonial project because it allowed colonialists to construct a reality and insistence on advanced thought, while at the same time engage in some of the more brutal and exploitative realities of transatlantic slavery, indentured servitude, and conquest.

Liberal institutions like law schools advance coloniality (Maldonado-Torres 2016, p. 5). Liberal legal education prides itself in training lawyers to think like lawyers when in actuality they are indoctrinated into European values. In order to dehumanize colonized subjects and invalidate their subjective experiences, objective theory, and the legal fictive universal, a reasonable person appears as a doctrine to normalize coloniality. Long after political colonization ended, this ideology remains entrenched in society and embedded in contract law through the continued application of the objective theory/reasonable person standard as historically constructed (Astrada and Astrada 2017, p. 200, Adebisi 2021, p. 444). Courts applying the reasonable person standard describe it positively as a "hallmark of the Anglo–American legal system" (Twp. of *Plymouth v. Hancock* 1999). In *Radtke v. Everett* (1993), acknowledging the reasonable person standard as part of "Anglo-American jurisprudence" the Michigan Supreme Court reviewing a hostile work environment case rejects a gender-conscious standard adopted by the appellate court and affirms the objective reasonableness standard to which *all* persons must conform. The court reasons that the objective standard is "flexible to incorporate gender differences," which reveals how coloniality is adept in allowing for heterogeneous narratives to be mediated through hegemonic systems of thought (Quijano 2000, p. 553). To illustrate this point further, the court writes approvingly of the generalized objective standard over one that considers the perspective of the plaintiff. The court writes that a gender-conscious standard eliminates "community standards and replaces them with standards formulated by a subset of the community" which could lead to the "fragmentation of legal standards." The Michigan Supreme Court's decision demonstrates that the objective standard indeed imposes an external community norm that fails to account for the perspective of the party claiming legal harm. While the court held that the plaintiff *did state* a hostile work environment claim, the rejection of a standard that considers the perspectives of the plaintiff for a Eurocentric community standard might defeat claims by others harmed by discrimination. Even where the law seems to provide favorable outcomes or legal protection to people of color, women, or other historically marginalized communities, the objective view ignores their differences. In short, this legal interpretation method is precisely the logic of colonialism – to valorize European civilization, universalize European values as rational and superior, and to discount, and render incognizable, the harms of marginalized communities, thereby justifying their subjugation.

> descolonizemos lo que nos enseñaron/decolonize what we were taught.
>
> *Ana Tijoux, Vengo*

Legal Pedagogies Integrating Decoloniality into Contracts

Decolonization theory represents a broad and wide-ranging field of thought and histories. Decolonization refers to a political and intellectual project whereby ideology, logic, and institutions of colonization and subordination of marginalized people are dismantled or challenged (Maldonado-Torres 2016). It refers to "rehumanizing the world" that "dehumanized subjects and communities" and to the "production of counter-discourses, counter-knowledge, counter-creative acts" that "open up multiple forms of being in this world" (Maldonado-Torres 2016, p. 10). Here, it is important to mention that there are different forms and histories of colonization, and a decolonial pedagogy must be attuned to those differences and processes of domination (Tuck and Yang 2012, pp. 4–5).

Contracts is a crucial site to introduce a decolonial pedagogy, given the confluence of the rise of the capitalist class, legal educators influenced by liberal political economists of the time and being the subject through which modern legal education was introduced. Further, because contract law is concerned with the legal ordering of economic resources and constitutes social relations through the enforcement of promises and agreements, it is ideally suited to illustrate to students how to imagine and reconfigure new social relations that are humanizing and emancipatory. However, illustrating the links to coloniality and its extension to the present day remains a pedagogical challenge. The description of contracts as solely involving private parties and US domestic law also allows the doctrine to elide decolonial scrutiny because coloniality is thought to be something of the past and a socio-economic process that took place outside of the US. Because neutrality, universality, and rationality are viewed as desirable for a modern legal system which has been normalized by coloniality, contract law remains insulated from any decolonial critique.

Teri McMurtry-Chubb is the first legal scholar known to this author to apply decoloniality within US legal education to legal writing as a method to upend the Western/Eurocentric epistemologies rooted in rhetoric, reasoning, and legal analysis (2019). That a decolonial framework would emerge among legal writing scholars who are often marginalized and occupy precarious positions within the segregated legal academy maintaining hierarchies between "podium" clinical and skills faculty is not surprising. In the context of legal writing, McMurtry-Chubb proposes methods of "counter-storytelling" or offering "oppositional discourses" as ways to relocate legal reasoning outside of the Eurocentric frame. She urges us to "decolonize Western rhetorical practices, the cannon and notions of canoncity throughout the law school curriculum" (McMurtry-Chubb 2019, p. 289). Decolonial scholars have also described this pedagogy of introducing oppositional discourse as "epistemic disobedience" (Velasquez Atehortua 2020, p. 157), which is intended to disrupt the hegemony of colonial knowledge. In this regard, decolonial pedagogies are dynamic, dialectical, and generative processes that allow for new ideas and methods to emerge.

In this chapter, I focus primarily on epistemic decolonization to challenge Eurocentrism and white supremacy, the hegemonic ideology through which coloniality gets reproduced (Quijano 2000, p. 549). I share three legal pedagogical methods to decolonize contracts: (1) introducing decolonial theories, (2) a praxis writing assignment, and (3) deconstructing a key contract case, *Raffles v. Wichelhaus* ("Peerless" ship case), which solidified objective theory in contract doctrine. Introducing critical theories can unmask the ways in which coloniality operates within the law to enable law students to detect how the law is operating in communities to maintain their subjugation and work toward dismantling those oppressive structures. In this regard, a decolonial pedagogy must link the classroom to the material lives of subjugated peoples and allow students to imagine social relations not based on domination and exploitation (Coulthard 2014, p. 13). In a heterogenous classroom, with students from varied lived experiences and identities, the introduction of diverse critical thinkers can resonate more strongly and activate their own methodologies of disrupting coloniality in legal education. Because coloniality was embedded into contract doctrine through the case method of modern legal education, deconstruction of the epochal *Peerless* case is essential to a decolonial legal pedagogy because it seeks to untangle coloniality from the foundation of the doctrine.

Decolonial Theories and Contract Doctrines

A core decolonial legal pedagogical method is grounding the doctrine in critical legal and political theories so as to animate questioning, curiosity, and consciousness among students (Velasquez Atehortua 2020, p. 162). Throughout the year-long contract course, I introduce students to different critical legal scholars as well as political theorists writing on feminism, racial capitalism, ableism, settler colonialism, and critical theories on class called Class Crit and invite students to learn contract law alongside these theories. I make my pedagogical choices transparent in my teaching philosophy to respond to common concerns that learning these theories takes away from "learning the law." My Pedagogical Philosophy that relates to critical theories states:

> I acknowledge that legal education has historically excluded and alienated many students based on their social identities and lived experiences. I teach foundational courses so that students gain competency on the subject but are also empowered to critique the doctrine. I do so with an explicit emphasis on critical legal theories. I believe that such an approach to legal education better prepares students to engage as public interest lawyers.

My philosophy makes clear that critical legal theory aids in their goal of becoming a lawyer. It challenges what the law is and what "thinking like a lawyer" means. The goal is to develop a pluralist habit of mind that questions what they are learning rather than wholesale adopting the doctrine and embedded ideologies. In this section, I share some approaches so as to concretize what may appear like a conceptual undertaking.

In this first method, I introduce first-year law students to decolonial and CRT theorists such as Kimberle Crenshaw's critique of objective theory, Patricia Hill Collins' Black feminist epistemology, Roxanne Dunbar-Ortiz's indigenous people's history, racial capitalism, and Walter Rodney's critique of economic development (Dunbar-Ortiz 2014). Black feminist epistemology is particularly instructive for a decolonial legal pedagogy because scholars like Collins empower students to ask *why* we believe what we believe to be true and how those truths shape action (Collins 2000, p. 252). To the extent doctrines represent truths about what the law is, critiques uncover those assumptions underlying the doctrine. Given constraints of time in the semester, I provide students with short excerpts of articles or may pull relevant quotes for discussion in class. These quotes/readings serve as "epistemic disobedience" or disrupters to the doctrine and unmask for the students the ways in which the colonial logic is extended.

I bring these counter-discourses into the classroom: through the Syllabus, in-class discussions, and a praxis exercise. I include specific prompts in my Syllabus, under the general column header Practice and Theory, and with specific questions on Theoretical Perspectives for doctrines that allow me to introduce and ground critical theories into the course. Examples of these prompts include:

> *What does the concept of racial capitalism add to our understanding of the doctrine? Can neoclassical economic theory or racial capitalism help explain discrimination faced by Black homeowners? What is the difference between the*

> *objective and subjective approaches to assent? Why does contract law opt for the objective approach? What are background assumptions the court makes about gender and work when applying the reasonable person standard? What does Dunbar-Ortiz' discussion of land add to our understanding of the parties' authority to "sell" or make a legal offer to sell land? If the courts will not look at the adequacy of consideration, does the doctrine of consideration permit discrimination in the market economy?*

In some respects, the teaching methods I employ may look no different than a "traditional" classroom in that students may read a relevant Restatement, UCC section, or a case. Once they understand the legal principle, they are asked to review that principle through the lens of a specific critical legal theory. The prompts guide students through their engagement with the legal theories and doctrine. They serve as guideposts for students particularly those for whom this may be the first time they are asked to engage in this type of critical legal reading.

For specific doctrines, I pair reading of cases with excerpts of a critical legal reading text. For an in-class discussion of the reasonable person, I share a quote from Walter Rodney's work. Specifically, I share: "A culture is a total way of life. It embraces what people ate and what they wore; the way they walked and the way they talked; the manner in which they treated death and greeted the newborn" (Rodney 2012, p. 34). I then ask students, if culture is so varied (and here Rodney is commenting on the diverse African cultures prior to European colonialism), then how could a reasonable person exist? Exposing the legal fiction of the mythical and mystical reasonable person as the arbiter of disputes through an anti-colonial writer allows students to begin to question other aspects of the doctrine, such as its function. It encourages them to explore other ways by which legal disputes can be resolved. Students draw from their lived experiences, including knowledge of how varied cultures resolve disputes. The durability of the reasonable person doctrine has been the unquestioned premise that there are no other alternatives to resolve disputes and an assumption that a subjective approach that takes into account the parties' actual realities is biased, as evidenced by the *Radtke* decision discussed above. In fact, it is the objective approach that consolidates one perspective at the exclusion of others. Rodney's quote on the pluralism of cultures calls into question the reasonable person.

For contract cases involving the sale of land, such as *Southworth v. Oliver* (1978), I assign Dunbar-Ortiz's chapter "This Land" from *A Indigenous People's History of the United States* to illustrate how any contract for the sale of land raises issues of settler colonialism. In *Southworth*, where students are introduced to the contract doctrine on what constitutes a legal offer, Dunbar-Ortiz surfaces that the legal "power" of the offeror in the US to sell land is premised on brutal "expropriation of lands and resources" and genocidal policy based on settler colonialism which continues to the present (Dunbar-Ortiz 2014, p. 7). The case set in Oregon, which had racial exclusion laws prohibiting Black people from settling in Oregon with threats of violence, also reveals how racism and settler colonialism work to provide white settlers access to land. Presented in this way, students are forced to grapple with settler colonialism and our accountability to stop this continued harm masked under the seemingly mundane doctrine of an offer.

Praxis Post: Reflection and Writing

Praxis is essential if any critical legal theories are to hold any influence in the legal profession (Lawson 1995, p. 369). "It is both theory and praxis that lead us to new ideas" (Adebisi 2021, p. 441). Integral to introducing key critical legal texts is to encourage the integration of theory–practice–reflection (Velasquez Atehortua 2020, p. 164). Praxis is reflection and action directed at the structures to be transformed (Freire 2005, pp. 125–126). So, *praxis*: integrating theory into the class empowers students to question the foundation of law, develop critical thinking skills, and direct that awareness to transform legal structures. In the context of a large first-year doctrinal course like contracts, where students typically learn the doctrine and then apply it to a hypothetical set of facts, there is no curricular space for students to reflect on the assumptions underlying the doctrine, its origins, and purposes. Just adding critical legal theories as "extra" reading even with the prompts I discuss above, without more, simply maintains those critical perspectives as if dangling in the periphery of the classroom. It also does not motivate students to consider how they would *act* in response to this new critical consciousness (Velez-Martinez 2015, p. 588). As such, "[c]ritical reflection on our pedagogical praxis has to be constant to avoid the peril of having students perceive our discourse as nothing more than empty words" (Velez-Martinez 2015, p. 588). Whereas critical legal theories like decoloniality provide students with a method of inquiry, praxis allows them to apply these insights to the doctrine they are learning and eventually to the practice of law.

To encourage students to affirmatively reflect on the assumptions of the doctrine that reinforces racism, sexism, and coloniality, they are required to submit an assignment I call Praxis Post. This assignment of 250 to 500 words asks students to "connect a theoretical perspective" to a case, doctrine, or current event. Students can answer in writing any of the prompts in the Syllabus or can write on what interests them. While I share one past example from a prior student, which is important for students who come from academic backgrounds where this type of inquiry is unfamiliar or discouraged, I do not require any structure or format to the post. This unstructured format allows for student agency within a highly regimented 1L curriculum, where in terms of writing they are already inculcated into the IRAC legal writing structure and European rhetoric (McMurtry-Chubb 2019) and to allow for multiple interpretations of the texts based on their subjective experiences. These praxis posts are shared on the course-management site so that students can read their peers' writings. The posts allow me to engage with students based on what awakens within themselves on the readings, as opposed to me imposing some banked set of knowledge they are supposed to derive from the readings. Citing Freire and the banking model of education, scholar Valasquez Atehortua writes on the value of "conscious-raising" reflections: students "write the texts as freely as letters to raise consciousness" (2020, p. 164). For example, two students self-identified as Afro-Asian/mixed race and Egyptian-American discussed how the reasonable person standard can disadvantage the Black community where the African American Vernacular English (AAVE) is used in contracts. They write (with slight modifications):

> Since African American Vernacular English (AAVE) is not widely accepted and is often viewed as ungrammatical … the different terms and slang may not be viewed as "reasonable." A juror could say that a Black individual should know of the meaning attached by the other party, but the other party would not have reason to know of the meaning of the AAVE slang, due to the lack of wide usage. The court may find that there is a contract and may enforce it in a way that disregards the intended meaning of the slang. If an individual uses slang such as "c note," "band," or "rack" to denote the amount of money they are offering in exchange, they may not be entitled to an enforceable contract. The negative view of AAVE held by jurors, judges, and even attorneys can be incredibly harmful to the Black community.
>
> Dub is a term that changes its meaning based on the context and tone of the individual speaking. In regard to the sale of marijuana, a "dub" is a description of weight/amount. Commonly used in dialogue as "Do you wanna cop a dub" dub in this circumstance is referring to the amount of marijuana wanting to be purchased. However, "dub," in NY, can also be used as a synonym to cancel. Saying "That's a dub" means you are canceling on plans or in disagreement with someone. In "an agreement between a buyer and a dispensary … buyer could use the term to cancel their transaction while the dispensary could have interpreted the term to mean the amount the buyer wanted to purchase."

These students highlight ways the reasonable person doctrine can disadvantage parties to a contract using AAVE by not enforcing contracts they actually intended to form or fail to protect them from unfair contracts under defenses such as the misunderstanding doctrine. While in a 1L class we do not have time to delve deeper into how these counter-discourses may impact lawyering, my hope in introducing these ideas in the first year with the praxis post is that these queries get picked up throughout the student's legal education, particularly in legal clinic.

Raffles v. Wichelhaus *Decolonial Redux*

Deconstruction, a practice of interpreting texts to demonstrate the ideological biases of legal doctrines, is a useful technique to introduce coloniality into discussions of contracts (Chase 1995, p. 61). Using *Raffles v. Wichelhaus* ("Peerless" ship case), a well-known contract class that stands for the objective theory under the case method of legal education (Gilmore 1974, p. 46) and providing historical context to the case, students are able to draw their own connections between colonialism and the doctrine. Briefly, the Peerless ships' case involves a dispute related to the sale of cotton at "fair market" price. The contract specified that the cotton would be arriving from Bombay on a ship named Peerless. There were two ships named Peerless ferrying cotton from Bombay to Liverpool, one departing in October and a second in December. The defendant argues that they contracted for cotton arriving on the ship departing in October, and the plaintiff asserts it was from the ship departing in December, which when arrived, they tried to deliver to the defendant who refused delivery. The claimant sued for breach of contract, arguing that the date of the ship was irrelevant. The issue before the court was whether the defendant should be bound by the agreement to buy the cotton of the claimant's *Peerless*. The Court found for the defendant on the grounds that because there were two ships named Peerless, which ship was intended was ambiguous (Simpson 1989, p. 291). Further, because there was no meeting of the minds as to which ship was intended, a contract was not formed.

Peerless illuminates how coloniality is embedded in contract law for several reasons. First, it is an integral part of the study of contract formation – described as one of the "best known old chestnuts of the common law" (Simpson 1989, p. 287). "No student of the law of contract could regard his education as complete without either reading the [Peerless ships] case" (Simpson 1989, p. 288). Next, while sparse judicial explanation of the case provides limited guidance on the *actual dispute* in the case, it has come to occupy doctrinal significance within contract law as reflecting the shift to the objective theory (Simpson 1989, p. 293). "[T]o the Holmesian ... the actual state of the parties' mind in Raffles v. Wichelhaus was irrelevant ... the true ground of the decision was not that the parties meant different things but that they said different things" (Gilmore 1974, p. 46). In fact, the ambiguity of the ships is belied by the elaborate records of voyages, agreements, and that the facts of the case could have been easily determined. The custom was that ships were not identified by names, but by captains (Simpson 1989, p. 295). Also, given the timing of these contracts, it is implausible that defendants contracted for cotton on a ship leaving in December (Simpson 1989, p. 315). This would have been known by the lawyers and parties involved in the case. So, by looking at the *actual facts* of the case, the plaintiff would have likely prevailed. Discounting the facts that question whether the defendant did mean to purchase cotton from the ship leaving

October and focusing on the existence of two ships named Peerless to create ambiguity of what was meant allowed the court to ignore the actual realities and context of this agreement. It is this method of analysis, of discounting lived experiences, while in Peerless involves merchants and not necessarily a marginalized group, which when applied to other contexts serves to extend the colonial logic into contract law.

Further, that the advancement of the objective theory of contracts rests on a commercial case during British colonialism, and at a time when England could not import cotton from the US due to the Civil War, points strongly to the colonial and racial foundations of the doctrine. The significance of the facts of the case, which involves a ship leaving from Bombay carrying cotton, is rarely if at all mentioned in law textbooks, evidencing links between both British colonialism and American slavery. Scholars Simpson and Gilmore relate the dispute to the American Civil War, where cotton was unavailable (Simpson 1989, p. 302; Gilmore 1974, pp. 35–39). The real reason for rejecting cotton was that the price had fallen below contract price. (Gilmore 1974, p. 41). Prior to that, southern US states were the source of cotton for England. Industries turned to India for cotton, and the price for cotton rose sharply and delivery was uncertain. It was speculated that a huge stock of cotton would be released from the US South if the war ended and that the prices would be lower, and this belief may have explained the defendant rejecting the shipment of cotton from India (Simpson 1989, p. 303). The contract at issue was less about whether the parties contracted for cotton on the same ship but instead sought to secure better prices of the product based on political speculations on the availability of the cotton from the US. The objective theory, which rests on externally circumscribed facts that are mediated through the fictive reasonable legal person, facilitates business and commercial interests because the externally imposed criteria can adjust private contracts to industry norms and business interests. In contrast, the subjective theory which focuses on an elaborate factual inquiry of the party's intent relegates the resolution of factual disputes solely to the parties and would impede business interests in shaping private contract law. In this regard, objective theory better serves the expansion of capitalism, and at that time, colonialism.

This legal analytical maneuver of discounting the actual state of the parties' mind, their realities, and the context of the dispute by imposing an external judgment of a reasonable person is the enduring feature of coloniality in contracts. It institutionalizes a legal doctrine that discounts the lived experiences of the colonized. The Peerless ships' case provides students a concrete way to understand how coloniality is foundational to contract law. While the application of the "reasonable person" doctrine may have broadened to include other perspectives, especially with the push by legal realists, ultimately, the legal analysis is limited to an externally mediated norm based on Eurocentrism. It is this *method of legal analysis* that needs to be decolonized such that people's realities are not separated into abstraction and their disputes are evaluated based on their lived realities. What should be put in place of the "reasonable person" standard is beyond the scope of this chapter, but there are scholars who point us toward some useful starting points. Ian Tapu advocates for a perspective on reasonable people that takes into consideration experiences of indigenous youth and how critiques of reasonableness omit colonial trauma of settler colonialism (Tapu 2020). Hernandez-Truyol, revealing that neutrality is a lie from the vantage point of a Latina lawyer and law professor, recommends a total replacement of those ideas with a "multidimensional one informed by the variety of experiences that describe the realities of fully diverse people" (Hernandez-Truyol 1994, p. 429). Naomi Cahn, while discussing the possibilities of a reasonable woman standard, ultimately concludes that instead of constructing one dominant doctrine to understand client experiences, we should develop a contextual standard that allows for multiple voices and images (Cahn 1992, p. 1435). My own experiences as a Bangladeshi-born immigrant to the US, Muslim, class-conscious, woman of color law faculty will not fully capture the multiplicity of lived experiences invalidated by doctrines like a reasonable person. Nonetheless, a multidimensional, pluralist decisional approach views parties holistically, and draws on their actual intentions and lived realities, is favorable to the narrow construction of the reasonable person standard where lives are evaluated based on Eurocentric norms. Such an approach would involve a robust, fuller factual inquiry and require courts to resolve disputes based on those inquiries. Such an approach would require judges to be attuned to the diversity of litigants before them. It would also require that the judiciary reflect the diversity of the litigants. Deconstructing the myths of objectivity, such as neutrality is threatening to the legal order upon which the entirety of the doctrine rests. But decoloniality does not seek to tinker at the edges but reimagine a legal system that is truly based on equality.

Conclusion

Objective theory and the reasonable person standard emerged as the contract doctrinal pathway to reinforce the superiority of European civilization, justifying the subjugation and dehumanizing of peoples around the globe. Specifically, the doctrine bifurcated reason and the determination of truth from the actual realities of the parties which legitimated the superiority of European civilization and justified subjugation of colonized peoples. Further, it allowed the law to ignore the realities of the parties, including their discrimination and subjugation. Long after slavery was legally abolished and political colonization ended, racism and coloniality remained in the doctrine with the continued application of the objective theory and reasonable person standard, enabling the law to assert its truthfulness, modernity, and even equitable role while racial and economic inequalities persisted. Thus, decolonizing contract law, which seeks to reestablish the humanity of all peoples, becomes an urgent and necessary task for legal educators. While the first-year legal curriculum remains resistant to changes, law professors can employ a critical praxis to teaching the doctrine by introducing key critical theorists and by deconstructing foundational contract cases. Student engagement with these critical theories can be deepened through a short writing assignment like a praxis post and other guided exercises so that the integration of these ideas does not remain at an abstract, peripheral level but encourages students to grapple with the complexities of the doctrine. A decolonial pedagogy gives students permission to engage in the "epistemic" disobedience necessary to imagine an emancipatory vision of the law.

Note

1 This chapter builds on a series of three blog posts I wrote on this topic for Contracts ProfBlog edited by Jeremy Telman. https://lawprofessors.typepad.com/contractsprof_blog/2020/07/guest-post-by-chaumtoli-huq-part-i-the-decolonial-framework.html;https://lawprofessors.typepad.com/contractsprof_blog/2020/07/guest-post-by-chaumtoli-huq-part-ii-freedom-to-contract-and-the-reasonable-man.html; https://lawprofessors.typepad.com/contractsprof_blog/2020/07/guest-post-by-chaumtoli-huq-part-iii-counter-hegemonic-narratives.html. Special thanks to Erin Quinn for her research assistance on this Chapter. Additional thanks to Andrea McArdle for reading an abstract of this article, gratitude to Barbara Lynn Atwell, Charles Calleros, Lynn Lu, Jeremy Telman, and Etienne Toussaint for reading drafts of this chapter and for their valuable comments. Thankful to Jamila Francisco and Rachel Kalta for their permission to include their comments in this piece.

References

Adebisi, Foluke, "Should We Rethink the Purposes of the Law School? A Case for Decolonial Thought in Legal Pedagogy", [2021] *Amicus Curiae* 428–449.

Astrada, Marvin and Scott Astrada, "Law, Continuity Change, Revisiting the Reasonable Person within the Demographic, Socio-cultural Political Realities of Twenty First Century", [2017] *Rutgers Journal Law and Public Policy* 14.

Atehortua, Juan Velasquez, "A Decolonial Pedagogy for Teaching Intersectionality", [2020] *New Jersey Coalition for Inclusive Education* 156.

Barnes, Wayne, "The Objective Theory of Contracts", [2008] *University of Cincinnati Law Review* 1119.

Cahn, Naomi R., "Looseness of Legal Language: The Reasonable Women Standard in Theory and in Practice", [1992] *Cornell Law Review* 1398.

Chase, Anthony R., "Race, Culture and Contract Law: From the Cottonfield to the Courtroom", [1995] *Connecticut Law Review* 1.

Collins, Patricia Hill, *Black Feminist Thought: Knowledge, Consciousness, and the Politics of Empowerment*, Routledge (2000).

Coulthard, Glen S., *Red Skin, White Masks: Rejecting Colonial Politics of Recognition*, University of Minnesota Press (2014).

Crenshaw, Kimberle, "Toward a Race-Conscious Pedagogy in Legal Education", [1998] *National Black Law Journal* 1.
DiMatteo, Larry, "The Counterpoise of Contracts: The Reasonable Person Standard and The Subjectivity of Judgment", [1997] *South Carolina Law Review* 293.
Dumont, Paul P., "Radtke v. Everett: An Analysis of the Court's Rejection of the Reasonable Woman/Victim Standard: Treating Perspectives That are Different as Though they are Exactly Alike", [1997] *Golden Gate University Law Review* 255.
Dunbar-Ortiz, Roxanne, *An Indigenous People's History of the United States*, Beacon Press (2014).
Fanon, Frantz, *Wretched of the Earth*, Grove Press (2004; reprint edition 2015).
Freire, Paulo, *Pedagogy of the Oppressed*, Continuum, New York (2005).
Gilmore, Grant, *The Death of Contract*, Ohio State University Press (1974).
Hernandez-Truyol, Berta, "Building Bridges – Latinas and Latinos at the Crossroads: Realities, Rhetoric and Replacement", [1994] *Columbia Human Rights Law Review* 369.
Kastely, Amy, "Out of the Whiteness: On Raced Codes and White Race in Consciousness, in Some Tort, Criminal and Contract Law", [1994] *University of Cincinnati Law Review* 269.
Lawson, Raneta J., "Critical Race Theory as Praxis: A View From Outside the Outside", [1995] *Howard Law Journal* 353.
Lugones, Maria, "Toward a Decolonial Feminism", [2010] *Hypatia* 742–759.
Maldonado-Torres, Nelson, "Outline of Ten Theses of Coloniality and Decoloniality", 2016 http://fondation-frantzfanon.com/outline-of-ten-theses-on-coloniality-and-decoloniality/
McMurtry-Chubb, Teri A. "Still Writing at the Master's Table: Decolonizing Rhetoric in Legal Writing for a "Woke" Legal Academy", [2019] *St. Mary's Law Review on Race and Social Justice* 255.
Munshi, Sherally, "Comparative Law and Decolonizing Critique", [2017] *The American Journal of Comparative Law* 207.
O'Gorman, Daniel P., "Learned Hand and the Objective Theory of Contract Interpretation", [2019] *University of New Hampshire Law Review* 63.
Perillo, Joseph M., "The Origins of the Objective Theory of Contract Formation and Interpretation", [2000] *Fordham Law Review* 427.
Quijano, Anibal, "Coloniality of Power, Eurocentrism, and Social Classification" in Anibal Quijano & Michael Ennis (eds), *Nepantia, Views from the South, Duke University Press* 2000, pp. 533–580.
Radtke v. Everett, 442 Mich. 368 (1993).
Raffles v. Wichelhaus, 2 H.& C. 906 (Court of Exchequer 1864). https://h2o.law.harvard.edu/collages/3676
Rodney, Walter, *How Europe Underdeveloped Africa*, Howard University Press (2012).
Semuels, Alana, "The Racist History of Portland, the Whitest City in America", [July 22, 2016] *The Atlantic*. https://www.theatlantic.com/business/archive/2016/07/racist-history-portland/492035/
Simpson, A.W. Brian, "Contracts for Cotton to Arrive: The Case of the Two Ships Peerless", [1989] *Cardozo Law Review* 11.
Southworth v. Oliver, 284 Or. 361 (1978).
Tapu, Ian F. "The Reasonable Indigenous Youth Standard", [2020/2021] *Gonzaga Law Review* 529.

Tuck, Eve and K. Wayne Yang, "Decolonization is Not a Metaphor", [2012] *Decolonization: Indigeneity, Education & Society* 1.
Twp. of Plymouth v. Hancock, 236 Mich.App. 197 (1999).
Velez-Martinez, Sheila, "Towards an Outcrit Pedagogy of Anti-subordination in the Classroom", [2015] *Chicago Kent Law Review* 585.

5

DEGREES OF COLONIALITY

Rethinking Property Law in (Northern) Ireland

Amanda Kramer and Alice Panepinto

Introduction

"Northern Ireland" (hereafter, NI)[1] is a unique space of contested coloniality where competing narratives permeate and are camouflaged in the law curriculum and the student body itself. The law curriculum in NI is premised on its current constitutional position within the United Kingdom (Dickson 2018). Given the surviving imperial legacies in the UK legal system, the law curriculum in NI has inherited various well-known problems that typify the laws of (former) imperial powers, as well as developing its own legal culture embedded in historic and political peculiarities. Consequently, the law taught in NI universities requires careful scrutiny through the lens of both global and local anti-colonial critique. As a (former) core module of the qualifying law degrees (LLB and MLaw) at Queen's University Belfast (QUB), "Contemporary Issues in Property Law" (CIPL) has offered opportunities to engage in this kind of reflection. The module covers a diverse range of topics and is designed to foster students' critical thinking about law in relation to power. As argued by Adebisi (2019):

> Critical thinking is at the core of legal study, yet failing to engage with 'marginalised issues' is an impediment to achieving critical thinking. When we do not account for the concerns of various groups that have been 'othered', we fail to achieve the positive possibilities of legal study. When our curriculum delivery fails to contextualise the information we transmit, we contribute to this othering.

With this in mind, the authors have sought to work towards decolonising the curriculum of CIPL, where legacies and current realities of colonialism and

DOI: 10.4324/9781003397885-8

white supremacy are hidden in plain sight. There is no agreement on the precise meaning of decolonisation, what it should look like and what form it should take. This chapter cannot contribute substantively to this complex debate: however, we are inspired by scholars like Gopal, Tuck and Yang, and Fanon, for whom decolonisation must involve a transfer of power back to Indigenous people; a return of stolen land and destruction of the processes created to initiate and continue this theft; the provision of meaningful, material reparations, and restitution to communities harmed by colonisation; and a "complete annihilation of the colonial order" (Gopal, 2021). Universities should not be exempt from this exercise; as argued by Gopal (2021), "the university cannot be decolonised independently of society and economy" but "if we take the production of knowledge seriously as a vital contributor to systemic transformation, then it would be equally perverse, indeed, harmful to leave the university out of endeavours to 'decolonise'". This chapter, therefore, hopes to contribute to this broader decolonisation project by moving towards decolonisation in our teaching, recognising that this is only a small part of the need for a broader dismantling of colonial systems to effect meaningful change. It provides reflections on the authors' experiences with attempting to decolonise CIPL as scholars racialised as "white" in a primarily "white" classroom, in a university in the Global North, in a place that has not been decolonised. We see this role as that outlined by Cartwright and Cartwright (2021), as educating in ways that challenge dominant ideologies and expose power structures in the creation and operation of the law.

Part 1 discusses the pedagogical context, the overview of the CIPL module, the complexities of decolonisation in NI, and researcher positionality. Parts 2 and 3 reflect on the authors' experiences of teaching "Colonialism/Land Grabbing" and "People as Property/Slavery". Selected relevant readings for each topic are presented alongside the authors' reasoning for selection and the contribution to the pedagogical context of the classroom. This discussion is framed within the broader purpose of this piece: moving towards an antiracist and decolonial legal pedagogy.

Part 1: framing the context

CIPL: learning objectives, place in the curriculum

CIPL has been, until very recently, a core module of the qualifying law degrees at QUB, the LLB (undergraduate) and MLaw (postgraduate).[2] It introduces students to the centrality of property in the history of "Western" legal traditions and critically unpacks the concept of property legally, socially, politically, economically, and culturally. Evolving notions of property run parallel with the histories of "Western" jurisprudence and underpin some of law's core assumptions. The module therefore encourages students to critically engage with the underlying factors that influence how property is conceptualised and understood. While the module aims and design do not foreground decolonisation per se, the module does include a session on colonialism and the lecturers have made a concerted effort to engage with decolonisation by adequately "contextualis[ing] the information we transmit" and providing the necessary information and tools for critical thinking (Adebisi 2019).

Two de/colonial encounters: local and global dimensions of colonialism in (Northern) Ireland

Talking about decolonisation in NI is complex, as the term and concept of colonialism is a taboo subject for various historical reasons with contemporary implications (O'Leary 2019). Efforts to decolonise the law school curriculum in NI are problematised by the discomforts around two coexisting dimensions of colonialism: the global and the local. Particular segments of the "ruling class" in NI have directly benefited from colonialism, reflecting its integration within the economy of the metropole for over half a millennium, including at the height of British imperialism (Wright 2013, 2019). At the same time, NI has been at the receiving end (Howe 2008) subjected to British colonialism since the Plantations in the Sixteenth and Seventeenth centuries, gradually integrated within London's jurisdictional control, and as a formal part of the United Kingdom since the 1921 partition (O'Leary 2019) (when the rest of the island of Ireland gained independence). Navigating these two seemingly contradictory dimensions is at the heart of the complex task of decolonising the law curriculum in NI, which requires a two-track effort. To echo Jonathan Jeffrey Wright (2013, p. 193), "encouraging an all-or-nothing mentality, in which Ireland must be either wholly colonial, or wholly non-colonial", is not helpful; these two intertwined dimensions must be appreciated together in their complexity.

The local dimension echoes the growing literature discussing how Ireland, including NI, was the first "trial" of organised British overseas (settler) colonialism embedded in an "ethos of superiority" towards the Irish (O'Leary 2019, p. 115). The Tudor conquest of Ireland (sixteenth century) and the Plantation of Ulster consolidated the grip of the British crown (a synonym for the state) over Ireland, including NI. After military conquest, law was key in the process of pacifying Ireland and establishing British sovereign control: Hans S. Pawlisch's (1985, pp. 4–5) study on law as an instrument of colonisation explains how English law and judicial strategies (backed up by military force) "locked a newly conquered country into a permanent colonial dependence". This two-stage approach – military conquest followed by legal imperialism – provided a blueprint for subsequent British colonialism worldwide (Pawlisch 1985).

This placed Ireland "systematically within the English empire, as a dependent territory that could not be easily controlled from London before the fiscal, military, and communicative powers of the UK state were strengthened in the early eighteenth century" (O'Leary 2019, p. 130). O'Leary (2019, p. 145) identifies the (partial) remedies to colonialism in Ireland in the "major shifts towards equality of natives and settlers that occurred from 1884 until 1912", the formation of the Irish Free State, and 1937 full sovereignty; for NI specifically, ending direct rule from Westminster and power-sharing arrangements contained in the 1998 Good Friday Agreement (GFA). However, McVeigh and Rolston (2021) identify these historical markers as part of the "unfinished revolution" against colonialism, arguing that colonialism remains embedded both North and South, with the most obvious manifestation of this being the continued existence of an Irish border. Law was a key factor in each of these pivotal stages. As such, teaching law in NI cannot be extracted from the historic and political context informed by the legacies of colonialism. NI constitutional law is the obvious topic where a decolonial lens is informative, but other subjects, including property law as discussed here, also benefit.

The global dimension of colonialism is the second element to consider in decolonising the law curriculum in NI. This takes stock of centuries of colonialism by white Europeans, including from Britain, in the Global South. In relation to Ireland, including NI, this dimension comes with an important caveat about British–Irish power dynamics described above but does not undermine the material advantage that its inhabitants (and public coffers) acquired through British imperialism (Dháibhéid et al. 2021). As O'Leary (2019, p. 139) sums up quite factually, "the Irish of many social classes were, of course, participants and beneficiaries in the extra-European British Empire". The literature reveals cross-community benefit: a Catholic family from Tipperary made their fortune in "the late seventeenth-century Chesapeake" (Virginia) exploiting the labour of their "growing slave work force" and a group of Ulster Scots in the Carolinas, "after clearing the land" and "fighting the Indians, … set about growing cotton and buying Africans from Charleston" (Rodgers 2016, p. 493–4). Much like the rest of the island of Ireland until partition in 1921, NI was an integral part of the British Empire, a predominantly white, Protestant and largely English-speaking area intertwined economically with the metropole, and where many inhabitants had similar aspirations of profiting from the exploitation of land and people overseas (Rodgers 2007; Roberts and Wright 2019). After partition, NI continued to play a role in the empire, in a manner that cannot be divorced from UK politics (Ollerenshaw 2008). Today, despite also being a historic recipient of British colonisation, the legacy of imperialism that brought wealth to (at least some in) NI based on slavery, land grabs, and exploitation elsewhere can no longer be ignored. For these reasons, the law curriculum (and other disciplines) in NI requires a frank reckoning with imperial legacies in NI, on the island of Ireland, and these islands more broadly.

Positionality vis-à-vis the curriculum and research interests

The QUB qualifying law degrees are designed to fulfil the academic stage of the legal qualification. Core undergraduate modules are delivered through lectures, supplemented by small-group tutorials; postgraduate modules are delivered through seminars incorporating more student-led learning. The programmes aim to improve students' knowledge and understandings of the module content, argumentation and critical analysis skills, engagement with appropriate learning resources, and written/oral communication skills – which is how the students are assessed. Like most law degrees, the curriculum is geared towards training people for, and maintaining particular standards within, the legal profession (Adebisi 2019).

Both authors engage with colonialism and postcolonial and decolonial theory within their own research. They identify as critical scholars, contesting positivist perspectives regarding the creation and operation of law, and bring these critiques into teaching practice. Panepinto researches international law and human rights "in context", specialising in the Middle East, and currently focuses on global and local law's complicity in entrenching colonialism in Palestine. Kramer's research interests straddle two relatively distinct areas: the consequences of Brexit, and postcolonial and decolonial theory. Her doctoral thesis explored the relationships between former European colonial powers and former African colonies through the mediums of international law and international institutions, using postcolonial and decolonial theory. Thus, the CIPL module allows for research-led teaching of the relationship between power and the law, in relation to colonialism, land grabbing, and slavery.

A & A: positionality vis-à-vis the student body and "outsiders" in NI

Both authors and the vast majority of CIPL students are racialised as "white", which has ramifications for the authors' role in decolonising and the ways they should design and deliver teaching that moves towards an antiracist and decolonial legal pedagogy. Cartwright and Cartwright contend that "the roles of those who have directly experienced racial oppression are different from the roles of those who have not, and that white academics must adopt a very different position when decolonising the curriculum from their colleagues of colour" (2021, p. 535). Thus, the authors use CIPL to encourage students to challenge dominant ideologies about the creation and operation of the law – to reveal power structures, such as white supremacy, built into the legal project, and expose the consequences.

Both authors are also "outsiders" in NI and "migrant academics" outside the local institutional norms. Neither author was born or raised in NI (both moved as adults), nor have a local accent or NI heritage – making both identifiable as "outsiders". Panepinto is half-English half-Italian, born in Egypt due to her parents' jobs in the Global South at the time. Kramer is a settler Canadian from the territories of the Anishinaabe people (Barker 2009). As outsiders, both Panepinto and Kramer have attempted to navigate NI's complex relationship to colonialism. Teaching about decolonisation requires an appreciation of this complex relationship and a careful elucidation of the perspectives on colonialism held by different NI communities. This outsider status accords the authors the advantage of being able to speak about the complexities of colonisation in the classroom and not automatically be categorised as "orange" or "green"[3] (Geoghegan 2008); as remarked by one NI colleague, "I could never discuss this in class". Nonetheless, outsiders may be oblivious (despite their best efforts) to certain nuances and sensitivities, so any pedagogical advantages that status confers may be tempered by actual or perceived inaccuracies in reading the local context.

Part 2: colonialism/land grabbing

The class on colonialism and land grabbing explores the core concepts of the doctrine of discovery and terra nullius. This section introduces these notions and provides examples of how a critical discussion of law's participation in colonialism and land grabbing is embedded in the core syllabus.

The legal foundations of colonialism: doctrine of discovery and terra nullius

The operation of English colonialism throughout history cannot be disentangled from law, and in particular the doctrines which provided the tools and mindset to justify and enable dispossession and subjugation. The doctrine of discovery (Miller et al. 2010) embodies "a set of legal principles that governed the European colonizing powers, particularly regarding the administration of indigenous land" formulated in the fifteenth and sixteenth centuries (Charles and Rah, 2019, p 15). Charles and Rah (2019, pp. 15 & 21) describe it as "rooted in dysfunctional theological imagination that shaped the European colonial settler worldview", initially used to affirm (and validate) the imperial ambitions of Portugal and Spain. The doctrine of discovery gave "theological permission for the European body and mind to view themselves as superior to the non-European bodies and minds"; it "created an identity for African bodies as inferior and only worthy of subjugation; it also relegated the identity of the original inhabitants of the land 'discovered' to become outsiders, now unwelcome in their own land" (Charles and Rah 2019, p. 21). This description reveals how the white, European colonial mindset racialised people "discovered" outside European spaces, and justified subalternity theologically, which was then either written into the law or used to colour seemingly neutral law for maintaining (white) supremacy in establishing and preserving title to land.

The related notion of terra nullius (nobody's land) (Zukas 2005; Fitzmaurice 2007) enabled non-European land "discovered" by Europeans to be lawfully appropriated. Benton and Straumann (2010, p. 11) consider terra nullius as "standing in for not a single doctrine but a legal orientation and a diverse set of practices" drawing on the Roman private law notion of res nullius (a thing owned by nobody) used by European colonial powers to justify claims to sovereignty of "discovered" lands. Far from being a precise, coherent rule, much like the doctrine of discovery, the notion of terra nullius was a normative framework that justified formal acquisition of title to Indigenous lands by European "explorers" and states.

These doctrines feed into what has been called "the international law of colonialism", employed "to subjugate Indigenous Peoples, … steal Indigenous lands, assets, and rights", and which "has impacted Indigenous Peoples from the onset of colonization to the present day" (Miller 2019, p. 35). As Miller sums up, "European powers primarily justified these acquisitions and their ambitions by ethnocentric allegations of cultural, racial, governmental, and religious superiority over the rest of the world". In the Americas, "under the aegis of 'discovery,' any claim to ownership of their lands by the Indigenous peoples of the Americas was discounted" (Medina 2019, p. 163). Nestor Medina plainly states that "one of the most insidious aspects of the Doctrine of Discovery was its inscription into law", supported by Roman jurisprudence and papal bulls to enhance its "'legal' character". For Medina (2019, p. 163), the various laws used by Spain "to establish sovereignty over Indigenous lands and peoples through 'legal' means" consequently "enshrined systems to keep Indigenous peoples indentured or enslaved and took away their 'rights' by ensuring that they did not have sovereignty over their own lands". What is particularly interesting for decolonial pedagogical purposes is the realisation that the laws governing private property have been (and can be) tools of international conquest and dispossession of local colonised peoples. In the CIPL syllabus, these twin doctrines are presented as part of the core concepts underpinning colonialism and land grabbing, explored through case studies, including those presented below.

Current lives of old land grabs

Ireland

The MLaw CIPL syllabus (2020–2021) included a chapter by Hans Pawlisch (1985) to discuss the legal history of colonialism and land grabs in Ireland. This is one of the most fascinating texts of Irish legal history Panepinto found to stimulate reflection on how the British grip on the island of Ireland developed through unique applications of law, allowing students to interrogate the character of the law in Ireland, including NI. The book traces the work of

Sir Davies, the solicitor-general (1603–1606) and attorney-general (1606–1619) of Ireland, who ushered in radical land law changes for transferring legal title of vast swathes of land to the Crown and its allies. As Pawlisch (1985, p. 14) sums up,

> Davies' formula for Ireland – 'to give laws to a conquered people is the principal mark of a perfect conquest' had established a paradigm for British conquest elsewhere. … Davies' judicial stance on Gaelic property rights laid the basis for an imperial formula that was fundamental in the creation of the British empire.

At the start of the Seventeenth century, eradicating significant parts of the local laws and customs as a form of colonial violence resulted in replacing the Indigenous system of land law in Ireland with a new system imposed by the conquering nation. Davies viewed the Gaelic landholding and succession norms, tanistry and gravelkind, as the main barrier to "the exercise of legal sovereignty in Ireland"; therefore, the extension of common law was a precondition for the assimilation of "an alien scheme of law and land tenure into the new state system" vested in the Crown (Pawlisch 1985, p. 55). This reading offers a dispassionate analysis of how Davies' dealings in Ireland trialled some of the key features of colonial land law used by Britain to expand its empire worldwide.

Pedagogically, this text was chosen because it is thought-provoking: in the NI law curriculum, the Land Law module is taught through the standard textbooks of English land law, with some relatively minor NI-specific add-ons. As such, it helps students think more critically about the law they are actually learning in a law school in NI as a result of British legal imperialism (to borrow from Pawlisch). Therefore, the primary learning aim is to offer students additional tools to understand the parameters of the law syllabus in NI through Pawlisch's historical analysis of why and how English common law was extended to the island of Ireland. Providing this sort of reading is important in the process of realisation that law is embedded in colonial histories and practices, in the hope that each student will approach their studies (and future legal careers) with a greater awareness of the imperial legacies of law in NI.

Canada

The LLB colonialism session taught by Kramer includes Canada as a "case" study. This session demonstrates to students that historical processes of colonisation had long-lasting and significant legacies and highlights that in Canada, settler colonialism never ended. The Canadian example allows for an interrogation of law's role in justifying and continuing colonisation, with a specific focus on conceptions of property and ownership. It also encourages students to apply this learning to other contexts and consider other places where colonisation did not end. This session uses the work of Borrows (2015) and Preston (2013) to explore key components of settler colonialism in Canada.

Indigenous scholar John Borrows (2015) examines *terra nullius* within the context of the colonisation of Canada, centring his analysis on a defining legal case: the *Tsilhqot'in Nation* decision. He reflects on the durability of *terra nullius* within this decision and lays out the judgment's strengths and weaknesses within the wider context of reconciliation. Borrows (2015) argues that the doctrine of discovery is ever-present within Canadian law and contends that, while the decision makes significant progress in recognising Indigenous title rights, it also perpetuates *terra nullius* as the "Crown still retains underlying title and paramount sovereign authority over these lands" (p. 740).

Preston (2013) emphasises the reality of settler colonialism in Canada by examining the Canadian tar sands (and associated pipeline) project opposition by Indigenous and environmental groups and responses by various levels of government, police and national security forces, and industry. Preston highlights the responses' interconnected nature (identifying these as neoliberal partnerships) and argues that they constitute one of many contemporary forms of white settler colonialism operating in Canada. She demonstrates that these partnerships "reveal how racism and settler colonialism fundamentally structure contemporary social and economic life" (p. 43), and details how the rights of Indigenous peoples over their lands (including that under treaty and unceded) have been continually violated to prioritise the settler government's economic interests.

These pieces inform many key themes and learning objectives in the lecture. Borrows (2015) demonstrates the law's role in maintaining settler colonialism and proposes strategies to move towards decolonisation, Indigenous sovereignty, and reconciliation. Preston (2013) demonstrates how public–private partnerships violate Indigenous rights and inflict ongoing colonial harms on communities. These pieces challenge students to see both obvious and insidious ways that settler colonialism operates, the law's role in this process, and to consider decolonisation strategies. They also provide the students with the knowledge for discussion tasks, one of which includes reflecting on colonialism in Northern Ireland. Typically, the students engage in this discussion tentatively and upon raising the question of whether they consider NI to be colonised, there is an audible reaction (which takes various forms, including gasps and laughter). We interpret this reaction as being due to the complexity and political associations of discussing colonialism in NI.

Contemporary land grabs

Palestine

The decolonisation of the law curriculum in NI includes situating law's ambiguous role in current contexts of post/coloniality worldwide, such as Palestine.

In the session on contemporary land grabs taught in 2020–21 on the MLaw Panepinto included readings by legal scholar Ahmad Amara and geographer Oren Yiftachel (Amara and Yiftachel 2014; Yiftachel, 2017), invited as guest speakers dialling in from Palestine/Israel.

Both pieces address the unilateral Israeli regulation of Palestinian land, focusing on the Bedouin communities in the Negev/Naqab (in present-day southern Israel), within the framework of settler colonialism. The readings reveal the "oppressive consequences of the interaction between law, land and identity", covering a "wide range of design, legal, regulative economic, ethnic and political decisions that together 'produce' societal space" (Yiftachel 2017, p. 243). Yiftachel (2017, p. 244) outlines the "charged context of Israel/Palestine where the settler Jewish state has extensively used legal and planning tools to seize, control and manage contested indigenous Bedouin lands". Against that backdrop, the doctrine of terra nullius – a legal concept as well as a "frame of mind typifying colonial and ethnocratic regimes" – strips "indigenous peoples of their culture, histories and codes of governance", allowing "the invading or expanding entity the power and legitimacy to define when and where land is considered 'empty', and hence who is a 'rightful' owner" (Yiftachel 2017, pp. 244–245). As such, the terra nullius doctrine becomes a tool to control ethnic and racial minorities.

The Negev/Naqab has been inhabited by Palestinian Bedouins from time immemorial, until it was taken over by the Israeli state in 1948 and, citing Yiftachel (2017, p. 245), "thoroughly Judaized". Despite the fact that the "historic Bedouin region was governed by well-established codes of ownership, partition, sales and conflict resolution", the new Israeli legal order drew selectively from Ottoman and British mandate law to deny and erase the "validity of a pre-state indigenous land system", devising the "Dead Negev Doctrine" to claim Indigenous land and effectively dispossess the Bedouin by making it impossible for them to prove their title to land in Israeli courts through their customary land system (Yiftachel 2017, pp. 247–248). The Israeli state policy of non-recognition of Indigenous title to land results in Palestinian Bedouin villages becoming "unrecognised" in the Israeli legal system; their existence in a "grey space" is then used as a pretext to deny basic infrastructure and services and to routinely demolish homes lacking Israeli-issued permits, which are almost impossible to obtain (Yiftachel 2017, pp. 247–248). Thus, applying settler-colonial land law carries serious human rights violations, highlighting the violent connotations of that legal system towards racialised minority groups.

In explicitly addressing law's centrality in enabling and entrenching colonialism, annexation and land grabbing, this session contributes to the efforts of anti-colonial pedagogy. In particular, focusing on the current mis/uses of property law and planning regulations drawing selectively on Ottoman, British mandate and Israeli law reveals how even today the dispossession of Indigenous populations can be presented in a "legalised" manner. The learning aim underpinning the inclusion of this topic in the CIPL syllabus is twofold: first, the doctrine of terra nullius is tested in a contemporary context where a settler-colonial state uses land grabs to dispossess Indigenous populations, showing the law's complicity in this violence. Second, these materials aim to stimulate reflection on how a contemporary, ongoing land grab might be reversed through decolonisation efforts, in contrast with consolidated historic land grabs.

Corporations in resource-rich countries

Moving towards decolonising the curriculum requires an exploration of neo-colonial practices; thus, Kramer examines "land grabbing" on the LLB module. While large-scale land acquisitions are often presented as providing economic and development opportunities to host governments, this session encourages critical engagement and examination of the variety of negative consequences, including, dispossession, gender inequality, violence and conflict, water supply depletion, and environmental destruction (De Schutter 2011). The lecture relies on Borras, et al.'s (2012, p. 405) definition of land grabbing:

> [C]ontemporary land grabbing is the capturing of control of relatively vast tracts of land and other natural resources through a variety of mechanisms and forms involving large-scale capital that often shifts resource use to that of extraction, whether for international or domestic purposes, as capital's response to the convergence of food, energy and financial crises, climate change mitigation imperatives and demands for resources from newer hubs of global capital.

Land grabbing is presented as inherently intertwined with capitalist and colonial structures. The assigned readings by De Schutter (2011) and Jurkevics (2022) engage with these debates and highlight how "property" and international investment law facilitate land grabbing.

Land grabbing occurs within the long history of "large-scale capture and monopolization of land" (Jurkevics 2022, p. 33). While this practice is not new, the transformation that occurred in 2007–2008 alongside the financial and world food price crises is markedly different. Students are introduced to the role of property law in land grabbing by De Schutter (2011), who argues that

> if the current challenge of large-scale land acquisitions leads to the globalisation of Western-style property rights, the ultimate result will be a more capitalised form of agriculture and more land concentration, when what we need instead is to democratise access to land and to support reforms that will benefit small-scale farmers.
>
> *(p. 506)*

Students consider the connection between colonialism and land grabbing by exploring Jurkevics' (2022) work, which identifies land grabbing as neo-colonialism through analysis of territorial sovereignty alienation. Central to this analysis is the facilitating role of international investment law. Jurkevics (2022) concludes that many land grabs alienate rule, as they involve situations where

> (i) contract clauses override domestic law or prevent the host state from regulating the investor's use of land; (ii) inhabitants are neither consulted nor included as parties to the contract; (iii) the purchaser gains unilateral control over resources and infrastructure; and (iv) the purchaser mimics sovereign power.
>
> *(pp. 34–35)*

Potential solutions are considered within the context of decolonisation. The students engage with Tzouvala's (2019) argument that the responsibilities placed on host governments, such as those emerging from "soft law" approaches, "are in tension with the legal legacies of colonialism" and "also with already existing 'hard' legal obligations of said states, and with the very state model promoted by the international financial institutions" (p. 236). This is connected with Jurkevics' (2022) proposals that the solution should not lie in the framework of territorial sovereignty due to embedded logics of capitalism and colonialism. Thus, students are pushed to radically rethink potential solutions to adequately recognise and counter the continuing operation of colonial structures.

Part 3: people as property/slavery

Teaching the extent of "old slavery"

One of the most harrowing features of property law is its application to human beings, including in the form of ownership of slaves. To address this, the CIPL curriculum at both LLB and MLaw features the infamous *Gregson and Gilbert* (1783) case as a historical example of how property law has purposefully enabled the deprivation of liberty through slavery and reduction of people to the status of cargo. *Gregson and Gilbert* is an insurance case "to recover the value" of 132 slaves thrown overboard the Zong ship, and not a property law case; its legal premise is, crudely, that Black people could be owned as chattel by white people under English law – and shipped as cargo. As such, in the late 1700s under English law "the owners of the Zong would have been responsible as private carriers for ordinary care of cargo on board – 'common care', or 'reasonable care'" (Oldham 2007, p. 314).

The facts of the case as well as the applicable law are shocking and difficult to read. The *Zong* massacre and related insurance case has been described "as the most infamous atrocity in the Atlantic slave trade" (Burnard 2019, para. 18). Abolitionist Granville Sharp who followed the proceedings rightly called for a murder investigation (Rupprecht 2008, p. 265). Yet at the time, the regulation of "human cargoes (slaves) in transit on the sea occupied a problematic, liminal position in maritime law – a position somewhere between personhood and property" (Webster 2007, p. 296). As Rupprecht (2008, p. 265) sums up, the case "exposed, very publicly, the extent to which British law had been corrupted by the nation's support of the transatlantic slave trade".

Recognising how British law enabled the slave trade and allowed such a massacre to occur in the first place and then dealt with it in court as an insurance claim and not a murder case is the explicit, immediate learning aim underpinning the inclusion of this case in the curriculum. The broader pedagogical outcome of teaching this case is implicit and longer-term: the Zong case has the power to confront a white (or almost exclusively white) classroom in Belfast with many of the commonly held assumptions about law being neutral and in principle correlated to substantive justice. The Zong case presents "the sea [as] a battlefield of domination where, in complicity with finance capitalism and insurance, law suspended the humanity of beings" (Quéma 2016, p. 95). Law played a key role in "the commodification of the body" (Haslam 2022): "processes and techniques of racialization required the legitimation of law" and "race was used to mark differences between who can be owned and who can own and who can own what" (Adebisi 2021, pp. 434–5).

The Zong massacre and its legal aftermath therefore remain seeped in the racialised, violent connotations of property law of the late 1700s, which legitimised slavery. Moreover, if the people thrown overboard had been white, this case would have reached the criminal courts, and would now be part of a criminal law curriculum instead of the property law syllabus. This is a crude way of teaching the law's role in "classic" colonial domination, but it remains an effective one. This is more so the case in the NI classroom, where British colonialism might be thought of as a thing pertaining to Britain, not Belfast, despite ample historical evidence (discussed earlier in this chapter) of individuals from NI profiting handsomely from the slave trade and plantations in the United States and the Caribbean.

Contemporary forms of slavery

These themes are also considered in the modern slavery lectures. The continued relevance of the concepts of property and ownership are made apparent through exploration of the legal definition of slavery and the relevant key cases of *Kunarac*, 2003; *Siliadin*, 2005; *Tang* 2008. While these cases identify the 1926 Slavery Convention as the legal definition of slavery, their interpretations vary significantly – hinging on whether slavery involves the *de jure* or the *de facto* exercise of the right of ownership over a person. While the judgments in

Kunarac and *Tang* both relied on the *de facto* exercise of the right of ownership, *Siliadin* maintained that the definition was only applicable in a *de jure* right of ownership over a person. While the *Tang* reasoning is now widely accepted, this debate alerts students to the importance of the conceptions of property and ownership in understanding and prosecuting modern slavery. The assigned reading by Allain and Hickey (2012) provides requisite knowledge to see this connection between property law and slavery and understand the debate within the historical context of the slave trade – a key learning outcome of the session.

The class also examines prominent anti-slavery legislative approaches. The students consider the UK Modern Slavery Act and some of its key provisions and reflect on its effectiveness within the broader policy context of the UK. Particularly, the work of Hodkinson et al. (2021, pp. 68–69) demonstrates that "when considered alongside the UK government's deliberate creation of a 'hostile environment' towards migrants, not least in the Immigration Acts of 2014 and 2016, state action to outlaw modern slavery is flawed, counter-productive and disingenuous". This piece also encourages reflection on structural contributors to modern slavery, such as the racism embedded in the UK's immigration policies – another learning objective of this lecture.

Next, focus shifts to provisions targeting businesses – particularly in relation to their responsibility for supply chains. The contrasting approaches taken within the French Duty of Vigilance Law and the Dutch Child Labour Due Diligence Law are presented and considered in relation to the central drivers of modern slavery. Here, the work of Banerjee (2021, p. 415) is emphasised, "just as historical slavery was an enabling condition of industrial capitalism, modern slavery is an enabling condition of global neoliberal capitalism". Banerjee's (2021) work encourages students to reflect on the connections between slavery (in all its forms), capitalism, and colonialism to assess the effectiveness of anti-slavery legislative approaches. This discussion is designed to highlight that domestic legislative approaches can never adequately combat modern slavery alone. It also helps the students to begin unpacking the connections made by Brown et al. (2021) between modern slavery and environmental degradation and climate change. The global economic structures established by capitalism and colonialism that attempt to consign the Global South to resource-extraction-based economies are the same forces that drive modern slavery and environmental degradation. Taken together, the continued patterns of exploitation by the Global North and the disproportionate consequences of these practices on the populations and environments of the Global South are highlighted and considered in relation to designing effective modern slavery responses.

Conclusion

Like all educational settings, the pedagogical context of qualifying law degrees at QUB is not exempt from the urgency of shining light on global systemic racism channelled and enhanced through legal instruments and legal education itself. Through their teaching on CIPL, Kramer and Panepinto have sought to contribute to the project of decolonisation in small but tangible ways. As white critical legal scholars in a majority white classroom, we have sought to implement decolonisation strategies in line with those suggested by prominent scholars, such as Adebisi (2019, 2021) and Cartwright and Cartwright (2021). Thus, we have consistently highlighted to the students the role of law in establishing, justifying, and continuing colonialism; the necessity of examining the context surrounding laws' creation and application; and strategies for imagining solutions to these problems that move towards decolonisation. We have also prioritised active learning techniques that provide a space for students to share their perspectives and ideas about these issues. The choice of content (i.e. core and additional readings for each topic) was meant to stimulate student reflection; in small-group teaching, expressing, and exploring reflection on the content was encouraged in class discussion and emerged in group presentations. The assessments for CIPL – an extended essay on some of the core themes/issues covered in the module – enabled students to engage and write about the dialectic between content/knowledge acquired, on the one hand, and reflexivity/critical thinking that emerged on the other. As a result, the two dimensions of colonialism spotlighted in CIPL teaching became evident in the learning that emerged from the essays produced.

It is hoped that by pursuing these strategies, students will see the operation of systemic racism and colonialism throughout the legal enterprise and, in doing so, expand their legal imaginations and work towards change. In the NI law classroom, conversations about decolonisation and the law seem to have been slow to develop; nonetheless, there is much to say about how law and colonialism are inextricably intertwined both in NI and overseas, especially in places connected in various ways to NI and its inhabitants through colonial structures. As educators, we have tried to incorporate readings in the curriculum of CIPL that stimulate reflection and discussion on these issues, in the hope that our students and graduates are mindful of the myth of law as a neutral toolkit in light of the legacies and continuing wrongs traced back to colonialism.

Notes

1 While we are using the term 'Northern Ireland' throughout this piece, we recognise that 'Northern Ireland' is a creation of the British Empire (imposed through the partition of Ireland) and that using this term itself can be seen to reinforce coloniality. We use this term for searchability, but we do not do so uncritically.
2 As of the 2022/2023 academic year, CIPL will no longer be a core module of the qualifying law degree at Queen's University Belfast.
3 'Green' and 'Orange' is local shorthand used to refer to the two largest communities in NI (broadly, nationalist, republican, and Catholic; and unionist, loyalist, and Protestant) and their respective political beliefs on NI as rightfully belonging in the Republic of Ireland or in the UK.

References

Adebisi, Foluke Ifejola, "Decolonisation and the Law School: Initial thoughts" (*Foluke's African Skies*, 22 July 2019): https://folukeafrica.com/decolonisation-the-law-school-initial-thoughts/

Adebisi, Foluke Ifejola, "Should We Rethink the Purposes of the Law School? A Case for Decolonial Thought in Legal Pedagogy" [2021] 2 *Amicus Curiae* 428–449.

Allain, Jean and Hickey, Robin, "Property and the Definition of Slavery" [2012] 61 *International & Comparative Law Quarterly* 915–938.

Amara, Ahmad and Yiftachel, Oren, *Confrontation in the Negev* (A study commissioned by the Rosa Luxembourg Stiftung, 2014).

Banerjee, Bobby, "Modern Slavery is an Enabling Condition of Global Neoliberal Capitalism: Commentary on Modern Slavery in Business" [2021] 60 *Business and Society* 415–419.

Barker, Adam J., "The Contemporary Reality of Canadian Imperialism: Settler Colonialism and the Hybrid Colonial State" [2009] 33 *American Indian Quarterly* 325–352.

Benton, Lauren and Straumann, Benjamin, "Acquiring Empire by Law: From Roman Doctrine to Early Modern European Practice" [2010] 28 *Law and History Review* 1–38.

Borras Jr, Saturnino M., Kay, Cristóbal, Gómez, Sergio, and Wilkinson, John, "Land Grabbing and Global Capitalist Accumulation: Key Features in Latin American" [2012] 33 *Canadian Journal of Development Studies* 403–416.

Borrows, John, "The Durability of Terra Nullius: Tsilhqot'in Nation V British Columbia", [2015] 48 *University of British Columbia Law Review* 701–742.

Brown, David, Boyd, Doreen S., Brickell, Katherine, Ives, Christopher D., Natarajan, Nithya, and Parsons, Laurie, "Modern Slavery, Environmental Degradation and Climate Change: Fisheries, Field, Forests and Factories" [2021] 4 *Nature and Space* 191–207.

Burnard, Trevor, "A New Look at the Zong Case of 1783" [2019] 76 *XVII-XVIII: Revue de la Société d'études anglo-américaines des XVIIe et XVIIIe siècles*.

Cartwright, Nick and Cartwright, T.O. "'Why Is It My Problem If They Don't Take Part?' The (non)role of White Academics in Decolonising the Law School" [2021] 54 *The Law Teacher* 532–546.

Charles, Mark and Rah, Soong-Chan, *Unsettling Truths: The Ongoing, Dehumanizing Legacy of the Doctrine of Discovery*, InterVarsity Press 2019.

De Schutter, Olivier, "The Green Rush: The Global Race for Farmland and the Rights of Land Users" [2011] 52 *Harvard International Law Journal* 504–559.

Dickson, Brice, *Law in Northern Ireland*, Hart 2018.

Fitzmaurice, Andrew, "The genealogy of terra nullius" [2007] 38 *Australian Historical Studies* 1–15.

Geoghegan, Peter, "Beyond Orange and Green? The awkwardness of negotiating difference in Northern Ireland", [2008] 16 *Irish Studies Review* 173–194.

Gopal, Priyamvada, "On Decolonisation and the University" [2021] 35(6) *Textual Practice* 873–899.

Haslam, Emily, "Archived Bodies: The Transatlantic Slave Trade and Abolition" in Didi Herman and Connal Parsley (eds) *Interdisciplinarities: Research Process, Method and the Body of Law*, Palgrave 2022, pp. 9–21.

Hodkinson, Stuart N., Lewis, Hannah, Waite, Louise, and Dwyer, Peter, "Fighting or fuelling forced labour? The Modern Slavery Act 2015, irregular migrants and the vulnerabilising role of the UK's hostile environment policy" [2021] 41 *Critical Social Policy* 68–90.

Howe, Stephen, "Questioning the (Bad) Question: 'Was Ireland a Colony?'" [2008] 36(142) *Irish Historical Studies* 138–152.

Jurkevics, Annam "Land Grabbing and the Perplexities of Territorial Sovereignty" [2022] 50 *Political Theory* 32–58.

McVeigh, Robbie, and Rolston, Bill, *Ireland, Colonialism and the Unfinished Revolution*, Beyond the Pale 2021

Medina, Nestor, "The Doctrine of Discovery, LatinXo Theoethics, and Human Rights" [2019] 21 *Journal of Hispanic / Latino Theology* 157–173.

Miller, Robert J, Ruru, Jacinta, Behrendt, Larissa, and Lindberg, Tracy, *Discovering Indigenous lands: The doctrine of discovery in the English colonies*, Oxford University Press 2010.

Miller, Robert J., "The doctrine of discovery: The international law of colonialism" [2019] 5 *Indigenous Peoples' JL Culture & Resistance* 35–42.

Nic, Dháibhéid, Caoimhe, Akhtar, Shahmima, Hassett, Dónal, Kenny, Kevin, McAtackney, Laura, McBride I., McMahon, Timothy G., and Ohlmeye, J., "Round table: Decolonising Irish history? Possibilities, challenges, practices" [2021] 45 *Irish Historical Studies* 303–332.

O'Leary, Brendan, *A Treatise on Northern Ireland: Volume II: Control*, OUP 2019.

Oldham, James, "Insurance Litigation Involving the Zong and Other British Slave Ships, 1780–1807" [2007] 28 *The Journal of Legal History* 299–318.

Ollerenshaw, Philip, "Northern Ireland and the British Empire-Commonwealth, 1923–61" [2008] 36 *Irish Historical Studies* 227–242.

Pawlisch, Hans S., *Sir John Davies and the conquest of Ireland: A study in legal imperialism*, Cambridge University Press 1985.

Preston, Jen, "Neoliberal Settler Colonialism, Canada and the Tar Sands" [2013] 55 *Race & Class* 42–59.

Quéma, Anne, "M. NourbeSe Philip's 'Zong!': Metaphors, Laws, and Fugues of Justice" [2016] 43 *Journal of Law and Society* 85–104.

Roberts, Daniel Sanjiv and Wright, Jonathan Jeffrey (eds), *Ireland's Imperial Connections, 1775-1947*, Palgrave 2019.

Rodgers, Nini, *Ireland, Slavery and Anti-Slavery: 1612–1865*, Palgrave 2007.

Rodgers, Nini, "Ireland, Slavery, Antislavery, Post-Slavery and Empire: An Historiographical Survey" [2016] 37(3) *Slavery & Abolition* 489–504.

Rupprecht, Anita, "'A Limited Sort of Property': History, Memory and the Slave Ship Zong" [2008] 29 *Slavery & Abolition* 265–277.

Tzouvala, Ntina, "A False Promise? Regulating land-grabbing and the post-colonial state" [2019] 32 *Leiden Journal of International Law* 235–253.

Webster, Jane, "The Zong in the Context of the Eighteenth-Century Slave Trade" [2007] 28 *The Journal of Legal History* 285–286.

Wright, Jonathan Jeffrey, "'The Belfast Chameleon': Ulster, Ceylon and the Imperial Life of Sir James Emerson Tennent" [2013] 6 *Britain and the World* 192–219.

Wright, Jonathan Jeffrey, "'A work purely local?': Narratives of Empire in George Benn's A History of the Town of Belfast" in Daniel Sanjiv Roberts and Jonathan Jeffrey Wright (eds), *Ireland's Imperial Connections, 1775–1947*, Palgrave 2019, pp. 143–168.

Yiftachel, Oren, “Terra nullius’ and planning: Land, law and identity in Israel/Palestine” in Gautam Bhan, Smita Srinivas, and Vanessa Watson (eds) *The Routledge Companion to Planning in the Global South*, Routledge 2017, pp. 243–254.
Zukas, Alex “*Terra Incognita*/*Terra Nullius*: Modern Imperialism, Maps, and Deception” in Gary Backhaus and John Murungi (eds), *Lived Topographies and Their Mediational Forces*, Lexington Books 2005, pp. 49–76.

6

TEACHING PROPERTY CRITICALLY IN DISPARATE PARTS OF THE FORMER BRITISH EMPIRE

Cristy Clark, Sarah Keenan, and John Page

Introduction

This chapter uses three case studies, two in Australian law schools and one in England, to explore the implications (and rich possibilities) of decolonising the curriculum of Property Law, a legal area with a reputation for arcane subject matters and a doctrinal, black-letter pedagogy. This reputation is mostly deserved. But it is also tragic, given that property and its laws are central to our spatial orderings, arbitrarily dictating where we belong, and where we do not (Waldron 1991). In the context of the former British Empire, property law was and still is a key means through which Indigenous people have been dispossessed of their land. Property's colonial underpinnings and enduring colonial structures enact a worldview that is exclusionary in operation and spatially unjust in effect, dividing up space and its finitudes along lines of race, class, gender, wealth, and power. In the settler colonial state, this worldview perpetuates the teaching of colonial laws from law schools located on stolen lands. It is from these starting premises that our discussions unfold.

The authors of this chapter are three non-Indigenous Australian property academics, based variously in Australia and the UK. We are theorists of *critical* property, and as circumstances permit, teachers of critical property law. In writing of our experiences in teaching property critically, we adopt the first person in describing each of our case studies, positioning ourselves within our respective law schools and faculties. Case Study I is the opening work of Sarah Keenan at Birkbeck, University of London. Cristy Clark of the University of Canberra Law School authors Case Study II. Case Study III closes with the observations of John Page at Southern Cross University. The chapter

DOI: 10.4324/9781003397885-9

concludes with a reflective discussion of a series of conceptual questions common to our case studies, questions with both practical implications and profound import.

Teaching property critically from the heart of the old Empire

Teaching Property Law in central London, my students are racially diverse and have a wide range of experiences with and knowledge of the former British Empire. At my first London job in 2012, I was surprised to find *Mabo v Queensland (no 2)* (1992) 175 CLR 1 on the curriculum, as it is, of course, an Australian case and the course is in English and Welsh property law. *Mabo* is the case, for the first time in common law history, which acknowledged that the continent now known as Australia was not empty and unoccupied, or *terra nullius*, when the British arrived in 1770. I have since found that a number of English courses teach the case because of the succinct history of common law property found in the judgment, and the way it brings the abstract concepts of radical title and tenure into sharp relief. Students with family connections in other former British colonies consistently find the case intensely interesting and choose to write their essays on it. My own understanding of the case and its positioning within British colonialism, and the ongoing process of decolonisation, have been deepened by reading it with London students.

Following initiatives by black students in South Africa, calls to 'decolonise the curriculum' in English universities began to be clearly articulated and heard in 2016 as the campaign to bring down the statue of white supremacist, mining magnate and educational philanthropist Cecil Rhodes from Oxford's Oriel College. Student movements across Britain have joined in the demand to have their curricula decolonised, which most universities have responded positively to, so much so that there is concern about the project being co-opted into a tokenistic programme of inclusion to be included in university marketing materials rather than meaningfully adopted through changes to knowledge production and pedagogy (Bhambra et al. 2018).

In my own position at Birkbeck School of Law, the university's acceptance of the need to recognise and remedy the colonising role played by courses which revolve around the perspectives and records of colonisers has empowered me to make more structural changes to how Property is taught to Law students. Previously, Property Law 1 (Land) was taught as a full-year (i.e. two-term, 20 teaching weeks) course, followed by Equity and Trusts in the same format the following year. I taught *Mabo* as part of the Property Law 1 course, along with Locke's theory of property and critical engagements with it, and a brief history of the colonial history of the Torrens system as a pre-curser to the English and Welsh land registration scheme. However, these topics felt added-in at the end of the year-long course. What I proposed, and what my School supported me in implementing, is a separate Foundations of Property one-term course to be taken prior to a one-term Land Law course, followed by Equity and Trusts. I have taught Foundations of Property in this format for the first time this year (2021/2022), to an overwhelmingly positive reception from students.

The Foundations of Property course aims to give students a historically grounded introduction to key concepts in English property law. The curriculum gives students a grounding in the feudal origins of many of these concepts, and an understanding of how those concepts have been developed, applied, and modified throughout the transition from feudalism to capitalism, including the key role that legal experimentation in the colonies had in making land more alienable. With a historically and politically grounded understanding of these concepts, my aim is that the course not only equips students for their studies on the following term's Land Law course – a more technical and applied course dealing with contemporary case law and legislation – but also makes them interested and keen to do so.

The course is presently organised into weekly topics as follows:

1. Feudalism and Possessive Derivative Title
2. Coverture, Primogeniture and the Patriarchal Family
3. John Locke, Enclosure and Colonialism
4. The Transatlantic Slave Trade and 1834 Compensation
5. *Mabo v Queensland*: Native title and terra nullius
6. The Common Law Mortgage in England and the Colonies
7. Torrens Title Registration
8. Property, Citizenship and the Criminalisation of Homelessness
9. How Property Became Intellectual
10. Crypto Currency and Value

Introducing concepts of radical and beneficial title, tenure, estate, and alienation in a historical context enables students to connect with the concepts in a grounded way as they are exposed to their original logic. I found that teaching coverture was an ideal way to introduce students to the Court of Chancery and the splitting of law and equity within property. Using Amy Louise Erickson's (2005) and Allison Anna Tait's (2014) work on coverture, students discussed how the legal disappearance of married women's personhood was countered by separate estate trusts enforced by the Court of Chancery. They were thus exposed to legal ownership being with one party while beneficial ownership lay with another, this being enforced via equity. We discussed the political economy of these cases: that it was upper-class women this was relevant to, and that less is known – at least from within the archives of legal knowledge – about working-class women's situations because they did not have property to litigate over.

Studying Locke's 'Of Property' in the context of his career as Secretary to the Lords Proprietor of Carolina, and author of its constitution which took for granted the existence of slave labour, enables a discussion of the origins of racism, without framing it as such. Students are faced with the establishment of a society and economy based on the designation of African and Native American populations as inferior and therefore with weak or absent property rights, or indeed as themselves capable of being rendered the object of property. Rather than framing this material as an introduction to understanding racism, which white students in particular can react defensively to, it is presented to students as an aspect of the history of English property law. This history then solidifies by examining the 1834 compensation of slaveowners upon abolition, the reassertion of colonial sovereignty in *Mabo*, and the increased alienability of colonial land via shifts in mortgage law and conveyancing practice (Torrens title registration). Looking at how homelessness was also criminalised in England and Wales invites students to draw connections between race and class, as they think through the social and legal consequences of not having property in land across different common law/British Empire contexts. The final sessions on the histories of intellectual property and cryptocurrency invite students to consider the different forms of abstract property and their relationship to value and concepts of trust.

Students were assessed via essay, which produced some brilliant, thoughtful reflections and broad-ranging evidence of an understanding of the political roots of property law. In class, students have been engaged with the material, both the social history and the legal concepts in the curricula. Students have emailed to thank me for teaching the material and expressed shock that they had not, for example, encountered the history of slaveowner compensation at any previous point in their education. Having developed the course in conversation with my colleague who teaches doctrinal Land Law the following term, my hope is that the grounded introduction to foundational property law concepts students have received this term will enable them to more easily connect with the contemporary manifestations of those concepts next term.

Indigenising the Property Law curriculum on Ngunnawal Country

When I took over the unit, the Property Law curriculum at my university (based on Ngunnawal Country – also known as Australia's capital city of Canberra) included one topic devoted to the impact of colonisation on Indigenous peoples and a brief overview of Native Title law, including *Mabo*. Though relatively brief, this topic did include a strengths-based overview of the diversity of Indigenous peoples and culture in Australia and a critical analysis of Native Title law, particularly in relation to the impact of the *Native Title Amendment Act 1998* (Cth) and the Howard government's '10-Point Plan' (which significantly wound back existing native title rights). Without time to explore the incongruities between Indigenous property law and Native Title (Watson 2017), it was particularly challenging in this context to overcome the dominant understanding that *Mabo* and the introduction of Native Title was an unquestionably positive development.

In 2021, the Canberra Law School established a Community of Practice to coordinate and drive the incorporation of Indigenous content, perspectives, pedagogy, and cultural competency into the law degree, using a whole curriculum approach. Property Law was identified as a key priority in this process, in recognition of the fact that the appropriation of land, and the legitimisation of this appropriation through law, is central to the colonial project (Harris 1993; Moreton-Robinson, 2015; Bhandar, 2018).

In renewing the Property Law curriculum, we identified a number of key priorities to further expand the Indigenous content and pedagogical approach, and to better integrate this content with the other topics covered in the unit. These included introducing property law pluralism – the reality that more than one legal system governs property in Australia, due to the fact that Indigenous property law continues to be practised and to have authority – and an explicitly critical approach to property law history from the beginning of the unit in order to create more conceptual space for Indigenous property law; explicitly teaching Indigenous property law and using it as a lens through which to understand and critique foundational common law property law principles; and ensuring that Indigenous scholarship was given greater prominence in the teaching materials. A further priority was to ensure that this pluralistic, critical approach and Indigenous property law content was reflected in the published unit learning outcomes and assessed in order to reduce the risk that it might be perceived as an 'optional extra' to the more technical 'prescribed areas of knowledge' that must be covered in Australian law schools (Law Admissions Consultative Committee, 2016).

The historically significant land rights case *Milirrpum v Nabalco Pty Ltd and the Commonwealth of Australia* (1971) 17 *FLR* 141 (Blackburn J) was used as a focal point for a number of learning activities and assessment tasks. *Milirrpum* preceded *Mabo* and is generally accepted to have paved the way for the recognition of Native Title in Australia – despite the judgment itself finding that such a concept had no foundation in Australian common law.

Students engaged in a collaborative process of annotating the entire (154 page) judgment to identify the parties; the facts of the case; key arguments raised by the claimants (representatives of the Yolngu peoples) and the respondents (a mining corporation and the Commonwealth government); the evidence; and the judge's determination of the key legal issues, including the existence, 'recognisability', and sophistication of the Yolngu legal system; and whether the plaintiffs held a 'proprietary' interest in the land that could be recognised by the common law (specifically under a doctrine of communal native title). This annotation exercise was supplemented by a documentary film made by the Gay'wu Group of Women (2019), 'Caring as Country: singing up sovereignties', which provides a Yolngu explanation and demonstration of their property law and ongoing relationship with Country.

For their mid-semester assignment, the students were asked to write a critical analysis of the judgment, using a selection of critical property law articles as an analytical lens, and to include a reflection on what they had learned through the process. Two of the five prescribed articles were written by Indigenous scholars, Professors Irene Watson (2017) and Mary Graham (1999), and critiqued the common law (particularly property law) from the perspective of Indigenous law. Both were explicit in their project of re-centring Indigenous perspectives and law by emphasising it as the 'standard' and the common law as the 'other'. The other three articles critiqued the colonial use of property law to attempt to simultaneously legitimise the appropriation of Indigenous land and delegitimise or erase Indigenous land rights (and, indeed, Indigenous peoples) (Keenan, 2017; Crabtree, 2013; Rose, 1998).

The students considered a wide range of issues in their papers and, particularly, their reflections, but a number of key themes emerged. These included comments that the assignment had expanded or challenged the student's understanding of both Australian history and property law, particularly by providing them with a better understanding of the impact of colonisation and colonial law, and its intersection with Indigenous law. Students also reflected that the assignment had prompted them to confront Australia's racism, challenged their belief that *Mabo* and Native Title had been positive (and that discrimination and injustice were issues of the past), and highlighted the need to decolonise the law – specifically property law. Students made specific mention of their appreciation for being exposed to a critical approach to law and to the politics of law and reflected that this had led them to reconsider its meaning and purpose. Finally, students commented favourably on the experience of (re)centring Indigenous perspectives, of having the opportunity to gain a better understanding of Indigenous law, and of being provided with an insight into a more sustainable approach to property that is not ownership or commodity based.

Overall, the changes would appear to have been successfully integrated into the unit and to have received a positive reception from students. Nonetheless, when the unit moved on to consider more of the technical aspects of common law property, such as indefeasibility, unregistered interests, and priorities, within the constraints of the 12-week teaching semester, the Indigenous content and critical lens essentially fell away. On reflection, it will be necessary to introduce further changes to the teaching (and particularly the pedagogical form) of these later topics to ensure that this more critical, pluralist approach is extended to all of the learning outcomes.

Teaching property critically in the neoliberal curriculum

This final case study explores the tensions, creative possibilities, and inevitable limitations that a decolonisation of property pedagogy offers in the (curiously contradictory) context of neoliberal curriculum reform. As is its ideological wont, the teaching and learning changes underway at my present institution, Southern Cross University, are radical, not incremental. At the time of writing, my law colleagues and I are confronted with the pressing task of converting 12 weeks of semester content into six weeks of intensive instruction under what is known as the 'Southern Cross Model' ('SCM'). The SCM is designed to be a point of marketing differentiation, a model that offers students 'flexibility' and 'timely completion' without sacrificing deep learning. Colloquially termed the '6x6', the model envisions six terms of six teaching weeks per calendar year. The University's website explains the SCM as 'empowering students to take greater control in shaping how they study across the year' with the 'shorter, more focused unit structure' enabling a 'greater sense of momentum and motivation as they achieve milestones quickly'. While this teaching 'reform' is ripe for separate scholarly scrutiny, here it merely provides a backdrop against which the project of decolonising property's curriculum offers different (theoretical and performative) possibilities – admittedly in the unlikeliest of contexts.

For legal educators, the SCM's greatest challenge lies in its delivery of the mandatory 'Priestley 11' areas of knowledge within six weeks, the prescribed (and highly prescriptive) content which law students must study to be admitted as legal practitioners in Australia's states and territories. Apart from Criminal Law and Contract Law (which remain as two discrete units), the other nine core Priestley 11 units, including Property, are required to 'intensify' their prescribed areas of knowledge into six weekly modules. The drive to intensify content delivery in the pursuit of student 'choice' and 'flexibility' (Pelizzon et al., 2022) offers up two possible oppositional outcomes. The first is a curriculum that continues to entrench the colonial paradigm, a pared-back offering that reinforces the status quo amidst subject-matter contraction, serving (ironically) to privilege the primacy of the content remaining that euphemistically 'makes the grade'. Educational designers contracted to assist academics in this 'transition' prioritise the checking off of mandated areas of knowledge (mortgages, co-ownership, Torrens title, etc.) against the compressed timeline. As Carol Rose intimates, in a different context, such a focus inevitably reinforces a doctrinal, black-letter approach to the study of law, and the conservatism that this mindset inheres (1998, 609–612).

The second possibility lies in the invocation of the critical, countering neoliberalism's radicalism with an inverse radical alternative. Seizing on the disruption that such major changes inevitably cause, this section scopes out an *other* property curriculum, one that works to de-centre property's colonial foundations and legitimise property pluralism. Of course, to undertake this task is to assume a deep understanding of the discipline taught, an expertise often lacking, given that large numbers of core units at my institution (and elsewhere) are taught by time-poor casual academics.

In reflecting on the (little-remarked) capacity of property academics to influence public policy, the work of American property historian Stuart Banner comes to mind. Banner writes of the late 19th-century entrenchment of the 'bundle of sticks' metaphor, claiming that its rise to dominance did not come about because of 'newspaper editorials or popular magazine articles insisting that property was or was not a relationship between people' (2011, 106). Rather, it was the consequence of a handful of influential professors, their pedagogical choices, and their privileged student cohorts. As Banner surmises, 'since all law students took a course in property, more and more of them would learn that property was not about things, it was about power over people' (Ibid). The bundle metaphor is particularly apposite to this discussion. It is the antithesis of context and the ancient relational understandings that are the hallmark of Indigenous relations with Country. Likewise, its inherent de-physicalisation is arguably 'one of the most significant contributions of modern Anglophonic law to anthropogenic environmental change' (Graham, 2021, 281). Albeit a tall order over six weeks, Banner's passing reflections underscore a motivation to re-write the Property unit in ways that disrupt orthodox understandings and methodologies and provide a more coherent narrative for the principles and doctrines under study.

Module 1 begins with the meaning and extent of property; canvassing orthodox theorists such as Blackstone, Locke, and Hohfield; the dominance of private property; and its values of exclusion, commodity, and alienation. However, the module equally focuses on contemporary critical theorists and legal geographers, their study of common law pluralism, and its overlooked links to space, place, and context.

Module 2 next shifts to law, equity, and co-ownership, explaining the evolution of equity as a response to the rigidities of the common law but also contextualising its rise by reference to the influence of powerful landholding classes in England. This module deals with prescribed content such as the creation and enforcement of legal and equitable interests in land. It also exemplifies the operation of equitable principles by using as case studies the running of the burden and benefit of restrictive covenants in equity, and the creation of equitable tenancies in common in contexts where joint tenants at law make unequal monetary contributions, conveniently differentiating the two. Module 2 highlights the herculean task of bringing together diverse areas within a tight remit. It also underscores the scant space to develop meaningful critical analysis.

Modules 4, 5, and 6 typify the problematics of the latter. Torrens title, mortgages, and leases each demand strict attention to mandated detail. The nuances of indefeasibility of title, the key exceptions, and the place of unregistered interests consume limited time, as does the nature of a Torrens mortgage, mortgagee remedies, and the power of sale on default, and so on for leases.

By contrast, Module 3 permits the greatest scope for inserting critical review into the curriculum. It starts with enclosure, citing the recent work of activists such as Nick Hayes (2021), and then highlighting enclosure's contemporary manifestations, including readings on private property and gentrification. It next shifts to the extinctive processes of erasure and dispossession; the rationales of *terra nullius*; the early, brutal logic of tenure in the Australian colonial context (typified by *Attorney-General of NSW v Brown*); and the 1971 judgment in *Milirrpum v Nabalco* (discussed above). It ends with the recognition of native title in *Mabo*, and its contemporary (in)adequacy as a 'colonial construct' to represent Indigenous relations with land (see e.g. Watson 2017). Module 3 ends with a mid-term assessment (worth 40%) that mirrors the assessment used at Canberra Law School.

As things turn out, I will not see the fruits of this neoliberal-induced labour. By the time this chapter is published, I will be in a different role and place, in Aotearoa New Zealand, overseeing one law school's part in a national curriculum re-design that aims to incorporate principles of tikanga Māori[1] into core units of legal study, including Property (Ruru et al., 2021). This exciting Aotearoan project is truly premised on de-centring colonial paradigms, offering new opportunities to teach property critically in an analogous settler colonial context, a project far removed from an ethos promoting 'student choice', 'flexibility', and 'achieving milestones quickly'.

Discussion

Our three case studies reveal a series of conceptual questions with important practical implications. Each study likewise implies that pedagogical content and form are of course related and that teaching different content necessarily requires an adjustment in how that content is taught. This concluding discussion reflects a shift in emphasis from content to pedagogy.

The first pedagogical implication goes to the distinction drawn between decolonising and Indigenising the curriculum. At first glance, these terms might appear interchangeable, at least in the Australian settler colonial context. However, we suggest that *undoing* colonisation is a process less likely to be co-opted by university managers since it demands 'root and branch' change rather than (potentially superficial) Indigenous inclusion or representation. A second raises the vexed problems of time and space; the crowded, prescriptive curricula mandated by Australian admission authorities compared to the more open-ended 'choices' available in UK law schools. And finally, as a corollary of both, is the recognition that the project of *teaching property critically* requires ongoing vigilance to avoid defaulting back to 'silo' mode, the habitual propensity to teach law subjects as disconnected from each other, and unanchored from their structural, societal, and political contexts. Each will be discussed in turn.

The tensions of decolonising versus Indigenising the curriculum

The terms 'Indigenising' and 'decolonising' are used inconsistently in both academic literature and policy documents. Indeed, the terms are often used almost interchangeably, making it difficult to determine how they might be distinguished. Canadian scholars Gaundry and Lorenz (2018: 218) respond to this lack of clarity by distinguishing between three meanings or 'visions of indigenisation', which they argue exist on a spectrum from 'Indigenous inclusion' through 'reconciliation indigenization' and finally to 'decolonial indigenisation'. Of these, they note only the '[d]ecolonial indigenization envisions the wholesale overhaul of the academy to fundamentally reorient knowledge production based on balancing power relations between Indigenous peoples and Canadians' (219). They also argue that while 'the Canadian academy has *rhetorically* adopted an aspirational vision of reconciliation indigenization, … [it] is in fact largely committed to Indigenous inclusion' (i.e. increasing the number of Indigenous students and faculty without making structural change) (ibid, emphasis in the original).

After surveying the literature (Kuokkanen, 2008; Tuck and Yang, 2012; Heleta, 2016; Smith, 2012), Gaundry and Lorenz (2018: 222–223) note an apparent consensus that genuine indigenisation must be a decolonial process but that universities have tended to adopt a more superficial approach and to act as 'guest-masters' by refusing to cede power. Here, in addition to power sharing, Gaundry and Lorenz (2018: 219–221) emphasise the importance of recognising ontological and epistemological assumptions and perceptions, rather than assuming Western ways of knowing are natural or neutral.

Similarly, Louie et al. (2017: 21), who are all Indigenous faculty members working in Canadian higher education, critique 'the superficial inclusion of Indigenous content' and emphasise the importance of reforming 'pedagogy in higher education through the use and valuing of Indigenous epistemologies and ways of knowing'. Drawing on Linda Tuhiwai Smith's (2012) work in her influential monograph *Decolonizing Methodologies*, Louie et al. (2017) describe the introduction of Indigenous pedagogies as 'effective decolonising practices'.

Writing from the standpoint of a UK-based law school, Matiluko (2020) brings a slightly different perspective to the concept of decolonising the university, while retaining an emphasis on decentring colonial 'modes of thought' or epistemologies. Where Matiluko (2020: 550) differs is that she focuses particular attention on also exposing the influence of Empire on existing prescribed texts, such as 'the writings of figures like John Stuart Mill, Jeremy Bentham and John Locke'. Matiluko (2020: 551–552) explains the importance of analysing how imperial history has influenced the development of law – including, for example, the role of private property and the doctrine of *terra nullius* in shaping colonial conquest – by arguing that this analysis will 'enable us to learn from the mistakes of the past', to disrupt coloniality, and to increase epistemic diversity in the classroom.

Overall, it seems that the risk of reduction towards Indigenous inclusion rather than decolonial Indigenisation might be reduced if the process is conceptualised as first and foremost one of decolonisation. While both 'Indigenisation' and 'decolonisation', like any term related to a process, are capable of cooptation by institutions, such cooptation may be more likely for 'Indigenisation' due to the present strength of liberal identity politics within university management strategies and its false equation of representation with racial justice. That is, if 'Indigenisation' is set as the goal for law schools without very clear definition of what it entails, it may be an easy managerial option to reach this goal by adding Indigenous writers to the curriculum and/or adopting an institutional interpretation of Indigenous pedagogy, rather than tackling the very structure of curricula and pedagogy within the context of ongoing colonial domination. Indigenous writers are diverse in approach and opinion; it would be possible to add reformist and conservative Indigenous writers to a curriculum in a way that allows an institution to claim they have 'Indigenised' without decolonising. The term 'Indigenising' is etymologically derived from the term 'Indigenous' which is used to describe a vast and diverse population. As Indigenous writers have noted, 'Indigenous' is itself a generalising, colonial term located within an Anglo-European epistemology: no Gurindji, Arrente, or Yorta Yorta people defined themselves as 'Indigenous' prior to the imposition of colonial rule (Watson, 2009). The 'Indigenous' identity category is the product of colonial power relations, and it is those relations – their reliance on and perpetuation of violent racial dominance – which must ultimately be addressed to achieve meaningful change.

'Decolonisation', while also capable of cooptation, might be more difficult to hollow out into a process of superficial inclusion/representation because – at least semantically – it specifically addresses the colonial process, demanding an undoing of that process. That the decolonisation of the university is a call used by student-led movements across the Global North also places this term within a genealogy of transnational activism, lending it to forms of solidarity across different colonial contexts. In a settler colonial context such as Australia, the undoing of colonisation will necessarily require the centring of Indigenous knowledge and pedagogies. It would also require that that knowledge and pedagogy be invoked for the explicit purpose of addressing and undoing the systems of racism which Australian law schools – being located on stolen land and teaching colonial law – presently rely on and perpetuate. Addressing and working towards the undoing of colonisation also invites solidarities between people suffering the violence of racial domination beyond the current borders of this colonial state. Australia, for example, is not only involved in the ongoing colonisation of Aboriginal and Torres Strait Island land but also in the contemporary colonial relations imposed on other areas of the Pacific such as Papua New Guinea and Nauru, and of the Arab states of the Persian Gulf in which the Australian military has been actively involved in the perpetuation of wars involving mass civilian death and dispossession. To decolonise property law in an Australian law school curriculum would require addressing these manifestations of Australia's coloniality, as well as its structural and ongoing theft of Indigenous land on the continent and its immediate surrounding islands.

Time and space: prescriptive curricula versus open-ended accreditation requirements

In another vein, our two Australian case studies illustrate the challenge of decolonising the curriculum where 'Priestley 11' core areas of study are highly prescriptive, leaving little scope (or time) for critical re-invention. In particular, the Southern Cross Model throws this dilemma into sharp relief, halving the typical Australian teaching semester from 12 weeks to six. By contrast, the freedom and flexibility inherent in the 'Foundations of Property' course at Birkbeck, University of London, suggests that open-ended curricula may be the natural 'friend' of reconceptualising property critically. Yet, the position is likely more nuanced and complex. As floated, intensifying the teaching calendar could equally unleash radical property theory as much as it simply condenses the *status quo*. And uncluttered, non-mandated curricula could equally be the end point of neoliberal higher education policy – as much as an opportunity for critical pedagogical reform.

This is the paradoxical context within which this particular discussion dwells. The common thread is neoliberalism, which drives the Southern Cross Model as much as it empties out the compulsory legal curriculum in the United Kingdom. In the former, it is about institutionalising 'customer/student choice' and privileging 'flexibility'. In the latter, the abandonment of the former qualifying law degree in favour of an open-ended model is the epitome of free market principles and facilitating competition in the sector.

Decolonising property requires coherence. Property's narratives only make sense, we argue, when contextualised to their colonial milieu. In Australia, prescriptive regulatory frameworks may prove a (practical) hindrance to this task, but such frameworks are not in themselves an impediment to decolonisation, especially where a broader interpretation of the Legal Admissions Consultative Committee ('LACC') Standards could conceivably justify different approaches. For example, the explanatory note to Standard 4.1 sets out 'a coherent sequence of units of study' as a guiding principle for the interpretation of LACC Standards (Accreditations Standards for Australian Law Courses 2018). Teaching property in an a-contextual vacuum produces the antithesis of coherence. However, teaching property in its colonial context makes sense of its often-arcane rules and doctrines and yields a *coherent* setting ripe for critical review and scrutiny.

In the UK, regulation's dearth neither 'rules in' nor 'rules out' the teaching of a decolonised property curriculum. But it does offer up a less cluttered space that academics may, if so minded and if supported by their individual School, populate with decolonised paradigms, the likes of the study of the patriarchal property-owning family or the transatlantic slave trade.

Conclusion: The ongoing risk of siloing and its consequences

In our opening case studies, we explored our individual attempts to teach Property Law outside of its traditional silos by contextualising it within a critical understanding of history, political economy, and legal pluralism. While this approach will sometimes be uncomfortable (and, indeed, should be) and will almost certainly involve resisting easy inclusion-based options, in addition to creatively navigating constraints around time and space in often crowded curriculums, it offers an opportunity for deeper learning. What the divergent Australian and UK examples depict is a shared understanding that notwithstanding differing regulatory, spatial, or temporal parameters and contexts, decolonising the curriculum offers up a rich, mostly untapped potential for re-thinking property critically – and coherently.

Acknowledgements

We would like to acknowledge and thank the editors and reviewers for their work on this chapter and the book project as a whole. We would also like to acknowledge and thank our colleagues for the contributions and collegial support they have provided to decolonising the curriculum of our Property Law units.

Note

1 'The right way of behaving in the Māori world, which also incorporates systems of Māori law and practice, and working with Māori stories as legal texts' (Jones, 2021, XX).

References

Banner, Stuart, *American Property: A History of How, Why, and What We Own* (Harvard University Press, 2011).

Bhambra, Gurminder K., Dalia Gebrial, and Kerem Nişancıoğlu, eds. 2018. *Decolonising the University*. London: Pluto Press.

Bhandar, Brenna, *Law, Land, and Racial Regimes of Ownership* (Duke University Press, 2018).

Crabtree, Louise, 'Decolonising property: exploring ethics, land, and time, through housing interventions in contemporary Australia' (2013) 31 *Environment and Planning D: Society and Space* 99.

Gaundry, Adam and Lorenz, Danielle, 'Indigenization as inclusion, reconciliation, and decolonization: navigating the different visions for indigenizing the Canadian Academy' (2018) 14(3) *AlterNative* 218.

Gay'wu Group of Women, *Caring as Country: singing up sovereignties* (2019) youtube.com/watch?v=H7usKj7_Yt8
Graham, Mary, 'Some thoughts about the philosophical underpinnings of Aboriginal worldviews' (1999) 3(2) *Worldviews: Environment, Culture, Religion* 105–118.
Graham, Nicole, 'Dephysicalised property and shadow lands', in R. Bartel and J. Carter (eds.) *Handbook of Space, Place and Law* (Edward Elgar, 2021).
Harris, Cheryl I., 'Whiteness as property' (1993) 106(8) *Harvard Law Review* 1707–1791.
Hayes, N., *The Book of Trespass: Crossing the lines that divide us* (Bloomsbury, 2021).
Heleta, S., 'Decolonising higher education: dismantling epistemic violence and Eurocentrism in South Africa' (2016) 1(1) *Transformation in Higher Education* 1–8.
Jones, Carwyn, 'Lost from sight: developing recognition of Māori law in Aotearoa New Zealand' (2021) 1(2) *Legalities: The Australian and New Zealand Journal of Law and Society* 162.
Keenan, Sarah, 'Smoke, curtains and mirrors: the production of race through time and title registration' (2017) 28(1) *Law and Critique* 87–108.
Kuokkanen, R., *Reshaping the university: Responsibility, indigenous epistemes, and the logic of the gift* (University of British Columbia Press, 2008).
Law Admissions Consultative Committee, *Prescribed Areas of Knowledge* (December 2016), at: https://www.legalservicescouncil.org.au/Documents/prescribed-academic-areas-of-knowledge.pdf
Law Admissions Consultative Committee, Accreditations Standards for Australian Law Courses, July 2018.
Louie, D.W., et al., 'Applying indigenizing principles of decolonizing methodologies in university classrooms' (2017) 47(3) *Canadian Journal of Higher Education* 16.
Matiluko, Oluwaseun, 'Decolonising the master's house: how Black feminist epistemologies can be and are used in decolonial strategy' (2020) 54(4) *The Law Teacher* 547.
Moreton-Robinson, Aileen, *The White Possessive: Property, Power, and Indigenous Sovereignty* (University of Minnesota Press, 2015).
Pelizzon, Alessandro, et al., 'Australian public universities: a crisis of governance', (2022) *Social Alternatives* (in press).
Rose, Carol, 'Canons of property talk, or, Blackstone's anxiety' (1998–1999) 108 *Yale Law Journal* 601–632.
Ruru, Jacinta, et al., Issues Paper, 'Inspiring National Indigenous Legal Education for Aotearoa New Zealand's Bachelor of Laws Degree: Phase One', 2021.
Smith, Linda Tuhiwai, *Decolonizing Methodologies: Research and Indigenous Peoples* (Zed Books, 2nd ed., 2012).
Tuck, E., and Yang, W.K., 'Decolonization is not a metaphor' (2012) 1(1) *Decolonization: Indigeneity, Education & Society* 1
Waldron, Jeremy, 'Homelessness and the issue of freedom' (1991) 39 *UCLA Law Review* 295.
Watson, Irene, 'Aboriginal laws and colonial foundation' (2017) 26(4) *Griffith Law Review* 469.
Watson, Irene, 'In the Northern Territory intervention: what is saved or rescued and at what cost?' (2009) 15(2) *Cultural Studies Review* 45–60.

7

TOWARDS DECOLONISING THE ORDINARY PERSON TEST IN LEGAL EDUCATION

Fady Aoun, Louise Boon-Kuo, and Tanya Mitchell

The intent of the 'ordinary person' doctrine, like objective legal standards more generally, is to promote consistency and equality in law, and ensure that people are held to the same standards despite their differences. Legal disciplines including defamation, negligence, trade marks, research ethics, and criminal law often assess what is expected of a hypothetical 'ordinary person' to determine specific legal questions. Yet it is more commonly expected that public law rather than private law teaching will engage with critical and anti-racist material. Drawing on our teaching practices in criminal law and trade mark law, this chapter argues that embedding anti-racist and anti-colonial approaches in doctrinal teaching has the potential to disarm sceptical students and presents an opportunity for an immediate and modest step towards 'decolonising' the curricula even in reluctant institutions.

Our argument unfolds in two main arcs. The first part of the chapter reflects on education scholarship in Australia, paying particular attention to the work of Indigenous legal scholars, to consider whether and how our approaches to teaching the ordinary person test might progress decolonial curricula goals in the Australian context. We use the word 'towards' in the title of this chapter to indicate that decolonisation is our aspiration, not a claim to achievement. This part discusses current debates about the Indigenous cultural competence (ICC) movement, as well as the classroom conundrums invoked through engagement with deeply racist material. We then identify the merits of the ordinary person test as a focus for anti-racist anti-colonial legal education. The second part of the chapter shares two case studies of teaching the 'ordinary person' test in (i) the partial defence of provocation in criminal law and (ii) assessing racist trade mark registrations. These case studies provide accounts of theory-informed

DOI: 10.4324/9781003397885-10

and adaptable classroom activities with four key angles—doctrinal, historical, contemporary, and the legal profession—and are offered as an invitation for teachers to consider how they might incorporate critique of the apparent race neutrality of the ubiquitous ordinary person test in their own law teaching disciplines.

Towards Decolonial and Anti-racist Law Curricula in Australia

Decolonisation has no single meaning in settler-colonial states such as Australia, where we, three non-Indigenous scholars, teach law. Decolonisation is often used to mean the return of stolen land and wealth to First Nations and the transformation of relationships between an imposed colonial legal system and ongoing First Nations sovereignties, laws, and life (see e.g. Tuck and Yang 2012). On this view, it is not possible to 'decolonise' the ordinary person test without a complete transformation of the current legal system in Australia. Some have argued that the production of knowledge about Indigenous peoples and the privileging of Western knowledge as superior is integral to colonial exploitation (Smith 2012, pp. 58–76). As education plays a crucial role in affirming the legitimacy and authority of knowledge, educators in settler-colonial states are inevitably involved in either upholding or dismantling the knowledge and cultural dimensions of the colonial project, thus making deliberate decolonising work both urgent and necessary (see also Adebisi 2021).

Scholarship on decolonising legal education and the ICC movement suggest several ways in which the knowledge, skill development, and practical considerations we draw upon in teaching the 'ordinary person' test in criminal law and trade mark law represent a step towards decolonial and anti-racist law curricula. Disrupting the law's presumed race neutrality and the notion of a singular knowledge system is central to this decolonial aim. While the examples we discuss in this chapter do not involve Indigenous cultural knowledge as it is conventionally understood, we incorporate published stories of lived experience, histories of resistance, and commentaries on the legal system told by Indigenous people and communities. In so doing, we follow the theoretical approach of scholars who treat knowledge of racism and colonialism as part of Indigenous knowledge that evolves at the 'cultural interface' between Western and Indigenous knowledge systems (Burns, Hong, and Wood 2019, p. 4; Nakata 2002).

ICC is not conceptually interchangeable with anti-racism or decolonisation. However, over the past decade, the ICC movement has influenced institutional projects within universities and law schools in Australia (Burns, Young and Nielsen 2018; Gainsford, Gerard and Bailey 2020) and operated as a platform for discussions of racism and colonisation. Many definitions (and alternate terms such as 'cultural humility') exist, but Universities Australia's *National*

Best Practice Framework for ICC in Australian Universities (2011, p. 48) definition of ICC has been influential:

> Student and staff knowledge and understanding of Indigenous Australian cultures, histories and contemporary realities and awareness of Indigenous protocols, combined with the proficiency to engage and work effectively in Indigenous contexts congruent to the expectations of Indigenous Australian peoples. Cultural competence includes the ability to critically reflect on one's own culture and professional paradigms in order to understand its cultural limitations and effect positive change.

Premised on the notion that cultural competence is possible without engaging in Indigenous demands for treaty and land rights, ICC arguably has 'flawed foundations' (Wood and Watson 2018, p. 10). Yet the diversity of projects under the banner of ICC means that the transformative potential of ICC rests on how it is mobilised, including the extent to which curriculum is driven by Indigenous peoples' struggle against racial subordination (Fredericks and Bargallie 2020, p. 305).

In teaching the 'ordinary person' test, we utilise learning activities intended to develop students' critical thinking and reflection on the presumed race neutrality of law. This kind of skill development has been identified as a guiding principle for embedding ICC in law programmes (Burns, Hong and Wood 2019, p. 20). Part of this involves simply building space for students to 'challenge preconceived notions of colonial thought and practices', which is said to comprise an important 'step' in decolonising law curricula (Gainsford 2018, pp. 7, 9; Gainsford, Gerard and Bailey 2020). This requires students to reflect on how their own subjectivity limits their thinking about the law and engage in activities that reveal how Anglo-Australian law orients a view 'through imperial eyes' (Smith 2012, p. 42). In so doing, we seek to grow critically engaged 'learners' not 'knowers' who understand that cultural competence is a process not a destination (Burns 2018, pp. 17–18).

In our experience, it is necessary to employ practical anti-racist education strategies to prepare the classroom for respectful listening and discussion. Launching into content involving Indigenous issues without preparing the classroom has 'often acted as magnet for the expression of racist attitudes', engendering pain and alienation for Indigenous students (Wood and Watson 2018, p. 9; Douglas 2005, p. 13), and other non-White students. As many scholars have noted, the reality in Australia is that we have not learned how to speak about race (Brown, Kelada, and Jones 2021; Moodie 2017), thus the role of the teacher is especially important here. Careful selection and explanation of material require ongoing critical self-reflection by teachers, as well as the time and space to be questioned by fellow teachers and to similarly challenge others

(Jivraj 2020, pp. 19–22). The teacher must include a content warning, which may be included in written material and in the classroom. This prepares students for difficult or potentially traumatic content and reassures them that the starting point is acknowledging realities of racial and colonial harm. Emphasising the anti-racist purpose for delving into offensive racist material or painful experiences of the legal system (Crenshaw 1988, p. 8) is important as it helps students understand how legal practices can produce or reproduce racial hierarchies and may inspire them to take up the mantle of responsibility for change. It also helps build the trust needed for genuine class discussion of challenging issues.

In the broader community, racial harm is often presented as an individual experience that results from individual prejudice. For this reason, orienting student attention to the *framework* of law is arguably an indispensable stage in preparing the class for discussion. This requires deliberate action because legal education conventionally seeks to teach students to 'think like a lawyer', a method that trains students to filter out facts deemed irrelevant by existing doctrine (Mertz 2007, p. 739). Moreover, explaining why we are questioning the supposed neutrality and objectivity of the law itself helps prevent students from dismissing discussion of racial dimensions as peripheral, biased, emotional, and 'unlawyerlike' (Crenshaw 1988, p. 5). Further, because the best learning environment is the product of collective effort (hooks 1994, p. 8), we ask students to recognise their part in creating the classroom dynamic.

While we hope our approach nudges towards decolonial goals, it does not include elements that Annette Gainsford (2018, p. 7) identifies as crucial 'steps' to decolonise the law curricula. These steps include forming strong ethical partnerships with Indigenous communities 'to support the teaching of cultural traditions and practices of Indigenous people', place-based learning, an Elders-in-Residence programme, and programmes of cultural immersion. While this whole-of-course approach to embedding ICC may be the gold standard, it is not immediately possible in most law schools because ethical partnerships take time. Our approach offers an achievable intervention that can be readily adapted to many conventional law courses.

The next part of chapter explains why destabilising the presumed race neutrality of the 'ordinary person' test in the public and private law domains of criminal law and trade mark law is valuable.

The Value of Challenging the Perceived Race Neutrality of the 'ordinary person' Test

Issues of race undoubtedly arise regarding the 'ordinary person' test. Commentators have pointed to problems with the 'ordinary person' as a construct who is 'always already white' (Blore 2018, p. 160), vulnerable to 'crude majoritarian understandings' (Burrell and Handler 2016, p. 167), and that when modified to be, for example, the 'ordinary Aboriginal person' can involve an 'oppressive process of construction' that results in defendants who are unable to meet 'the threshold test of authenticity' (Douglas 2006, p. 208). In reflecting on an analogous objective standard, the 'reasonable man', Patricia Tuitt argues that we should understand this construct as a conceptual institution that is 'most susceptible to the influences of the more subtle, indirect and institutionally inscribed forms of racial stereotyping' (Tuitt 2004, p. 38). The flexibility of the test can reify commonality as reasonableness and thereby operate as a vehicle for colonial and racial knowledge and norms (Tuitt 2004, p. 40). In this way, legal constructs such as the 'ordinary person' and 'reasonable man' can operate as a form of institutional racism, producing racial inequality through mechanisms and practices that are colour-blind and not contingent upon individual prejudice and racist intent (Bonilla-Silva 2013, p. 3).

Challenging the apparent race-neutral 'ordinary person' is a worthwhile strategy towards decolonising legal education for several reasons. First, legal doctrine is regarded as an important 'hook' for teaching ICC and should guide curriculum design (Gerard and Gainsford 2018, p. 17 citing Nakata 2002). As Annette Gainsford, Alison Gerard, and Kim Bailey (2020, p. 68) state, '[I]f we simply "add on" Indigenous perspectives without making authentic and rigorous connections to law, there is a serious risk that students will view the content as tokenistic and irrelevant'. Moreover, given that colonial and racist practices have often been lawful practices, a focus on interpreting statutes (and case law) naturally turns attention to the law's impact on the lived experience of Aboriginal and Torres Strait Islander peoples (Gerard and Gainsford 2018, p. 2). Anchoring Indigenous perspectives in the subject areas required for professional accreditation (known in Australia as the 'Priestly 11') addresses the objection that there is no space for Indigenous content in the curriculum (Gainsford, Gerard, and Bailey 2020, p. 68, Burns, Hong, and Wood 2019, p. 18).

Second, our case studies show that the 'ordinary person' legal standard, which is used in both public and private law, plays a crucial role in affirming the myth of legal neutrality. Theoretically, counter-storytelling offers a means of toppling this foundational myth that has institutionalised a reality in which racial hierarchy appears unremarkable (Delgado 1989, pp. 2412–2413). Storytelling is 'fundamental' to Indigenous cultures and methods of teaching (Watson 2022, p. 1) and thus enables a further layer of learning. Counter-storytelling may involve bringing in alternate narratives of events and drawing attention to what is included and excluded in legal interpretive structures.

Third, there is pedagogical value in challenging the race neutrality of a hypothetical standard that appears in multiple law units across the law degree. Encountering critical perspectives in stage one of a law degree as well as in final year units allows for the spaced repetition that has been shown to facilitate students' ability to apply learning to new situations (Sites 2019). Grappling with such perspectives in diverse disciplines—in commercial law units and public law units—reinforces the legitimacy and persuasiveness of the broader questions raised by discipline-specific study.

Lastly, focusing on the construct of the 'ordinary person' across multiple units magnifies its impact as a strategic institutional intervention. The ICC literature emphasises that both 'bottom-up' and 'top-down' approaches are necessary for curricula reform (Universities Australia 2011, pp. 21, 26, 42; Burns, Hong, and Wood 2019, pp. 18–19). Developing subjects by individual teachers helps address the documented perception that ICC is anathema to the law core curricula and outside the expertise of teachers (Burns, Hong, and Wood 2019, p. 18) and can be used as a model for other units (Universities Australia 2011, p. 241). Institutional approaches to course-wide programme reform enable a more ambitious, coherent, scaffolded reform but involve longer timeframes for development. Our approach is placed somewhere between these models. We connect teaching across disciplines and subjects as an example of a grassroots-initiated, micro-scaffolding of a sustained critique of a legal doctrine, as a step towards decolonising the curricula.

Gender, Race, and Provocation in Criminal Law

Provocation (now called 'extreme provocation' in NSW) is a partial defence that reduces murder to manslaughter if the provocative conduct could have induced an ordinary person to lose self-control to the extent of forming an intention to kill or (in NSW) inflict grievous bodily harm on the deceased (in NSW see s 23 *Crimes Act 1900* (NSW)). It is a controversial doctrine and has been abolished in Victoria, Tasmania, Western Australia, and South Australia. As mentioned above, the objective test is designed to ensure that all persons are held to the same standard, 'notwithstanding their distinctive personality traits and varying capacities to achieve the standard' (*Hill* (1986) 25 CCC (3d) 322 at p. 345 per Wilson J). The defence has always been controversial, and the ordinary person has evolved in response to changing social attitudes (Brown et al. 2020, p. 926). Consequently, a study of provocation is ideal for exposing the reality that objective standards are not race neutral. It also provides an opportunity to examine the intersectionality of race and gender.

The partial defence of provocation originated at a time when it was socially acceptable for men to use violence to defend their honour. However, to prevent the defence from being used to excuse 'cold blooded' killings where there had been no loss of self-control, the common law required that the act causing death immediately follow the provoking conduct. Delay was thought to allow the blood to 'cool', thereby rendering any subsequent killing a product of the controlled formation of an intention to kill (see Crofts and Loughnan 2013 for a history of the defence).

In the 1980s, a series of cases in Canada and Australia (e.g. *Lavallee* (1990), 55 C.C.C. (3d) 97, *Hill* (1986) 25 CCC (3d) 322, and *R v Hickey* (14 April 1992) (Supreme Court of NSW) [unreported]) involving women charged with murdering their intimate partners in a context of prolonged domestic violence exposed the gendered nature of the ordinary person test and the immediacy requirement. Juries struggled to understand why the ordinary person would not 'just leave' such a relationship, and the requirement that the accused's act causing death be an immediate response to the provoking conduct did not reflect 'female patterns of behaviour' (Crofts and Loughnan 2013). As King CJ explained in *R* (1981) 28 SASR 321 at 326:

> The deceased's words and actions in the presence of the appellant on the fatal night might appear innocuous enough on the face of them. They must, however, be viewed against the background of brutality, sexual assault, intimidation and manipulation.

Women who killed their intimate partner in circumstances of domestic violence became known in criminal law as 'battered women', and a practice developed of tendering expert psychological evidence of 'battered woman's syndrome' (BWS) to show juries that the accused's behaviour in such a context is 'intelligible and explicable' (Stubbs and Tolmie 1995, p. 131). While well-intentioned, feminist scholars have criticised this approach for pathologising women, effectively making the defence conditional upon women's perceived learned helplessness, rather than addressing the patriarchal social structures that contribute to male violence, and the limited options for women to escape it (Stubbs and Tolmie 1995, p. 131). However, Julie Stubbs and Julia Tolmie note that this is only part of the story for Aboriginal women for whom BWS replicates colonial harm.

Aboriginal women in domestic violence situations face barriers to seeking the protection of the criminal justice system that are not present for non-Aboriginal women. It has been shown that the criminal justice system has repeatedly failed to protect Aboriginal women, with police often not responding to requests for help, or subjecting women to racism and further violence (Stubbs and Tolmie 1995, p. 134). Stubbs and Tolmie list further reasons why Aboriginal women are unable to trust the criminal justice system:

> Many women have a sympathy and loyalty for the Aboriginal men in their community and a fear of what will happen to them in a hostile, white criminal justice system. Community pressure may also make it difficult for women to involve the criminal justice system. The reluctance of some Aboriginal women to invoke the criminal law for their own protection against male violence is informed by a history of over-policing and over-criminalization of Aboriginal peoples…
>
> *(1995, p. 135)*

Demonstrating these dynamics for students reveals to them how the supposedly neutral ordinary person standard can be racist in practice. If juries do not understand these dynamics, there is a risk they will find an Aboriginal woman's choice to remain in a violent relationship—rather than seek protection from the criminal justice system—as unintelligible and inexplicable, thus resulting in her conviction.

Provocation also presents an opportunity to show students that 'ethnocentric assumptions' within legal processes can produce racist outcomes (see Eades 1992). *R v Kina* [1993] QCA 480 is an egregious example of this point. On 20 January 1988, Robyn Kina stabbed her partner, Anthony Black, who died from his wounds. After a trial that lasted less than a day, she was convicted of murder and sentenced to life imprisonment with hard labour. Her lawyers ran a two-pronged defence. The first was that she did not intend to kill the deceased or cause him grievous bodily harm. The second was the defence of provocation. Ms Kina appealed the trial judge's refusal to leave the issue of provocation to the jury, but her appeal was dismissed because there was 'no evidence of what occurred in the room prior to the stabbing…' and therefore no evidentiary basis for a provocation defence (*R v Kina* [1993] QCA 480, p. 4). There was no such evidence because Ms Kina had felt unable to discuss with her male barrister the abuse, both physical and sexual, that she had suffered in her life, generally, and at the hands of Anthony Black:

> I was unable to tell him about the rape and abuse that Tony had subjected me to and which had driven me to breaking point. I just couldn't talk about it. So traumatized was I by the memory of my unbearable suffering and by the thought of disclosing my shameful secret that I preferred to face a murder charge knowing that the sentence was imprisonment.
>
> *(Kina 2005, p. 69)*

The work of Diana Eades (1992), a socio-linguist, shows how an Aboriginal woman like Ms Kina might be silenced by the criminal justice system. As Stubbs and Tolmie explain, the 'questionnaire' style of information gathering used in the adversarial system is not 'culturally appropriate amongst Aboriginal English speakers as a means of eliciting significant and/or personal information. Such speakers use indirect and circumspect methods of information gathering and rely on reciprocity of exchange' (Stubbs and Tolmie 1995, p. 136). The direct questioning style used in examination in chief and cross-examination has been shown to confuse Aboriginal English-speaking witnesses and/or shut them down (Stubbs and Tolmie 1995, p. 145–149).

For Robyn Kina, the criminal justice system's lack of cultural competence produced a grave injustice, and her story provides a salutary lesson for law students. After her trial, the Australian Broadcasting Corporation took an interest in Ms Kina's story, interviewing her on the television shows 7.30

Report and 4-Corners. This prompted lawyers to re-examine her case. On 24 May 1993, they delivered a petition of pardon on her behalf to the Queensland Attorney-General who then referred the matter to the Supreme Court of Queensland. The Court quashed the conviction and ordered a new trial, but the Director of Public Prosecutions declined to run a second trial and the charges were subsequently withdrawn. Ms Kina was released after serving six years in prison. In 2005 her voice was heard when she published her story in a collection of essays on race, gender, and the prison-industrial complex (Kina 2005, pp. 67–71).

This brief analysis illustrates the potency of an anti-racist analysis of the partial defence of provocation for destabilising the myth of race neutrality, not only of objective standards in legal doctrine but of the legal system itself. It also shows law students, however, that the law can adapt to changing social standards, giving them the tools and an understanding of how they might effect positive change should they move into the profession.

Contesting Race Neutrality and Racist Imagery in Trade Mark Law

There is something deeply unsettling about sharing and then deconstructing racist commercial symbols in a classroom. However, there can be no more effective way of dismantling supposedly race-neutral legal constructs, such as those surrounding the 'ordinary person', which is invoked in determining the registrability of trade marks. Revealing and discussing these state-sanctioned racist trade marks and their underlying tropes calls into question the racist constructs, bureaucratic processes, and legal infrastructure, leading to their registration and projection into the Australian public sphere and elsewhere. It also exposes the role of traders and the consuming public in driving their proliferation.

From an educational and pastoral standpoint, adopting this confronting approach requires sensitive and sustained preparation of the classroom with the appropriate content warnings in anticipation of the release of unsafe racist vectors. Some important steps can be taken here. The educator must signpost the course trajectory in the first class, then develop, and encourage student resilience and maturity in engaging with these materials. Most importantly, students must be given an opportunity—but not compelled—to engage with this material and be supported following such exposure. In particular, the voices of minority groups must be given sufficient opportunities to be heard, to avoid committing unintentional but potentially jarring racial microaggressions (Sue et al. 2008, p. 330).

In the class in which students are to be exposed to racist, hateful, and bigoted symbols and their underlying tropes, such as that depicted in Figure 7.1, students must be warned of what is to come and given a meaningful opportunity to vacate the room at *any* time should they so wish and, importantly, be

FIGURE 7.1 Kitchen & Sons' Trade Mark (Commonwealth of Australia, *Trade Marks Register*, 1920).

supported in that decision. But a race-critical reading of the legal processes (including government gazetting or 'publication' of applied-for trade marks) and legal tests that facilitated the registration of plainly racist trade marks buttressed by counter-storytelling helps best to support the students' own learning.

Colonial and post-Federation Australian trade mark legislation provided for the denial of registering trade marks considered 'scandalous' or 'contrary to law or morality'. While there has not been an explicit statutory reference to 'morality' since 1955, present-day legislation retains the prohibition on registering 'scandalous' trade marks (*Trade Marks Act 1995* (Cth), s 42(a)). There is little case law and few Australian Trade Mark Office decisions that flesh out the meaning of this provision, so one is guided mainly by the Trade Marks Manual of Practice and Procedure, which is effectively a practical guide to Trade Mark Examiners (administrative decision-makers) and traders.

In the Manual, we encounter the amorphous 'ordinary person' which, when combined with various dictionary definitions of the word 'scandalous', suggests a legal standard in determining the registrability of trade marks: that is, the Registrar must decide 'on behalf of the ordinary person, whether a trade mark should be regarded as shameful, offensive or shocking, and therefore be rejected' (IP Australia 2022, Pt 30.2.1). The Manual then notes that this 'ordinary person should not be credited with either a very thick or very thin skin' (IP Australia 2022, Pt 30.2.3). The historical record reveals that the colour of the skin here matters (see generally Aoun 2019). For instance, the repetition of racist stereotypes applied to registered trade marks regarding cleaning products juxtaposing dirt/cleanliness, the colourfastness of blacking or paint indicates that stepping into the shoes of the putative ordinary person reveals they possess the trappings of Whiteness and racist ideologies.

Put simply, race neutrality was a myth. The Trade Marks Register contains many deeply racist trade marks, including those lionising imperialism, that were obviously not considered 'immoral' or 'scandalous'. Such registrations support Patricia Loughlan's contention that the ordinary person test 'discriminates against and marginalises minority groups' (Loughlan 2005, p. 39). To help square this historical ledger, then, we need to deconstruct the ordinary person to understand why racist text and imagery secured state-sanctioned registration and functioned effectively as valuable commercial symbols with the full protection of the law. There were legal mechanisms through which such trade marks could be challenged, but those mechanisms were not triggered.

One effective anti-racist educative technique is to reimagine these historical trade marks and challenge their registration from the perspectives of the minority group(s) referenced. Vivid imaginations are not required here. Students need not look far to find historical sites of intense resistance. For instance, Jack Patten and Bill Ferguson in the course of advocating for civil rights for Aboriginal Australians rallied against harmful racial stereotypes and caricatures circulating widely in advertising and mass media (Patten and Ferguson 1938, p. 10), yet these voices did not appear to resonate with decision-makers, traders, or the wider populace.

Building on this approach, students can then be exposed to more recent examples of commodity racism (see generally McClintock 1995) and encouraged to interrogate the deeply entrenched structural racism driving such racial stereotypes or what Stuart Hall calls 'racialised regime[s] of representation' (Hall et al. 1997, p. 269). These exercises may also be used as a vehicle for critical race self-reflection and challenging one's own racist predispositions. Stephen Brookfield reminds us of the importance of:

> getting Whites to accept that in a racist world in which they have been bombarded with racial stereotypes all their lives, and in which the ideology of White supremacy has been internalized at a deep level, [and recognising that] it would be remarkable if racism was not alive and well within them.
>
> *(2015, p. 113)*

The advantage of pointing out the normalisation of racism in this way is that one moves past fruitless discussions over 'White guilt and constantly attempting to prove [one's] goodness', instead creating the necessary space to 'get on with the work of trying to understand just how a normalized racism manifests in [one's] life' (Brookfield 2015, pp. 113–4).

The in-class discussion generated by this exercise reveals the law's inability or unwillingness to conceptualise and appreciate the racial harm (including racial subordination) it perpetuates, thereby contributing to oppression and a denial of certain rights. Racial harm was not considered actionable, even if it was identified in the first place (Tuitt 2004, pp. 37–54). The exercise also exposes how trade mark law prioritises trader pecuniary interests above all other interests and is oblivious to the concomitant harm inflicted on groups referenced by impugned marks.

These issues dovetail into broader concepts reflected in the Manual that are arguably premised on a misreading of Farwell J's judgment in *Re Ellis & Co's Trade Marks* (1904), an English case that denied rectification proceedings brought by the Society of Friends (also known as 'Quakers') to remove the QUAKER word mark from the UK Trade Mark Register in relation to certain alcoholic goods. The main grounds for rectification were that the mark was 'scandalous' and was 'liable to deceive the public'. The Manual cites the case in support of two propositions: first, that 'a "sentimental objection" is not enough for grounds for rejection to be raised under [s 42(a)]' and second, that 'the standards to be adopted when evaluating grounds for rejection are in how the ordinary person is going to react to the mark, whether that person is Muslim, Christian, Quaker or any other religion, race, or persuasion' (IP Australia 2022, Pt 30.2.3).

As for the first proposition, Farwell J's observation related not to any assessment of what constitutes a 'scandalous' mark but to the complainants' inability to satisfy the standing requirements. The applicants were not 'persons aggrieved' since total abstinence was 'not one of the tenets of the Society of Friends' but mainly because '*no legal damage* [could] accrue to the Society of Friends, or to that portion … who are total abstainers, from the use of the [QUAKER mark]' (*Re Ellis & Co's Trade Marks* (1904) 21 RPC 617, 620 (emphasis added)). The second proposition in the Manual—tracing the ordinary person to *Re Ellis & Co*—is more bewildering and problematic. It is bewildering because nothing in the judgment supports this claim; it is merely a bureaucratic invention. It is also problematic because, as Robert Burrell and Michael Handler (2016, p. 167) observe, it 'appears to suggest that no great weight should be placed on the fact that the mark in question is especially offensive to a particularly religious or racial group'.

Despite an increased sensitivity to denying racist trade mark applications (IP Australia 2022, Pt 30.2.9), the above discussion sets out the continued challenges faced by minority groups in contesting troubling marks. The Manual has of course been amended to prohibit the registration of 'Indigenous Knowledge trade marks' and offer stronger guidance by directing that objections be raised where there are applied-for marks that have 'religious, spiritual, or cultural significance'; are 'sacred or secret'; or are 'derogatory or otherwise promotes intolerance, racism, or violence' (IP Australia 2022, Pt 30.2.13). A more appropriate approach worth considering in class is to examine the New Zealand experience following the adoption of a *legislative* prohibition of registering trade marks that are likely to offend a significant section of the community, especially Māori Peoples (*Trade Marks Act 2002* (NZ), s 17).

Before leaving this discussion, another effective yet controversial technique worth mentioning is to run a counternarrative whereby minority groups seek to register trade marks such as 'FIGHTING WHITIES: EVERYTHING IS GONNA BE ALL WHITE' replete with stereotypical representations of Whiteness (UNC, Fighting Whities Basketball Team, 2002). In this scenario, White students must convince Others as to why registration ought to be denied, and it is hoped that this role reversal can engender cultural humility and empathy.

Conclusion

Challenging widely held assumptions about law's supposed race neutrality in teaching and learning environments requires both perseverance and patience. A threshold issue that must be trounced is recognising this as an entrenched problem and then being conscious of the various ways in which this is manifested in the legal system. In this chapter, we reflected on our classroom efforts in deconstructing the 'ordinary person' test. Its racial dimensions present a potent source for challenging its supposed neutrality. Its prevalence similarly offers opportunities for classroom resistance in private and public law, in compulsory and elective units, and in early or late-degree subjects. Put another way, the 'ordinary person' test provides the opportunity for race-critical and anti-colonial approaches to be integrated into core and elective subjects. Another strength of focusing on this test lies in its generative capacity to foster collaborations with fellow teachers in support of micro-scaffolding as modest steps towards anti-racist and decolonial approaches in legal education. Given the repetition of narratives of colonial domination and objectification (Fanon 2008), we view repetition of critical approaches to the test across the law degree as indispensable in dislodging learned deference to the legal status quo.

Acknowledgements

This chapter was written on the land of the Gadigal of the Eora nation, where sovereignty was never ceded. We pay respect to the knowledge embedded forever within the Aboriginal Custodianship of Country. We wish to acknowledge the many stimulating conversations we have enjoyed with scholars both inside and outside the academy about the possibilities for disrupting colonialism and what good teaching looks and feels like. We are also indebted to the brilliant Sydney Law School students we have taught in our respective courses and the teaching and research insights arising from those productive exchanges.

References

Adebisi, Foluke, "Should We Rethink the Purposes of the Law School? A Case for Decolonial Thought in Legal Pedagogy", [2021] 2.3 *Amicus Curiae* 428–449.

Aoun, Fady JG, "Whitewashing Australia's History of Stigmatising Trade Marks and Commercial Imagery", [2019] 42.3 *Melbourne University Law Review* 671–736.

Blore, Kent, "'Lindsay v The Queen': Homicide and the Ordinary Person at the Juncture of Race and Sexuality", [2018] 39.1 *Adelaide Law Review* 159–201.

Bonilla-Silva, Eduardo, *Racism Without Racists: Color-Blind Racism and the Persistence of Racial Inequality in America*, Rowman & Littlefield Lanham, Maryland 2013 (4th edition).

Brookfield, Stephen D., *The Skillful Teacher*, Jossey-Bass, San Francisco, 2015 (3rd edition).

Brown, David et al. (eds), *Criminal Laws: Materials and Commentary on Criminal Law and Process of NSW*, The Federation Press, Alexandria 2020 (7th edition).

Brown, Lilly, Kelada, Odette and Jones, Dianne, "'While I Knew I Was Raced, I Didn't Think Much of It': The Need for Racial Literacy in Decolonising Classrooms", [2021] 24.1 *Postcolonial Studies* 82–103.

Burns, Marcelle, Hong, Anita Lee, and Wood, Asmi, *Indigenous Cultural Competency for Legal Academics Program Final Report* 2019.

Burns, Marcelle, "Are We There Yet? Indigenous Cultural Competency in Legal Education", [2018] 28.2 *Legal Education Review* 1–29.

Burns, Marcelle, Young, Simon and Nielsen, Jennifer, "'The Difficulties of Communication Encountered by Indigenous Peoples': Moving Beyond Indigenous Deficit in the Model Admission Rules for Legal Practitioners" [2018] 28.2 *Legal Education Review* 1–27.

Burrell, Robert and Handler, Michael, *Australian Trade Mark Law*, Oxford University Press, South Melbourne 2016 (2nd edition).

Commonwealth of Australia, *Register of Trade Marks* (May 1920 – September 1920) vol 29, 395 (Trade Mark No 28395 for Class 47 (candles, common soap and other laundry preparations)).

Crenshaw, Kimberle Williams, "Toward a Race-Conscious Pedagogy in Legal Education", [1988] 11 *National Black Law Journal* 1–14.

Crofts, Thomas and Loughnan, Arlie, "Provocation: The Good, the Bad and the Ugly" [2013] 37.1 *Criminal Law Journal* 23–37.

Delgado, Richard, "Storytelling for Oppositionists and Others: A Plea for Narrative", [1989] 87.8 *Michigan Law Review* 2411–2441.

Douglas, Heather, "Indigenous Legal Education: Towards Indigenisation", [2005] 6.8 *Indigenous Law Bulletin* 12–15.

Douglas, Heather, "Assimilation and Authenticity: the 'Ordinary Aboriginal Person' and the Provocation Defence", [2006] 27.2 *Adelaide Law Review* 199–226.

Eades, Diana, *Aboriginal English and the Law*, Queensland University Law Society, Brisbane 1992.

Fanon, Frantz, *Black Skin, White Masks*, Pluto, London 2008.

Fredericks, Bronwyn and Bargallie, Debbie, "An Indigenous Australian Cultural Competence Course: Talking Culture, Race and Power" in Frawley, Jack, Gabrielle, Russell and Juanita Sherwood (eds), *Cultural Competence and the Higher Education Sector Australian Perspectives, Policies and Practice*, Springer, Singapore 2020, pp. 295–308.

Gainsford, Annette, "Connection to Country: Place-Based Learning Initiatives Embedded in the Charles Sturt University Bachelor of Law", [2018] 28.2 *Legal Education Review* 1–14.

Gainsford, Annette, Gerard, Alison, Bailey, Kim, "'Yindyamarra in Action': Indigenous Cultural Competence as Core Business Within Legal Education and Law Schools" in Hill, J. Harris and R. Bacchus (eds), *Teaching Aboriginal Cultural Competence: Authentic Approaches*, Springer, Singapore 2020, pp. 61–74.

Gerard, Alison, and Gainsford, Annette, "Using Legislation to Teach Indigenous Cultural Competence in an Introductory Law Subject", [2018] 28.2 *Legal Education Review* 1–19.

Hall, Stuart et al. (ed), "The Spectacle of the Other", in *Representation: Cultural Representations and Signifying Practices*, Sage Publications, London, 1997, 223–290.

hooks, bell, *Teaching to Transgress: Education as the Practice of Freedom*, Routledge, 1994.

IP Australia, *Trade Marks Manual of Practice and Procedure l*, 20 April 2022.

Jivraj, Suhraiya, *Towards Anti-Racist Legal Pedagogy: A Resource*, University of Kent, UK, 2020.

Kina, Robbie, "Through the Eyes of a Strong Black Woman Survivor of Domestic Violence: An Australian Story" in Julia Sudbury (ed) *Global Lockdown: Race, Gender, and the Prison-Industrial Complex*, Taylor & Francis Group, 2005, pp. 67–71.

Loughlan, Patricia, "Oh Yuck! The Registration of Scandalous Trade Marks" [2005] 61 *Intellectual Property Forum* 38–42.

McClintock, Anne, *Imperial Leather: Race, Gender and Sexuality in the Colonial Conquest*, Routledge, New York, 1995.

Mertz, Elizabeth, *The Language of Law School: Learning to Think Like a Lawyer*, Oxford University Press, Oxford, 2007.

Moodie, Nikki, "Decolonising Race Theory: Place, Survivance and Sovereignty", in Greg Vass et al. (eds) *The Relationality of Race in Education Research*, Routledge, Milton, 2017, pp. 33–46.

Nakata, Martin, "Indigenous knowledge and the cultural interface: underlying issues at the intersection of knowledge and information systems", [2002] 28 *IFLA Journal* 281–291.

Patten, Jack and William Ferguson, "Aborigines Claim Citizen Rights! A Statement of the Case for the Aborigines Progressive Association", [1938] *The Publicist* (Sydney).

Sites, Brian, "Learning Theory and the Law: Spaced Retrieval and the Law School Curriculum", [2019] 43 *Law & Psychology Review* 99–132.

Smith, Linda Tuhiwai, *Decolonizing Methodologies: Research and Indigenous Peoples*, Zed Books, New York, 2012.

Stubbs, Julie and Tolmie, Julia, "Race, Gender, and the Battered Woman Syndrome: An Australian Case Study", [1995] 8.1 *Canadian Journal of Women and the Law* 122–158.

Sue, D.W., Capodilupo, C.M., Holder, A.B., et al. "Racial Microaggressions in the Life Experience of Black Americans", [2008] 39.3 *Professional Psychology: Research and Practice* 329–336.

Tuck, Eve and Yang, K. Wayne, "Decolonization is Not a Metaphor", [2012] 1.1 *Decolonization: Indigeneity, Education & Society* 1–40.
Tuitt, Patricia, *Race, Law, Resistance*, Glasshouse Press, London, 2004.
UNC, Fighting Whities Basketball Team, 2002 https://web.archive.org/web/20050306163550/http://www.fightingwhites.org/
Universities Australia, *National Best Practice Framework for Indigenous Cultural Competency* (2011).
Watson, Nicole. *Aboriginal Women, Law and Critical Race Theory: Storytelling from the Margins*, Palgrave Macmillan, Cham 2022.
Wood, Asmi, and Watson, Nicole, "Mirror, Mirror on the Wall, Who Is the Fairest of Them All?" [2018] 28.2 *Legal Education Review* 1–16.

8

REINVENTING WRONGS

A Subversive, Anti-Racist Pedagogy for Tort

C. P. McGrath

Introduction

The role of Tort in law school curricula is often paradoxical. As an oft-compulsory subject, Tort enjoys a privileged position. It cannot be avoided, and its customary model of delivery presents a considerable but necessary challenge for many students. Yet it is constituted, on any measure, by the stuff of everyday life, and so may be thought intuitively more accessible; it invites us to understand how we frame and respond to often unconscious behaviours deemed the cause of negative outcomes. Furthermore, in the English common law tradition, Tort, perhaps more than other subjects, impacts beyond its subject matter. It plays an integral part in helping students understand the very mode of analytical thought that underpins that legal tradition itself. As such, designing a model of Tort teaching that highlights and responds to an anti-racist imperative must take account of these characteristics. Here, I draw on aspects of Kishimoto's broader framework for defining anti-racist pedagogy, which highlights that '[a]nti-racist pedagogy is not about simply incorporating racial content into courses, curriculum, and discipline. It is also about *how* one teaches, even in courses where race is not the subject matter' (Kishimoto, 2018). Given change must be both structural and substantive, there are particular pedagogical challenges in approaching Tort with these goals in mind. Nevertheless, there is good reason to be optimistic about how this might be achieved in a way that both enriches and enlivens the Tort classroom. The customary model of Tort can be reframed as a space within which anti-racist pedagogy can be fruitfully enlivened without sacrificing Tort's broader contribution to intellectual development. Three particular challenges flowing from Tort's

DOI: 10.4324/9781003397885-11

traditionally compulsory, national, and judicially driven nature will be outlined before both structural and substantive design strategies are explored.

The Tort Teacher's Three Challenges

In designing a model of anti-racist Tort pedagogy, three particular challenges stand out:

The first is the reality of Tort's position as a compulsory subject and the regulatory framework and learning outcomes that inform that. Teaching Tort entails a necessary degree of regulatory instrumentalism, given that the immediate *market* value of a law degree for many students in the UK lies in the fact that any Tort module will likely aim to satisfy the respective requirements of key regulators as the academic stage of qualifying to practice. Both the Law Society and the Bar Standards Board had, until the autumn of 2021, specified Tort as one of the subjects that constituted the compulsory 'Foundations of Legal Knowledge' of a Qualifying Law Degree (Bar Standards Board and Solicitors Regulation Authority, 2014, 19). It was left to individual institutions to define for themselves the 'key elements and general principles' of these subjects, with more granular details left unspecified. With the advent of the Solicitors Qualifying Examination—stage one of which focuses on 'Functioning Legal Knowledge'—whilst the basic need for a compulsory Tort element remains for qualification to both forms of practice, there is now, on the solicitors' side, defined content that needs to be addressed if a provider wishes to provide the same benefit, in the form of the 'core principles of tort'. This covers negligence, remedies and defences, vicarious liability, occupiers' liability, product liability, nuisance, and the rule in *Rylands v Fletcher* (Solicitors Regulation Authority, n.d.). These core principles are further unpacked into a list of specific issues within each topic and, as such, now represent the minimum expected coverage. Any effort to implement an anti-racist Tort pedagogy in the UK must recognise those basic boundaries (Efron 2016, 310). Yet, this leaves open what other topics may be included and neither limits nor specifies the critical frameworks that can be drawn on in approaching these topics. If the raw content of a Tort module is now, understandably, less flexible, how that is framed remains within the bailiwick of those teaching and learning it.

Likewise, Tort demands an *intellectual* instrumentalism. The common law tradition is characterised both by a particular set of normative choices about its rules, but in the form of binding precedent and reliance on analogical reasoning, by a particular intellectual framework and conception of the formal sources of law, one that emphasises the stability of often long-held positions and the power of initial categorisation. Again, it is a necessary product of legal education that students are socialised into these choices and forms of reasoning (discussed powerfully in the context of colonisation by Baxi, 2003). Nevertheless, this need not mean that existing hierarchies of reasoning, which are of necessity deeply intertwined with law's colonial legacy (Graziadei, 2019, 451), are simply replicated without scrutiny or, as is often the case in the customary model of Tort, grappled with unconsciously *whilst* learning Tort's substantive rules.

The second challenge in part responds to the first. Traditional Tort teaching tends towards a narrow focus on national systems and strongly emphasises mastering black-letter law. As the link between Tort's syllabus and practice demonstrates, knowledge of *what* the law is represents the primary learning outcome. This is understandable. The regulatory environment that requires Tort to be taught necessarily focuses efforts not on Tort-in-the-abstract but, rather, Tort *in a given system*. Tort is thus bound to a degree of *national* instrumentalism, and it cannot be disputed that the '*what*' of a legal subject represents a key learning outcome, even if, for the English common law, identifying the '*what*' is often far from straightforward.

Thus, the third challenge flows from the substance of Tort as driven by judicial decision-making. Given the volume of materials to be grappled with, the frequently slippery nature of the content and the absence of a fixed overarching structure within which to place them, Tort can be particularly unwieldy (generally Weir, 2006; Goldberg, 2008). That Tort can, at times, appear to be a movable feast understandably challenges students and can be, ultimately, deeply off-putting. For teachers these challenges are mirrored in balancing the appropriate extent of a syllabus and an effective pedagogical pathway through it.

Focusing on the objectives of teaching any core subject is important. In part, the goal is to help students understand the content and application of key principles. Viewed more holistically, the central task is better understood as helping students think like a lawyer within and be aware of the relevant values and boundaries of the given subject. Learning Tort means learning how to think *like* a Tort lawyer (borrowing from Fritz's nuance, Fritz, 2013). Tort's (in) famously fuzzy qualities ask an act of faith from many students, to trust that what it is to think like a Tort lawyer can actually be defined. Highlighting the analogical nature of this process in curriculum design is important as it forces us to ask: what it is that constitutes that analogue of Tort in the first place? Much modern scholarship resists any assumption of Tort's formlessness, pushing back against the idea, as Goldberg wonderfully puts it in doing so himself, that 'Torts is a class not a subject' (Goldberg, 2008, 1273). That this view is relatively modern however simply emphasises the less structured period on which it builds (Morgan, 2013, 28). Goldberg himself decries treating the 'alleged formlessness of tort law' as an opportunity to diminish Tort teaching as an exercise in 'adjudicative policymaking'. He is clearly right to do so. The claim developed here, however, echoing Wriggins (2021) is that there can be meaningful pedagogic virtue in embracing this formlessness: an anti-racist pedagogy of Tort does not abandon Tort's irreducible nature as a law of civil wrongs, rather it steps towards it and, in subverting the customary model outlined above, enriches reflection on Tort itself.

Finding a Pedagogical Foothold

Drawing on Kishimoto, developing an anti-racist pedagogy of Tort will involve both structural and substantive subversion of the customary model. In practice these are likely to be closely intertwined but will be discussed separately here for clarity. Any single strategy outlined below may be adopted initially, and what is discussed is by no means exhaustive. Rather they are intended to offer immediate, practical strategies for both module and syllabus design.

Subversive Structural Design

It is important to consider not only how what is commonly taught might be re-approached but how the customary model of a Tort module can be harnessed to create space to centre an anti-racist pedagogy. Building from the first and second challenges identified above, the customary model is characterised by three key features: 1) it is inward-looking, 2) it emphasises black-letter law over critical engagement, and 3) it structures Tort through what Brownsword—in a different but similarly disruptive context—labels a coherentist mindset. One, as he puts it, where, '…what matters above all is the integrity and internal consistency of legal doctrine' and where 'the focus is on the recognised legal concepts categories and classifications … accompanied by a certain reluctance to abandon these' (Brownsword, 2021). The underlying aim of the customary model and much modern Tort scholarship is to provide a convincing account of Tort's supposedly innate normative characteristics and explain how everything comfortably fits together (see generally Hedley's critiques of this approach, 2018). Boundaries are presented as firm, well defined; the judicial role is often minimised; Tort is neat.

Subverting any aspect of this customary model is to consciously challenge a set of choices about what constitutes Tort and how best it can be engaged with by learners. We suggest that an anti-racist pedagogy for Tort must create suitable space for critical engagement with the tacit values and normative positions reflected in those black-letter sources, view Tort through a pluralist rather than national framework, and highlight the consequences of these choices, some of which are explored in the following section.

Critical engagement with the law is a necessary aspect of good legal teaching but can be demanding in the context of Tort. As an often first-year subject, students are learning to learn law in the first place, whilst also learning Tort. This can leave little space, to draw on contextual frameworks external to the law. The sources can be sufficiently challenging on their own terms to slow any developing outward critical engagement. As such, what critical space there is is often inward-looking, channelling engagement towards customary coherentism. Classes may have to be formally given over to engaging with relevant critical literature (with suggestions in the following section) or space otherwise found for direct engagement. One practical strategy for the latter may be introducing a coursework element to allow students, with appropriate scaffolding, to explore relevant critical frameworks. In such a way, and at the cost of additional assessment needs, shifting some part of summative assessment to this format may act to both incentivise students to engage generally, where a choice of frameworks is available, and offer a less pressured assessment space for reflective engagement.

As to how a Tort syllabus might be restructured to emphasise an anti-racist pedagogy, we suggest that the natural starting point is to reject the coherentist inertia of the customary model and instead start by investigating the ways in which Tort often failed and fails to capture types of wrongs. As noted, the foundation for action here is the fluidity of what constitutes the fruitful study of Tort to begin with. Whilst the customary model might work through particular Torts and general principles; or perhaps a pattern that tracks the required mental state of the defendant—moving from intentional, to negligent, to strict forms of liability—an anti-racist pedagogy can start impactfully from the interests protected and the hierarchy Tort adopts here. This is, of course, far from a novel intellectual perspective with both classic (Cane, 1997) and recent work considering these topics (Murphy, 2022), but it seldom appears as a model for course design. One plausible explanation for this is that the case law does not neatly distinguish between given Torts and given interests. The messy, overdetermined nature of Tort means various Torts might respond when the same interest is engaged. There is an obvious challenge in grounding the relevant Torts that a student might engage with when starting from an interests-based approach. Yet, starting there trains attention on where and how the boundaries of recognised interests *are* drawn, pressuring the basic assumptions that Tort creates when presented as an extant, given structure of recognised wrongs. Doing so naturally creates space for critical engagement between the is and ought of present Tort rules. Substantive ways in which these boundaries might be highlighted and explored are discussed in the following section, regardless of how a module is structured, but it bears considering that this can be addressed structurally as a matter of design as well and, in doing so, grounds Tort explicitly in the very wrongs that it recognises, or, more pertinently, does not, rather than their various further requirements.

The last but most challenging structural strategy subverts the single-minded, national focus of most Tort courses. This naturally uses a course's structure to engage narratives of legal colonisation and its impacts. Given the value of comparative study in core subject is flagged in the relevant literature (Zweigert and Kötz, 1998), the challenge here lies in articulating why this is of *particular* value in the context of anti-racist Tort pedagogy. Three arguments stand out here, one historical-contextual, one conceptual, and one practical.

The historical-contextual argument builds from the recognition that the benefit of a comparative approach to legal studies includes the ability to better contextualise one's own legal system and the choices in its construction and operation (Sebok, 2007). Subverting the tacit; national endorsement of Tort's customary model—that one's own legal system represents the necessary and correct way to think about the form and substance of Tort—better empowers students to recognise and critique ostensibly neutral decisions about the structure and substance of law-making in Tort. For the English common law, exploring this pluralist context naturally highlights the inevitably entwined relationship between the global spread of the common law and England's imperial ambitions (Graziadei, 2019; Zweigert and Kötz, 1998, 218ff), with similar patterns evident in other legal traditions (Siems, 2022, 110). Whilst, classically, the comparative study of private law might look to engage systems across the civil/common divide, given their shared historical root, the global life of the common law itself provides a natural pool of systems from which a pluralist, comparative approach to Tort in the classroom can be developed. The roots of such comparative study of Tort law across the common law world reflect the ambitions of one of its leading, and arguably only, scholars to date, John G Fleming (Sappideen and Vines, 2011) but likewise, in foregrounding the spread-by-colonisation of one legal tradition, what Baxi describes as the egregious error of remaining '…complicit with the politics of organized amnesia of law as a form of conquest' may be avoided. Awareness of why a significant portion of the legal world shares a common root cannot be avoided. Whilst focusing on the positive law of such systems provides a degree of comparative engagement sufficient to subvert Tort's customary model, the practical argument set out below highlights that the choice of which legal systems within that pool to draw on is an important aspect of subverting the customary model here.

Turning to the conceptual argument, this has two strands. The first is that even just adopting the familiar functionalist method of comparative legal studies (Michaels, 2019)—which focuses students on legal responses to problems shared across systems—such an approach to teaching Tort presupposes dialogic exploration in the classroom of how that underlying, supposedly shared problem is conceived, and, in identifying potentially distinct responses across systems, opens a critical space to explore them; as Sebok notes of a comparative approach generally, 'Using comparative materials can help students see something that is easily missed' (Sebok, 2007). In the context of this chapter, focusing on what it is that Tort law in a given system actually responds to mutually reinforces the idea of adopting an interest-focused approach to Tort, whether intending to reach beyond a single system or not. Second, a pluralist, comparative approach may also train attention more obviously on what Baxi calls the 'sociolegal genre' of comparative analysis, where questions naturally arise as to the 'production of difference within, between and across legal cultures, especially through the prisms of legal/juridical pluralisms' (Baxi, 2003, 46). As is well understood (see generally Chamallas) and as explored further in the following section, finding impactful ways to re-view existing choices and categorisations is central to substantive subversion of the customary model, and foregrounding this type of analysis—thinking about law in plural rather than the monomaniacal terms—naturally supports an anti-racist course design goal here. To the extent that a module allows for assessment by coursework, where these aspects can be further explored beyond the classroom, there is, again, a mutually supportive feedback loop available from a course designer's perspective.

Finally, once the decision has been made to introduce a pluralist element, there remains the practical issue of what this entails. We have suggested that one means of doing so that engages important historical and contextual discourse is to focus on the global common law legal tradition. Here, two choices present themselves: where within that legal tradition to look for relevant materials and whether the positivist, transplanted common law legacy is the best or only topic to explore? As to the former, whilst in the likes of Australia, Canada, and New Zealand, there are common law systems that have more clearly developed away from the English inheritance and where copious materials are available, teaching Tort from a pluralist, common law perspective offers the chance to highlight the experience of systems from the Global South depending on the materials available. This is not without potential risk: the narrower the range of materials available, or the greater the extent to which the focus is only on the bare decisions of the courts without the opportunity to further contextualise or engage with relevant secondary literature, the greater the risk of losing nuance. Whether something is better than nothing here is a key choice a course designer is likely to find themselves faced with and, again, opportunities to selectively deploy a comparative element within overall module design may be advantageous in limiting the focus to where sufficient materials on a topic can be found. As to the latter, in many cases, the English common law operated through a policy of indirect rule in a dualist fashion, parallel alongside or otherwise co-opting an existing traditional legal order (Bennett, 2019, 671). Engaging with those existing original structures as part of a compulsory tort law course works in part to critique that operation, acknowledges the national pluralism it often created in a given system (Cottrell, 1988; Bussani 1996) but, importantly, also works to highlight and reinforce the key lesson that Tort is '…at the same time a product and constituent of the very cultural framework in which it is embedded' (Bussani and Infantino, 2015 with numerous references to non-Western patterns of Tort). On the model suggested here, paying heed to both the ways in which the state-driven common law model has diverged across the globe and how the *same* issues are approached by indigenous systems creates space for foundational 'Tort' issues—what is harm? who is it that is harmed? what remedies are available and to whom? (reflected in Dagbanja, 2021)—to be approached from an engaging, critical perspective where the priors of one system are not assumed to hold for others and both the tutors' and students' own assumptions must be reflected upon rather than merely received (Kishimoto, 2018). The value of breaking out of a single-system mindset is then not only that there is obvious pedagogic value to learners but that in the choices that are made over where the intellectual eye is trained, valuable insights may be drawn from understanding functional equivalents to Tort rooted in indigenous and customary cultures—and the relationships between them—that have gone overlooked (Davies and Dagbanja, 2009). Likewise, with indigenous communities around the globe engaging Tort in response to a range of harms rooted in the legacy of colonisation, there is a range of case studies available that can now be drawn on to explore how national Tort laws can respond to that legacy (Thalia, 2012; Jivraj, 2020).

This section ends on a cautionary note. The case for a refocused, rebalanced, and re-presented model of Tort teaching centring anti-racist frameworks has been set out. Some aspects of this, particularly the push towards pluralist and critical engagement by necessity, ask much of both Tort students and teachers. Given the compulsory nature of the subject, this suggests, finally, that there is merit in approaching course design to be merely minimally compliant with the relevant regulatory framework so as to allow as much space as possible within that to engage those frameworks. Torts or, indeed, *interests* falling beyond this irreducible core may need to instead be offered, if at all, in a further, optional module. The tension is obvious: breadth or critical depth. The case could, of course, be made for offering the richer, critical engagement suggested here as an advanced module, retaining the full customary model of Tort teaching for the compulsory element. The decision here speaks to the ambition of a given institution, many of whom expressed their solidarity in the wake of reaction to George Floyd's murder (Otobo, 2020): is working towards anti-racist legal pedagogy in fact only—optionally—for some, or for all?

Tort's Subversive Substance

Whilst the structure-focused strategies identified in the preceding section are primarily means of re-imagining the customary model of Tort teaching, this section turns to subverting that model's substance, whether accompanied by structural changes or not. Again, the strategies below reinforce the central claim that foregrounding an anti-racist pedagogy reinforces and richly engages innate features of Tort. Likewise, they highlight Kishimoto's model of treating anti-racist pedagogy as an integrated rather than additive aspect of the curriculum and reflects an optimism about the capacity to highlight anti-racist discussion in subjects where race has been less obviously central (Kishimoto, 2018; Gadson, 2020). In designing towards that, it is suggested that the topics below, many but not all of which naturally arise in the design of any Tort module, may be impactfully re-presented through an anti-racist lens. What follows are practical suggestions for topics and issues to consider in the classroom, building on the excellent work already available here (see Jivraj, 2020).

At its broadest, Tort deals with a particular species of civil wrongs tied to a particular set of remedies offered to wronged individuals. Whilst some of the wrongs that would undoubtedly comprise the minimum irreducible core of a Tort module are intuitively easier to recognise—contiguous bodily interests protected against negligent interference may be more straightforward to grasp than the more nebulous sense of interference with quiet enjoyment protected by private nuisance—this basic starting point of what wrongs Tort recognises at all raises an interesting foundational question. No doubt the colonial project and the subjugation that accompanied it involved countless individual wrongs perpetrated on populations subject to it, but does the banner under which these acts were carried out suggest an additional wrong here? If so, does it differ from a *tortious* wrong? Tort selects the behaviours and consequences for which remedies are available, after all. The legal philosophical literature here interrogates whether a distinct account of the wrongfulness of colonisation can be identified (see Renzo, 2019 and references there). Contrasting this with Tort's settled boundaries offers one way to fruitfully interrogate the lop-sidedness of what wrongs Tort recognises, and why. Likewise, an excellent starting point—and one that enhances an existing strand of Tort teaching—can be found in interrogating the role of compensation schemes as vehicles for capturing particular wrongs that existing Tort structures might struggle with. This can now be explored using the experience of the Windrush Compensation Scheme, established in the UK in 2022 'to compensate individuals who have suffered loss in connection with being unable to demonstrate their lawful status in the United Kingdom' (Home Office, 2022). Ask, why does *Tort* struggle here? If Tort's wrongs reflect some shared understanding of social order, what is gained or lost by offering compensation through a system parallel to but distinct from Tort?

Tort's conceptual surface neutrality has long been identified as a potential pressure point for exploring the tacit, but powerful ways in the common law tradition creates anything but neutrality in practice. Again, much mastery of Tort can be gained from exploring *why* Tort so often adopts an objective stance and the consequences of that. Rooted in a closely related critique of the same conceptual choices, Conaghan is surely right to observe that in offering a 'rational' arbiter—one conceived at one time in the mind of the jury and now, most often by a single county or High Court judge—against which behaviour might be measured, the reality is that the embodied person of Tort models 'an adult, able-bodied, white man' despite the ostensible goal being to construct a model, 'as race-less as it is sex-less' (Conaghan, 2003, n. 98). The impact of this inertial pull towards objectivity has been explored extensively in the literature on Tort in the United States, notably in Chamallas and Wriggins' joint and individual work, and good footholds for exploring analogous issues in a UK class might be found in their extensive output (Chamallas, 2022, 2010; likewise Wriggins, 2005; Chamallas and Wriggins, 2010). It is generally understood that there is less research on these topics in core subjects in the UK (albeit see Jivraj, 2020) and settled doctrinal differences between Tort in the US and English common law may explain this, but this simply redirects classroom focus back to primary sources, again, empowering UK students to engage directly and critically with key materials and unpack these differences. In interrogating the distinction between courts demanding an ethical standard of behaviour over one rooted in praxis, students might ask whether Tort's race-neutral stance can be justified. Elsewhere, in deciding, say, in private nuisance, what constitutes unreasonable interference, how do we account for clashing cultural habits? Would the often spice-laden air of east London always have been so welcomed and, if not, could Tort guard against a claim succeeding because of tacit racism in policing this boundary? Might, given the era, it have mattered that it was an *Italian* restaurant in *Sanders-Clark v Grosvenor Mansions Co Ltd* [1900] 2 Ch 373? How could Tort's conceptual structure avoid this if so? Likewise, the general irrelevance of motive in Tort can be powerfully explored in the classroom. This again highlights the outer boundaries that Tort draws, selectively pushing overt consideration of race-based wrongs into other areas of the law and signalling that *racist* harm is not obviously Tort's immediate concern over harm *simpliciter*. Likewise, consider *Morrison v Mohamud* [2016] UKSC 11 where the clearly racist motive of the defendant's employee in attacking the claimant was held irrelevant for the purposes of the latter's vicarious liability. Is it progressive that motive appears irrelevant if the employee is acting within the bounds of their so-called field of activities, or, in seemingly divorcing these questions, do we risk privileging an employer who takes no steps to police such behaviour and might then rely on it to limit their own liability (from another angle, see *Allay (UK) Limited vs Gehlen* [2021] ICR 645)? Finally, consider *Constantine v Imperial Hotels Ltd* [1944] 1 KB 693, where the claimant, a renowned West Indian cricketer on tour in England, was refused lodging by the defendant. That he recovered damages for breach of his right to accommodation rested not on the 'much unjustifiable humiliation and distress' he suffered, as Birkett J put it, but on the defendant's status as common inn; does Tort truly capture the wrong there? What would be so greatly sacrificed if it did?

Often overlooked, the role of remedies offers potentially interesting material here in again uncovering the underlying implications and constrained nature of Tort's choices, given the remedy for most past wrongs is, bluntly, money. Students might explore the role of aggravated damages as a means to capture *racist* tortious wrongs (note, Learie Constantine was denied substantial damages on the authorities as they stood), or, as Jivraj perceptively notes, the risk that a system of Tort reparation geared, as it is, towards settlement may, in practice, amplify existing structural disadvantages rooted in race—and often entwined with class—to the effect that some potential claimants recover lower sums in similar situations or are simply unable to risk an unsuccessful outcome at trial. The same can be said of involving students in legal clinics where they may develop a better sense of to whom the idealised doctrinal picture offered in Tort books is actually available in practice (see Wriggins, 2020, 2021) emphasising disparity in the availability of liability insurance). Students might explore whether and how we would re-approach the wrongs Tort recognises if different remedial opportunities were on offer. Would the general reticence to protect 'mere' upset be ameliorated by developing remedial structures rooted in incentivising apology and conciliation rather than living in the fear of floodgates that imposing monetary remedies conjures (Brutti, 2020)?

This highlights a final substantive issue worthy of exploration in the classroom: the *common*-ness of the common law of Torts hinges on an assumed division of labour between the institutions of law-making. As the product of judicial development, Tort can struggle with rules that hinge on contextual particularity rather than an abstract generality. If the fear is that existing Torts are ill-suited to meaningfully capture wrongs rooted in race in that they often rely on *generalised* categories of tortious wrongs rather than specific, contextual wrongs—on which further UK-focused research is needed—students could engage with the role of *statutory* law-making in Tort as a better means of reflecting the necessary context here. Again, working towards an anti-racist pedagogy here does not sacrifice important themes and topics within existing Tort teaching—of which interplay between the common law and statutory rules is surely one—rather it reframes them as an enriching means of exploring the subject.

The Reasonable Tort Teacher's Response

This chapter has identified three challenges in the customary model of Tort teaching that an anti-racist pedagogy for Tort must address. Some, such as the regulatory environment, are less malleable than others and must be accepted as necessary context. Nevertheless, this still leaves a good space within which to work. In identifying a pedagogical foothold, we have explored two broad categories for action. The first, and more radical, looks to subvert the structural design of the customary model by encouraging a critical, pluralist and interests-focused approach to Tort. The second looks to subvert the likely substance of customary courses by highlighting particular topics central to Tort where an anti-racist perspective can be readily adopted. The distinction drawn between these categories is not neat; matters of structure and substance are entwined; the way defines the what. The distinction is drawn here to help separate the more far-reaching structural strategies, which might need greater practical effort to implement, from those which may be easier to implement within existing course structures. Equally, the preceding should bolster optimism that an anti-racist pedagogy for Tort may be meaningfully enabled in *different* ways. The strategies above are intended only as a practical toolkit for course design; they are prescriptive neither in whole nor in part and they represent, at best, initial waypoints for further innovation. Likewise, this chapter has highlighted the need to be realistic about what can be done within the bounds of a compulsory, often first-year course, with the consequence that course design building on the strategies identified above may have to be selective in what can be achieved. It may be necessary to develop an elective, advanced module where parts of Tort pared back from a re-conceived compulsory module can be explored. As always, individual course design should be viewed against, and feedback into, the design of the curriculum as a whole, no less so here (Thalia, 2012).

Finally, central to everything preceding has been the claim that Tort is well-placed to refract, amplify, and engage the issues that an anti-racist pedagogy highlights in a way that both enriches the classroom and learners' engagement with Tort itself. In adopting the language of subversion, it is vital to realise that what is being subverted is not the subject of Tort itself, far from it but rather an approach to Tort teaching that privileges an inward-looking, coherentist mind-set. The strategies identified here seek to more fully embed Tort in the world. Such engagement represents a proactive step towards enlivening an anti-racist pedagogy and, as the strategies above demonstrate, Tort teachers should be optimistic that this can serve to enhance rather than diminish what Tort offers those who engage with it.

Acknowledgements

My grateful thanks to the editors of this volume along with other contributors to it who offered helpful feedback on earlier drafts of this work. All errors remain my own.

References

Bar Standards Board and Solicitors Regulation Authority, *Academic Stage Handbook* (2014).

Baxi, Upendra, "The Colonialist Heritage" in Pierre Legrand and Roderick Munday (eds) *Comparative Legal Studies: Traditions and Transitions*, Cambridge, CUP, 2003, 46–75.

Bennett, TW, "Comparative Law and African Customary Law" in Matthias Reimann and Reinhard Zimmermann (eds), *The Oxford Handbook of Comparative Law*, Oxford, OUP, 2nd edn, 2019, 652–680.

Brownsword, Roger, *Law 3.0*, Routledge, London, 2021.

Brutti, Nicola, "An Incentive-based approach to Apologies and Compensation" in Prue Vines and Arno Akkermans (eds) *Unexpected Consequences of Compensation Law*, Hart, Oxford, 2020, 165–182.

Bussani, Mauro, "Tort Law and Development: Insights into the Case of Ethiopia and Eritrea" (1996) 40 *Journal of African Law* 43–52.

Bussani, Mauro and Infantino, Marta, "Tort Law and Legal Cultures" (2015) 63 *The American Journal of Comparative Law* 77–108.

Cane, Peter, *The Anatomy of Tort Law*, Hart, Oxford, 1997.
Chamallas, Martha, "Gaining Some Perspective in Tort Law: A New Take on Third-Party Criminal Attack Cases" (2010) 14 *Lewis & Clark Law Review* 1351–1400.
Chamallas, Martha, "Race and Tort Law", in Devon Carbado, Emily Houh, and Khiara M Bridges, *The Oxford Handbook of Race and Law in the United States*, Oxford Online, 2022.
Chamallas, Martha and Wriggins, Jennifer B, *The Measure of Injury: Race, Gender, and Tort Law*, NYU Press, New York, 2010.
Conaghan, J, "Tort Law and Feminist Critique" (2003) 56 *Current Legal Problems* 175–209.
Cottrell, Jill, "The Functions of the law of Torts in Africa" (1988) 31 *Journal of African Law* 161–184.
Dagbanja, Dominic N, "Customary tort law in Sub-Saharan Africa" in Mauro Bussani and Anthony J Sebok (eds) *Comparative Tort Law*, Elgar, 2nd edn, 2021, 443–468.
Davies, Julie A and Dagbanja, Dominic N, "The Role and Future of Customary Tort Law in Ghana: A Cross-Cultural Perspective" (2009) 26 *Arizona Journal of International and Comparative Law* 303–333.
Efron, Yael, "The Pentalectic Sphere as Means for Questioning Legal Education - Towards a Paradigm Shift" (2016) 95 *Arizona Summit Law Review* 285–378.
Fritz, Christian G, "Teaching Legal History in the First Year Curriculum" (2013) 53 *American Journal of Legal History* 379–383.
Gadson, Marcus, "Legal Education in the Era of Black Lives Matter" (2020) 69 *Journal of Legal Education* 637–642.
Goldberg, John, "Ten Half-Truths about Tort Law" (2008) 42 *Valparaiso University Law Review* 1221–1276.
Graziadei, Michaele, "Legal Transplants" in Matthias Reimann and Reinhard Zimmermann (eds), *The Oxford Handbook of Comparative Law*, Oxford, OUP, 2nd edn, 2019, 442–473.
Hedley, Steve, "The Rise and Fall of Private Law Theory" (2018) 134 *Law Quarterly Review* 214–238.
Home Office, Windrush Compensation Scheme Rules (2022). https://www.gov.uk/government/publications/windrush-compensation-scheme-full-rules
Jivraj, Suhraiya, "Towards Anti-Racist Legal Pedagogy: A Resource" (2020) https://research.kent.ac.uk/decolonising-law-schools
Kishimoto, Kyoko, "Anti-racist pedagogy: from faculty's self-reflection to organizing within and beyond the classroom" (2018) 21 *Race Ethnicity and Education* 540–544.
Michaels, Ralf, "The Functionalist Method of Comparative Law" in Matthias Reimann and Reinhard Zimmermann (eds), *The Oxford Handbook of Comparative Law*, Oxford, OUP, 2nd edn, 2019, 345–389.
Morgan, Jonathan, *Contract Law Minimalism*, Cambridge, CUP, 2013.
Murphy, John, "Tort's Hierarchy of Protected Interests" (2022) 81 *Cambridge Law Journal* 1–28.
Otobo, Osaro, "UK Universities' Response to Black Lives Matter" (2020) https://halpinpartnership.com/halpin-sector-report-uk-universities-response-blm
Renzo, Massimo, "Why Colonialism is Wrong" (2019) 72 *Current Legal Problems* 347–373.
Sappideen, Carolyn, Vines, Prue (eds) *Fleming's The Law of Torts*, Thompson Reuters, 10th edn, 2011.

Sebok, Anthony J, "Using Comparative Tort Materials to Teach First-Year Torts" (2007) 57 *Journal of Legal Education* 562–578.
Siems, Mathias, *Comparative Law*, Cambridge, CUP, 3rd edn, 2022.
Solicitors Regulation Authority, SQE1 Assessment Specification, https://sqe.sra.org.uk/exam-arrangements/assessment-information/sqe1-assessment-specification
Thalia, Anthony, "Frameworks for Including Indigenous Issues in Tort Law Subjects: Case Study of Stolen Generations Litigation" (2012) 4 *Ngiya: Talk the Law* 30–45.
Weir, Tony, *Tort Law* Clarendon Law Series, Oxford, 2nd edn, 2006.
Wriggins, Jennifer, "Torts, Race, and the Value of Injury, 1900–1949" (2005) 49 *Howard Law Journal* 99–138.
Wriggins, Jennifer, "Teaching Torts with a Focus on Race and Racism" (2020) *Race and the Law Prof Blog*. https://lawprofessors.typepad.com/racelawprof/2020/02/teaching-torts-with-a-focus-on-race-and-racism-by-professor-jennifer-wriggins-sumner-t-bernstein-pro.html
Wriggins, Jennifer, "How to Include Issues of Race and Racism in the Torts Course for First Year Law Students: A Call for Reform" (2021) 23 *Rutgers Race & the Law Review* 259–298.
Zweigert, Konrad and Kötz, Hein, *An Introduction to Comparative Law*, Oxford, OUP, 3rd edn, 1998 (trans Tony Weir).

PART III

Public Law

International Law, Human Rights, and the Courts

9

UNMASKING INDIGENOUS INVISIBILITY

Reforming and Decolonising the Pedagogy of *Terra Nullius*

Asmi Wood

Since the British's arrival on the Continent now called Australia, colonial versions of English law have sought to deny the existence of Indigenous peoples while legitimising their own claims to the Continent. Law and its pedagogy have facilitated the denial of non-Anglo, non-Christian civilisations. The glacial pace of change has had a detrimental impact on Indigenous populations. Deeply flawed and racist pedagogy that created generations of law makers, judges, and lawyers is part of the reason for the slow change of Anglo-Australian law with respect to the humanity and rights of Indigenous Peoples. Thus, a reform of legal pedagogy is likely to have a positive impact on race law and relations in Australia. This chapter examines how law schools have adapted and what they can further do to effect social change.

Further, a settler-colony such as Australia, which the UN General Assembly terms a metropolitan colony, is where colonisers reside geographically alongside the colonised Indigenous peoples. Such colonies are not directly controlled by the 'mother country'. Decolonising such societies faces additional hurdles, not least because of demographic changes effected to create majorities that will find decolonisation detrimental. This chapter examines both the law and how law can be reformed in the context of race, so that decolonisation, or perhaps more realistically a form of self-determination for Indigenous peoples, can still occur in Australia. Decolonisation of Australian society is unlikely to occur in practice until what this entails for the law, and more importantly for settlers, whose interests are far better protected than those of Indigenous peoples, is more carefully articulated for settler-colonial societies. Decolonising legal education in the context set out above, and in a non-instrumental or self-serving manner, will be an important instrument in decolonising society as a whole.

DOI: 10.4324/9781003397885-13

Introduction: Reforming Law through Legal Education as a Path to Indigenous Self-Determination

Indigenous peoples *alone* do not enjoy equality in Australia (Constitution, French 2003). This chapter is an exercise in both critique and suggesting reform in the legal pedagogy of Australian law schools, touching on the treatment of Aboriginal and Torres Strait Islander peoples, the Indigenous peoples of the Australian continent ('Continent'), and also a peaceful path to decolonisation and self-determination for Indigenous peoples.

Decolonising or reforming law fully, that is, accommodating changes that will provide for the legitimate rights of Indigenous peoples, within the constraints of the High Court and the limits of Anglo-Australian law, is akin to satisfying Shylock's demand for his pound of flesh without spilling that proverbial drop of blood. As in the tale, there is in the interim, a more reasonable, practical 'solution', although perhaps not one that greatly pleases the stronger colonising party and its supporters, because it calls for the sharing of sovereignty and the recognition of Indigenous norms and then identifies some initial avenues for reform within the constraints of Anglo-Australian laws.

This chapter briefly examines the meanings of 'colonisation' and 'decolonisation', as accepted in international law. It then suggests what law teachers can and cannot reasonably do within their university teaching programmes to promote justice for Indigenous peoples. The chapter argues for three things:

(i) the collective development of a closer version of the 'truth' of the ongoing process of colonisation;
(ii) speeding up the processes of comprehensive recognition, including constitutional recognition, as a next step in carving out a place for self-determined Indigenous peoples in their appropriate 'bodies politic', and promoting *de novo* approaches to treaty based on free, prior, and informed consent ('FPIC') as set out in the *United Nations Declaration on the Rights of Indigenous Peoples* ('UNDRIP'); and
(iii) encouraging emerging lawyers to abandon the coercive practices of the past, to stop promoting the legal fictions that legitimise ongoing colonisation and to help rectify past wrongs.

This approach to legal pedagogy will give lawyers (and law students who choose not to practice law) a truer and deeper understanding of colonisation, meaning a fairer acceptance of the legal, social, and cultural attributes of colonisation, and its detrimental effects on Indigenous peoples. Lawyers have a particular legal and ethical obligation to develop reasonable but specific legal skills to work with Indigenous peoples, particularly if they choose to help them to recover from the attacks on their civilisations and to truly promote Indigenous self-determination and agency.

A Short History of a White Continent

'Aboriginal and Torres Strait Islander peoples' is the most common term to describe Indigenous peoples of the Continent. These are clearly colonial terms: terminology variously used by settler states to refer collectively to a range of tribes and peoples, who often identify separately (*Love v Commonwealth* (2020) 270 CLR 152 ('*Love*')). The use of these terms is not uncontentious. This chapter generally employs the phrase 'Indigenous people/s', used by consensus in the 2007 *UNDRIP*.

In *Mabo v Queensland [No 2]* (1992) 175 CLR 1 ('*Mabo*'), nearly two centuries after the initial 'acquisition' of the Continent, a principled High Court – one that did justice as best it could within its own legal constraints – finally denied that the continent was *terra nullius* through the acknowledgement that the Continent was populated by 'civilised peoples' at the time of British claims. While this was a momentous and important turning point for relations between the white majority and Indigenous peoples, the substrate on which property law rests remains substantially undisturbed. In *Mabo*, the Court recognised a 'new' property law interest in the form of native title for Indigenous peoples, a significant achievement. Yet three decades later, the accrued property interests, privilege, and prosperity of the majority – that was supported by the legal fictional theory of *terra nullius* – largely remain undisturbed. If justice is to be served, 'the people' and the international community must force Australia to address outstanding issues as it has done in other colonised nations.

The High Court in *Mabo* did not offer an alternative theory for the acquisition of territory or for the British's claim of sovereignty. Indeed, in contradistinction to the British and their successors' unsupported claims of sovereignty, *from an Aboriginal perspective, 'sovereignty always was and always will be theirs'* (Wood 2021). However, 'fracturing law's skeleton' – a major concern for the High Court in *Mabo* – should not breed fear amongst the majority. In a historical sense, Australia has developed a very particular Anglo-centric, insular form of race law. This law is based on the idea that the British first arrived at an uninhabited Continent, a continent that could therefore be 'settled' according to the prevailing international law, precisely because it denied the existence of Indigenous peoples. Thus, Anglo-Australian law can only be altered by the Australian Parliament; therefore, it does not provide a fair framework for treaty.

Alternatively, the British version of common law permits a degree of pluralism, as demonstrated by their Lordships at the Privy Council, in deciding on cases involving Hindu and Islamic laws; for example, the exposition of Lord Parker provides for the laws of 'Shia Mohamedans' in *Hamira Bibi v Zubaida Bibi (1916) 43 IA 294*. British or imperial law provides a broader and more pluralistic understanding of the common law, law that encompasses international law. Therefore, it is not easily amenable to amendment by the colonisers alone (*Vienna Convention on the Law of Treaties* 1969, Article 27). This broader notion of the common law is arguably a reasonable halfway point as an initial legal framework on which to commence negotiations for treaty (Wood 2021). It should be actively taught to law students as a plausible alternative to the current Anglo-Australian common law, as a fairer legal basis for treaty framework. Considering Indigenous notions of law, as part of the framework, would be a better and fairer next step but is not politically feasible at present.

Reforming Law without 'Fracturing Law's Skeleton'

The acknowledgement that *terra nullius* was a legal fiction in *Mabo* was a limited one because of the High Court's inability to simultaneously 'fracture the skeleton of the law'. For non-Indigenous lawyers, stopping short of 'fracturing law's skeleton' is, arguably, a non-negotiable limit set by the High Court. These limits apply to non-Indigenous lawyers. However, Indigenous lawyers will not and should not be held to domestic standards when engaged in the process of decolonisation, which *ipso facto* is an attempt to remove, replace, or amend the system itself (see *Legal Consequences of the Separation of the Chagos Archipelago from Mauritius in 1965 (Advisory Opinion)*, International Court of Justice, 2019) ('*Chagos AO*').

Indigenous lawyers and Elders, as members of a colonised group, legitimately can resist colonial laws' restraints (see Judge Sebutinde, *Chagos AO*). Further, they will bring to bear their lived experiences of racism and colonialism in articulating and shaping their self-determined communities. Thus, Indigenous peoples alone must self-determine what, if any, compromises they will collectively make in locating that fulcrum that gives best effect to their legitimate aspirations, while taking into account the key concerns of the majority. As Indigenous lawyers, we represent our clients and stakeholders as any other reasonable lawyer following the ethical standards of conduct that are normalised in the common law legal community. There is, however, an additional dimension to the work, which is legal emancipation from the coloniser's legal system.

Following the *Mabo* decision, the status of the Australian common law, while now recognising the prior existence of Indigenous peoples, arguably only saw them as British subjects (Senate and House of Representatives 1902). In the more recent *Love* case, the majority of the High Court recognised the existence of separate, and in this case distinct, Indigenous body/bodies politic ('body politic'). *Love* tacitly acknowledged that Indigenous peoples' laws and normative systems pre-dated Anglo-Australian common law and were independent from the British. This crucial acknowledgement provides a legal foundation for different peoples cohabiting on the Continent to enter into agreements, such as treaties under their own normative systems. Consequently, the High Court's recognition in *Love* has provided a 'space' in the common law where Indigenous laws, ways, and norms can change and also be developed as foreshadowed by Brennan J in *Mabo* but moderated and subject to customary international norms. Recognition affords Indigenous peoples an opportunity to develop this multi-communal body politic independently and to do so as self-determined peoples. The right to self-determination as reflected in Articles 73 and 74 of the United Nations ('UN') Charter is now a universally accepted norm (*Chagos AO* and *Western Sahara (Advisory Opinion)*). Training lawyers of the future to recognise and work comfortably with Indigenous peoples as independent, self-determined peoples provides an excellent opportunity for the development of productive, harmonious coexistence of these bodies politic and helps decolonise legal pedagogy.

Decolonisation in International Law

In the broader global context of national liberation, the early phase of decolonisation focused on the grant of political independence of distant colonies (the so-called blue-water colonies), recognised and precipitated by the *UN General Assembly 1960 Decolonisation Declaration*, generally leading to UN membership. Notwithstanding the UN's then primary focus on 'national liberation' as the paradigm for decolonisation, the *1960 Decolonisation Declaration* nonetheless envisaged the ultimate decolonisation of 'all peoples' who were subject to alien domination. It is also interesting to note that the minority in *Love* attempted to characterise Aboriginal people as 'alien', in contrast to international law, where it is the coloniser that is alien. It is acknowledged that decolonisation, even in non-settler and 'blue-water' colonies, has not yet been given full effect, other than for the element of majority rule. Aboriginal people in Australia are a minority and, consequently, majority rule across the nation is unhelpful to Indigenous self-determination.

In contrast to the 'blue-water' colonies, Australia is what the UN General Assembly and international law have termed a 'metropolitan colony' or a settler-colony as it is perhaps better known in Australia and Aotearoa (Alfredsson 1987). A metropolitan colony is where the colonisers, complete with the institutions of their 'mother country', reside alongside the colonised Indigenous peoples. Such colonies are not directly controlled by the 'mother country' but maintain deep and abiding connections with it. Decolonisation, leading to independence in the meaning of self-determination in the UN Charter, is beyond what is reasonably possible at present without 'fracturing the skeleton' of Anglo-Australian law. Therefore, Indigenous peoples, like other colonised peoples in the world, should seek international support to achieve a lawful form of self-determination as understood in international law and subject all relevant processes to international supervision (see *Chagos AO*) so a fairer outcome becomes possible.

Australian domestic law and pedagogy tightly circumscribe definitions of crucial terms such as 'people'. In domestic law, the term 'people' appears in the preamble to the *Constitution* (Quick and Garran 1901). The notion of *terra nullius* and section 127 of the Constitution mean that 'the people' must exclude Indigenous peoples, at least at the moment of federation. Initial exclusion of Indigenous people from Parliament's jurisdiction (race power) confirms this. The Constitution has not been amended to recognise Indigenous peoples; thus, the constitutional meaning of 'people' as confirmed by Justice Gageler in *Love* in an 'individualistic' sense, as opposed to 'a people' in the meaning of a nation or tribe, must apply in Anglo-Australian law. On the other hand, the term 'peoples' in the meaning of the UN Charter arguably means a group that possesses international legal personality (Wood and Gardiner 2020). The domestic definition of 'people' is an impediment to self-determination and continues to preserve non-Indigenous privilege; consequently, a fair settlement cannot be based on the Anglo-Australian legal framework alone.

The British and their successors clearly will not benefit from decolonisation leading to independence, or even Indigenous self-determination based on proper Indigenous consultation. Consequently, they resist change. That is, at present, it is not in the interests of the colonial state to allow decolonisation, or unfortunately, even FPIC-based self-determination under some form of international supervision. Pragmatically, therefore, a form of internal self-determination might be what is possible in the current environment. Contemporary treaties could reflect this version of self-determination. At the same time, it would also be unethical and wrong for Indigenous peoples of today to completely bind posterity to agreements based on significant contemporary limitations.

Imperial and Anglo-Australian laws have played a significant role in the colonisation of the Continent resulting in detrimental consequences to Indigenous peoples. This includes the oppression of Indigenous peoples, especially through the notion of 'race', a broad constitutional subject matter power ('race power') under section 51(xxxvi) of the Australian Constitution. In Australia, lawyers – almost all of whom are educated at Australian law schools – ensure that law primarily operates for the benefit of the British and their successors. There is, therefore, a tension between teaching positive law as a colonising and destructive force or, alternatively, a sanitised, instrumentally constructed, and benign version of colonisation and history or by using truncated definitions of 'decolonisation'. The disingenuous nature of such positions becomes particularly evident especially when juxtaposed against an emerging version of what actually transpired during colonisation.

The master will not easily allow Indigenous peoples to possess the tools to bring down his own house, or more obliquely stated by the High Court, the tools '*to fracture the skeleton of principal which gives the body of our law its shape and internal consistency*'. There is also less internal university resistance – compared to other contexts – to teaching a truncated meaning of 'decolonising', as is the current practice in law schools. However, this *de minimus* form of 'decolonisation' is a very small subset of its fuller meaning at international law. The question for law teachers, therefore, becomes how (and how far) can issues so closely related to the ongoing colonisation of the Continent reasonably be discussed and taught within the pedagogy of law schools? That is, how can teachers produce the next generation of lawyers to be the best and most effective at working *with* Indigenous peoples, while doing so with clear declarations of their own standpoints?

Colonising Pedagogies – Considering the Objections Raised by Law Teachers

There are many excellent non-Indigenous colleagues working in this space, and their work is acknowledged. However, teaching law's true impact on Indigenous peoples sometimes encounters a strong counter-current, often in the form of a coercive assimilationist streak. Consciously or otherwise, these countercurrents often use the language of promoting human rights 'for' Indigenous people but do so strictly in their own superior image. The optics of this are largely invisible to non-Indigenous peoples but can create significant angst in class for Indigenous students (Kruk-Buchowska and Wood 2019). An example of this is the continued teaching of property law, purely based on British notions of what was 'lawfully' acquired in a settled colony. This approach is *prima facie* incompatible with the High Court's admission that Indigenous people had previously populated the Continent and did not hand sovereignty over land to the British Crown. The High Court's decision in *Mabo* has not changed the legal curriculum other than to add 'native title' as a new common law interest in real property.

A colonised approach to pedagogy shows how law was, and still is, able to maintain and to continue to promote its harmful fictions, while adopting at the same time the language of 'progress' and 'humanity'. Thus, 'the law', as-is, is also self-limited as to how much change it can bear before fracturing its own skeleton. Anglo-Australian common law intrinsically *cannot* address important issues such as competing claims of 'sovereignty'. In *Yorta Yorta Aboriginal Community v Victoria* (2002) 214 CLR 422 ('Yorta Yorta'), the joint judgment of Gleeson CJ, Gummow and Hayne JJ stated: 'Deny[ing] the acquisition of sovereignty … that is not permissible [for a Chapter III Court]'. Nevertheless, these fundamental, contested matters can reasonably be discussed by students in the safety of a classroom as they affect the law that lawyers are required to protect and promote. Approaching, negotiating, and overcoming the *limits of Anglo-Australian law* should be left to Indigenous peoples, especially to their Elders, who will determine the compromises that will be made in negotiations. The views of Elders – assisted by their lawyers – could be set out in binding treaties/agreements formulated under neutral legal frameworks (meaning laws that cannot unilaterally be altered by the stronger party). In doing this, they should be able to rely upon the best-informed legal expertise of their lawyers, whether Indigenous or non-Indigenous (see Wood and Gardiner 2020).

All lawyers must, within the Court's constraints, advise and act in their client's best interest. To be able to do this in the case of an Indigenous client, whose actions might shatter 'the law's skeleton', lawyers must first know and understand what constitutes these 'best interests' in a deep and nuanced way. To this end, such knowledge should ideally be made a mandatory graduate attribute for law students and, thus, a formal task for law teachers. Some law teachers argue that the legal curriculum is already too full to include 'substantive Indigenous content'. Others sometimes claim that they are 'uncomfortable' with teaching 'Indigenous content' This is clearly a vacuous statement as no one is asking them to teach Indigenous legal content (Anglo-Australian law concedes the existence of no such thing!) but rather to encourage students to take a critical examination of their own law and legal claims. The real questions for those making such and similar arguments are: what should I include and what should I exclude from the law course I teach? Should I ignore the legal fictions with respect to Indigenous people and the 'settlement' of white people on the Continent, and on which the current majority body politic thrives?

Law in a Land of Fictions

In Australia, law is largely taught as a professional course, preparing students for legal practice. At law school, law is presented as a benign, civilising force, treating people equally, fairly, and with dignity. Law presents as a morally sound force treating the ruled and ruler alike through notions such as the 'rule of law'. The Constitution, however, specifically permits under section 51(xxxvi) the continued detrimental treatment of Indigenous peoples alone (see *Kartinyeri v The Commonwealth* (1998) 195 CLR 337 and French 2003). However, law schools seldom qualify their 'equality before the law' discussions, further promoting Indigenous invisibility by omission. Since colonisation, legal fictions, generally and uncritically, can under Anglo-Australian law, be passed off as 'fact' (see Keane J in *Love*). Further, soon after the legal fiction of *terra nullius* had been denied, all the lands alienated by the Crown between 1788 to 1975 were retrospectively legitimised through the doctrine of extinguishment; this reversed the onus of proof onto Aboriginal people to prove that they had occupied land as required by the *Native Title Act 1993* (Cth) (e.g. *Yorta Yorta*).

In this context, Indigenous peoples are largely invisible except as statistics (Australian Law Reform Commission, *Pathways to Justice* 2018). In *Love*, Justice Keane relies on the 'fact of settlement'. However, if the Continent was not 'substantially empty' – an inescapable implication of *Mabo*, 'settlement is not legally possible, and consequently, results in a very questionable 'fact'. This continuation of past fictions is arguably the consequence of teaching what is untrue at universities. As argued elsewhere, it puts great lawyers in an impossible situation (see Wood 2021). Keane J's 'fact of settlement' was a crucial factor in his decision to exclude the two Aboriginal men from their sacred lands, thus potentially compounding, revisiting, and amplifying the injustices of the past. Law based on such fictions is taught uncritically in law schools to successive generations of lawyers, including the present generation of law students. In the overwhelming majority of law schools, the in-class safety of re-examining these legal fictions, anecdotally anyway, is denied to the majority of the cohort. Generally, the transparent aim is that of maintaining British supremacy, including by promoting assimilation, invisibility, or dispossession. The reasoning is ensconced in legal language but always with sufficient ambiguity to provide plausible deniability. Thus, Indigenous invisibility and oppression persist.

In the alternative, what usually passes for Indigenous content in class includes a 'deficit discourse', where Indigenous detention, gaol statistics, conditions, and recidivism are endlessly re-examined. While some discussion is arguably necessary, this is not all that is necessary. Systemic problems that need to be highlighted are politely avoided in a manner enough to quell the students' doubts on the veracity of history taught in law schools but arguably not enough to spark their interest to delve deeper into the mysteries of these legal fictions. Law teachers can highlight the fictions or at least require students to examine such propositions critically so that they may be more reflective than their predecessors in their future careers. The colonial version of law and history, however, is only part of the story. There is a truer, more balanced view of law, one that will more clearly emerge with truth-telling. This more comprehensive truth is what our students deserve to learn and not the limited view of law aimed at assuaging the guilt of the majority, protecting their privilege, and glossing over the unacknowledged theft of land on which the prosperity of the majority depends. *Mabo* acknowledged that 'their [Indigenous peoples'] dispossession underwrote the development of the nation [Australia]'. More recently, a closer version of what actually transpired over the years has been emerging (often referred to by Indigenous peoples as 'truth telling'). Very slowly, this is beginning to counter the fictional, colonial version of 'truth'. This objective of truth-telling in law, however, is often cluttered or obfuscated, even by supporters of Indigenous rights. It is the present law, lawyers, and law teachers who perpetuate the current fictions. These and other fictions largely remain part of the standard legal curriculum. Lawyers and supportive teachers should not condone the ongoing colonial project because otherwise, self-interest conspires to hide mainstream 'shame'. As long as these fictions remain unchallenged, they allow the many beneficiaries of the ongoing crimes against Indigenous communities to feign ignorance or to 'get away' with wilful blindness. It clearly remains in their broader interests to do so for the longest possible time.

Remedies: Legal and Political

Contemporary Anglo-Australian law remains a key tool of colonisation and therefore, 'as-is', is not likely to provide a fair framework for substantial redress.

As a next immediate step, however, it remains within the law's remit to ameliorate the worst effects of colonisation, while simultaneously creating time, opportunity, and 'space' for Indigenous peoples to develop their own self-determined responses to history. In order to facilitate this, non-Indigenous law teachers reasonably could focus on these practical issues. On the other hand, a superficial approach to 'decolonisation' continues to give succour to the worst excesses of colonisation while maintaining the *status quo ante*. The High Court has declined jurisdiction in determining the lawfulness over the acquisition of territory, including the rejection of, in its opinion, poorly framed Aboriginal counterclaims (*Coe* 1979). This nonetheless means that all domestic avenues for legal remedies have been exhausted on, at least, two key issues: sovereignty and the acquisition of territory. Exhausting all legal domestic avenues is generally a prerequisite for accessing international remedies, including for issues related to human rights (Trindade 1983). Therefore, the High Court's position leaves either a political solution or international legal avenues as the remaining, practical, peaceful options for seeking a negotiated solution to these and other fundamental outstanding legal issues. In the international plane, this allows Indigenous peoples to access a broader range of remedies under international human rights laws than are available under domestic law alone. Encouraging law students to examine these broader sources and the possible content of remedies in the safety of a classroom setting is something that law teachers can reasonably and ethically do as a step towards justice for Indigenous peoples. Further, Parliament is *not obliged* to use the broad oppressive 'race power' but does so arguably to seek electoral and political advantage. The 'race power' ensures that *as a matter of right* Indigenous peoples do not enjoy formal (and certainly not substantive) racial equality even as against non-white immigrants (French 2003). At present, fair and equitable solutions to outstanding issues between Indigenous peoples and the settler-colonial state are unlikely to gain majority support in Parliament; however, the law community can also play a positive role, and hence the importance of focusing on legal pedagogy. Teaching law students the importance of settling 'unfinished business' (Barclay 2008) and adequately equipping them to assist with this will perhaps induce them to use their skills and knowledge for Indigenous clients in seeking these remedies.

Setting Baseline Definitions for Teaching

Discussion around teaching law in a more balanced way might appear somewhat vague to those not consciously familiar with settler-colonialism. However, until relatively recently, 'unassimilated' Indigenous people were excluded from education, society, and most Western/colonial institutions in Australia (*Shaw v Wolf* (1998) 163 ALR 205, O'Brien and Gale 2007; Gardiner-Garden 2000). A consequence of this exclusion is that Indigenous modes of knowledge transmission are still unfamiliar to and thus do not meet the 'standards' required by Western educational institutions. This was, and is, a natural consequence of colonisation, which privileges the British and their institutions. Nevertheless, Indigenous knowledges and pedagogies are gradually finding their way into the broader educational system. This is a slow process and must be given time and active support to trickle into the consciousness of the majority of law students. White historians, while clearly not always supportive of Aboriginal accounts of history, have also documented cases including massacres, dispossession, child removals, murder, and treachery, in a way that was acceptable to the white academy (Reynolds 1989, 2021; Kercher 1998; Gammage 2012). Although these accounts are necessarily subjective, they can sometimes be helpful in pursuing justice in the courts (*Trevorrow Case* and *Akiba v Queensland (No 3)* (2010) 204 FCR 1). While settler accounts should continue to be taught alongside Indigenous epistemologies and accounts, the balance should be recalibrated to allow students to hear all sides of these histories.

However, one of the inhibitors of progress is the absence of 'baseline' terminology, conflating Indigenous issues in common law, international law, race law, human rights law, and law on self-determination, which usually speak to widely different disciplines. Thus, terminology used in this context can appear to be imprecise at times. Teaching 'race law' in Australia is also relatively recent and adopts terminology from a range of disciplines related to both Indigenous issues in Australia and overseas. Inconsistent terminology can result in imprecision or worse, misunderstanding. Consequently, there is a need to establish some broad definitions including on race, colonisation, decolonisation, constitutional recognition, and treaty that could be included in the broader legal pedagogy in discussing the place of Indigenous peoples. Clear definitions can create a broad, common baseline for understanding.

What Lawyers and Law Teachers Cannot Do

Lawyers, including many law teachers, are officers of the Court in Australia and must undertake to uphold the integrity of the law (clearly including its 'skeleton'). Their duty to the Court is arguably the reason why the Court in *Mabo* did not venture to replace 'the system' even while undermining Britain's legal basis to the underlying claims to territory. This is a limit which the High Court, and therefore other non-Indigenous common lawyers, could not reasonably be required to cross. If the undertaking to the Court is taken at its ordinary meaning, lawyers could not advocate for decolonisation within the meaning of international law and is arguably a reason why they teach 'decolonisation' in its truncated form. Decolonisation must require the fracturing of or perhaps even 'shattering' of the current legal system 'as is' because it supports the colonial structure, including the oppressive racist elements of law and its associated institutions. Law has kept Indigenous civilisation invisible and even now denies their sovereignty. The presumption of Aboriginal sovereignty must surely, at least *prima facie*, be a consequence of the High Court's denial of *terra nullius* (Wood 2021).

What Lawyers and Law Teachers Can Do?

Lawyers, teachers, and students, relatively easily, can work out what change the system will bear before it 'fractures its skeleton'. The question then becomes how far along this trajectory politics and society will tolerate as 'reform' before self-interest slows or stops the process. Law teachers and students can work out these 'outer limits', taking into account the exigencies of their own times. The teaching of race law is not a regular or fixed item in Australian law programmes and is itself an area for reform which will help to create a deeper and better understanding of White Australia's own legal and racial history.

At present, the vast majority of law teachers are not Indigenous and consequently cannot speak 'for' Indigenous countries. To help overcome this gap, teachers sometimes give 'Elders'/Indigenous people a small (often unpaid) 'guest lecture' spot. Law teachers can help to correct this by formally incorporating the voices of recognised Indigenous Elders (who are both valued and paid) in law programmes. For the lawyers of the settler majority, working within 'the system' to improve conditions for Indigenous people at law is the most practical approach, reflecting the approach to pedagogy recommended. The majority of students, including in classes covering 'Indigenous peoples, law and society', remain largely non-Indigenous. This provides teachers with an opportunity to reach out to the leaders of tomorrow and urge them to consider fairer outcomes for Indigenous peoples.

Law schools and programmes can, and should, provide all students with a truer, more balanced version of legal history. There are well-known difficulties in recruiting Indigenous lawyers for law programmes. Law classes can still, however, incorporate high-quality, Indigenous input. If done properly, this will further raise the baseline knowledge on Indigenous peoples and issues. Law schools and teachers can also make law programmes safe spaces for Indigenous students. Indigenous law students as a cohort appear not to enjoy equality at present, not least because of the fictions and racial stereotyping they have to confront at law schools (Kruk-Buchowska and Wood 2019). Anecdotally, many Indigenous students say that law teachers perpetrate such abuse in class (often through ignorance), something that teachers can help ameliorate within the current regime (Kruk-Buchowska and Wood 2019).

In this vein, the current, arguably superficial, approach to race relations in law schools often fails to promote a deeper, more sophisticated, and nuanced knowledge of Indigenous ontologies. Critical examination of legal issues such as the creation of treaties supporting self-determination, sovereignty, and Indigenous agency should at least be put to law students as possible ways of reversing historical wrongs. This will offer students an opportunity, in the safety of their classes and under guidance, to consider deeply, peaceful means of settling the many outstanding issues and injustices, and to consider alternative legal paths leading to a just future. A crucial and safe first step for lawyers is to press for full racial equality under law. *Prima facie*, formal equality can be achieved by rescinding the 'race power', which currently allows Parliament to make unequal laws that are detrimental to Indigenous peoples (Wood 2016). The rescission of the 'race power' will make the 'lawful oppression of Indigenous peoples' more difficult and could easily be discussed in current arrangements in classes on constitutional law. Of course, the insidious effects of race are deeply embedded in the current system.

Conclusion

Australia has a distinct form of colonisation, which differs from the colonisation processes with which the UN is acquainted. Decolonisation will, therefore, not be identical to the processes that the UN has dealt with under the *Decolonisation Declaration*. Settler-colonialism in Australia is unique even among the CANZUS group, countries including Canada, Australia, New Zealand, and the United States. These states have a similar but not identical, colonial history. Australia is unique as prior human occupation of the Continent was only recently recognised at law, and its legal consequences are still in the process of being negotiated. While decolonisation in Australia is an existential issue for Indigenous peoples only, there still is a chasm in understanding between the protagonists. A fair decolonisation process will not be possible until this gap in understanding is minimised. In terms of decolonisation, closing this understanding gap in the legal, social, and cultural attributes of British colonisation on the Continent, is crucial and is a necessary condition before decolonisation can begin in a principled, non-perfunctorily, or non-instrumental manner that will lead to a just and fair peace where Indigenous peoples will be equal at law.

A key argument of this chapter is that law school curricula should reflect a version of legal history that shows the past in a more balanced and truthful way, one that does not perpetuate self-serving legal fictions that continue to legitimise and perpetuate past atrocities. Law schools should encourage lawyers of the future to acquire a deeper knowledge of Indigenous societies, to rectify past wrongs, and to gain a level of competence to work constructively with Indigenous Elders and communities. This would include how best to develop and frame strong, precise, legally enforceable agreements for establishing lasting relations for the future, based on fair and equitable legal frameworks that do not unilaterally disadvantage the weaker parties. While this chapter discusses decolonisation broadly within the current limitations of the Australian law curriculum, it stops short of a discussion leading to the 'fracture of the skeleton' of the common law. It posits that, if necessary, this is not a step that should create fear, but rather an opportunity, for developing Anglo-Australian common law more equitably for the future.

Indigenous people also need time to recover from the continuing ravages of colonialism and need the space to do this. An Inuit Elder once said at an informal gathering in Canada that she hoped that her people, and especially the young, would not just speak of Inuit ways but live, speak, behave, and 'be Inuit within those traditions as they evolve into the future. Many Indigenous Elders concur with this sentiment. Colonisation has had an impact in Australia similar to that experienced by this Inuit Elder's community. Recovery of Indigenous ways ravaged by colonisation will not be easy, and it will take time, space, and opportunity to recover in its contemporary forms.

Some preliminary changes for consideration include:

a) seeking racial equality in the *Constitution* and in law in practice;
b) promoting the legal study of Indigenous recognition and legal personality that will permit discussions of issues such as sovereignty, self-determination, and treaty between self-determined peoples; and
c) promoting Indigenous agency, including FPIC embedded through all levels of decision-making concerning Indigenous peoples.

Past actions of lawyers and approaches ensconced in the legal pedagogy, which remain until today, have covered the eyes of lawyers to injustice and permitted the usurpation and dispossession to continue *even after* the recognition of the existence at law of an Indigenous population (Allam 2021). On the other hand, a truer version of history is slowly developing. While the tide has very slowly started to turn, law teachers can, and should, help speed up the process. At a minimum, they can avoid impeding the progress by advocating change based on their own self-interests. On the other hand, such self-serving behaviour should be discouraged by the law school leadership and respectfully called out by students.

In the meantime, truth-telling will make law students consider issues including law, colonisation, self-determination, and treaty anew. A revised legal pedagogy should promote a truer view of history, while simultaneously urging moderation and generosity on the part of Indigenous leaders and Elders in the actual exercise of their own power. *This will take time, but time is also of the essence.* Teachers can help to set the stage for this current generation of law students by informing them and encouraging students to truly stop, reflect, and help reverse the damage of past thefts, crimes, dislocation, and dispossession. This will not happen to those who do not belong to the majority Anglo-Saxon, and related races cannot base their calls for racial equality in the *Constitution.* Gaining racial equality however will allow the peoples who now share this Continent to begin along that long road to the decolonisation of a deeply entrenched settler-colonial society.

References

Alfredsson, Gudmundur, 'The Right to Self-Determination and Its Many Manifestations' in Ruth Thompson (ed), *The Rights of Indigenous Peoples in International Law: Selected Essays on Self-Determination* (University of Saskatchewan, Native Law Centre, 1987) 53.

Allam, Lorena, 'Pat Dodson slams Morrison government for rejecting key element of Uluru Statement from the Heart', *The Guardian* (online, 16 March 2021).

Barclay, Paul, *Unfinished business – Mick Dodson*, ABC Radio National Big ideas Programme, 17 August 2008. https://www.abc.net.au/radionational/programs/bigideas/3199658

Gammage, Bill, *The biggest estate on earth: How Aborigines made Australia* (Allen & Unwin, 2012).

Kercher, Bruce, 'R v Ballard, R v Murrell and R v Bonjon', (1998) 3(3) *Australian Indigenous Law Reporter* 410–425.

Kruk-Buchowska, Zuzanna and Asmi Wood, 'Indigenous experiences of higher education — the role of the ANU Tjabal Indigenous Higher Education Centre' (2019) 1 *Australian Aboriginal Studies* 51.

O'Brien, Lewis Yerloburka and Gale, Mary-Anne, *And the Clock Struck Thirteen: The life and thoughts of Kaurna Elder Uncle Lewis Yerloburka O'Brien* (Wakefield Press Adelaide, 2007).

Quick, John and Robert Garran, *The annotated constitution of the Australian Commonwealth* (Angus and Robertson, 1901).

Reynolds, Henry, *Dispossession: Black Australians and White Invaders*, (Allen & Unwin, 1989).

Reynolds, Henry, *Truth-Telling: History, sovereignty and the Uluru Statement* (NewSouth, 2021).

Senate and House of Representatives, Debates, Vol. IX 10 April 1902, 11,580 (A P Mathieson (WA); Commonwealth, *Parliamentary Debates*, House of Representatives, 24 April 1902, 11980] (Mr Isaacs (Indi).

Trindade, Cançado, *The application of the rule of exhaustion of local remedies in international law: Its rationale in the international protection of individual rights* (Cambridge University Press, 1983).

Wood, Asmi and Christie Gardiner, *Identifying a Legal Framework for a Treaty between Australia's First Peoples and Others* (Australian Institute for Common Roots, Common Futures International Indigenous Governance, Rowman & Littlefield, 2020).

Wood, Asmi, 'Australia and pandemics v BLM: No, Love Lost (at the High Court) Part II' (2021) 46(4) *Alternative Law Journal* 314.

Wood, Asmi, 'Constitutional Recognition and Racial equality' in Jennifer Nielsen, Simon Young and Jeremy Patrick (eds), *Constitutional Recognition* (Federation Press, 2016) 103.

10

DECOLONISING CIVIL PROCEDURE

Court Process as Continuing Colonisation and Tool for Indigenous Justice

Kate Ogg

Introduction

Civil procedure, a compulsory law course in Australia, is often considered a technical and practical subject devoid of politics or prejudice. However, because it is the law governing how disputes are brought before and adjudicated by courts and tribunals, it is, in many respects, the 'rules of the game' that are predominately 'written by straight, white men' to 'privilege them and disadvantage others' (Cartwright and Cartwright 2020, 538). In this chapter, I reflect on my, sometimes clumsy, attempts to begin a process of decolonising civil procedure curriculum at the Australian National University (ANU).

Drawing on Iseke-Barnes' (2008) description of decolonisation, I discuss the first part of this journey, which involves inviting students to analyse the role procedural law plays in civil cases brought by Indigenous Australians challenging colonial laws and policies. Students explore how rules relating to aspects of civil procedure such as limitation periods, jurisdiction, class actions, pleadings, appeal, settlement, and costs perpetuate discrimination and colonisation but also how Indigenous Australians have used these colonial legal processes to attain recognition of historical and continuing injustices. I share students' reactions to these additions to course content, which provide a poignant twist on Reynolds' (2000) famous provocation: Why Weren't We Told?

Despite these curriculum changes, the process of decolonising civil procedure pedagogy has barely begun. To go further on the decolonisation journey requires fundamental changes to the regulation of Australian law degrees. Civil procedure curriculum cannot be properly described as 'decolonised' until there is a commitment to legal pluralism by way of teaching both colonial and Indigenous forms of dispute resolution on their own terms. This crucial objective

DOI: 10.4324/9781003397885-14

nevertheless creates an ethical conundrum for civil procedure teachers operating in the existing regulatory context. This is because it may conflict with another important objective for the legal profession: increasing the numbers of Indigenous barristers and judges. The teaching of civil procedure, which provides the gateway to these career paths, brings these tensions to the fore and indicates that curriculum reform needs to occur at a broader and deeper level than changes to individual courses.

Throughout this chapter, when I discuss individual First Australians, I note their Country (if known). When referring collectively I use the terms 'Aboriginal and Torres Strait Islander', 'Indigenous', 'First Nations', and 'First Australians' interchangeably. There are mixed opinions amongst Indigenous Australians as to preferred terminology (Watson and Douglas 2021). As a non-Indigenous Australian, it is not my place to take a position. I intentionally use all commonly employed terms to reflect the diversity of opinions amongst First Nation Australians.

What is 'decolonisation' in the pedagogical context and where am I on the decolonisation journey?

I am not entirely comfortable with describing the changes I have made to the civil procedure curriculum at the ANU as 'decolonial'. The structure and content of law degrees in Australia are heavily regulated by the legal profession. There are 11 compulsory subjects and the regulatory bodies are highly prescriptive as to what must be taught in these courses. The following must be taught as part of the civil procedure curriculum: adversarialism, costs, service, jurisdiction, parties, pleadings, discovery, early resolution of litigation, judgment, appeal, enforcement, alternative dispute resolution, and party and practitioner obligations (Law Admissions Consultative Committee 2016). Alternatively, the subject must

> embrace the general study of civil procedure and alternative dispute resolution relevant in the State or Territory. The law concerning jurisdiction, the initiation and service of process, the definition of issues through pleadings and judgment and enforcement should all be included.
>
> *(Law Admissions Consultative Committee 2016, 5)*

This imposed framework is colonial. It presupposes that the prime form of civil dispute resolution in Australia is litigation. There is no acknowledgement that Australia is a legally pluralistic society in which First Nation laws that address disputes are practised by First Nation communities across the country (see Spiers-Williams 2022). First Nations methods of managing conflict could be taught as 'alternative dispute resolution', but this positions First Nations laws as 'alternative' to the dominant colonial legal system. Further, the notion that conflict management can be split between criminal law and procedure (another compulsory subject) and civil dispute resolution poses challenges to teaching Indigenous law. First Nation legal scholars opine about being asked to write about 'Indigenous criminal law' or aspects of 'Indigenous civil law' because these distinctions, foundational to many Western legal systems, are simply not reflected in First Nation laws (Spiers-Williams 2022).

Iseke-Barnes (2008, p. 320), a Canadian First Nation scholar, describes Indigenous education as 'self-determined' and 'engages distinctive Indigenous methods, structures, and content'. Due to the regulatory requirements imposed on Australian law teachers, self-determination cannot be achieved in the context of a compulsory course, and opportunities for engaging Indigenous methods, content, and knowledges are limited. While this may be a pessimistic position, it is important not to make unfounded and misleading claims that certain pedagogical reforms are 'decolonial' when they reproduce colonial knowledge and structures (Tuck and Yang 2012). Nevertheless, scholars in Australian law schools can start on a process of decolonisation when teaching compulsory courses. Iseke-Barnes explains that:

> A step in the process of defeating colonial power is to recognize this power, how it is structured into an integrated system, and to begin to disrupt it through knowledge of how the system works. With this knowledge the system can be challenged and dismantled.
>
> Indigenous scholars provide strategies that can be used in the process of decolonizing by recognizing the structures of colonization, meanwhile strategizing and engaging in practices and processes that disrupt colonial power.
>
> *(Iseke-Barnes 2008, pp. 123–124)*

The reforms I have made to the course civil procedure at the ANU (discussed in the next section) can be considered the beginning of a process of decolonisation in the sense Iseke-Barnes (2008) describes. The rules of civil procedure are highly technical and can come across to students as tedious and politically neutral. Yet from the first lecture I invite students to contemplate the ways in which procedural law may be discriminatory and implicated in a broader and endemic process of continuing colonisation by focusing on the experiences of Indigenous Australians as civil litigants. I also highlight how First Australians have used these colonial processes to challenge colonial laws and practices. In doing so, I encourage students to both recognise structures of colonisation and how, through knowledge of how these colonial systems work, they can be disrupted.

My discussion of curriculum reform is not intended to be a presentation of 'best practice' in decolonising pedagogy in the civil procedure context. Akin to Cartwright (Cartwright & Cartwright 2020, p. 542), I view my journey towards decolonial teaching practice as a 'stumbling mess'. The purpose of discussing class exercises is to reflect on the attempts that I, as a white, cis-gender academic, have made to decolonise the civil procedure curriculum, including my mistakes (however well-intentioned). My view is that one of the most important skills that non-Indigenous academics need to foster to move towards decolonial teaching practice is humility. We must critically reflect on our efforts to decolonise our course content and pedagogical methods, acknowledge to ourselves and our students when we get things wrong, and invest in a continuous process of learning in order to improve.

Humility is not a skill that comes easily to academics, especially in law. We are socialised to be the 'expert' and to defend robustly our positions in the face of critique. The practice of 'winning' by sheer force of vigorous, one-sided argumentation and conceding ground is developed in high school debating societies, reinforced in law school mooting competitions and modelled in academic conferences. Thus, the process of decolonisation must start with decolonising ourselves (Spiers-Williams 2022) and relinquishing power (Cartwright & Cartwright 2020). Developing and modelling a sense of humility as a law teacher is a key and challenging part of this process.

By proffering that decolonising pedagogy starts with decolonising ourselves, I am not suggesting that decolonisation can be achieved solely by changes to individuals' attitudes or increasing diversity within the academy and legal profession. Settler colonialism imposes structures of discrimination and racism (Wolfe 1999) that modifications to pedagogy and the profession, no matter how fundamental and radical, cannot undo. Yet, many scholars who have benefitted from colonialism (in particular, non-Indigenous residents of settler colonial states) feel a responsibility to do 'all *within one's power* to dismantle unequal and unjust structures that produce privilege and disadvantage' (Biermann 2011, p. 387, my emphasis). The tensions inherent in attempting to decolonise civil procedure curriculum in Australia, outlined below are a microcosm of the larger disjunctions between recognising the entrenched, structural forces of colonialism and the responsibility of individual scholars to make changes that are within their power and spheres of influence.

Why weren't we told?

When I started my academic career in 2013, I was circumspect of the position some scholars take that the curriculum is 'too crowded' and 'there is not enough time' to include Indigenous perspectives. At the time, the requirement was that the civil procedure course provide a *minimum* of 36 contact hours over a 13-week semester. The course we delivered provided 60 hours of contact time. This allowed for teaching material beyond the compulsory requirements. In 2021, I was told that the course could only have a *maximum* of 36 contact hours across a 12-week semester, which reduced the contact time by 24 hours.

To maintain a focus on Indigenous justice and still cover the required content, I draw on litigious disputes initiated by Indigenous Australians and use them as case studies for dual purposes. First, I place these cases in their historical, social, legal, and political context and highlight why First Nations people had to turn to colonial courts. Second, I use these cases to walk the class through the far less exciting but still important procedural aspects of the litigation. I start the course with a lecture on cases initiated by Indigenous plaintiffs who were removed from their families as part of what is now known as the Stolen Generation. The first procedural hurdle these litigants faced was limitation periods. All stolen generation plaintiffs brought their cases outside the limitation period, and in the overwhelming majority of cases, courts refused to exercise their discretion to extend the limitation period on the grounds that to do so would prejudice the defendant (in most cases the Commonwealth or a state). Students are asked to question the extent to which the overwhelmingly white, male judiciary attempted to understand the reasons why these plaintiffs had taken a long time to initiate court proceedings. To provide a broader picture of the colonial context and, in particular, how discrimination operates beyond individual decision-making and is entrenched at all levels of law and policy, I highlight that in some Australian states, limitations periods have been removed for particular plaintiffs, such as those who contracted asbestosis. Thus, a person on a construction site in New South Wales in 1961 who was exposed to asbestos has no time limit applied to their claim, but this is not the case for an Indigenous Australian who in the same year was removed from their family as part of policies now well-accepted to constitute a genocide (see Human Rights and Equal Opportunity Commission 1997).

Another aspect of civil procedure the class critically analyses with reference to stolen generation civil litigation is the role of pleadings. Textbooks inform students that pleadings are designed to define the issues for trial. They assist with the efficient administration of justice because they indicate the matters for argumentation and those that lay outside the dispute. I invite the class to explore whether the rules of pleadings fracture the historical narrative that stolen generation plaintiffs want to present. For example, in *Cubillo and Gunner v Commonwealth* (2000, [1369]) the judge found Ms Cubillo's testimony unreliable and described it as 'rambling [and] non-sensical' because she could not confine herself to the issues pleaded. For many First Nation litigants, the story they want to tell traverses issues that are addressed in the pleadings and those that lay outside the matters determined by the pleadings to be in dispute (Llewellyn 2002).

The Stolen Generations cases are a fundamental part of Australia's legal history. Most Australian students studying law in the 21st century have at least a basic understanding of the history of the Stolen Generations. Unlike older Australians, they would have been taught about this dark part of Australian history (the effects of which are still felt today) as part of their primary and secondary education.[1] What astounds me is that every year I ask my students if they know about these Stolen Generation cases. I have never had a single student raise their hand across the ten years that I have taught this course. At the ANU, civil procedure is the last compulsory course taught in the programme, and most LLB students have completed four to five years of law school before they enter my classroom. Before I introduced these cases as part of the civil procedure curriculum, we were most probably graduating law students who had no knowledge that laws and policies regarding the removal of Indigenous children from their families had been litigated in state and federal court systems. These cases raise complex and significant questions of tort, fiduciary duty, and constitutional law that could be covered in the relevant compulsory courses. This absence indicates that curriculum reform has to happen at the broader programme level in addition to individual academics making reforms to their specific courses. In the same way that primary and secondary schools consider what aspects of Indigenous history must be part of the curriculum, law schools need to consider what moments in the nation's legal history must be part of our compulsory subjects.

Can the master's tools dismantle the master's house?

While exposing the prejudicial operation of civil procedure law is important, I am reticent to portray civil litigation to my students as a site that cannot deliver justice on some level to First Nation Australians. This would risk creating, in Indigenous and non-Indigenous students alike, a defeatist attitude. For Indigenous students, this could feel quite disempowering. While the civil litigation system may be colonial and discriminatory, in some situations it is the only forum available to agitate for Indigenous justice. When I introduce the Stolen Generation cases to the class, I start by referring to the 'Bringing Them Home Report', which investigated stolen generation laws and policies (Human Rights and Equal Opportunity Commission 1997). The Report concluded that these laws and policies were a form of racial discrimination and constituted a genocide. Two of its main recommendations were that compensation be provided and that the Commonwealth provide an official apology. At the time, the Commonwealth government did not act on these recommendations. Indigenous Australians initiated civil action partly due to frustration with this lack of action (Marchetti and Ransley 2005).

Another case we examine where Indigenous plaintiffs had no option but to resort to litigation is a class action brought in the Federal Court against the State of Queensland for stolen wages (*Pearson v Queensland* 2017). Until well into the 20th century, states and territories across Australia implemented laws and policies that robbed Aboriginal and Torres Strait Islanders of their wages (Kidd 2007). These laws and policies permitted Indigenous Australians to be paid only a small part of their wages (Kidd 2007). The remainder were to be paid at a later date. Most Indigenous Australians affected by these laws and policies never received their full wages (Kidd 2007). Many lived in poverty as a result, and this started a cycle of intergenerational poverty (Kidd 2012). First Nation Australians have engaged in numerous campaigns to have their wages paid in full plus interest and an acknowledgement that these wages were stolen (Kidd 2007). In Queensland, the government established a compensation scheme, but the amounts offered were paltry (Kidd 2007). With successive Queensland governments refusing to provide meaningful compensation, litigation was the last resort.

I use the stolen generation cases, stolen wages class action, and a case brought in the ACT Supreme Court I refer to as the 'genocide case' (Re Thompson Ex Parte Nulyarimma 1998) to highlight that, in some contexts, the master's tools can dismantle, or at least unsettle, the master's house. The case of *Trevorrow v South Australia* (2007) was potentially a turning point in stolen generation civil claims. Mr Trevorrow was removed from his family as a young child. He was outside the limitation period, but the Supreme Court of South Australia exercised its discretion to extend the limitation period. The Court's reasoning demonstrates, in comparison to earlier jurisprudence, a greater awareness and understanding of the reasons why stolen generation plaintiffs could not have brought their action within the time allowed under the relevant limitation provisions (*Trevorrow v South Australia* 2007, [262–264]). Further, the appeal judgment acknowledges that courts have an important role to play in adjudicating these claims beyond delivering individual justice to the parties in each case:

> [I]n our opinion there is a definite public interest in persons like Bruce Trevorrow being able to have their claims decided by a court. The widespread concern about the policies of the past, and about the manner in which they were administered, support the circumstances being exposed to public scrutiny, and the Court having the ability to consider what was done, whether it was done validly and properly, and with what consequences. That public interest, in this context, is an interest of justice.
>
> *(South Australia v Lampard-Trevorrow 2010, [461])*

The stolen wages case in the Federal Court of Australia (*Pearson v Queensland* 2017) is a valuable case study for civil procedure teachers because it provides an opportunity to explore some of the technical aspects of civil procedure (class actions, the differences between open and closed classes, and the role of settlement) alongside a lesser known fight for Indigenous justice. While all of my domestic students know about the stolen generations, very few are aware of the stolen wages saga. I use the stolen wages case to highlight to students the utility of class actions by explaining that it would have been incredibly difficult to bring these claims on an individual basis. Many of the victims of stolen wages laws and policies would not be in the financial position to sustain litigation against the State of Queensland or risk an adverse costs order. Any individual claims would have been vigorously defended by the State of Queensland and the legal and evidentiary aspects of these claims were highly complex. This would mean that the costs of bringing the case would most probably have been equal to or would have outstripped the damages awarded in the event a plaintiff was successful. I use this case to walk my students through how a class action can alter the power dynamics between parties by turning a 'David and Goliath' battle into a 'Goliath and Goliath' conflict. I explain that the class action negates individual risk to the class members (they do not have to pay legal fees in the same manner as a regular action and are not liable for adverse costs orders).

I also use the stolen wages case to highlight that open classes enable plaintiffs who may not be aware of the case to benefit from any settlement or award of damages. Further, the Court's decision to allow the lead plaintiff's application to make the class an open as opposed to closed class (*Pearson v Queensland* 2017) provides an opportunity to explain to students the nature and role of interlocutory applications and interlocutory orders. An examination of the open class order handed down by the Federal Court also allows the class to examine the role of colonial courts in Indigenous struggles for justice. The Federal Court, in making the open class order, recognised that many Indigenous Australians affected by Queensland's wage laws and policies are 'elderly, poorly educated, lack legal and commercial sophistication and live in relatively isolated locations' (*Pearson v Queensland* 2017, [14]). While this may be true of some or many of the class members, I invite students to think about how the decision represents Indigenous Australians. It certainly sidelines the highly strategic and sustained advocacy on behalf of Indigenous leaders who have fought for decades to achieve justice on this issue and the courageous actions of the lead plaintiff, Hans Pearson, who was instrumental in initiating the case and took on significant risk in doing so.

The settlement in the stolen wages case (*Pearson v Queensland* 2020) provides an opportunity for students to critically engage with the notion of case management, out-of-court settlement, and alternative dispute resolution in the colonial context. On the one hand, the opportunity to settle out of court and the increasing role of the courts in encouraging settlement may make civil litigation more appealing to Indigenous Australians in their fights for justice. Out-of-court settlement removes the need to give oral testimony, which can be traumatising. It can also result in plaintiffs receiving damages and a sense of resolution much earlier than continuing until judgment. However, the rise in out-of-court settlement and the cost rules that provide incentives to parties to settle reduce the possibility of receiving a judgment and establishing a precedent (Genn 2012). This is significant in the stolen wages context. Aboriginal Australians and Torres Straight Islanders who worked in states and territories other than Queensland and had their wages stolen do not have a judgment from the Federal Court that would have provided an important precedent in their fights for justice and compensation. Of course, the role of judgment and precedent-setting is a complex question in the context of strategic litigation (Duffy 2018). A judgment in favour of the State of Queensland in the Federal Court would have diminished the chances of obtaining compensation for stolen wages in other states and territories.

The 'genocide case' similarly provides an opportunity to introduce students to foundational concepts in civil procedure law and examine litigation as a site of continuing colonisation as well as a tool for Indigenous justice. In my view, this is one of the most significant civil cases in Australian history and yet remains relatively unknown. It began when a group of First Australians, led by Wadjularbinna Nulyarimma, asked the registrar of the ACT Magistrates Court to issue arrest warrants for John Howard (then the Prime Minister of Australia) and other high-profile politicians on the charge of genocide. The registrar refused on the ground that there was (at the time) no crime of genocide in Australia. Ms Nulyarimma and others then filed an application in the ACT Supreme Court seeking a writ of mandamus compelling the ACT Magistrates Court registrar to issue the arrest warrants. I use this juncture in the case to highlight to students the different ways of commencing a civil proceeding. We explore the difference between an originating application and an originating claim and why it was appropriate to use a written originating application in this matter.

The questions to be answered in this application were whether a genocide occurred in Australia and whether genocide was (at the time) criminalised in Australia. Two aspects of the procedure are relevant to how the Court determined these questions. First, the applicants were unrepresented, but a barrister appeared as *amicus curiae* to assist the Court in identifying the correct legal arguments and submissions. This provides a platform to discuss the experience of being an unrepresented litigant, courts' treatment of unrepresented litigants, and the nature and role of *amicus curiae*. When the proceeding was being heard, Judge Crispin agreed to hear oral testimony in the Aboriginal Tent Embassy. Judge Crispin explained that many of the applicants wanted to give oral evidence but felt uncomfortable doing so in a courtroom setting (Re Thompson Ex Parte Nulyarimma 1998, [7]). This provides an opportunity to discuss with the class the different ways in which evidence is collected as part of a civil proceeding and, in particular, how oral evidence is given.

The Court found that, as a matter of fact and law, a genocide had occurred in Australia (Re Thompson Ex Parte Nulyarimma 1998, [78]). However, the Court ultimately concluded that the crime of genocide did not exist in Australia because, despite Australia having ratified the Genocide Convention, at the time Ms Nulyarimma's application was heard, there was no domestic law criminalising genocide (Re Thompson Ex Parte Nulyarimma 1998, [73]). As an international lawyer, I am keen to share with the class my critique of Justice Crispin's reasoning on this point. However, I must show restraint because this is not an international law or criminal law class. Students have become accustomed to learning law in a siloed fashion and are uncomfortable with different areas of law merging in a single course. Dividing the teaching of law in this manner frustrates a full exploration of the experience of First Australians as civil litigants and their attempts to use colonial laws and processes (including international law) in their struggles for justice.

What the class instead examines is whether the ACT Supreme Court's judgment can be considered a victory for Indigenous justice.

Most students take a glib view of the judgment's recognition of genocide but ultimate conclusion that no remedy was available to the First Nation applicants. However, one year I was fortunate to have a senior Aboriginal law woman in my class. She had a much more positive view of the judgment. She spoke to the class about how important it was to her personally and the communities she belonged to for a colonial court to recognise that a genocide had occurred in Australia.

Reflection, honesty, and change as part of decolonising pedagogy

Teaching the above cases across a period of almost a decade has also taught me lessons about the nature of decolonisation in the university context. As noted earlier, one aspect of decolonisation is decolonising the self: an incessant process or self-awareness, learning, and change (Spiers-Williams 2022). This reflective exercise has resulted in changes to the way I have presented First Nations-led civil litigation to my students. When I first started teaching the 'genocide case', I overemphasised and misrepresented the *amicus curiae's* role. I used to tell students that the *amicus curiae* translated the applicants' allegations into recognisable legal arguments that the Court could hear and determine. However, I realised that this treatment of Ms Nulyarimma and the other applicants was incredibly condescending. I had assumed, incorrectly and without any basis, that Ms Nulyarimma and others involved with the case had no knowledge of the law of genocide. Further by presenting the *amicus curiae's* role in this way, I was delivering a 'white saviour' version of Ms Nulyarimma's application. Akin to the way Atticus Finch is often presented as the white hero who did his best to save a grateful Tom Robinson (Moore and Pierce 2007), I presented a version of the genocide case in which the barrister, trained in colonial law, took a misguided and unmeritorious claim and gave it legal credibility. I still discuss the *amicus curiae's* role but focus on the technical rules of pleading and why self-represented litigants benefit from lawyers trained in colonial law ensuring that their arguments are pleaded in a manner acceptable to a court or tribunal.

When I first started teaching civil procedure in 2013, there was minimal scholarship on the genocide case. Then in 2015 Professor Irene Watson, a legal scholar from the Tanganekald, Meintangk Boandik First Nations Peoples of the Coorong and the south east of South Australia, published her acclaimed book *Raw Law*. Watson was involved in the application as an intervener and in *Raw Law* she shares her story of the case and analysis of the outcome. Re-reading *Raw Law* for the purpose of writing this chapter has made me realise that I have made another error in my analysis of Ms Nulyarimma's application and one that stemmed from my bias as a non-Indigenous academic. The applicants' submissions with respect to a genocide taking place in Australia focused on native title legislation. I told my class that the application could have been dealt with summarily because native title legislation has no relevance to the crime of genocide. As an international lawyer, I felt that I was on safe ground. Indeed, the part of the judgment that considered whether a genocide occurred in Australia did not refer to native title (Re Thompson Ex Parte Nulyarimma 1998, [74–78]). However, Watson's (2015) account of the applicants' arguments revealed nuances in Indigenous understandings of native title and genocide that I had been ignorant of and overlooked on my first reading. Watson (2015, p. 114) explains that amendments to native title legislation in 1998 made it more difficult for First Australians to care for country, and 'the severance of this relationship is in itself an act of genocide'. Again, I realised that I have been presenting a narrative of this case in which colonial law and colonial-trained actors delivered justice to First Australians and, in doing so, I had prioritised colonial understandings of international law.

This leaves me at a critical juncture in what should be a continual process of decolonising the self and decolonising pedagogy. Having come to this realisation about how my colonial background and legal training have coloured the way I have presented this case in the past, should I acknowledge this the next time I teach civil procedure? Should I apologise for not listening to the Indigenous voices that were available to me and pledge to do better? This will not be easy. Teachers are supposed to be the experts. As a female, I do not have the privilege of the immediate and unquestioning sense of authority and respect that students (of all genders) bestow on white, male academics (Mitchell and Martin 2018). Yet, unless we as scholars model humility to our students, unless we demonstrate that it is not only acceptable but necessary to acknowledge our mistaken assumptions and colonial bias, I doubt that the legal profession can become more inclusive or take the radical steps needed to continue on a process of decolonisation.

Indigenising course content: regulatory boundaries and ethical dilemmas

To take decolonisation further in the context of teaching civil procedure would require building in to the curriculum Indigenous law on dispute resolution. This would be challenging in the context of the current regulatory framework – as discussed earlier, while colonial law segments criminal and civil law, First Nation laws do not operate along the same divide. It also presents ethical conundrums. Indigenous law on dispute resolution is not covered in any Australian civil procedure textbooks with the exception of one, which devotes less than three pages to the topic (see Collins, Demeter and Douglas 2021). The literature on Australian First Nation approaches to disputes is sparse but as part of researching for this chapter I came across some scholarship I intend to use in future iterations of the course (Lavelle 2005; Behrendt and Kelly 2008). Nevertheless, to devote half the course to Indigenous approaches to dispute resolution would require asking Indigenous colleagues to give guest lectures or calling on Indigenous elders from outside the university sector. The former is problematic in the context of First Nation academics being given large teaching and service loads due to the need to have an 'Indigenous perspective' and consequently not progressing in their careers because of reduced capacity to publish (Page and Asmar 2008). The latter is unlikely to be supported in the current climate of strained university budgets. Initiatives to employ more Indigenous academic staff are important in this respect.

Further, mastery of civil procedure is essential for a career at the bar. The most common pathway to being appointed as a judge in Australia is to have a career as a barrister. There is a recognition of the need to have more First Nation barristers and judges (see, e.g., NSW Bar Association 2013). In the context of reduced teaching hours in Australian universities, I am reticent to decrease the time allowed for learning the technical rules of civil procedure (however dull). Indigenous students are less likely than non-Indigenous students to have opportunities outside law school to develop these skills because they are less likely to have family in the legal profession. Only 0.8 per cent of solicitors in Australia are Indigenous (Law Society of NSW 2021), and in 2018 it was estimated that there were only 20 Indigenous barristers (Walsh 2018).

Commencing a career at the bar is a risky adventure in the Australian context. Unlike obtaining a position as a graduate solicitor, there is no clear pathway to starting out (it is often about 'who you know'), mentoring is ad hoc, and work and payment are intermittent. Not having the opportunity to study civil procedure law at university in depth may be another factor deterring Indigenous law students from a career at the bar. ANU has strong links with the legal profession, and in the civil procedure course we are increasing opportunities for students to learn practical skills from experienced barristers. While all students find these sessions useful, I suspect that they are of particular value to Indigenous students contemplating a career at the bar and with ambitions for a judicial appointment – many of whom are first in family to attend university (O'Shea et al. 2017). This indicates the need for more flexible approaches to law degrees that allow students to tailor their learning to suit their professional aspirations.

Reflecting on the lack of Indigenous representation at the bar and judiciary for the purpose of writing this chapter has prompted another idea for decolonising civil procedure that I intend to employ in future iterations of the course. Civil procedure rules are not created by legislators but by committees made up of judges, barristers, and litigation solicitors. Given the underrepresentation of Indigenous Australians in the legal profession, it is highly likely that there is no or limited Indigenous influence on the drafting and reform of civil procedure rules. While law students are aware of the lack of diversity in federal and state and territory legislatures, drawing students' attention to how these rules are created and who creates them is an important pedagogical step in creating awareness of how power and privilege operate at all levels of law making.

Conclusion

The aim of this chapter was to highlight how a seemingly dry, practical, and apolitical compulsory law course can be used to expose processes of continuing colonisation and how knowledge of these colonial systems can be harnessed to disrupt and challenge them. My objective was to describe the changes I have made to the civil procedure curriculum at ANU and the extent to which they could be considered 'decolonial'. However, the process of writing this chapter stimulated additional ideas that I have shared and intend to implement in the course in coming years. Contributing to this collection on decolonising pedagogy was the first time I have taken the opportunity to write about my teaching. As an academic with a full-time and ongoing position, this is a luxury I can afford. Increasing administrative, teaching, and service demands and pressure to publish as well as insecure employment conditions for many academics often leave little or no time for deep reflection on pedagogy. Those who take on the additional workloads associated with curriculum reform and decolonisation may be stymying their career advancement, especially if it interferes with research time. While we have sabbaticals for focusing on research, we do not have sabbaticals for reflection on and reinvigoration of pedagogy. A genuine commitment to decolonising pedagogy, or beginning or continuing processes of decolonisation, may require allowing teachers to take time out of the classroom.

Note

1 It is important to emphasise that Indigenous Australian children are still being removed from their families at a much higher rate than non-Indigenous children (Davis 2019).

References

Behrendt, Larissa and Loretta Kelly (eds), *Resolving Indigenous Disputes: Land Conflicts and Beyond*, Sydney, Federation Press 2008.

Biermann, Soenke, "Knowledge, Power and Decolonization: Implication for Non-Indigenous Scholars, Researchers and Educators", [2011] 379 *Indigenous Philosophies and Critical Education: A READER*, 386–398, Counterpoints.

Cartwright, Nick and T.O. Cartwright, "'Why Is It My Problem If They Don't Take Part?' The (Non)Role of White Academics in Decolonising the Law School", [2020] 54 *The Law Teacher* 532–546.

Collins, Pauline, Dalma Demeter and Susan Douglas, *Dispute Management*, Cambridge, Cambridge University Press 2021.

Cubillo and Gunner v Commonwealth [2000] FCA 1084.

Davis, Megan, *Family is Culture Final Report: Independent Review into Aboriginal Out-Of-Home Care in NSW*, 25 October 2019.

Duffy, Helen, *Strategic Human Rights Litigation: Understanding and Maximising Impact*, Bloomsbury Publishing 2018.

Genn, Hazel, "What is Civil Justice For? Reform, ADR and Access to Justice", [2012] 24 *Yale Journal of Law and Humanities* 397–417.

Human Rights and Equal Opportunity Commission, *Bringing them Home: Report of the National Inquiry Into the Separation of Aboriginal and Torres Strait Islander Children from their Families*, April 1997.

Iseke-Barnes, Judy, "Pedagogies for Decolonising", [2008] 31 *Canadian Journal of Native Education* 123–148.

Kidd, Rosalind, *Trustees on Trial: Recovering the Stolen Wages*, Aboriginal Studies Press, Canberra 2007.

Kidd, Rosalind, "Aboriginal Workers, Aboriginal Poverty", in Natasha Fijn, Ian Keen, Christopher Lloyd and Michael Pickering (eds), *Indigenous Participation in Australian Economies II: Historical Engagements and Current Enterprises*, ANU E Press, Canberra 2012, pp. 171–180.

Law Admissions Consultative Committee 2016: https://www.legalservicescouncil.org.au/Documents/prescribed-academic-areas-of-knowledge.pdf

Law Society of NSW 2021: https://www.lawsociety.com.au/sites/default/files/2021-07/2020%20National%20Profile%20of%20Solicitors%20-%20Final%20-%201%20July%202021.pdf

Lavelle, Keren, "Ancient Ceremony Transformed into Cross-Cultural Mediation Training", [2005] 43 *Law Society Journal* 22–23.

Llewellyn, Jennifer, "Dealing with the Legacy of Native Residential School Abuse in Canada: Litigation, ADR, and Restorative Justice", [2002] 52 *University of Toronto Law Journal* 253–300.

Marchetti, Elena and Janet Ransley, "Unconscious Racism: Scrutinising Judicial Reasoning in 'Stolen Generation' Cases", [2005] 14 *Social & Legal Studies* 533–552.

Mitchell, Kristina and Jonathan Martin, "Gender Bias in Student Evaluations", [2018] 51 *Political Science & Politics* 648–652.

Moore, Wendy and Jennifer Pierce, "Still Killing Mockingbirds: Narratives of Race and Innocence in Hollywood's Depiction of the White Messiah Lawyer", [2007] 3 *Qualitative Sociology Review* 171–187.

NSW Bar Association 2013: https://nswbar.asn.au/circulars/2013/may/rap.pdf

O'Shea, Sarah et al., *First-In-Family Students, University Experience and Family Life: Motivations, Transitions and Participation*, Palgrave MacMillan 2017.

Page, Susan and Christine Asmar, "Beneath the Teaching Iceberg: Exposing the Hidden Support Dimensions of Indigenous Academic Work", [2008] 37 *The Australian Journal of Indigenous Education* 109–117.

Pearson v Queensland [2017] FCA 1096.
Pearson v Queensland (No 2) [2020] FCA 619.
RE Thompson Ex Parte Nulyarimma [1998] ACTSC 136 (upheld on appeal: Nulyarimma v Thompson [1999] FCA 119).
Reynolds, Henry, *Why Weren't We Told? A Personal Search for the Truth about our History*, Penguin Books, Sydney, 2000.
South Australia v Lampard-Trevorrow (2010) 106 SASR 331
Spiers-Williams, Mary, "Challenging Settler-State Legal Fantasies: Basic Precepts of First Law", in Peter Cane, Lisa Ford and Mark McMillan (eds), *The Cambridge Legal History of Australia*, Cambridge University Press, Cambridge, 2022.
Trevorrow v South Australia [No 5] (2007) 98 SASR 136
Tuck, Eve and K. Wayne Yang, "Decolonization is Not a Metaphor", [2012] 1 *Decolonization: Indigeneity, Education & Society* 1–40.
Walsh, Katie, "One Barrister's Battle to Increase Indigenous Lawyer Numbers", 1 February 2018, *Australian Financial Review*.
Watson, Irene, *Raw Law: Aboriginal Peoples, Colonialism and International Law*, Routledge, New York, 2015.
Watson, Nicole and Heather Douglas, "Introduction", in Nicole Watson and Heather Douglas (eds), *Indigenous Legal Judgments: Bringing Indigenous Voices into Judicial Decision Making*, Routledge, New York, 2021, pp. 1–22.
Wolfe, P., *Settler Colonialism and the Transformation of Anthropology: The Politics and Poetics of an Ethnographic Event*. Cassel, London, 1999.

11

TEACHING INTERNATIONAL LAW AGAINST RACISM AND EMPIRE

Ntina Tzouvala

Introduction

'We are teachers of international law'. Such was the opening line of one of the most high-profile public interventions by international lawyers. These were the first words of the letter published by the *Guardian* on the eve of the invasion of Iraq in 2003 proclaiming that 'war would be illegal' (Bernitz et al. 2003). Even though the letter did not discuss further the signatories' pedagogical role, the figure of the teacher functioned as source of both authority and duty: the teacher was positioned as a public intellectual, one that has both the right and the duty to speak out in support of the truth, as they best know it, especially when the truth was being publicly manipulated by governmental sources and friendly media. Of course, as many have acknowledged since, these were not just any teachers: the signatories were based in the most prestigious universities (Oxbridge and a handful of high-ranking London universities), and they were of European or Antipodean origin (Craven et al. 2004, p. 370). No Iraqi or Middle Eastern scholars were included in the list of signatories. Nevertheless, the point remains: in what many saw as a low point for international law, being a law teacher was considered the most relevant qualification even though the signatories also had brilliant records of practice and research.

Even though the letter's indirect reference to pedagogy can be dismissed as a rhetorical move, I think that it captures a deeper truth about international law teaching. International legal practice (understood here as appearing in court and giving legal advice) is more limited than its domestic counterparts and, shockingly, even more geographically and demographically concentrated in the hands of a few (heavily white and male) barristers and solicitors in New York, London, Paris, and Geneva. In addition, the limited role of adjudication in

DOI: 10.4324/9781003397885-15

international law and the limited engagement of most domestic courts with the field mean that teaching is for most of us the most obvious way of engaging with a broader audience and effecting the consciousness and (perhaps) practice of people beyond the handful of our peers who read our work.

This search for relevance, along with the fact our teaching is not as embedded in one jurisdiction as that of our domestic law colleagues, means that discussions about pedagogy have been common amongst international lawyers, especially critical ones, at least since the turn of the century (Orford 1998; Simpson 1999; Otto 2000). TWAIL scholars (Third World Approaches to International Law) have played a significant role in these debates in an effort to bridge the gap between our radical and creative scholarship and our oftentimes surprisingly conventional teaching (Sen 2020; Eslava 2020; Al-Attar 2021). As demands to decolonise the university have now entered law schools, this growing body of literature and practice interacts with, is enriched, and is challenged by the initiatives of our own students, who raise urgent questions about their education (Tan 2021).

In this short contribution, I will not offer novel theoretical insights. Rather, I will reflect on my own experience as someone who has been teaching international law in various capacities for over a decade. In particular, I will focus on my recent experience of convening a large compulsory international law course arguing three things: first, the perceived tension between doctrinal rigour and theoretical engagement might have a kernel of truth, but it has been greatly exaggerated. In fact, when we stop perceiving the role of the international lawyer as one that systematises and rationalises the rules, it becomes necessary that we acknowledge the profound impact of racism and imperialism on the discipline. In so doing, many things that do not make much sense if approached as a-historical expressions of universal reason actually become comprehensible. Second, I will contend that one need not be ready for a radical overhaul of their course in order to implement concrete changes immediately. Rather, modest changes in conventional curricula can bring race and coloniality at the centre of classroom discussions and course assessments. My third point is intimately linked to the second: a large proportion of our students are eager to have these discussions and, in fact, they will be having them with or without their teachers. This eagerness is not universal or equally spread across cohorts, and it does not guarantee that there will be no pushback or complaints. However, it indicates that even limited work can bring about substantial change.

Introductions

It is customary for people writing within the traditions of TWAIL, critical race, or decolonial theory to explicitly situate themselves within their subject in an effort to challenge false universalism and the mystified – and therefore unaccountable – authority of the scholar-teacher. It is also customary that these introductions usually focus on what lawyers call one's 'protected characteristics': gender, race, sexual orientation, religion, maybe class background, or perhaps migration status. I have no doubt that one's position within these relationships influences one's engagement with the law in a world that is built around these axes of oppression. However, when I do think about myself, it is other relationships and experiences that have shaped the way that I interact with international law in general and with its teaching in particular. For example, it seems highly relevant to me that I was a 'red-diaper baby': my family and broader family were committed left-wingers with various degrees of association with the Greek Communist Party. Growing up in this context meant that I did not exactly choose my politics and, therefore, I did not choose to engage with international law through the prisms of racism, imperialism, and capitalism either, especially if we take 'choice' to entail a fully conscious and fully free process of rational decision-making. I simply have no idea how to think about my field without these concepts (Fakhri 2012, p. 12). A second, and very different experience, that still influences my teaching is that I received – and overall appreciated – a formalist legal education. Legal education in Greece was and remains formalist and structured around both memorising and rationalising legal codes. This is an approach also adopted by progressive legal scholars and practitioners, including by many who end up working overseas. In a country with only three law schools, appointments are limited and tightly controlled ensuring methodological uniformity. More broadly, though, in a context where state and capital violate the law systematically – rather than occasionally – a 'culture of formalism' (Koskenniemi 2002, p. 500) has historically operated as an effective(ish) way of resisting power in fields such as human rights, administrative law, migration and refugee law, or labour law. Even though my own engagements with progressive legal formalism have been brief and mostly unfortunate, this background has had a profound influence on the way that I teach law. A third influence has been that both my mother and most of our close family friends were high school teachers. As a result, I grew up in an environment where discussions about teaching, the duties of the pedagogue, and the role of politics in the classroom and its interaction with other imperatives were commonplace. I remember distinctly my mother's concerns about what to do with competently written but racist student essays both when these students were her own and when she did anonymised marking for university-entry exams. This background does not necessarily mean that I landed where my mother or family friends did, but I entered university teaching with an understanding that dilemmas and tensions would arise and that there was no chance that I could resolve them satisfactorily by myself. Rather, talking to others – both in formal and informal contexts – was essential. This chapter is, then, one small part of this ongoing dialogue. Finally, few things have influenced my legal and pedagogical consciousness as deeply as the realisation that upon moving to Australia in 2016 I became both an economic migrant and a settler. Being originally from Greece and having left in the midst of the financial crisis, I understood myself and my people as having been at the receiving end of imperialism, be it British, US, or German. This perception had to shift: migration in Australia – as well as in other settler colonies – has and continues to be a way of deepening and legitimising Indigenous dispossession. Therefore, even though my self-understanding as culturally and politically different from my 'Anglo' colleagues is as strong as ever, coming to appreciate my duties as a migrant teacher who is also a settler has been a long, arduous, and complicated process (Xavier 2018).

On small pebbles and big ripples

I have been a teacher of international law for quite some time. However, one experience stands out for the unique challenges and opportunities that it presented: convening and delivering all the lectures (but none of the tutorials) for a compulsory LLB/JD course of over 470 students. My convenorship and lecturing role meant that I had full control over the course's content. At the same time, the fact that international law is a core course in my department without being part of the qualifying law degree meant that I had the big cohort that comes with the former without the limitations that accompany the latter. These were then ideal circumstances for creating a course that placed race and imperialism at the heart of my teaching. At its face, my course did not deviate much from a standard public international law course: I started with the subjects of international law and then explored its sources before discussing law-breaking, including state responsibility and international dispute settlement. I devoted two lectures to the prohibition of the use of force before wrapping up the course with jurisdiction, and immunities, and I devoted explicitly one lecture to theory, focusing on feminism and TWAIL. The tutorials, which were taught by casual staff, followed this order and centred around a combination of theoretical reflections (where imperialism was addressed directly at times) and problem-solving exercises that tended to be more technical. Similarly, the assessment was split between theoretical reflections and an exam involving problem-solving.

Many teachers of international law have raised the question of textbooks and have lamented the dearth of critically orientated teaching materials and the gap between the flourishing of critical international law and our textbooks' ongoing commitment to Eurocentrism (Jones & O'Donoghue 2022, pp. 86–93). This is undeniably true. However, I also agree with Hindi and al-Attar in their conclusion that important distinctions can be drawn between relatively orthodox textbooks (Hindi 2021; Al-Attar 2021, pp. 184–7). In discussing teaching international law in and for Palestine, Hindi has compared and contrasted the leading textbooks by Shaw and Crawford. He found that the latter is more appropriate for Palestinian students as it adopts a nuanced – if conventional – position on the matter of the occupation, while Shaw is known to have advanced pro-Israel arguments (Hindi 2021). It then 'pays' to devote some time to perusing available textbooks and deciding which one might facilitate a critical approach to teaching without necessarily being a critical piece of work itself.

My own course relied on Gleider I. Hernández's, *International Law*.[1] This textbook adopts a formalist orientation, but it does so while discussing at length the imperialist (and to a lesser extent, racist) roots of the discipline and emphasising how power asymmetries continue to influence it in the present. For example, in discussing the disputed doctrine of 'specially affected states' in relationship to the emergence of customary international law, the textbook emphasises that the doctrine has become a way of rationalising the disproportionate weight given to powerful (usually Western) states in the process of identifying custom in the areas of international economic law or jus ad bellum, without affording the same weight, say, to Pacific states when it comes to the adverse effects of nuclear weapons (Hernández 2019, pp. 37–8). Even though the book frames the issue as one of power without delving into questions of race and coloniality that are obviously present in these examples, it offers an important starting point for both teachers and students to have this conversation.

Students often show (undue) deference to textbooks as *the* authoritative statements of the field, as guidance not necessarily about what to think but certainly what to think about (Bernandino 2021, p. 295). For this reason, choosing them wisely can facilitate our efforts to reform our courses. Besides choosing the best amongst orthodox, universally framed textbooks, as I propose above, another option is adopting a textbook with a regional/national focus, especially when it comes to Global South educational settings. Such textbooks are not always available or even critical (Mbengue & Akinkugbe 2023, pp. 11–13). However, the adoption of a national/regional framework can enable teachers to construct a course that does not treat international law as a neutral and universal system of rules but as a historically grounded way of managing encounters between political communities. Once this becomes the starting point of teaching, it is easier to also explain that these encounters have not been symmetrical and that imperialism and colonialism were – and continue to be – at the heart of international law and its core concepts.

In my case, 'placing' international law involved a dual move: first, thinking about Australia as a settler colony (Watson 2015; Wood 2020) and, second, treating it as a 'sub-imperial' force in the Pacific (Storr 2018) and inviting my students to reflect on the role of international law in both contexts. In so doing, I tried to disrupt the common (and heavily racialised) move of imagining Australia as an outpost of Britain or of the (white) Commonwealth and tried to emphasise its legal entanglements with Indigenous peoples on the continent and the Pacific. I did so both by tweaking the traditional curriculum and by teaching the traditional curriculum using examples of settler colonialism and the Pacific. For example, it is common practice that international law courses open with one session dedicated to states and 'other subjects' of international law. The way that this usually works out is that the class ends up being devoted to states and, to a lesser extent, to international organisations while everyone else (and notably, the individual) gets a brief mention towards the end of the class. This traditional approach reifies and naturalises the state as the only imaginable form of political association – a move that has been critiqued by postcolonial, Marxist, and other critical scholars in international law (Pahuja 2011; Parfitt 2019).

For this reason, I decided to devote two sessions to the subjects of international law: the first one dealt with statehood coupled with self-determination while the second focused on international organisations and Indigenous peoples. This could be thought of as a compromise: on the one hand, I ticked the boxes of addressing the significance of the state and went through the conventional criteria of statehood (territory, population, government, independence, etc.) while also teaching my students about the expansion of international legal personality as confirmed by the International Court of Justice (ICJ) in the *Reparations for Injuries* Advisory Opinion. On the other, I relativised this common move in two ways. First, by introducing self-determination as a core component of my first lecture, my students got to discuss what and who is statehood for and whether it is an appropriate vehicle for realising self-determination in every context. We did so by discussing the past and present of self-determination as crystallised in the ICJ's *Chagos Archipelago* Advisory Opinion. By assigning parts of the Advisory Opinion for the first class of the course, I foregrounded imperialism and colonialism as core concepts – rather than peripheral considerations – for the course. Unsurprisingly, my students were dismayed by the process that led to the detachment of the Chagos Archipelago from Mauritius. At the same time, the Advisory Opinion led my students to contrasting conclusions: some considered it a redemptive moment for international law. Others flagged that this was 'too little, too late' and it has not (yet) resulted in the return of the Archipelago. I generally tried not to take too firm of a position in such class discussions but rather acted as a facilitator. In this instance, my main contribution was to push both groups to think about the Chagossians themselves and how they were impacted both by the separation and by the Advisory Opinion, given their ongoing marginalisation both in the UK and in Mauritius.

In linking this discussion to the second session that focused on Indigenous peoples, I discussed how historically self-determination-as-statehood was confined to what came to be known as 'saltwater/bluewater colonialism' excluding Indigenous peoples who found themselves within settler colonies both in the Global North and in the Global South. I was pleasantly surprised to see that at least some of my students were familiar with the UN Declaration on the

Rights of Indigenous Peoples (UNDRIP) and that they were keen to discuss its impact both on international law and on the daily lives of Indigenous peoples. These discussions had a dual effect: first, they persuaded at least some sceptical students about the relevance of international law as a legal field. As Australia is in the midst of a political debate about Indigenous constitutional recognition and self-determination (Synot 2019), discussing these concepts early on enabled my class to grasp the far-reaching nature of the subject and its impact on matters that they are familiar with and care about. Second, this small tweaking of the curriculum 'denaturalised' international law's state-centrism, at least to an extent. Even though we did not delve into the Eurocentric character of statehood as a political unit, some students went down this path for their first assessment that required them to write short, independently researched essays as responses to a number of prompts. One of the provided prompts discussed this Eurocentrism inherent in the statist doctrine of sources (Parfitt 2014, p. 298), and it was refreshing to see that at least some of the students were able to draw these links by questioning whether the universalisation of the state-form was actually as emancipatory as earlier generations of international lawyers assumed it to be. That said, I did not necessarily tackle this issue directly in class. This omission arguably created a gap between those students who were already interested in the topic and were willing to research it further and those with no preexisting familiarity with or commitment to postcolonial theory or Third World and/or anti-racist politics.

This split between the students was an ongoing issue. Students were generally divided into three groups: first, a significant percentage did not attend the live lectures but listened to the recordings (which are mandatory in my institution) and mostly focused on attending the tutorials. This was either due to insufficient interest in the subject or, creating further complications, because of conflicting obligations, especially work commitments. Financial need and the perception that a good law degree is not enough anymore but needs to be supplemented by work experience leads a significant percentage of our students to undertake paid work. This creates new dilemmas for teachers. Generally speaking, I try to run my lectures in a highly interactive and conversational way. The idea is to reclaim the lecture not as a space of one-way transmission of knowledge but as a space for 'critical civic participation' (Tokumitsu 2017). To that end, I used my two-hour slot to introduce the basics and contextualise relevant debates, while encouraging student participation throughout the lecture.

This is an approach that is generally appreciated by those students who are physically present. However, I received complaints that I dedicated too much time to questions and to dialogue with students. The recording did not catch properly those who sat away from the microphone. This, combined with the fact that it is less than ideal listening to a recording of people having a lively and largely unstructured dialogue, meant that those who relied on recordings had a strong preference for a more traditional lecture where I would provide information in a more one-directional and linear way. That is to say that a combination of technological form (recordings) and political economy (institutional desire/need to accommodate students who do not attend lectures) can have a conservative impact on our pedagogical approach. Efforts to give students more control over their learning and to cultivate an ethos of collective inquiry, rather than professorial authority, can be undermined by measures that are otherwise touted as progressive by university administrators.

As noted above, students who attended in person were generally appreciative of the conversational format and a significant percentage asked questions and made comments on a regular basis. Active students were generally divided into two groups: one group was detail-orientated and interested in the mechanics of international law, while the other was much more concerned with 'big picture' questions with race and coloniality being at the centre of their interests. Both groups were respectful towards each other and me. I also need to point out that the former group was not hostile towards discussions about race or colonialism. In fact, they often agreed with many of the critical points raised. However, they were only interested in these discussions if they could help them understand the finer points of doctrine. This was easy to address insofar as I agree with Jones and O'Donoghue that to not understand imperialism is not to understand international law (Jones & O'Donoghue 2022, p. 93). Reversely, students with an interest in race and coloniality often adopted a position very close to that of international relations realism. They often adopted a 'Great Power' outlook towards international law doubting its 'lawfulness' and seeing it as a tool that powerful states fully control and can violate without consequence. These students were not particularly interested in the details of the law sometimes leading to doctrinally over-ambitious or even outright implausible political critiques.

The way that I tried to draw together these two groups and their different interests was to emphasise international law's indeterminacy and to show that it is through its details and technicalities that international law's racism and Eurocentric biases play out in practice (Tzouvala 2020, pp. 35–42). To do so, I emphasised the role of the law's interpreters, be it judges, academics or legal counsels, and asked my students to conceptualise international law as a never-ending dialogue between states, corporations, international organisations, bureaucrats, individuals, Indigenous peoples, etc. 'Dialogue' did not imply equality between participants (dialogues rarely do) and did not guarantee democratic decision-making or optimal, rational outcome. Rather, the idea of international law as dialogue allowed me to question rules-centrism and to present as many views as possible (especially the views of subaltern actors) on each doctrinal question.

For example, when discussing circumstances precluding wrongfulness in the law of state responsibility, some students raised the issue of the narrow construction of the defence of necessity by courts and tribunals (Hernández 2019, p. 266).

This was a great opportunity to reflect on the institutional role, identities, and ideological commitments of judges, arbitrators, and scholars who opted for this narrow construction of the exception, which is, arguably, supported but not mandated by the relevant legal texts. Taking things one step further, we discussed whose interests were protected and whose were undermined by such a narrow construction of the rule. In particular, students were concerned about the implications of such interpretations in the era of climate change and how it can subsume the interests of the most vulnerable populations to those of investors or powerful states. This is, of course, one limited example. However, it shows that one can teach students about the prevailing opinion without reifying it into an eternal, supposedly rational and universally accepted rule. By placing conflict and dissent at the centre of one's teaching, teachers can draw out the divergent material interests as well as the diverse ontologies and cosmologies inherent in different international legal arguments.

Leaning on indeterminacy as a pedagogical tool is not always easy, not least because students of different politics and sensibilities are resistant to this approach. Even though my students appreciated the conversational format, they often wanted me to have the final word and conclude the conversation by giving them the 'correct' answer. Curiously, this desire was present across both groups that I identified above. Ultimately, it became clear that many students were more comfortable with the idea that international law is Eurocentric and racist than with the idea that international law is not a set of readily identifiable rules but a historically specific and institutionally embedded way of arguing about international affairs. Ultimately, I realised that one of the biggest challenges for international law teachers is how to draw out the field's politics and biases without at the same time falling back to a formalist conception of international law as rules only sprinkled over with anti-racist, anti-imperialist, and decolonial politics. This is an approach that is appealing, due to its simplicity and because it fits with the prevailing conception of law as rules, but it is neither accurate nor, ultimately, emancipatory, as it elevates the teacher into the depository of 'correct' answers.

Decolonising legal pedagogy?

Even though I am pleased with my experiment of introducing TWAIL as a core part of my legal teaching, I would not claim that I 'decolonised' my course, or even that I am in the process of so doing. First, the international law that I taught my students is just one system of ordering inter-communal relations in this continent and, in fact, one that arrived and was imposed violently. At the same time, Indigenous peoples in Australia have a long and sophisticated tradition of ordering inter-communal relations amongst themselves and between themselves and others. This tradition survived colonisation and is a core manifestation of Indigenous sovereignty (McMillan 2014). I acknowledged this limitation during the first session of the course; this acknowledgement did not make the problem disappear. Even though I rhetorically emphasised legal pluralism beyond (Eurocentric) international law, my teaching in practice concentrated on pluralism and struggles *within* its confines. Arguably, this is an understandable choice, given the educational context and my own training, but it poses a hard limit to claims about 'decolonisation'.

This limitation was also evident in my efforts to place my course in the context of Australia's role as a Pacific (imperial) power. I do this especially in the context of international dispute settlement by focusing on cases brought by or against Australia or cases that are of direct interest to the country. A common point of reference was the ongoing (as of early 2023) effort of Pacific states led by Vanuatu to obtain an advisory opinion from the ICJ on the legal obligations of states related to climate change (Wewerinke-Singh et al. 2021). This was both a way of highlighting the ongoing relevance of the discipline and showing the complicated relationship of Global South states and subaltern peoples with its institutions. For example, it was one way of complicating the understanding of those students who were interested in racism and coloniality and tended to treat international law as a ploy of powerful, white-majority states. Initiatives such as those of Vanuatu put pressure on their account and made them think both about legal ideology and about tactical engagement and struggle within international law. At the same time, in so doing I (mostly) ignored Pacific scholars and activists who have shown ambivalence or even outright hostility towards international law as a tool for justice and emancipation. For instance, commenting on this very initiative Samoan legal scholar Dylan Asafo has expressed reserved support for the effort to obtain an advisory opinion reminding us that a just solution for climate change demands 'a world beyond international law' (Asafo 2022).

This is a position that I largely share. A decolonised international legal order would not be a mere variation of the present one. This is not to say that some form of stable regulation of interactions between different political communities is not desirable or necessary. It does, however, mean that the version of international law that emerged during the last quarter of the 19th century in tandem with the revival of imperialism and the expansion of capitalism could not survive a profound reconfiguration of the international economic and economic order and the ideological and epistemological notions that underpin it. There are undeniably intelligent, valuable, and emancipatory elements embedded in modern international law, primarily thanks to the struggles of the oppressed (Rajagopal 2003). However, modern international law's emphasis on statehood as the most legally relevant form of political organisation, its entanglement with the protection of private property and foreign investment, its conception of sovereignty as domination over and exploitation of nature, and its protection of humans as individuals are both conceptually and, materially, products and ongoing enablers of colonial relationships of exploitation, domination, and dispossession.

I am not certain that one can centre this radical approach in one's teaching and still teach something that is recognisable as 'international law'. We can highlight injustices and encourage critical engagement; we can bring to the forefront struggles and creative usages of the field; and we can, even, encourage our students to push the limits of the discipline, but within the context of university teaching we will largely remain within the confines of Eurocentric international law. Pushing at the limits of the field is no small feat. However, I am doubtful that we can meaningfully 'decolonise' the subject in the process of teaching it. This is for two reasons: first, the limitations of the university as an institution and, second, the limitations of teaching and discourse as a way of bringing about social change. Starting from the latter, I obviously believe in the emancipatory potential of pedagogy – my involvement in this volume being proof of this. At the same time, I think that we should not overstate the importance of teaching. Bureaucratic constraints, professional habits, money incentives, market pressures, and the de-politicising norms and rules that underpin the legal profession, mean that even the most radical legal education can only have limited effects on legal practice. These effects are worth fighting for insofar as they can make a huge difference in the lives of both our students and their future clients, but they should not be exaggerated or disembedded from the broader material and professional context. Second, the university can and has been a place of questioning the status quo, but it is far from an ideal space of radical learning, questioning, and changing society. Even before its current marketisation, the university relied on ideas of merit, disciplinary expertise, separation from 'lower' forms of learning, and professional accreditation that do not sit comfortably with a radical egalitarian agenda and a desire to undo the material and epistemological consequences of colonialism and imperialism. When it comes to law faculties in particular, their existence as separate departments relies on and reproduces the idea of law as a separate, and, in fact, superior form of social regulation and of the existence of lawyers as a separate professional class with privileged access to power. In this context, educating conscious or even radical international lawyers would still require that we educate, well, international lawyers, thereby, reproducing some of the most deeply embedded elements of racism, coloniality and class rule.

Conclusion

Teachers of international law are perhaps amongst the luckiest when it comes to anti-racist and decolonial critique, partly because our subject is so obviously the product of empire and white supremacy. Drawing from decades of critical literature but also cultivating the critical instincts of our students can help us implement modest but impactful changes even in the context of traditional curricula. The obviously political nature of the subject facilitates a more dialogical approach to teaching, and the decentralised nature of the international legal order can be a way to decentre our own authority as teachers: refusing to give our student the *one* correct answer is not the same as cultivating nihilism or avoiding rigour but rather it can become one way of making sense of the international legal order as a form of (asymmetrical) dialogue and contestation in which the teacher is a participant rather than an impersonal, all-knowing observer.

If I am right in arguing that relatively small interventions can produce substantial change, then this transformative path is open both to critical international lawyers and to others who may not conduct critical research per se but care about racism, coloniality, and imperialism. One need not depart from their entire agenda and conception of law all at once, and one need not over-burden themselves in a context where workloads are already unsustainable. Rather, existing work coupled with the sheer interest and enthusiasm of our own students can go a long way towards creating an international legal pedagogy that confronts the dark past and present of our discipline and even aspires to create a better future. It is, precisely, these cracks, these openings for contestation and transformation that give me hope in dark times.

Note

1 Here I need to acknowledge that the textbook's author was my PhD supervisor.

References

Asafo, Dylan 'Climate Justice Demands a World Beyond International Law' (CIL Dialogues, 12 September 2022), available at: https://cil.nus.edu.sg/blogs/climate-justice-demands-a-world-beyond-international-law/

Al-Attar, Mohsen (2021) 'Must International Legal Pedagogy Remain Eurocentric' *Asian Journal of International Law* 11(1) 176–206.

Bernandino, Ana Luisa (2021) 'Going by the Book: What International Law Textbooks Teach Us Not to Know' in Andrea Bianchi et al., *International Law's Invisible Frames: Social Cognition and Knowledge Production in International Legal Processes* (Oxford UP) pp. 293–307.

Bernitz, Ulf et al., 'War would be illegal' (The Guardian, 7 March 2003), available at: https://www.theguardian.com/politics/2003/mar/07/highereducation.iraq

Craven, Matthew, Simpson, Gerry, Marks, Susan and Wilde, Ralph (2004) We are teachers of International Law. *Leiden Journal of International Law*, 17(2) 363–374.

Eslava, Luis (2020) 'The Teaching of (Another) International Law: Critical Realism and the Question of Agency and Structure' *The Law Teacher*, 54(3).

Fakhri, Michael (2012) 'Introduction – Questioning TWAIL's Agenda' *Oregon Review of International Law* 14(1) 1–16.

Simpson, Gerry (1999), 'On the Magic Mountain: Teaching Public International Law' *European Journal of International Law*, 10, 70–92.

Jones, Henry and Aoife O'Donoghue (2022) 'History and Self-Reflection in the Teaching of International Law' *London Review of International Law* 10, 71–103.

Hernández, Gleider I. (2019) *International Law* (Oxford UP).

Hindi, Ata R. (2021) 'A Palestinian Perspective on Teaching International Law' (TWAIL Review, 12 March 2021), available at: https://twailr.com/a-palestinian-perspective-on-teaching-international-law/

Koskenniemi, Martii (2002) *The Gentle Civilizer of Nations: the Rise and Fall of International Law 1870–1960* (Cambridge UP).

Mbengue, Makane Moïse & Olabisi D. Akinkugbe 'The Criticism of Eurocentrism and International Law: Countering and Pluralizing the Research, Teaching and Practice of Eurocentric International Law' in *The Oxford Handbook of International Law in Europe*, Eds., Anne Van Aaken, Pierre D'Argent, Lauri Mälksoo (2023).

McMillan, Mark (2014) '*Koowarta* and the Rival Indigenous International: Our Place as Indigenous Peoples in the International' *Griffith Law Review* 23 110.

Orford, Anne (1998) 'Embodying Internationalism: The Making of International Lawyers' *Australian Year Book of International Law* 19(1).

Otto, Dianne 'Handmaidens, Hierarchies and Crossing the Public-Private Divide in the Teaching of International Law' (2000) *Melbourne Journal of International Law* 1(3).

Parfitt, Rose (2014) 'The Spectre of Sources' *European Journal of International Law* 25(1) 297–306.

Parfitt, Rose (2019) *The Process of International Legal Reproduction: Inequality, Historiography, Resistance* (Cambridge: Cambridge University Press).

Rajagopal, Balakrishnan (2003) *International Law from Below: Development, Social Movements and Third World Resistance* (Cambridge UP).

Sen, Rohini (2020) 'Teaching International Law in Asia: The Predicated Pedagogue' (Afronomicslaw, 24 September 2020), available at: https://www.afronomicslaw.org/2020/09/24/teaching-international-law-in-asia-the-predicated-pedagogue

Storr, Cait (2018) ''Imperium in Imperio': Sub-Imperialism and the Formation of Australia as a Subject of International Law' *Melbourne Journal of International Law* 19(1) 335.

Pahuja, Sundhya (2011) *Decolonising International Law: Development, Economic Growth and the Politics of Universality* (Cambridge UP).

Synot, Eddie (2019) 'The Universal Declaration of Human Rights at 70: Indigenous rights and the Uluru Statement from the Heart' *Australian Journal of International Affairs* 73(4) 320–325.

Tan, Jing Min (2021) 'The many layers of invisible labour in decolonising the academy' (TWAIL Review, 12 March 2021), available at: https://twailr.com/the-many-layers-of-invisible-labour-decolonising-the-academy/

Tokumitsu, Miya 'In Defense of the Lecture' (Jacobin, 26 February 2017), available at: https://jacobin.com/2017/02/lectures-learning-school-academia-universities-pedagogy/

Tzouvala, Ntina (2020) *Capitalism as Civilisation: a History of International Law* (Cambridge UP).

Watson, Irene (2015) *Raw Law: Indigenous Peoples Colonialism and International Law* (Routledge).

Wewerinke-Singh, Margaretha et al. (2021) 'Bringing Climate Change before the International Court of Justice: Prospects for Contentious Cases and Advisory Opinions' in Ivano Along et al. *Climate Change Litigation: Global Perspectives* (Brill) 393–414.

Wood, Asmi (2020) 'Self-Determination under International Law and some Possibilities for Australia's Indigenous Peoples' in Laura Rademaker, Tim Rowse (Eds), *Indigenous Self-Determination in Australia: Histories and Historiography* (ANU Press, 2020) pp. 269–292.

Xavier, Sujith (2018) 'Loving, Working, and Living on Stolen Land: People of Colour, Settler Colonialism & White Supremacy' available at: https://reconciliationsyllabus.wordpress.com/2018/12/08/loving-working-and-living-on-stolen-land-people-of-colour-settler-colonialism-white-supremacy/

12

DIVESTING RELIGION FROM RIGHTS

Teaching Freedom of Religion through Anti-Racist Pedagogy

Sahar Ahmed

Introduction

The pedagogical case study this chapter explores is of my teaching of the Right to Freedom of Religion in International Human Rights Law to secondary school students. This choice to focus on teaching outside the university classroom is also informed by my positionality. When I started doctoral research here in Ireland and wanted to teach (having had extensive teaching experience in Pakistan already), I was informed that postgraduate students who do not have an undergraduate law degree from Ireland cannot teach within the law school for a perceived lack of knowledge of Irish law. This was the first time that my identity as a scholar from the Global South proved to be an obstacle in my academic ambitions because the racialised nature of this 'rule' was apparent – as the only woman of colour in the department, the fact that I was unable to teach was stark. Obstinance prevailed, however, and I was eventually allowed to teach Fundamental Rights and Freedoms in Irish Constitutional Law. However, to my disappointment, the teaching was only for seminars (or tutorials), which meant that I was constrained by not only the syllabus set by the lecturer, but I was also limited to teaching a set question, with virtually no wiggle room as to how I taught it. Even from my limited contact hours with students, I was able to clearly see the impact my mere presence in the classroom was having.

These mostly white undergraduate students had never been taught by a non-white person. My Black and Brown students had never been taught by someone who looked like them. My Muslim students had never been taught by a Muslim teacher. I started receiving emails from students, asking me questions about readings and cases they were studying which they did not agree with, and

DOI: 10.4324/9781003397885-16

asking me about my opinion on them. I fondly recall a particular email asking me for my 'hot take'. The students were eager to learn from an alternative perspective, but my precarity as both a casual worker and an immigrant worried me as to the extent I could take liberties with the set syllabus. The self-sustaining nature of the colonised academy is thus apparent, and, as I discuss below, the only opportunity I (as a Brown, Muslim scholar) was afforded to develop a curriculum that addressed the colonial and racist worldviews that have become embedded in International Human Rights Law was through a student outreach programme for secondary schools, run by my university.

This chapter explores that teaching through self-reflection and contemplation. However, I must admit the challenge such an exercise has proven to be. My training as a legal practitioner and academic did not feature self-reflexivity, either of myself or of those whose work I read. Therefore, any writing that centres my own active voice is uncomfortable and alien. But 'courting discomfort is necessary' and if 'decolonisation is about knowledge, epistemologies, ways of knowing and being known' (Adebisi 2019) then I need to make myself known. As Adebisi says, '[D]ecolonisation requires us to be specific. The passive voice does not work here'.

I am a Muslim woman from Pakistan. My legal education has been in both Pakistan and England, where I trained as a barrister. I proceeded to undertake a PhD in the Republic of Ireland, which is where I now live and work as a lecturer. I am an immigrant. These realities and identities are important because not only do they situate me, the person, but they contextualise my learning and teaching. When I teach the Law here in Ireland, I teach it through my Brown body and self, firmly rooted in my Muslimness. It is also how I understand the Law for myself and society around me. This chapter, therefore, is an introspective exercise where I use my experience of teaching the Right to Freedom of Religion in Ireland to secondary school students to inform a new pedagogical approach to the topic. My perspective is informed by the lived experiences of not only myself but also the students who graciously shared theirs with me.

The 'access' (or outreach) programme required all instructors to teach their own area of expertise evidenced from their specific PhD topics. As someone who was researching the Right to Freedom of Religion under International Human Rights Law and Islamic jurisprudence, I knew what my course was limited to. But studying the intersection of religion, law, and Human Rights, in Europe, was and continues to be deeply pertinent. Recent cases that involve Muslim women and the right *vis-á-vis* clothing have taken up an inordinate amount of time on the airwaves all over the world. Having developed a sizeable Muslim population over a very short amount of time and that to a large extent as a result of its own uncomfortable colonial legacy, seeing Europe get to grips with this unprecedented demographic shift through its jurisprudence on the Right to Freedom of Religion provides ample food for thought for this discussion. The role of colonialism which ties Europe to Muslim-majority countries, and which informs immigration patterns from those former colonies to Europe, is an arguably intentionally ignored facet in mainstream discourse around Freedom of Religion. Add to this the setting of a classroom in Ireland, an island which has experienced (and continues to face in the North) centuries of colonial oppression, religious and sectarian turmoil, and an interesting new 'emergent' form of Church–State separation, and it becomes obvious that whilst it may have been a necessity, Freedom of Religion was and remains a dynamic choice of topic to teach through an anti-racist pedagogy.

The right to freedom of religion, as a subject, as it is understood in the contemporary legal classroom (Irish or otherwise), is heavily influenced by overtly Christian (specifically liberal Protestant) ideas of what religion is, as evidenced repeatedly in the jurisprudence of European and other international courts (Ahmed, 2022). There are numerous judgements involving Muslim women and their right to wear the hijab and/or niqab in public, Sikh men wearing turbans in public, orthodox Christian denominations holding public ceremonies, Jehovah's Witnesses and their refusal to participate in certain aspects of public and private life on the basis of faith being rejected, and the lack of religious status being afforded to 'new religions' like Scientology (see, inter alia, Danchin, 2011; Fox, 2020). What the jurisprudence demonstrates is that anything falling outside the category of 'religion' as per the liberal Protestant understanding based on belief and ritual practice as the external manifestation fails to get protection under International Human Rights Law (IHRL). There is a dire need to divest and decolonise this concept. Those who are harmed the most from this (*vide* Muslim women and veils) are minoritised and racialised people who are already at the margins of these societies, being further pushed away due to this lack of protection.

This presents several difficulties in the classroom as well, where a teacher trying to teach Human Rights Law is faced with trying to teach the colonial, racist context that the International Human Rights apparatus operates in, while also trying to make sure the students do well in a system that does not give any weight to this contextual understanding. This chapter considers a critical approach to understanding what religion is, from a legal and jurisprudential perspective, and the protection its manifestation and practice should be entitled to. It does so through reimagining a decolonisation of the teaching of the Right to Freedom of Religion as a part of the larger IHRL module, using an anti-racist lens, in which I use my lived teaching experience to offer an alternative engagement with the text of the law that reflects and centres the lived experiences of practitioners of minoritised religions.

Before discussing my own teaching, I would like to give some context regarding the nature of the Right to Freedom of Religion as found in international law, illustrating the need for why, in the absence of a legal and cultural revolution which reconfigures the IHRL system, the way 'religion' is understood and taught in the classroom needs to be addressed (and changed). There are a few assumptions regarded as truths that this chapter works on. First, human rights are seen as the product of European history: a history of religious wars, religious treaties, and the gradual development of both a legal and philosophical field of thought on this topic. Second, this conception of Human Rights is not neutral. They have been formulated since the 1940s with as great a degree of universality and applicability as possible, endeavouring to leave sufficient scope to allow states to implement them in their own ways, according to the laws of the land and the customs and mores of its people; however, their original conception stems in form from a particular liberal, Protestant, Western European mode of thought, and this heritage has influenced the current form Human Rights take, both in terms of Freedom of Religion and more generally. As Fox explains, within this context, neoliberal democracies are the most to blame for the rise in government-based religious discrimination more generally, and against Muslims and Jews, specifically (Fox 2020). These realities become difficult to reconcile, however, with what the popular narrative tells us about how IHRL is meant to protect the vulnerable through the systems it has in place. The reality is that IHRL is predicated on neo-colonial Western ideas of 'rights', couched in concepts of 'saving' the Global South. The right to freedom of religion, within such a system, is no different (as I discuss below in the context of the TWAIL movement).

The International Human Rights regime's conception of 'religion' in legal terms is limited to the idea of 'belief', which very specifically privileges Christianity over other overtly communitarian religions which visibly and obviously 'manifest' themselves, for example, Islam and Sikhism. Therefore, there is always going to be an inherent bias in favour of Christianity in how international courts (like the European Court of Human Rights; henceforth 'the Court') understand what religion is and what its 'manifestation' means to different adherents (Ahmed, 2022). As a result, to adjudicate on non-Christian worship according to a Christian rubric is misguided at best, and harmful to the religious freedoms of non-Christian believers, at worst.

The harm is compounded by how religion becomes 'racialized'. As Masuzawa (2005) notes, the 'racialization' of the non-European and non-Christian into various distinct categories (always as an 'other') has also been an important factor in how the East and 'its religions' came to be seen through Orientalist ideas of being inferior and uncivilised. It is further useful to think of 'racialisation' through Jivraj's explanation 'to mean a particular form of understanding and/or of representing persons perceived as alien to the 'home' environment, namely Christian Europe' (2016, 9). And while Jivraj's rubric examines how notions of secularity actually 'mask a Christianised normativity' (Jivraj, 2016, 39) in judicial conceptualisation within the English legal system, it proves to be a useful parallel when assessing religion within IHRL as well.

The issue of Islamic veiling is a particularly important one in this context. The recent decisions of the Court indicate that the Court accepts that the wearing of a veil for Muslim women constitutes manifestations for the purposes of Article 9. As Evans observes in the case of *Şahın v Turkey*, the Court 'chose not to draw on the distinction in the *Arrowsmith* case between acts which are motivated by religion or belief but fall short of being a manifestation of religion or belief'. (Evans, 2010). Instead, when dealing with a case that involves attire, the Court presumes that there *is* a manifestation and acknowledges that there *is* interference in that manifestation and then considers whether that interference is justified. We observed this in the case of *Mann Singh v France*, where an observant Sikh lost his claim to appear in his driver's licence photograph with his turban and with the numerous cases of Muslim women wearing the hijab and/or the niqab.

From the perspective of, for example, deeply observant Muslims, this separation of belief and practice is wholly artificial; due to the inextricability of the internal and external for Muslims, many religious obligations *require* adherents to display their faith. Therefore, religious expression becomes a much more complex and multifaceted medium compared to other forms of expression. No matter how much the law may distinguish between the 'internal' and the 'external', for an observant Muslim woman who wants to cover her head, her internal belief system is indivisible and intertwined with her external manifestation of said belief system. Expression is not a choice but rather a religious injunction. It is important to recognise that this is the case for Muslim students of the law in Europe (or Sikh students, or students of many other faiths). This disjunct between their faith and the way the Law (mis)understands their faith will be immediate and obvious. A pedagogy that recognises and grapples with this disjunct is vital for academic and legal discourse, and these students can go on to challenge the hegemonic assumptions the Court makes but only if they are taught that that disjunct is real, not imaginary or a product of the student's inability to fit in.

An anti-racist pedagogy requires that this unbalanced relationship, and the emergent understandings of race, creed, and racialised religion, be talked about and taken into account in the classroom when looking at how European law deals with the Other. Otherwise, no accurate or equitable understanding of the law can be possible.

'Divesting' Religion from the Colonisation of 'Law' – Considering TWAIL through an Anti-Racist Approach

'Religion' as a concept, as understood within the Western, European legal canon has a very clear legal heritage that considers 'religion' to be understood through a Christian lens. This Christian lens is white – and there are shades to whiteness in this context too – consider for instance that white Protestant

Christians in the United States traditionally do not consider Catholics truly Christian (Butler, 2021). Consider also the sectarian element in the Troubles in Northern Ireland, with a different kind of Protestant hegemony. But a detailed discussion of this is beyond the scope of this chapter. It would be fair to say that religion, therefore, is a heavily colonised concept, and the legal understanding of the right to freedom of religion is also through a colonial conception. This invariably disadvantages and 'others' those adherents of religions that fall outside this colonial concept. Communitarian religious groups, overwhelmingly communities of colour, fall outside it. And the very real consequences of falling outside this periphery is to be denied by law the right to manifest religious belief in ways they want.

There is already a vast and ever-growing body of literature on TWAIL (Third World Approaches to International Law) that challenges the Eurocentrism inherent in international law and the way it is taught. TWAIL scholars have been asking questions about what a 'new' and decolonised system of international law would and can look like (Fakhri, 2012) and recognise that

> the teaching of international law is myopic. There is a culture of sanitising international law of all its vices (Judeo-Christian imageries seem to be all pervasive) and the only permissible ones are the ones that do not topple its eurocentric character.
>
> *(Sen, 2020)*

'Europe without racism is not Europe at all' (Al Attar, 2022) because 'racism, as we understand it today, was devised to justify the dehumanisation of the peoples whose lands and bodies Europe coveted'. Therefore, international law, a system that has come about as a direct result of 20th-century European modernisation and globalisation 'legitimised imperial violence, colonial conquest, and scientific racism'. But as Al Attar cogently points out, while international law's racism is a building block for TWAIL scholarship, anti-racist pedagogy is still underexplored within it. Critical race theory and TWAIL have much to learn from each other (Gathii, 2020), and critical legal scholars are beginning to use the tools that social justice theory deploys, for example. But there is much work to be done in this regard.

If the IHRL system, as a part of international law as a whole, needs to be reformed, the way it is taught needs to be reformed. This chapter suggests starting with the way 'Religion' and the Right to Freedom of Religion is taught by taking an anti-racist pedagogical approach, as defined by Kyoko Kishimoto.

'Anti-racist pedagogy centres and contextualises systemic racism in academic engagement' (Al Attar, 2022). My teaching of Freedom of Religion in secondary schools has been an exercise in trying to develop a potential roadmap for how to insert anti-racist pedagogical tools into the way international human rights in general and more specifically, how Freedom of Religion can be taught in Law Schools, using Kishimoto's synthesis of what anti-racist pedagogy is and should be, viz:

> 1) Incorporating the topics of race and inequality into course content,
> 2) Teaching from an anti-racist pedagogical approach, and
> 3) Anti-racist organising within the campus and linking our efforts to the surrounding community.
>
> *(Kishimoto, 2018)*

Reflections on Course Development and My Teaching Experience

The place where I was given an opportunity to be creative and attempt to employ innovative anti-racist pedagogical tools was through an access programme run by my university. The programme I took part in partners with secondary schools around Dublin to provide a small number of internally selected students with a short university-style module taught by a PhD tutor. The idea is for secondary school students from 'disadvantaged' backgrounds to gain the benefit of experiencing what university education is like, to spark an interest in potential future subjects they might like to study, and to equip them with the kinds of knowledge and skills that their counterparts in more well-resourced schools might be receiving. The PhD tutor is tasked with creating a short course, run over a few months, based on their area of doctoral research, but geared towards being taught to younger students.

When presented with the opportunity to apply for this programme, I realised that this might be my only chance at 'curating' and developing the kind of content I really wanted to teach. Having been selected, I created a course called 'Religion and the Law: The Human Right to Freedom of Religion', focusing on Europe and the European Court of Human Rights. My experience of teaching this course has proved to be instrumental in developing what I believe is an anti-racist approach to teaching Law and Religion in International Human Rights Law (or European Human Rights Law), specifically, but also across subjects like Constitutional Law in Ireland and one that I am planning on implementing as a university lecturer in Ireland.

The experience of teaching Freedom of Religion in Irish secondary schools has been revealing in terms of the varied student responses to this anti-racist pedagogical approach, and the differing teaching strategies I had to adopt to help students relate to, and engage in good faith, the questions at hand. This was also informative in terms of my developing a more nuanced way of thinking about teaching religion within law through an anti-racist lens.

Some of the schools I have taught in have had extremely diverse student bodies, often with more than half the class consisting of Black students. Most of these students were from migrant families and said they were preparing to go to college. This is not something I was emotionally prepared for.

Universities in Ireland, despite an ever-increasing diverse student body, are predominantly white. My classrooms have always been white. Intellectually, I was aware that secondary schools in certain areas will have a sizeable non-white student population but I was not prepared for being confronted with predominantly Black and Brown faces staring back at me whilst I teach. Getting used to this meant allowing myself to be more disarmed and vulnerable than I had allowed myself to be in a classroom before, allowing myself to *see* myself in my students and perhaps letting them see themselves in me.

The teachers at these schools, however, were predominantly white (which was unsurprising). This informed the way the students interacted with both me and the material I was teaching them – one of the first things one of the Black students said to me was that she had never been taught by a teacher who was not white. It was noticeable that she was apprehensive about saying this – visible in her body language – her tone also seemed concerned at how I might take this. As Memon and Jivraj (2020) write, '[I]t is no surprise that students experience a sense of dysphoria rather than belonging, without ostensible institutional support and few staff of colour' and I can imagine saying something like this must have felt bold and scary. Questions of race are not common in any classroom in Ireland, let alone one in secondary school.

The course was designed to run over eight weeks, with the first class being an introduction to Human Rights. Usually, this would involve a short lecture with ample opportunity for the students to ask questions, interject as and when they need to. All the classes in this course are meant to be fairly open-ended to allow students to engage as freely as possible with the material, but due to this being introductory, the first tutorial was particularly unstructured, and keeping in mind the age of the students, particularly basic. In one of my predominantly Black classrooms, however, this proved to be a very interesting exercise because as soon as I asked the students what they thought we would be studying, based just on the title of the course and their handbook (a 'book' all tutors are expected to create for each student, aimed at their educational level, with activities, exercises, and detailed explanations of the course content but also how to study for the assessment), the students responded in a way unlike what I was used to. Each girl – unprompted – stood up and at length gave accounts based on news that she had heard on TV, conversations with family elders, neighbours, and her own moral compass on what human rights are; what she believes they are supposed to be; and how the world at large has failed people. All their examples were heavily informed by their racial identity and their experiences of being Black in Ireland. This was mind-blowing to me because the structure of the first tutorial completely changed even in its unstructured form. I could no longer give a lecture, even if I had wanted to, because the class was completely taken over by these students offering first-hand testimony and bringing their identities and evidently epistemological knowledge to the classroom.

These secondary school students had a very clear, well-developed understanding of the concept of human rights, even before we discussed religion. I realised at this point that the way this course would be taught had to change. While I chose not to change the overall learning objective of each tutorial, I decided to restructure each tutorial to begin with what I call Student Testimony. This does not necessarily have to be a personal and involved account of any sort but allows students to start a class discussion and set the tone, which informs the delivery of the content that follows. It sets the narrative for how information is given to them. This became a very effective tool, particularly in the second tutorial when Freedom of Religion was introduced. These students, predominantly from migrant backgrounds, overwhelmingly came from faith-based communities. Many Irish classrooms I have taught in at the secondary school level have been primarily comprised of (often very devout) Christians. This was an interesting challenge because these non-white students had very strongly held personal opinions and convictions about what religion is, what it means to them, their families, their communities, and how their racialised and marginalised communities worship and pray in a relatively homogenous white Ireland. And yet, their faith-based convictions were that of the majority. Even those who did not come from Catholic backgrounds were Christian. For a course that was developed to show how religion as understood by IHRL is heavily Christian, and disadvantages anything else, I was concerned that these students from devout Christian backgrounds would not take this well. However, the aforementioned method of inviting Student Testimony at the start of the class proved to be incredibly useful because these students by virtue of their racialised identity lived in somewhat ghettoised neighbourhoods, which were very religiously diverse. They had friends from many different religious backgrounds, whom they related to by virtue of their shared racial identity. Their 'testimonies' gave them space to voice their anger at how their Muslim friends in school, who wore hijabs that did not conform to the strict rules of uniform, were asked to remove them. They felt this was a gross violation of their friends' right to manifest their religious beliefs freely. Student-led discussions like these at the start of each class allowed a natural springboard towards discussion of seminal case law, which I had chosen to specifically reflect direct or indirect racial inequality or discrimination. The aforementioned cases involving Muslim women's right to veil in public from around Europe were suddenly *personal* for my students.

However, no matter how successful the techniques of Student Testimony, student-led discussion, and student activities could be, these techniques were not uniformly suited to all school environments. I have also taught in extremely under-resourced schools in very socioeconomically disadvantaged neighbourhoods, where the students were predominantly white and Irish, and came from working-class backgrounds with no family history of university attendance, and broadly speaking the students had no interest in university. The students in these environments were mindful of who was teaching them and were happy to learn but would also make it very clear that the reality of the communities they come from is one of anger and hostility at the way the state has left them behind to, as they believe, better accommodate immigrants. (This is a rising sentiment particularly in working-class Dublin neighbourhoods, as seen from the recent protests (late 2022/early 2023) by locals in East Wall and Ballymun against asylum seekers being housed there.) But this was also a cohort of students who were very 'online', very aware of social justice movements on social media, aware of Black Lives Matter, and aware that they were being taught by a Muslim teacher. And while a Catholic ethos did inform their upbringing and had a strong presence in their neighbourhoods, these were students from a community that had a real and sustained anger at the Catholic Church and did not lead with their religious identities. I wanted to follow the same pedagogical approach I had planned to use but was concerned about facing sustained racism and anger fuelled by the anti-immigrant rhetoric I had already heard in the first few minutes of being in such classrooms. Therefore, while I still had student-led classrooms, and still implemented student-led activities, I put in prompts that were meant not to interrupt them but to encourage them to stop for a minute and think. The format remained the same, but I went from being an observer during these classes to being a moderator. By framing the content through a critical class consciousness that nudged the students to think of *who* was making the laws and passing the judgements and critiquing the hegemony of the elite (Kearney and Reynolds, 2016), the students were able to empathise with the religious and racial 'other'. Bringing in an intersectional analysis allowed me to use an anti-racist approach, effectively.

When asked at the end of the course whether my students would consider applying to study Law at university, my Black students overwhelmingly said yes (I do not know whether they actually did apply when the time came but their enthusiasm for the Law not only made this experience more worthwhile for me but I believe accomplishes what the programme sets out to do, at least in spirit – to allow these young people to see themselves pursuing multitudes of paths). My working-class white students, however, were not entirely sold. Most of them said that they did not see the 'point' in going to university, let alone study something like Law and Human Rights, despite finding the topic very interesting. And whilst this is purely anecdotal from my time, since, as an Assistant Professor of Law at one of the largest law schools in the country, I see an exponential rise in ethnic and racial diversity amongst my students, but I do not see the same from within diverse class backgrounds. I believe that an anti-racist pedagogical approach has the potential to make the study of Law, in general, more accessible to students from *all* marginalised backgrounds because of its unique capacity to offer an intersectional dissection of the issues that affect *all* students. We as legal educators owe it to our students to at least try.

Conclusion

For secondary school students, linking our anti-racist classroom to the wider community, as Kishimoto advises, was a theoretical exercise, with discussions around social media campaigns. But the fact that I propose adopting an anti-racist pedagogical approach to university law subjects in *Ireland* is an important point to reflect on. Ireland has always had a strong ethos of resistance whether it be against British imperialism or privatisation by the State (Fletcher, van Heelsum, and Roggeband, 2018), and the substantive content of the law has drastically changed to reflect this over the past century (Cahillane, 2012). The role of religion in law has also had a huge shift (Howlin and Costello, 2021; Rooney, 2021), from anti-colonial struggle centring Catholicism, to strong breaks from religion in the form of constitutional changes (e.g. the recent referendum in 2018 that removed the ban on blasphemy from the Constitution). And while Irish academia and higher education are *very* white, important conversations on 'decolonising the Irish' have started here (Alderson, 2019), this time challenging Irish involvement in British imperialism with our very own version of Rhodes Must Fall in the form of calls to rename Trinity College Dublin's Berkeley Library, named after the philosopher and bishop George Berkeley, a famous enslaver (Trinity's Colonial Legacies Project). With this context in mind, adopting an anti-racist pedagogical approach to teaching *anything*, let alone Freedom of Religion under International Human Rights Law, not only becomes possible but imperative. The connections and points of solidarity across campus and community are many and alive and we must develop them.

References

Ahmed, Sahar, *The Right to Religious Freedom under International Human Rights Law and Islamic Jurisprudence: A Re-Interpretation*, Trinity College Dublin School of Law, 2022.

Al Attar, Mohsen (2022) "'I Can't Breathe': Confronting the Racism of International Law" in Afronomicslaw.org https://www.afronomicslaw.org/2020/10/02/i-cant-breathe-confronting-the-racism-of-international-law/

Adebisi, Foluke, (2019) "Decolonisation & the Law School: Initial thoughts" in African Skies https://folukeafrica.com/decolonisation-the-law-school-initial-thoughts/

Alderson, Aedan, "Decolonizing the Irish: The International Resistance and Entrenchment of the Global Irish Diaspora" [2019] 9 *Studi irlandesi. A Journal of Irish Studies* pp. 369–386.

Butler, Anthea, *White Evangelical Racism: The Politics of Morality in America*, The University of North Carolina Press, Chapel Hill 2021.

Cahillane, Laura "Anti-Party Politics in the Irish Free State Constitution" [2012] 35 *Dublin University Law Journal* [pp.]

Danchin, Peter G, "Islam in the Secular *Nomos* of the European Court of Human Rights" [2011] 32 *Michigan Journal of International Law*.

Evans, Caroline, "Individual and group religious freedom in the European Court of Human Rights: Cracks in the intellectual architecture" [2010] 26(1) *Journal of Law and Religion* pp. 321–343.

Fakhri, Michael, "Questioning TWAIL's Agenda", [2012] 14 *Oregon Review of International Law*.

Fletcher, Cory, van Heelsum, Ana and Roggeband, Conny, "Water privatization, hegemony and civil society: What Motivates Individuals to Protest About Water Privatization?" [2018] 14(3) *Journal of Civil Society*.

Fox, Jonathan, *Thou Shalt Have No Other Gods Before Me: Why Governments Discriminate against Religious Minorities*, Cambridge University Press, Cambridge 2020.

Gathii, James Thuo, "Writing Race and Identity in a Global Context: What CRT and TWAIL Can Learn from Each Other" [2020] 67 *UCLA Law Review* pp. 1610–1648.

Howlin, Niamh and Costello, Kevin (eds), *Law and Religion in Ireland, 1700-1970*, Palgrave MacMillan, London 2021.

Jivraj, Suhraiya, *The Religion of Law: Race, Citizenship and Children's Belongings*, Palgrave MacMillan, New York 2016.

Kishimoto, Kiyoko, "Anti-Racist Pedagogy: From Faculty's Self-Reflection to Organizing within and beyond the Classroom" [2018] 21(4) *Race, Ethnicity and Education* pp. 540–554.

Masuzawa, Tomoko, *The Invention of World Religions, or, How European Universalism was Preserved in the Language of Pluralism*, University of Chicago Press, Chicago, 2005.

Memon, Ahmed Raza and Jivraj, Suhraiya, "Trust, courage and silence: carving out decolonial spaces in higher education through student–staff partnerships" [2020] 54(4) *The Law Teacher* pp. 475–488.

Kearney, Michael and Reynolds, John, "Palestine and the Politics of International Criminal Justice" in *The Ashgate Research Companion to International Criminal Law*, Routledge, Abingdon 2016.

Rooney, James, *Judicial Culture and Social Rights, A Comparative Study of How Social Rights Develop Within Common Law Legal Systems*, Trinity College Dublin School of Law, 2021.

Sen, Rohini, (2020) "Teaching International Law in Asia: The Predicated Pedagogue" in Afronomicslaw https://www.afronomicslaw.org/2020/09/24/teaching-international-law-in-asia-the-predicated-pedagogue/

13

PEDAGOGY AS ADVOCACY

The Role of Anti-Racist and Decolonial Pedagogy in Advancing Social Justice

Gulika Reddy

Introduction

No form of education is politically neutral (Freire, 1968; hooks, 1994). Education has been used as an oppressive tool by those in power—states, institutions, individuals—to hold on to and reinforce power structures. We see this in the way history is taught (or not taught) around the world. There are intentional efforts to use education as a means to teach historical narratives that serve the oppressor and the colonizer. Yet, education can also be a tool for liberation (Jones, 2020, p. 204) and a powerful site of social justice advocacy. It can be a space to address ongoing human rights abuses as well as a space to work toward the prevention of future harms and transform existing power structures. Paulo Freire and bell hooks, for instance, imagine education as a practice through which oppressed people can find liberation. In addition to developing anti-racist and decolonial pedagogies, they also advocated for a broader liberatory project inclusive of anti-capitalism, anti-imperialism, and other efforts that challenge existing power structures. Similarly, the pedagogical examples in this chapter draw on the theories of anti-racist and decolonial pedagogy, as well as other forms of pedagogy, including liberatory pedagogy, critical pedagogy, feminist pedagogy, and identity literacy.

This chapter explores the role of education in addressing discrimination and advancing social justice through two case studies. The first is an example of anti-racist pedagogy in India that would come to inform my legal pedagogy in the United States. It highlights the role of pedagogy in fostering critical thinking and empowering students to prevent and respond to discrimination within and beyond their classrooms. The second explores the potential of a decolonial approach to clinical teaching to both nurture reflective and critical lawyers and

DOI: 10.4324/9781003397885-17

reconfigure power imbalances within the human rights field. It uses examples of how the seminar and clinic projects in two distinct regions allowed students to undertake inner work around identity while contributing to external, systemic change.

While this book is about anti-racist and decolonial legal pedagogy, many of the forms of pedagogy I practiced, particularly in the early years of my career in India, took place long before I heard those words. Over the past several years, I have observed how these forms can be truly embodied to effect change. I have also observed the ways in which they have been co-opted or used as buzzwords but not embodied in actions or practice. While this chapter refers to certain pedagogical terms, the emphasis throughout is on the *purpose and mode* of the teaching and action, rather than the genealogy of specific terms. I say this explicitly to acknowledge the many practitioners and educators I have been fortunate to learn from in the Global South, who engage in creative, reflective, and effective advocacy and pedagogy, and who may use different terms to describe their work and teaching.

Using tools of anti-racist pedagogy to address discrimination in India

The first part of this chapter offers an example of how education can be a space to address the limits of legal interventions. Growing up in India, I felt frustrated by the normalization of discrimination. I imagined the law to be a powerful instrument for social change, and this motivated me to go to law school. I spent the first few years of my career focused on redressing multiple forms of discrimination through litigation, with a specific focus on gender-based violence. While several laws recognize women as equal through the provision of rights to address systemic violence, a patriarchal approach to implementation continues to be pervasive in the judiciary (Menon, 2004, p. 4). This became apparent in my work as a litigator as I witnessed judges suggest that women "adjust" to their abusive circumstances or marry their rapist for a "happy conclusion" (Gowen, 2015). These attitudes reflected deeply entrenched biases that exist in society.

In order to address bias in the judicial system, I conducted capacity-building workshops for lawyers and judges that were designed to build their capacities to address discrimination and bias in the judiciary. At those workshops, it was clear that shifting entrenched attitudes is hard and socialization begins early, so I decided to focus on prevention. I started Schools of Equality, a nonprofit that runs activity-based programs in schools to shift attitudes that perpetuate discrimination. It is a multi-year program that is offered to students from first grade to high school. The program is run by a team of facilitators from across disciplines—including people trained in psychology, education, law, development studies, and social work.

Although our work does not specifically focus on race, our classroom approach is similar to different components of anti-racist pedagogy. Kyoko Kishimoto (2018) describes three elements of anti-racist pedagogy in the context of the United States—(1) including race and inequality in course content, (2) an anti-racist approach to teaching and pedagogy, and (3) anti-racist organizing within campus that is integrated with the local community. These three components have aided Schools of Equality's work toward shifting attitudes and preventing discrimination even in a different geopolitical context where the principal axis of oppression is not race but discrimination based on caste, religion, sexuality, gender, and other dimensions of identity. Discrimination based on skin color in India is widespread, and yet it differs from colorism in the West in the way that it "hides behind various other variables" including religion, caste, and class (Mishra, 2015, p. 725). While the landscape of caste discrimination, racism, and religious exclusion looks different in the varied regions of the subcontinent, scholars have noted the links between them (Chakravarti, 2018; Illaiah, 2005; Anandhi, Jeyaranjan, & Krishnan, 2002). Historically, some groups of people belonging to lower caste groups converted to Christianity, Islam, or Buddhism in the hope of facing less discrimination (Illaiah, 2005; Ambedkar, 1936). However, this did not always happen. Instead, they found themselves at the receiving end of majoritarian violence and exclusion because of the intersection of their identities.[1] Therefore, identity must be understood through an intersectional lens as the failure to do so can further harm already marginalized groups (Crenshaw, 1991). As Kimberlé Crenshaw (1991), a scholar on critical race theory and Black feminist theory, explains, "When one discourse fails to acknowledge the significance of the other, the power relations that each attempts to challenge are strengthened (p. 1282)."

Classroom engagement: Reflecting on identity

There are clear parallels between Kishimoto's first element of anti-racist pedagogy—discussing racial identity and inequality—and the goals of the Schools of Equality curriculum. The curriculum creates spaces in school for students to reflect on and discuss questions of identity particular to the Indian context as well as how inequality manifests for specific populations. Such reflections guide community-led action. Facilitators at Schools of Equality conduct weekly sessions during the school year where students aged 6 to 18 examine and discuss ways to challenge and shift inequalities entrenched in society, such as gender bias, class, caste and racial discrimination, and religious intolerance. The sessions are designed to encourage students from a young age to introspect and examine their own attitudes and unconscious biases and, as a consequence, question and shift notions of power and privilege related to identity.

The second element is an anti-racist approach to teaching. Kishimoto (2018, p. 546) describes how such an approach fosters critical analytical skills, develops students' awareness of their social positions, and creates a sense of community in the classroom. The sessions in the first trimester are designed to do this. The classes are focused on the self, to enable students to examine their own social position and make connections between their lives and the themes discussed in class (Kishimoto, 2018, p. 547). The focus on the individual, and on each student, deepens one's awareness that we are all impacted by and/or implicated in issues related to discrimination, and these are not issues that are external to us. This creates both individual and collective impetus to work toward change.

In one exercise, for instance, students in small groups discuss which of their identities they most strongly identify with and why. Using examples from their lived experiences, they then discuss all the identities that came up in the small group and whether they feel marginalized or privileged due to those aspects of their identity. The purpose of this exercise is to ensure that students approach their reflection and advocacy through an intersectional lens since race, caste, gender, class, and other dimensions of identity often intersect in the context of social hierarchy and inequality (Karn, 2021, p. 357). Advocacy that fails to account for the ways in which multiple forms of identity overlap and intersect in the context of discrimination will not be effective. For instance, colorism in India cannot be addressed without addressing gender and caste (Geetha, 2022), and gender-based violence, as well as access to justice for women, differs based on class, caste, geography, and religion (Dey & Orton, 2016).

We have found that as a result of this and other exercises, students in the class became much more aware of the ways in which their words and actions had harmed others in the class. For instance, students from religious minorities described the harmful impact that the "jokes" made by other students had on them. Students also shared how derogatory comments about the color of their skin as well as caste decreased their sense of safety and belonging. Through these exercises, students examined how social constructs around identity can become the basis of discrimination. The idea that identity is socially constructed is not intended to minimize the challenges associated with it but to draw attention to the fact that such construction is "social and political rather than inherent or static" (Sealey-Ruiz, 2011, p. 26).

When students learned about the harmful impact they had, it led to greater empathy in the classroom. They discussed ways in which these social constructs could be challenged and shifted. This reduced the incidence of discrimination and fostered a stronger sense of community in the schools we work in. This reduction was reported to us both in the form of anonymous surveys students filled out at the end of the program as well as by the school administration and counselors who receive complaints about discrimination and bullying.

An anti-racist approach to teaching also involves decentering authority (Kishimoto, 2018, p. 549). Through the design of the exercise, in which students are in small groups alongside a facilitator, the authority of the facilitator is decentered and peer learning is privileged. The name of our non-profit, Schools of Equality, is itself a play on the term "schools of thought"—intended to create learning environments for students to critically examine issues related to identity based on their own perspectives rather than through prescriptive instruction. In the classroom, we see our role as facilitators, and our goal is to facilitate dialogue and create a container for learning rather than offering instruction (Sethi, 2022, pp. 81–82). This container should ideally be within the "zone of productive disequilibrium" (Heifetz, Linsky, & Grashow, 2009, pp. 32–33). Heifetz et al. (2009) define this zone as an "optimal range" of discomfort, which provides a sense of urgency for people to act and yet is not so overwhelming that it can result in the avoidance of doing difficult but necessary work. The role of a facilitator is to hold space for students to sit with the range of emotions, including discomfort, that might arise as they grapple with their own social positions. In doing this, it is important for the facilitator to account for differing life experiences and trauma in the classroom and acknowledge the fact that these themes have a different impact on each student (Jivraj, 2020, p. 21).

Lastly, anti-racist pedagogy prioritizes humility, self-reflection, and self-awareness on the part of the teacher, particularly as these relate to awareness of their power and positionality (Kishimoto, 2018, p. 551). It is important for educators to undertake internal work as well as seek external training to ensure they are conscious of their own biases (Sethi, 2022, p. 81). With recognition that this is a lifelong process and a necessary precondition to facilitating productive conversations about identity and power, we have weekly facilitator learning circles to allow for ongoing individual and collective reflection.

Effecting change beyond the classroom: Preventing, challenging, and redressing inequalities

Part of the vision of Schools of Equality is creating spaces where students feel empowered with the knowledge and tools necessary to effect change, particularly in a context where the wisdom and imagination of young children is not always leveraged and valued. This pedagogical approach is similar to efforts that move beyond "passive anti-racism" to active efforts seeking change (Wetzel, 2010), and the third component of Kishimoto's definition of anti-racist pedagogy, which involves organizing within and beyond campus. It is also aligned with models of liberatory education that emphasize the importance of not only teaching students about structural oppression but also giving them the space to enable change (Jones, 2020, pp. 205–206).

In the second trimester, sessions are focused on creating rights awareness and examining the impact of social institutions on equality. Human rights education is "insufficient" when it is limited to simply teaching rights (Ahmed, 2014). The curriculum recognizes that it should instead "guide students through experiential human rights education" (Ahmed, 2014), and the final trimester of the curriculum is focused on taking action. It is similar to the element of anti-racist pedagogy that encourages students to apply theory to practice (Kishimoto, 2018, p. 546). In this trimester, students draft their school constitution, plan campaigns, and organize events to help build communities of respect. This allows them to not just be aware of their rights but also take active steps to claim them (Ahmed, 2014) and support others to advocate for their rights.

Students at Schools of Equality have implemented strategies that both address ongoing human rights violations and prevent future harms. They have challenged and changed discriminatory rules in their schools that enforced gendered participation in sports. They have also led successful public education campaigns to shift discriminatory attitudes. These efforts have taken the form of theatre, photo exhibits, art installations, and working with journalists. As an example, some students created an art installation in the city for people to walk through in order to highlight the impacts of street and sexual harassment. Another set of students created graphic novels for children that examine racism and sexism. As a result of such interventions, students have expressed how the arts have served as a way to engage a wider audience in conversations about rights and justice.

While acknowledging that direct intervention is not always feasible and can depend on one's identity and positionality, some students who have witnessed discrimination have powerfully intervened in public and private spaces in order to effect change. One student who noticed harassment on a public bus stepped in, deescalated the situation, and spoke to the conductor to see that the perpetrator was removed from the vehicle. Additionally, parents have recounted how their children have constructively raised and changed power dynamics in the household and initiated discussions about how to prevent and respond to discrimination resulting from multiple, overlapping aspects of identity in their communities. Witnessing students experience internal transformation and advancing external change makes me hopeful about the role of education in promoting just and equitable societies.

Many of the goals of anti-racist pedagogy, including creating spaces for reflection and discussion about identity and power, have informed not just my approach in the classroom in India but also to teaching law school students in the United States how to engage in critically-responsive human rights advocacy.

The potential of decolonial pedagogy to address unequal power dynamics in the human rights field

The human rights field seeks to address systemic and structural oppression caused by power imbalances, and yet these power imbalances are often mirrored within the field. (Knuckey, Reddy, & Parrin, forthcoming). While working in India, I was confronted with how agenda-setting was driven by lawyers rather than community needs. When I moved to the United States, I saw how these concerns were exacerbated in transnational advocate–community relationships, with advocates frequently exerting supremacy over impacted communities as well as Global South advocates. There was an unsettling disconnect between the stated values and practice in the human rights field. While many actors in the Global North know and speak the language of human rights critiques—including failing to engage in client-centered lawyering and unequal power dynamics between international NGOs and local NGOs—their practices and attitudes replicate many of them. This mode of human rights advocacy has "significant negative effects" both on advocates in the Global South and the human rights field (Knuckey, Reddy, & Parrin, forthcoming). Effects include "reproducing hierarchies and undermining fundamental human rights principles of equality and empowerment," which "risks ineffective human rights work that is not adequately tailored to the needs of those directly impacted by abuse" (Knuckey, Reddy, & Parrin, forthcoming).

As I had in India, I turned to educational spaces as a site of advocacy, a space to address this hypocrisy in the human rights field. Over the past four years as a human rights clinician, I have grappled with the question: how can we use a decolonial approach to legal education to nurture reflective, critical lawyers and to reconfigure power imbalances within the human rights field?

Education is an area that has been greatly discussed in decolonization discourse, given its imbrication with coloniality (Shahjahan, Estera, & Surla, 2022, p. 74). Human rights education can be valuable due to its "transformative potential" (Coysh, 2014, p. 89). At the same time, it can be "problematic in the way it can ignore and sustain the political conditions of injustice" (Coysh, 2014, p. 89) and has been the subject of critique (Aldawood, 2020). An important critique is the Eurocentric understanding of human rights knowledge and expertise (Barreto, 2013, p. 3), and treating non-Western knowledge as "simplistic or substandard to Eurocentric knowledge" (Aldawood, 2020, p. 4). This colonization of human rights negatively impacts its ability to serve as a "tool for social transformation" (Aldawood, 2020, p. 5). Curriculum and pedagogy play a central role in formalizing or marginalizing systems of knowledge production (Shahjahan, Estera, & Surla, 2022, p. 74), and therefore education is an important site for decolonization. Decolonization demands an inclusion of "epistemologies, ways of knowing, lived experiences, texts and scholarly work that have been previously excluded from our disciplines" (Adebisi, 2018). A decolonial approach to pedagogy would involve intentionally examining and deconstructing existing hierarchies, and drawing on multiple knowledge systems, "with a particular focus on amplifying the voices currently underrepresented in the curriculum" (Warner, Tran, Arboine, Morrison, & Tran, n.d., p. 3). It is important, however, that making space for alternatives is done in a way that does not further replicate hierarchy through notions of "local-global, researcher-researched, and university-community" (Dutta, 2018, p. 273).

The ways in which human rights is taught—in black-letter law classes and through experiential learning—has the power to reproduce problematic colonial advocacy practices by centering Western knowledge. However, it also has the power to disrupt and replace current modes of harmful practices with a decolonial approach to advocacy that centers the knowledge and expertise of impacted communities. Clinics are experiential law classes where students participate in an intensive skills-based seminar where they learn core human rights skills, which they then apply while working on projects to advance justice globally. Clinics can and should be spaces where decolonial approaches to advocacy are taught and practiced.

Decolonial pedagogy in clinics: Fostering critical thinking, self-reflection, and solidarity

Between 2018 and 2022, I was one of the instructors of the Smith Family Human Rights Clinic at Columbia Law School. During those years, my co-teachers and I thought about how a decolonial approach to pedagogy can strengthen both the syllabus and classroom discussion by constantly questioning who is reflected in the syllabus, how classes are conducted, and how students are evaluated in a way that does not privilege certain forms of education and knowledge.[2]

In our syllabus, we intentionally included different sources of scholarship and knowledge—from academic writing and human rights documents to op-eds and videos from scholars and practitioners around the world. In the seminar, we taught a class on key critiques of the human rights field. One critique is that the human rights movement can depict impacted individuals as "victims" in need of a "savior" (Mutua, 2001) and treat human rights professionals as "heroic" and victims as "passive" (Kennedy, 2002, p. 111). As a result, human rights advocacy can objectify, displace, and disempower impacted individuals and communities (Knuckey et al., 2020). Another critique is that there are "persistent asymmetries" of power between Northern and Southern NGOs, and human rights work can reinforce these power imbalances (Evans & Rodríguez-Garavito, 2018, p. 23) (Knuckey, Reddy, & Parrin, forthcoming). We see these "asymmetries" reflected in several ways, including in terms of which organizations receive the most funding (Klugman, Daniel, Dora, Jallow, & Azambuja, 2017). The purpose of the class was to deepen students' awareness of critiques of the human rights field as well as create space for them to identify ways to mitigate and overcome these pressing critiques in their own advocacy.

As collaborative partnerships are an essential part of human rights advocacy, we also taught a class on human rights partnerships that are built on decolonial approaches and values. It is critical to move beyond Euro-American knowledge and center the power, expertise, knowledge, and agency of marginalized and impacted communities. In class, we collectively examined how to develop strong, equal partnerships with our project partners, and ways in which we could jointly conduct decolonial human rights advocacy.

In addition to discussing field-wide critiques, it is important to create spaces for students and supervisors to look inward and examine our own positionality and identities, how it impacts our work and relationships, and our role as lawyers within the systems in which we work. It is also important to think about our identity and positionality within our classroom. My co-teachers and I started the academic year with a full-day retreat focused on building community through conversations about identity. At this retreat, I introduced some of the exercises from the Schools of Equality curriculum, including the exercise centering identity and lived experience. This reinforced the importance of critical thinking, reflective practice, and empathy. We then discussed two core questions: how can we make sure that everyone feels they can fully embody their identities and participate in the clinic? What are specific things we can actively do or avoid doing? We started the year with this exercise to emphasize the importance of investing in and building relationships to help sustain ourselves while doing human rights work and to create a sense of community within the clinic.

Students have shared that, in contrast to the sometimes isolating and disempowering nature of law school, spaces that foster a sense of community and belonging have a profound impact on their educational experience. It is important, however, to ensure that creating a sense of community is a result of, rather than in tension with, ensuring all students are able to bring their full selves and identities. The purpose of decolonial education is to ensure that educational environments are designed such that all students have the opportunities necessary to thrive (Warner, Tran, Arboine, Morrison, & Tran, n.d., p. 3). One way we addressed the possible tension between individual identity and community was by having explicit conversations about this while co-creating group agreements that set out intentions and guidelines for how the groups would engage with each other. Students included "engaging in productive conflict" as well as "practicing kindness instead of niceness" in their group agreements. They discussed how creating an environment where there is space to have difficult conversations rather than trying to be "nice" and avoiding necessary conflict is one way to ensure that every individual can bring their full selves, which in turn, deepens the overall sense of community.

In addition, my co-supervisors and I developed and taught a class entirely focused on identity. This signals the critical importance of engaging with this theme and underscores the importance of reflecting on one's own identity and positionality as a prerequisite for engaging in ethical and effective advocacy. It also helps challenge the hierarchy of skills law schools can sometimes have that place higher value on technical legal skills as compared to reflective capacities. In one of the classroom exercises, we individually reflected on the ways we have confronted discrimination within and outside law school. We shared a set of readings of other law students describing how they have experienced discrimination in law school and asked students to select an example that resonated with them or to choose a personal experience to reflect on. We also asked them to reflect on how they think the marginalized individual, the perpetrator, and the bystander felt in the example they chose, after which they discussed their individual reflections in small groups. Finally, in a larger group, we discussed the kinds of practices, actions, and behaviors that caused harm. We asked the students to describe in a few words what the specific action or behavior was that caused harm. This process helped build a class-wide understanding of varying types of discriminatory practices—from physical harm to prejudice and stereotyping based on identity.

By unpacking and discussing concrete discriminatory practices, we explored an individual's feelings within a specific moment of harm, to understand the impact of discrimination on that individual and build greater empathy. We discussed why we were having a conversation about feelings, particularly in a law school context—where emotion and feelings are frequently deprioritized—and explained how the ability to make connections between feelings and systemic analysis is an important capacity that human rights advocates need. In developing a greater understanding of the impact of discrimination on individuals, we are better able to respond to their emotions and needs as advocates and allies. It also allows us to understand the harmful impact of our actions or inactions if we are perpetrators or bystanders and change such behavior.

Additionally, while teaching other classes where we focus on human rights skills, it is important to mainstream discussions about identity and highlight the importance of reflecting on one's identity in all aspects of our advocacy. I know from my experience as a lawyer and clinic supervisor that engaging in this form of inner work around identity is a necessary precondition to engaging in human rights work. For example, while working in Kashmir, I have grappled with how my identity as an Indian can, on the one hand, facilitate access to a region that is not open to international researchers and, on the other, present challenges in gaining the confidence of those who are understandably critical of the Indian state's role in the conflict. This has made building trust and deep relationships through honest conversations about identity both critical and rewarding. My teaching therefore prioritizes supporting students in engaging in similar conversations and building strong, lasting relationships with project partners. This is necessary to be able to conduct interviews, human rights investigations, and engage in the forms of advocacy we teach in the seminar.

Decolonial legal practice as critically-responsive advocacy

While teaching critiques and classes on identity, my co-supervisors and I were confronted with a second question: how do you teach students critiques of the human rights field as well as make space for them to undertake inner work around identity in a way that helps them engage in more thoughtful and transformative work but does not result in decreased engagement? While discussing critiques, some students expressed anger and frustration with how the field operates, others expressed a sense of validation, and some expressed feeling "stuck" and unsure of how to navigate the critiques. They saw the critiques as pressing and accurate but were not sure how to mitigate and overcome them. Often the nature of the reaction depended on the identity and lived experiences of the student. My co-teachers and I found that even this feeling of being "stuck"—stemming from well-founded discomfort—was a teaching and learning moment, where it is imperative to build the muscle to sit with the discomfort before moving forward to determine the best course of action. In some situations, there may be an intentional decision not to act, but even this should be made jointly with our project partners and impacted communities.

One way we addressed the need to be both critical and constructive was by teaching the critiques alongside critically-responsive advocacy. This enabled students to grapple with the critiques and think about ethical, transformative, and sustainable modes of action. Collectively engaging in conversations about critiques as well as discussions on identity and power allowed us to focus both on *what* we achieve and *how* we do it—who leads and what values guide our engagement with communities. For instance, my clinic students supported a local women's group[3] to directly engage in advocacy at the UN, which can be rare in international advocacy spaces. In a different conflict-affected region, my students adopted a participatory action research process to ensure the work was community-led. By creating mutual exchange mechanisms throughout the process, students were able to effectively build equal partnerships and work in solidarity with impacted communities.

In the conflict-affected region, students studying in that region shared that their universities deliberately did not allow courses that fostered critical thinking or research as they thought it would lead to resistance against the existing authoritarian regime. I therefore adopted a participatory action research model to enable students in the region to engage in research themselves. This model also helps mitigate the critique that the human rights field is extractive—with advocates flying in and out of contexts to conduct research without crediting the work of local actors. The participatory action research model involves impacted individuals and communities leading the process of producing and using knowledge (Pain, Whitman, & Milledge, n.d., p. 2). This mode of action is decolonial in practice in the way that it centers the knowledge and wisdom of impacted individuals rather than Western actors. My clinic students conducted participatory action research that was led by impacted individuals and communities.[4] This meant that all stages of the research process were led by our partner organizations. The research questions were identified by members of the community, and all the research tools, including the interview guide, focus group guide, and surveys, were jointly developed and implemented by the students and project partners.

Our work with a local women's rights group in a different region resulted from our clinic's desire not to replicate advocate-centered narratives. As a graduate student, I attended a conference at the United Nations Office in Geneva and was struck by the composition of the panels. They were all primarily Global North "experts" speaking about human rights issues in the Global South. When I asked why no one from the regions or communities being discussed was on the panels, an organizer plainly told me that people from those regions do not speak English and that hiring an interpreter would limit the time for discussion. The irony of their response was that the region in question was a former British colony where English is fluently spoken by advocates. Yet, even if that was not the case, their condescending attitude highlighted not only the shameful lack of agency offered to impacted individuals but also revealed the imperialist attitudes with which communities in the Global South are regarded. It also ignored legitimate concerns about whether the motivations of lawyers are truly aligned with those of the communities they "represent." As explained by Spivak, it is worth acknowledging that we see issues related to lack of agency, even in the Global South; there can be a "real epistemic discontinuity" between human rights advocates in the Global South and "those whom they protect" (Spivak, 2004, p. 527). Spivak also explained the role of education in this problem and how the Southern elite are often educated in Western academic institutions (Spivak, 2004, p. 527).

Those running educational spaces have a responsibility to ensure that they are taking active steps to challenge and shift harmful modes of advocacy instead of entrenching these modes of practice. One way to do this in the context of clinics is community-led advocacy. While preparing a speech for a panel at the same UN forum a few years later, I thought about how students could support our partners to write it in their own voice by drawing on Marshall Ganz's public narrative framework. Ganz (2008) describes the importance of individuals telling their own stories: "Telling about a story is different from telling a story. When we tell a story we enable the listener to enter its time and place with us, see what we see, hear what we hear, feel what we feel" (p. 11). Ganz explains the components of a public narrative as follows:

> ...public narrative is composed of three elements: a story of self, a story of us, and a story of now. A story of self communicates who I am – my values, my experience, why I do what I do. A story of us communicates who we are – our shared values, our shared experience, and why we do what we do. And a story of now transforms the present into a moment of challenge, hope, and choice.
>
> *(p. 1)*

Using the broad structure of public narratives offered by Ganz, we asked our local project partner, who leads a women's rights organization questions related to her "story of self." For instance, what motivated her to do the work she did? We also asked about her "story of us"—in what ways had she worked in coalition with other civil society groups in her region, and what were the parallels with similar movements in other parts of the world? And finally, what is the "story of now"? What is she calling on different stakeholders to do, and why now? In what ways could she compel the audience at the UN to act? Through multiple conversations between the students and project partners, we were able to co-write a speech in the words of our project partner, which she then delivered at the UN. Throughout this process, my students learned how to conduct advocacy at the UN as well as how to engage in rightsholder-centered lawyering and support our partners to engage in advocacy themselves. We did this not only for ethical reasons but because the work is much more effective as a result.

Transnational lessons on the role of pedagogy in advancing social justice

As a teacher, I often reflect on how grateful I am to be a part of a classroom that is a space of hope and imagination. I am constantly energized by the ideas each student brings to the classroom, and hopeful when I witness their inner transformation that results from collective learning and unlearning. I am also inspired when I witness the external change students are able to foster alongside impacted communities. However, teaching is something that I happened upon. It was only a few years after practicing as a human rights advocate that I found myself repeatedly turning to education as a space to reimagine the human rights field.

Working alongside students from various age groups and countries, and with different life experiences has taught me some important lessons. The first has been to constantly reflect on the purpose of education, the goals of the human rights field, and how these two can meaningfully intersect. As a teacher, it has been important to ensure that the educational goal of equipping students with a wide range of skills and capacities through experiential learning furthers, rather than impedes, community needs. Adopting an anti-racist and decolonial approach to pedagogy enables necessary alignment between community needs and student learning goals. When we operate at the intersection of these goals, we are able to nurture empowered, reflective, and creative advocates who engage in ethical, innovative, and community-centered advocacy.

The second lesson is the need to ensure that conversations about identity and power are not limited to a theoretical discussion about anti-racism or decolonization but instead inform how students interact with each other and the communities they work with. It is critical to create a classroom environment where everyone is able to bring their full selves (Aryee-Price, Fernandez, & Rogers, 2020, p. 217) and fully participate (Sturm, Eatman, Saltmarch, & Bush, 2011, p. 5). These conversations about identity and power, while sometimes challenging, are necessary to create such an environment. They also have a transformative impact on relationships in the classroom and with project partners, which in turn has a significant impact on the effectiveness of the work.

The third and most important lesson is the need to embody anti-racist and decolonial values rather than just talking about them. It is critical to ensure that those values are practiced within the classroom and reflected in who is in the classroom, whose scholarship is discussed (Rigney, 2020, pp. 514–515; Jivraj, 2020, p. 21), who teaches, what is taught, what is valued and incentivized, what methods of evaluation are used, and how power plays out in the classroom (Jivraj, 2020, p. 21). In embodying anti-racist and decolonial principles, we can ensure that our values are mirrored in our work toward greater equity in legal education, the practice of law, and in the communities we are a part of, and work alongside.

Acknowledgements

Assistant Professor and Director of the International Human Rights and Conflict Resolution Clinic, Stanford Law School. Many thanks to Makina Moses, Anjli Parrin, Benjamin Hoffman, Sarah Knuckey, Archana Venkatesh, Radhika Santhanam, Anchita Dasgupta, Nabila Khan, Shanna Ramadhanti, Elias Passas, Emily Ekshian, Katie Siler, Taryn Marks, Rachel Shields, Aneliese Castro, Kai Wiggins, Jenny Moroney, and Andrés Suarez. I am incredibly grateful to my students, project partners, and co-teachers with whom I have had countless conversations about various themes in this chapter over the years. I am also very grateful to the editors of this book for their generous and thoughtful comments. This one is for Nanu, my grandfather.

Notes

1 This is clear from the fact that the category "Dalit Christian" and "Dalit Muslim" exists in the Indian census.
2 This part of the chapter refers to my work at Columbia Law School where I was a Clinical Teaching Fellow (2018–2020), Senior Clinical Teaching Fellow (2020–2021), and the Acting Director (2021–2022) of the Smith Family Human Rights Clinic.
3 The location is kept anonymous for security reasons.
4 The location is kept anonymous for security reasons.

References

Adebisi, F. I. (2018, May 7). Retrieved from African Skies: https://folukeafrica.com/decolonization-law-race-the-legal-curriculum-slsa-2018/

Ahmed, K. (2014, May 5). *Rethinking human rights education.* Retrieved from Mail & Guardian: https://mg.co.za/article/2014-03-05-rethinking-human-rights-education/
Aldawood, D. (2020). Decolonizing approaches to human rights and peace education higher education curriculum. *International Journal of Human Rights Education*, 3(1), 1–31.
Ambedkar, B. R. (1936). *1891-1956. Annihilation of Caste: An Undelivered Speech.* New Delhi: Arnold Publishers, 1990.
Anandhi, S., Jeyaranjan, J., & Krishnan, R. (2002). Work, Caste and Competing Masculinities: Notes from a Tamil Village. *Economic and Political Weekly*, 4397–4406.
Aryee-Price, A. O., Fernandez, M. C., & Rogers, C. (2020). Not Just in February! Reflection Questions to Make Black Lives Matter Every Day in Your Classroom. In D. Jones, & J. Hagopian, *Black Lives Matter at School: An Uprising for Educational Justice* (pp. 214–218).
Barreto, J.-M. (2013). *Human Rights from a Third World Perspective: Critique, History and International Law.* Cambridge Scholars Publishing.
Chakravarti, U. (2018). *Gendering Caste: Through a Feminist Lens.* SAGE Publications Pvt Ltd.
Coysh, J. (2014). The Dominant Discourse of Human Rights Education: A Critique. *Journal of Human Rights Practice*, 6(1), 89–114.
Crenshaw, K. (1991). Mapping the Margins: Intersectionality, Identity Politics, and Violence against Women of Color. *Stanford Law Review*, 43, 1241–1299.
Dey, A., & Orton, B. (2016). Gender and Caste Intersectionality in India: An Analysis of the Nirbhaya Case, 16 December 2012. In *Gender and Race Matter: Global Perspectives on Being a Woman (Advances in Gender Research, Vol. 21)* (pp. 87–105). Bingley: Emerald Group Publishing Limited.
Dutta, U. (2018). Decolonizing "Community" in Community Psychology. *American Journal of Community Psychology*, 62, 272–282.
Evans, P., & Rodríguez-Garavito, C. (2018). Introduction: Building and Sustaining the Ecosystem of Transnational Advocacy. In *Transnational Advocacy Networks: Twenty Years of Evolving Theory and Practice* (pp. 8–24). Bogotá, Colombia: Dejusticia.
Freire, P. (1968). *Pedagogy of the Oppressed.* 30th anniversary ed. New York: Continuum, 2000.
Ganz, M. (2008). *What Is Public Narrative?* https://changemakerspodcast.org/wp-content/uploads/2017/09/Ganz-WhatIsPublicNarrative08.pdf
Geetha, U. (2022, August 2). *Colourism, Gender, and Caste: Skin Colour Shaming Is Intersectional and Cannot Be Addressed in Isolation.* Retrieved from Feminism in India: https://feminisminindia.com/2022/08/02/colourism-gender-caste-skin-colour-shaming-is-intersectional/
Gowen, A. (2015, July 9). *Why an Indian judge thinks rapists should marry their victims.* Retrieved from The Washington Post: https://www.washingtonpost.com/world/asia_pacific/why-an-indian-judge-thinks-rapists-should-marry-their-victims/2015/07/08/606f8998-23e5-11e5-b621-b55e495e9b78_story.html
Heifetz, R., Linsky, M., & Grashow, A. (2009). *The Theory Behind the Practice: A Brief Introduction to the Adaptive Leadership Framework.* Harvard Business Press.
hooks, b. (1994). *Teaching to Transgress: Education as the Practice of Freedom.* New York: Routledge.
Illaiah, K. (2005). *Why I Am Not a Hindu.* Samya.
Jivraj, S. (2020). *Towards Anti-racist Legal pedagogy: A Resource.* https://research.kent.ac.uk/decolonising-law-schools/wp-content/uploads/sites/866/2020/09/Towards-Anti-racist-Legal-Pedagogy-A-Resource.pdf

Jones, D. N. (2020). The Black Lives Matter at School Pedagogy. In D. Jones, & J. Hagopian, *Black Lives Matter at School : An Uprising for Educational Justice*. Haymarket Books.

Karn, K. (2021). Gendered Racism in India. *International Journal of Law Management & Humanities*, 4(2), 355–364.

Kennedy, D. (2002). The International Human Rights Movement: Part of the Problem? *Harvard Human Rights Journal*, 15, 101–125.

Kishimoto, K. (2018). Anti-racist pedagogy: from faculty's self-reflection to organizing within and beyond the classroom. *Race Ethnicity and Education*, 21(4), 540–554.

Klugman, B., Daniel, R., Dora, D., Jallow, M., & Azambuja, M. (2017, December 4). *Addressing Systemic Inequality in Human Rights Funding*. Retrieved from Open GlobalRights.

Knuckey, S., Hoffman, B., Perelman, J., Reddy, G., Ancheita, A., & Jain, M. (2020). Power in Human Rights Advocate and Rightsholder Relationships: Critiques, Reforms, and Challenges. *Harvard Human Rights Journal*, 33, 1–55.

Knuckey, S., Reddy, G., & Parrin, A. (forthcoming). *Decolonizing Human Rights Advocacy*. Oxford University Press.

Menon, N. (2004). *Recovering Subversion: Feminist Politics beyond the Law*. Orient Blackswan.

Mishra, N. (2015). India and Colorism: The Finer Nuances. *Washington University Global Studies Law Review*, 14(4), 725–750.

Mutua, M. (2001). Savages, Victims, and Saviors: The Metaphor of Human Rights. *Harvard International Law Journal*, 42, 201–245.

Pain, R., Whitman, G., & Milledge, D. (n.d.). *Participatory Action Research Toolkit: An Introduction to Using PAR as an Approach to Learning*. Research and Action.

Rigney, S. (2020). Creating the Law School as a Meeting Place for Epistemologies: Decolonising the Teaching of Jurisprudence and Human Rights. *The Law Teacher*, 54, 503–516.

Sealey-Ruiz, Y. (2011). Learning to Talk and Write about Race: Developing Racial Literacy in a College English Classroom. *English Quarterly*, 42(1), 24–42.

Sethi, R. A. (2022). Reflective Journal: Curricular Deficits, Pedagogical Challenges and Constructing Community in a Non-Traditional Law School Class. *Roger Williams University Law Review*, 27(1), 57–88.

Shahjahan, R. A., Estera, A. L., & Surla, K. L. (2022). "Decolonizing" Curriculum and Pedagogy: A Comparative Review Across Disciplines and Global Higher Education Contexts. *Review of Educational Research*, 92(1), 73–113.

Spivak, G. (Spring/Summer 2004). Righting Wrongs. *The South Atlantic Quarterly*, 103(2/3), 523–581.

Sturm, S., Eatman, T., Saltmarch, J., & Bush, A. (2011). *Full Participation: Building the Architecture for Diversity and Community Engagement in Higher Education*.

Warner, C., Tran, D., Arboine, J., Morrison, C., & Tran, D. (n.d.). *Decolonising Pedagogy and the Curriculum*. https://www.arts.ac.uk/__data/assets/pdf_file/0035/228986/AEM-Decolonising-pedagogy-and-the-curriculum-PDF-224KB.pdf

Wetzel, M. M. (2010). 'That Really Hit Me Hard': Moving beyond Passive Anti-racism to Engage with Critical Race Literacy Pedagogy. *Race Ethnicity and Education*, 13(4), 449–471.

PART IV

Socio-legal Education

Designing Subjects That Address Complicities of Law with Power

14

INSPIRING ANTI-RACIST LAWYERS THROUGH CLINICAL LEGAL EDUCATION

Sumayyah Malna

Introduction

Clinical legal education (CLE) provides an ideal forum in which to surface anti-racist legal practice in higher education. Its proximity to the profession via live pro bono casework (supervised by qualified lawyers) and academic consideration of social justice means that students are engaged in considering access to and administration of justice on both a micro level (for their client) and on a macro level (for whole communities). Critical consideration of the impact of laws and policies on marginalised groups is integral to CLE's pro bono legal offering.

Through this chapter, I will provide reasoning for inspiring the anti-racist lawyers of the future through CLE, from a UK perspective. I will consider the importance of teaching critical race theory ("CRT") as part of the CLE curriculum. I will demonstrate how CLE allows students the opportunity to analyse law, policies, and practices through an anti-racist and intersectional lens that can identify discriminatory outcomes of measures that do not overtly appear to be so. CLE provides space for reflection on difficult issues such as personal racial biases and is well-placed to equip students with the tools to deconstruct these. It allows students to examine the impact of systemic and judicial racism on the actors within the legal system and consider potential anti-racist legal, policy, and institutional solutions. Students have the chance to critically consider whether the government provides sufficient resources to ensure meaningful participation and representation of racialised minorities – for all actors within the system – whether they are the defendant, the lawyer, the victim, or the judge.

Racialised minorities experience drastically different outcomes in our experience with the justice system than our white counterparts. For instance, we are

DOI: 10.4324/9781003397885-19

an over-represented population throughout the criminal justice system, more likely to be stopped and searched, remanded in custody at the Crown Court, and disproportionately represented in prisons. Harrowingly, almost half of all homicide victims aged 15–17 are Black (Ministry of Justice, 2020). Elsewhere, the coronial system deals with a significantly disproportionate number of deaths of people of colour in police custody where restraint or use of force is a feature or where mental-health-related issues are a feature (INQUEST, 2022).

Within the civil landscape, medical lawyers practise in an arena where Black mothers are four times more likely to die in childbirth (MBRRACE-UK, 2021) with ethnic inequalities also evident across mental health services, and within the NHS workforce itself (NHS Race and Health Observatory, 2022). There is evidence of race disparities in immigration detention, with 90% of Australian nationals being released before spending 28 days in detention, in comparison to 40% of Jamaican nationals and 60% of Nigerian nationals (Runnymede, 2021). Within the legal profession itself, Black and Asian people make up only 18% of the profession, yet 35% of those who were hauled through the disciplinary tribunal were from these communities (Hyde, 2020).

Racialised minorities also make up a significant proportion of those who seek pro bono services in the UK. LawWorks (2021) reports that 53% of pro bono clients were from the "Black and minority ethnic community" in stark contrast with Census data (2011), which found that only 13% of the population identified as "Black, Asian, Mixed or Other ethnic group". Clearly, there is an issue to be addressed regarding why racialised minorities find themselves at much greater need of pro bono legal services than the white population. This is perhaps partially explained by data from the House of Commons Research Briefing on poverty in the UK, which found that, after housing costs, 55% of Bangladeshi households and 47% of Pakistani households were in poverty. For Black families, this figure is 40%. Only 19% of white households find themselves in poverty after housing costs are applied (Francis-Devine, 2021).

Given University law clinics provide 48% of the pro bono legal services in England and Wales (Sandbach and Grimes, 2020), CLE is well-placed to provide space for students to consider access to justice for communities (Nicolson, 2015), as exposure to real clients allows students to gain an awareness of the obstacles many face in obtaining legal representation. Indeed, student representation via law clinics is likely to be a means of last resort for many clients who cannot afford private legal representation and who do not qualify for Legal Aid. Being exposed to social injustices (inherent in the provision of pro bono legal advice in a state where government provision of Legal Aid is lacking) provides a gateway to "social justice movement lawyering" (Sandbach and Johnson, 2019).

Kendi's (2019) well-established definition of anti-racism provides a simple starting point for students to acknowledge and understand the existence of racial disparities in the system. He contrasts racist policies and anti-racist policies ("policies" here including laws) and goes even further to state no policy (and therefore no laws) are race-neutral, giving formal definition to the way that certain laws and policies disproportionately discriminate against racialised minorities. He writes,

> A racist policy is any measure that produces or sustains racial inequity between racial groups. An antiracist policy is any measure that produces or sustains racial equity between racial groups. By policy, I mean written and unwritten laws, rules, procedures, processes, regulations, and guidelines that govern people. There is no such thing as a nonracist or race-neutral policy. Every policy in every institution in every community in every nation is producing or sustaining either racial inequity or equity between racial groups.

As bell hooks (1994) wrote, we should have the "willingness to be responsible, not to pretend that [we] do not have the power to change the direction of our students' lives". Our classrooms are places of possibilities, where we should demand of everyone "an openness of mind and heart that allows us to face reality even as we collectively imagine ways to move beyond boundaries, to transgress". In them sit the future judges, policy makers, and senior partners whose actions will mould both the law and the system. The opportunities are there for teachers of CLE to advance the progression of anti-racism through our teaching practice, by inspiring the next generation of anti-racist lawyers, and, ultimately, contributing to the construction of an anti-racist justice system.

CLE: A unique space for anti-racist practice in legal education

CLE is, broadly, the study of the law through the experiential learning methods offered through university law clinics (via live or simulated cases), often alongside associated lectures and seminars. Students undertake pro bono legal work under professional supervision, with guidance and feedback given on the dynamics and details of running each case. Despite this common underpinning, university law clinics vary widely. Some are education-oriented (where the education of students is the ultimate priority); others are social justice-oriented (where the unmet legal needs of the local community are the ultimate priority) (Nicolson, 2006). The type of clinical activity undertaken also varies widely; from advice-only clinics to full representation, and including specialist clinical projects, placements, or StreetLaw endeavours (Kerrigan and Murray, 2011).

CLE's constructivist approach to teaching provides a unique opportunity to expose students to anti-racist thought which will stay with students and form part of their identities as future lawyers in three ways. First, through the deeper learning that the experiential learning model provides; second, through the overt use of reflective practice; and third, through the opportunity it provides to critically analyse justice in practice.

The pedagogical benefits of live case experience are well established, allowing students to transcend the lower levels of learning (remembering, understanding, applying), and reach the higher levels (analysing, evaluating, creating) (Bloom, 1979). Kolb's (1984) experiential learning theory further underlines the benefits, as acting as an advisor to a real client allows knowledge to be created "through the transformation of experience". Kolb considers there is a cycle of concrete experience (interviewing a client, researching the law, providing advice), reflective observation (considering their role, what went well, what did not, and why), abstract conceptualisation (learning from the experience, considering their experience in light of relevant theories, drawing conclusions), and active experimentation (trying out what was learned with their next case – or when they enter the profession).

Placing students in a complicated case context enables them to gain competencies that the sole analysis of abstract legal doctrine does not offer (Givelber et al., 1995), such as proactive problem-solving, conflict management, and empathetic approaches to client communication (Giddings and Weinberg, 2020). Accessing these skill sets whilst fostering this deeper level of learning as the norm leads students to adopting a "mindset of questioning, rather than unthinking acceptance" (Coper, 2010), priming students well for critical theoretical thought during classroom discussions.

Reflecting upon an experience is essential in order to transform that experience into learning, before it is lost or forgotten (Boud, Keogh and Walker, 1985), and indeed forms part of Kolb's learning cycle. Reflective practice is a significant part of CLE, often forming part of formative or summative assessments. Students are encouraged to reflect on their actions and the progress of their cases, including reflection on ethical issues and the wider legal landscape. Life-long learning is established through self-awareness, examination of assumptions, and critical evaluation of students' own responses to their casework (Finlay, 2008), with the student then using these insights to improve their future work. Providing specific space for students to undertake such metacognitive thought – particularly relating to assumptions, biases, and conceptions of self – naturally indicates an ideal provision of space for anti-racist thought.

CLE often provides students with the opportunity to critically analyse justice in practice through consideration of – for instance – theoretical bases of social justice, or access to justice and the role that law clinics play in these contexts. There is space to take this much further to ensure that the CLE curriculum is adequately integrating anti-racist thought and practice into its curriculum. Two of the potential ways I consider this can be done are as follows:

1. Using CRT to understand the client, the self, and the system.
2. Critically considering the impact of judicial racism and lack of diversity within the judiciary.

Using CRT to understand the client, the self, and the system

In considering a move towards anti-racism, law clinics mapping critical race theory onto clinical pedagogy is essential in order for students to truly appreciate the impact of race on clinic clients (Hayat, 2021). The aim of CRT is to ensure that the importance and impact of race are fully appreciated by society and that any discussion of rights gives due credence to the rights of oppressed communities. One of its primary pillars is therefore the acceptance of the existence of racism and that racism is the standard, lived, daily experience of racialised minorities. Other essential pillars are that race is a social construct which has no biological or genetic basis and that systemic white-dominance benefits both the white working class and white elites – whether that is psychically or materially (Delgado et al., 2017).

Given that race is a central factor in understanding a client's experience of the law (Russell, 1992), curricula dealing with justice which consider class as the sole vector of oppression for clinic clients are limited and fail to fully appreciate how race and class intersect (Crenshaw, 1991) to determine outcomes for clients and wider communities. There are missed opportunities for future lawyers to consider race as a defining factor in the way in which racialised minorities experience the justice system. Without presenting these opportunities responses to issues raised in discussions are likely to be white-centric. Given the way CLE establishes a solid basis for the furtherance of social justice once students enter the profession (Byron, 2014), this is a significant omission – particularly when considering equal justice as "central to the legitimacy of the democratic process" (Rhode, 2004). An intersectional and anti-essentialist approach is necessary to ensure the impact of race is recognised, and the voices of racialised minorities are not silenced (Harris, 1990); any other approach would be racist.

The theoretical frameworks provided by CRT should be used to assist students in their reflective thought – acknowledging and deconstructing biases, assumptions, and norms – and to provide an academic basis upon which to understand clients as complex and unique beings, existing within a system of hierarchies and inequity (Goldfarb, 1992). An anti-racist approach to clinical practice would necessarily involve the recognition that legal systems and doctrine are not infallible and that certain laws and policies perpetuate racial inequity.

Students of CLE are in a unique position where they are not just learning about the law and theory, they are actioning it, and creating solutions for their client – which necessarily indicates the deeper levels of learning reached through clinical practice. Understanding and applying CRT is therefore essential to developing anti-racist lawyers. I consider two potential ways in which to do this within the CLE curriculum below: encouraging and allowing space for metacognitive thought to allow students to deconstruct their own assumptions on race, and teaching interest convergence and surfacing understanding of racialised paternalism.

Metacognitive thought and deconstructing assumptions

The way in which CRT involves considering clients in their own unique context will contribute to the development of greater empathy and client-centredness in running cases (Johnson, 2005). In considering integrating critical theories (to include CRT and feminist legal theory) into CLE, Johnson proposes students undergo a case simulation, supported by scholarly readings. In promoting anti-racist practice, readings on CRT will be crucial in shaping the student's approach. The aim is to prompt students to reflect on the way they run the "case", target the assumptions and biases that they hold, and identify the subsequent impact on the case. The exercise also prompts critical analysis of legal and governmental organisations and provides the opportunity for students to reflect on power, privilege, and agency (as student advisors and future lawyers). Taking inspiration from Johnson, I have taught this in the past through facilitating role plays of an initial client interview, followed by analysis of two bits of evidence: one a statement of the client and the other a report of the local council. I then prompt a discussion on which piece of evidence the students thought was more reliable, and why they might hold these thoughts, along with the reflective discussion aimed at targeting assumptions and biases, mentioned above.

Unlike Johnson, however, I propose that the race of the simulated client should not be ambiguous; it should be as clear upon reading the simulation instructions as it would be in practice. Otherwise, the simulation fails to centre race as a key concept which influences the lawyer/client relationship and the client's experiences with the justice system – and therefore is limited in its ability to strengthen anti-racist thought and practice. Without centring race in this way, there is a lack of overt space for students to critically analyse racist policies or actions of the institutions involved in the case, or to specifically direct their attention to reflecting on the way race influences the power dynamics with the lawyer/client relationship as well as within the legal system itself.

Surfacing more than one vector of oppression for the simulated client provides students with an example-based opportunity to consider the marginalised intersections the client occupies; particularly how those marginalised by race and class have fallen victim to measures of austerity that have drastically curtailed access to justice (Adebisi and Jivraj, 2021). Using a simulated (or real client) example provides an opportunity for students to move away from abstract discussion and consider concrete examples of how racism and capitalism disproportionately impact those who require access to justice.

Teachers can, of course, surface race as an issue within reflective discussion, even if it is not explicitly referred to in a simulation. This may be an inherently more difficult approach as we, as a society, struggle to talk about and address our own assumptions about race; no one wants to openly admit to racial biases or racist thought. Teachers and students alike, despite best intentions, may well limit discussions on race for fear of creating uncomfortable learning environments and steer the conversations towards a topic they are more comfortable discussing, such as class. bell hooks' view is that teachers should not be encouraging students to take risks in confessing in the classroom if teachers themselves are not willing to do. She considers this to be coercive use of power (hooks, 1994).

Being able to identify our assumptions on race is essential to anti-racist lawyering. It is only in accepting the existence of these assumptions that we are able to suitably deconstruct them and create an oppositional dialogue – otherwise, we continue to perpetuate cycles of racial inequality and feed into racialised power hierarchies. Without surfacing this line of thought, we are preventing our students from accessing introspective and metacognitive thought processes to enable them to identify and deconstruct the assumptions they hold. A future lawyer who considers they have absolutely no biases or assumptions on race is only going to perpetuate structural inequalities. Pedagogical thought has continually demonstrated the value in reflective thought converting experience into learning, and, in the experiential learning context of CLE, the opportunity for serious reflection on racial biases and the impact on the student's relationship with the client, as well as the client's relationship with the legal system, presents itself well.

That said, teachers should be careful of the nature of their learning environments before introducing thought on personal racial biases and assumptions (their own or the students'). The classroom environment would require a strong degree of trust between all present to enable everyone to feel secure in the conversation. This may necessarily depend on how far into the course CRT is taught, the size of the class, and the relationships between the students themselves. Without an environment that fosters trust, students of colour may well feel triggered, further marginalised, or "othered" upon hearing the biases and assumptions held by their teachers and peers. Regard should be given to the fact one in four students experience racial harassment at university (EHRC, 2019), which adds another difficult layer to combat when considering the pedagogy of teaching CRT within CLE.

The way forward may be to open discussions on assumptions and biases held by people *generally*, including analysis of structural inequalities within the legal system within the classroom, with reflection on *personal* biases and assumptions done privately, or anonymously via reflective journals to ensure they suitably deep and genuine to be deconstructed. Open classroom discussions on race may prevent this sufficiently deep reflection.

Peters and Bryant (2014) address the difficulties in talking about race. They consider there are three principles for teachers to adhere to when discussing race in a clinical setting:

1. Embrace tension as an inevitable and constructive part of the learning process.

2. Create non-judgemental environments, attribute meaning according to the speaker's intention (rather than the listener's perception), and give everyone the chance to be heard.
3. Choose the direction of discussion, cultivate it in a way that furthers racial justice, and take responsibility for that choice.

Their detailed delve into these principles is worth reading for any teacher serious about instigating conversations on race safely and effectively.

Building on Bryant's (2001) article "The Five Habits: Building Cross-Culture Competence in Lawyers", Bryant and Peters (2022) have provided suggested teaching materials to assist in teaching a critical approach to CLE. The use of their Doubting/Believing spectrum – first, At Rest – categorising example of belief and doubt on a numerical scale of 0–100, and then, In Motion – using simulated case scenarios – may provide a way to incrementally encourage students towards a mindset open enough to truly examine personally held biases and assumptions. Peters and Bryant acknowledge some of the limitations in open class discussion in this respect and suggest students note down their own positions on the scale privately. Their suggested approaches and materials for teaching about cross-cultural lawyering in CLE (which summarising here would do no justice) also provide many opportunities for students to reflect on their own identities, how this relates to the client, the impact on lawyering, and the context and system within which they both find themselves.

In summary, teachers should facilitate the following: prompting discussion on race, centre race as a significant factor influencing lawyering, provide a toolkit via CRT to talk about and analyse it, encourage reflection on both generally held biases (in class) and personally held biases (via reflective journal), and instil confidence in critiquing systems of powers.

Interest convergence and racialised paternalism

Students of CLE should give due consideration to the autonomy/paternalism spectrum; to what extent is it acceptable for clinical advisors to make decisions for their clients? A paternalistic approach may well further the client's interests – but lawyers may also be paternalistic in order to pursue their own interests or those of other parties or communities (Nicolson and Webb (1999). Power dynamics between student advisors and clients will vary depending on the unique make-up of the social groups within which they both sit (including race).

Hierarchies of race and paternalistic action go hand in hand, in that there is dominant group (white people) and a subordinate group (all other racialised people) (Jackman, 1994). Racialised paternalism means that the white dominant group aims to improve outcomes for the subordinate group, but that there is a belief that the subordinate group is unable to improve their own outcomes without the dominant group's interference (Moore, 2020). Translating this into the lawyer/client relationship with a CRT lens, a white lawyer will be more likely to act paternally where their client is a person of colour.

A hierarchy of race means that some racialised groups will find themselves at a higher level of the hierarchy than other racialised groups. It is those groups who are considered "model minorities", or who have a greater proximity to whiteness who will find themselves in these higher echelons. What this means is that a lawyer of colour is not exempt from racialised paternalism; they can still be impacted by racial biases and act comparatively more paternal to a client from a different racial group to one they themselves inhabit.

"White saviourism" is a term that is traditionally used to explain the phenomenon of white people travelling to countries in the Global South with a view to aiding and improving outcomes for the communities they travel to. Although intentions may seem pure, white saviourism is form of racism – borne from constructions of white supremacy. It presumes that those who are white and privileged can save those who are Brown or Black. White saviours are intrinsically paternalistic in their offerings of help – often ignoring the socioeconomic, political, and geographical reasons for oppression. The issue of white saviourism informing racialised paternalism should be raised in a clinical context, given that over half of all clinical clients are racialised minorities. Students should see the difference in paternally running a case presuming it helps a subordinated client versus allowing the client autonomy to run it in conjunction with them. Not all CLE students are white, but the application of racial hierarchies (as above) nonetheless applies. Teachers should facilitate students' conception of the lawyer/client relationship – prompting reflection on white saviourism in a clinical context and encouraging deconstruction of presumptions that students are in a better position than their clients and hence able to "save" them.

Reflection and deconstructing assumptions are essential precursors to anti-racist practice when decision-making on a clinical case. Considering the appropriate position on the autonomy/paternalism spectrum for each client would necessarily involve accepting the existence of racialised paternalism and white saviourism, examining biases and assumptions as set out above, reflecting on actions taken, and moulding future behaviour in light of this. When reflecting on autonomy and paternalism, students should also be exposed to the concept of interest convergence (Bell, 1980) and how this interacts with racialised paternalism to influence the actions that an individual may make but also the actions of institutions in implementing racist laws and policies. Case simulations can be used within the CLE classroom to address both of these points or reflective discussion on students' current live cases.

Interest convergence is the concept that "the interest of blacks in achieving racial equality will be accommodated only when it converges with the interests of whites" (Bell, 1980). Common law judgements and development of law and policy will therefore only promote equality when they serve the purposes of the white dominant group. Lawton (2015) extrapolates this theory into a clinical context alongside consideration of the theory of granting power. The theory of granting power raises the question as to whether power is truly granted if those who grant the power retain the ability to remove it. Students therefore become members of the group of power when enabling clients to reach desired legal outcomes by assisting with their cases. Lawton considers several questions when considering her position of power when supporting clients on housing cases:

> …do I ever really relinquish my shared power particularly when I, as their counsel, determine what information is sufficient for them to make a well-informed decision? Or, am I, as a member of a group with influence, willing to assist low- and moderate-income individuals to become homeowners because our interests now converge?

Taken together these theories raise several themes to be explored in CLE classes:

1. Understanding autonomy, paternalism, racialised paternalism, and white saviourism, and reflecting on one's own assumptions and actions and working to deconstruct them.
2. Considering whether favourable outcomes for clinical clients are only reached when student and client interests converge.
3. Considering whether student/client interest convergence with a client of colour influences the extent to which lawyering is paternalistic.
4. Considering interest convergence and racialised paternalism in relation to government-granted legal aid.
5. Considering whether law clinics can contribute to racial equity or whether they are perpetuating it by the very provision of pro bono support.

At the centre of these discussions should be the main pillars of CRT and the understanding of Kendi's definition of racist policies.

Critically considering the impact of judicial racism and lack of diversity within the judiciary

CRT's central tenet that racism exists and is an ordinary daily experience of people of colour naturally leads to the proposition of racism within the judiciary. The Lammy Review (2017) was instrumental in bringing to light the real impact of judicial racism on outcomes for people of colour in the criminal justice system. Lammy found racial disparities in magistrates' verdicts and sentencing decisions, although, interestingly, found that racism did not appear to have substantial impact on the decisions of juries (he essentially theorises that the difference in viewpoints and the prolonged group discussions leads to, what CRT would call, the deconstruction of assumptions). Other, more recent publicly commissioned reports have underlined the continuing existence of judicial racism and the lack of attempt in any qualitative investigation by the relevant organisations to strive for change, despite being faced with harrowing statistics such as BAME offenders being 240% more likely to receive a prison sentence (Brown, 2022).

Barrister Leslie Thomas KC talks at length on the manifestations of judicial racism in practice, including the racial disparities in the criminal court and the use of racialised evidence, judicial decisions which silence race where Black people are victims, and the legal profession itself (Thomas, 2021). His lecture (available publicly on YouTube) is a fantastic resource for introducing the concept to students in a way that grounds it in practice-based examples.

Classroom discussions on judicial racism should flow naturally from any of the proposed pedagogical methods discussed in this chapter and arguably should form an essential part of CLE if we are indeed shaping the minds of the future judiciary. Racial biases are often internalised, rather than conscious, and therefore fail to be acknowledged by judges who are unaware of their presence (Lawrence, 1987). This is why metacognitive thought is so essential to anti-racist practice.

Discussions on judicial racism should be underpinned by readings on formalism, legal realism, and racial realism, to provide suitable theoretical frameworks to support academic thought. Formalism is the concept that laws are a priori neutral, and objective, and judges can therefore apply them with consistent outcomes, whereas a legal realist approach would consider that case outcomes would be influenced by the judge's values, assumptions, and biases (Bix, 2019). Bell's (1992) concept of racial realism goes further, by determining that formalist models accept the current racial power structure as proper, which would subsequently lead to racialised minorities never truly having their legal rights upheld. Judges preserve the racially unequal status quo and make case decisions which continue to subordinate racialised minorities.

Although Lammy and Brown both cite lack of diversity within the judiciary as an issue in the racial disparities they unearthed, Genn (2010) considers that the two matters are unrelated. I disagree with Genn and contend that the points are necessarily related – although increased diversity may not lead to improvements in racial disparities. If there is an established lack of racial diversity within the judiciary, then the fundamental issue is that the judicial system is racist. Take, for example, the "secret" consultation process which involves the Judicial Appointments Commission consulting with current senior judges for recommendations on new judicial appointments (Fouzder, 2021a). Lawyers of colour are less likely to be recommended by senior judges and therefore the racially unequal status quo is upheld (demonstrated in Figure 14.1). It is no

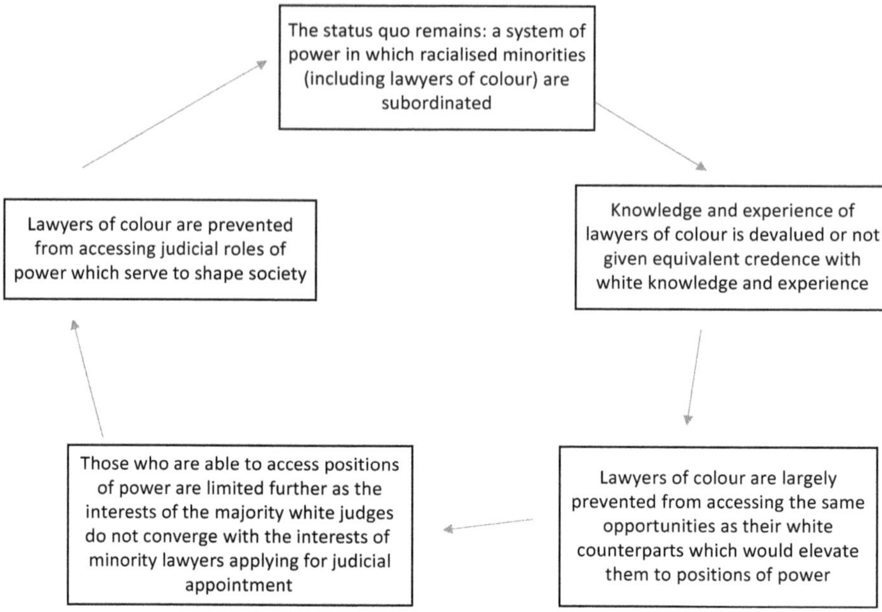

FIGURE 14.1 A critical view on the link between institutionalised racism in the judiciary and the lack of judicial diversity.

wonder that lawyers cite racism as a barrier to their career progression (Fouzder, 2021b).

Although we cannot be sure whether improving racial diversity will *directly* correlate with improved case outcomes for racialised minorities in the UK (as absolutely everyone, even people of colour hold racial biases), the acceptance of the lack of judicial diversity being a strong indicator of the institutionally racist judicial system may push us a step closer to an anti-racist judiciary. It will get us no way near the goal of corrective justice, but it would be a step in the right direction – as such acceptance would necessarily involve those in judicial roles of power, making the link between the social construction of race and structural inequalities in the judiciary.

Another question for classroom discussion therefore is whether a judge who is a racialised minority holds less of an incentive to uphold a racially unequal status quo than a white judge. I consider it is arguable, given promoting a lawyer of colour to the judiciary will also involve intersectional issues, such as class, and will depend on the degree to which those judges of colour assimilate with the white majority in order to be accepted as a member of their dominant community. Ultimately, people of colour do not automatically make better anti-racists.

CRT holds the key to deconstructing judicial racism, in the way in which it compels us to examine our biases and actively work to undo them. Although not speaking directly about CRT, Leslie Thomas considers that judges accepting their own prejudices and working to ensure they do not influence their decision-making is the first step in combating judicial racism. He also suggests mandating training on race for all judges, and I propose that this is taken one step further, in that judges should be thoroughly educated on CRT and engaged in compulsory reflective practice. This would be a great top-down measure, along with students being taught CLE as part of their legal education.

Considering judicial racism and lack of diversity within the judiciary provides CLE students with a space to understand racism at an institutional level. Accepting judicial racism means that students can apply their critical lenses to unpick judicial decision-making and understand the shaping of a hierarchical society, as well as considering the extent to which lack of diversity in the judiciary impacts these. By equipping students with the anti-racist tools to recognise judicial racism and the theories behind this, we are placing students in an informed position should they decide to take up judicial office in their careers. In conjunction with the tools to deconstruct assumptions, and avoid racialised paternalism, CLE teaches students an array of skills to equip them to be the anti-racist lawyers and judges, which our legal system so desperately needs.

Conclusion

The justice system is flawed, but, as law teachers, we are part of that system. This chapter outlines just a few ways in which CLE teachers can use experiential learning techniques to educate students in an anti-racist approach to lawyering. We have a duty to equip the next generation of lawyers with the anti-racist tools to influence, change, and reinvent the system. We should be unafraid of confronting racist realities when constructing our curriculum and should embody anti-racist practice in our own teaching methods. Indeed, the profession itself has started to respond to racist concerns, and a guide for anti-racist lawyers in the criminal justice system now exists to support practical efforts for change (Howard League for Penal Reform, 2021).

It is time for CLE to play a role in educating and empowering our students in a way that gives them the tools to identify, challenge, and change the legacy of systemic racism within the legal sector and in the administration of justice.

References

Adebisi, F., & Jivraj, S. (2021). Racism as Legal Pandemic: Thoughts on Critical Legal Pedagogies. In D. Cowan & A. Mumford (Eds.), *Pandemic Legalities: Legal Responses to COVID-19 – Justice and Social Responsibility* (1st ed., pp. 65–78). Bristol University Press.

Bell, D. (1980). Brown v. Board of Education and the Interest-Convergence Dilemma. *Harvard Law Review*, *93*(3), 518–533.

Bell, D. (1992). Racial realism. *Connecticut Law Review*, *24*(2), 363–380.

Bix, B. (2019). *Jurisprudence: theory and context* (Eighth). Thomson Reuters, trading as Sweet & Maxwell.

Bryant, S. (2001). The five habits: building cross-culture competence in lawyers. *Clinical Law Review*, *8*(1), 33–108.

Boud, D., Keogh, R., Walker, D. (eds) (1985). *Reflection: Turning Experience into Learning*, London: Kogan Page.

Bloom, B. S. (1979). *Taxonomy of Educational Objectives, Handbook 1: The Cognitive Domain*. New York: David McKay. In Fry, H. *et al.* (2009) *A handbook for teaching and learning in higher education: enhancing academic practice*. 3rd edn. New York: Routledge.

Brown, D. (2022). *Identifying disproportionality in the Avon and Somerset Criminal Justice System*. https://www.avonandsomerset-pcc.gov.uk/wp-content/uploads/2022/01/Identifying-Disproportionality-Report.pdf

Bryant, S., & Peters, J. K. (2022). *Five Habits of Cross-Cultural Lawyering and More*. https://fivehabitsandmore.law.yale.edu/

Byron, I. P. (2014). The relationship between social justice and clinical legal education: a case study of the women's law clinic, faculty of law, University of Ibadan, Nigeria. *International Journal of Clinical Legal Education*, *20*(2), 563–563.

Coper, M. (2010). Educating lawyers for what? Reshaping the idea of law school. *Penn State International Law Review*, *29*(1), 25–40.

Crenshaw, K. (1991). Mapping the margins: intersectionality, identity politics, and violence against women of color. *Stanford Law Review*, *43*(6), 1241–1299.

Delgado, R., Stefancic, J., & Harris, A. (2017). *Critical race theory: an introduction* (Third, Ser. Critical America). New York University Press.

EHRC (2019). *Tackling Racial harassment: Universities challenged*. https://www.equalityhumanrights.com/en/publication-download/tackling-racial-harassment-universities-challenged

Finlay, L. (2008). *Reflecting on 'Reflective practice'*. Practice-based Professional Learning Paper 52, The Open University.

Francis-Devine, Brigid (2021). *Poverty in the UK: statistics*. House of Commons Library.

Fouzder, M. (2021a). *Secret soundings for judiciary must go, says Boyce*. Law Gazette. https://www.lawgazette.co.uk/news/secret-soundings-for-judiciary-must-go-says-boyce/5109706.article

Fouzder, M. (2021b). *Racism and bias "barriers to career progression", say black lawyers*. LawGazette. https://www.lawgazette.co.uk/news/racism-and-bias-barriers-to-career-progression-say-black-lawyers/5109497.article

Genn, H. (2010). *Judging civil justice* (Ser. The Hamlyn lectures, 2008). Cambridge University Press.

Giddings, J., & Weinberg, J. (2020). Experiential Legal Education. In: C. Denvir, ed., *Modernising Legal Education*. Cambridge University Press.

Givelber, D. J., Baker, B. K., McDevitt, J., & Miliano, R. (1995). Learning through work: An empirical study of legal internship. *Journal of Legal Education*, *45*(1), 1–48.

Goldfarb, P. (1992). Beyond cut flowers: Developing a clinical perspective on critical legal theory. *Hastings L.J.* 43, 717.

Harris, A. P. (1990). Race and essentialism in feminist legal theory. *Stanford Law Review*, *42*(3), 581–616.

Hayat, N. B. (2021). Freedom pedagogy: Toward teaching antiracist clinics. *Clinical Law Review*, *28*, 149.

hooks, bell. (1994). *Teaching to transgress: Education as the practice of freedom*. Routledge.

Howard Legal for Penal Reform, (2021). Making Black Lives Matters in the criminal justice system. A guide for antiracist lawyers. Howard Legal for Penal Reform. https://howardleague.org/wp-content/uploads/2021/06/A-guide-for-antiracist-lawyers.pdf

Hyde, J. (2020). *Huge disparity in BAME solicitors taken to, SRA figures show tribunal* https://www.lawgazette.co.uk/news/huge-disparity-in-bame-solicitors-taken-to-tribunal-sra-figures-show/5106786.article

INQUEST, (2022). *BAME deaths in police custody* https://www.inquest.org.uk/bame-deaths-in-police-custody

Jackman, M. R. (1994). *The velvet glove: Paternalism and conflict in gender, class, and race relations*. University of California Press.

Johnson, M. E. (2005). An experiment in integrating critical theory and clinical education. *American University Journal of Gender, Social Policy & the Law, 13*(1), 161–185.

Kendi, I. X. (2019). *How to be an antiracist*. Bodley Head.

Kerrigan, K., & Murray, V. (2011). *A student guide to clinical legal education and pro bono*. (K. Kerrigan & V. Murray, Eds.). Palgrave Macmillan.

Kolb, D. A. (1984). *Experiential learning: Experience as the source of learning and development*. Englewood Cliffs, NJ: Prentice-Hall.

Lammy, D. (2017). *The Lammy Review. An independent review into the treatment of, and outcomes for, Black, Asian and Minority Ethnic individuals in the Criminal Justice System*. https://assets.publishing.service.gov.uk/government/uploads/system/uploads/attachment_data/file/643001/lammy-review-final-report.pdf

Lawrence, Charles R. III (1987). The Id, the ego, and equal protection: Reckoning with unconscious racism, *Stanford Law Review 39*, 317–388

Lawton, J. D. (2015). Who is my client? Client-centered lawyering with multiple clients. *The Clinical Law Review* 22, 145.

LawWorks (2021). *LawWorks Clinics Network Report. Analysis of clinic activity between January 2020-December 2020*. https://www.lawworks.org.uk/sites/default/files/files/LawWorks-Clinics-Report-2020-web.pdf

MBRRACE-UK (2021) – *Saving Lives, Improving Mothers' Care* https://www.npeu.ox.ac.uk/assets/downloads/mbrrace-uk/reports/maternal-report-2021/MBRRACE-UK_Maternal_Report_2021_-_FINAL_-_WEB_VERSION.pdf

Moore, S. (2020). *The Road to Hell: How Race Paternalism Shapes Political Behaviour*. https://deepblue.lib.umich.edu/handle/2027.42/163012

Ministry of Justice (2020). *Ethnicity and the Criminal Justice System* https://www.gov.uk/government/statistics/ethnicity-and-the-criminal-justice-system-statistics-2020/ethnicity-and-the-criminal-justice-system-2020

NHS Race & Health Observatory (2022) *Ethnic Inequalities in Healthcare: A Rapid Evidence Review* https://www.nhsrho.org/wp-content/uploads/2022/02/RHO-Rapid-Review-Final-Report_v.7.pdf

Nicolson, D. (2006). "Legal Education Or Community Service? The Extra-Curricular Student Law Clinic". *Web Journal of Current Legal Issues*. [2006] 3 Web JCLI.

Nicolson, D. (2015). Legal education, ethics and access to justice: forging warriors for justice in a neo-liberal world. *International Journal of the Legal Profession, 22*(1), 51–69.

Nicolson, D., & Webb, J. S. (1999). *Professional legal ethics: critical interrogations* (Ser. Oxford scholarship online). Oxford University Press.

Peters, J. K., & Bryant, S. (2014). *Talking about race*. In Bryant, S., Milstein, E. S., Shalleck, A. C., *Transforming the Education of Lawyers: The Theory and Practice of Clinical Pedagogy*. Carolina Academic Press.

Rhode, D. L. (2004). *Access to justice*. Oxford University Press.

Runnymede, (2021). *England Civil Society Submission to the United Nations Committee on the Elimination of Racial Discrimination* https://assets-global.website-files.com/61488f992b58e687f1108c7c/61bca661b8abd33d2f6f579c_Runnymede%20CERD%20report%20v3.pdf

Russell, M. (1992). *Entering Great America: Reflections on Race and the Convergence of Progressive* Legal Theory and Practice, 43 Hastings L.J. 749.

Sandbach, J., & Grimes, G. (2020). *Law School Pro Bono and Clinic Report 2020*. https://www.lawworks.org.uk/sites/default/files/files/LawWorks%20Law%20Schools%20Report%202020_0.pdf

Sandbach, J., & Johnson, C. (2019). *Impacting Justice: The contribution of clinical legal education and law school clinics to pro bono and access to justice in England and Wales*. LawWorks. Paper for the European Network for Clinical Legal Education and International Journal of Clinical Legal Education Conference.

Thomas, L. (2021). *Judicial Racism and the Lammy Review*. https://www.gresham.ac.uk/watch-now/judicial-racism

15

DECOLONIZATION AND ANTI-RACISM IN CRIMINOLOGY

Student Perceptions on Faculty Teaching Practices

Tamara O'Doherty, Helene Love, and Marsha-Ann Scott

Introduction[1]

Decolonizing higher education curriculum is important because classrooms are primary sources of socialization and can serve as spaces to transform the way teachers and students think and operate outside of the classroom (Xasan 2017; Hollinrake, Hunt, Dix & Wagner 2019; Evans-Winters, & Hines 2020; Hall et al., 2021). But what do students think about instructors' efforts to decolonize and/or introduce anti-racism into law courses?

In this chapter, we explore how our colleagues in a Canadian undergraduate criminology department translated the objective to teach about "social inequities as they relate to law" into specific pedagogical choices in their classes. We surveyed students across several law courses to learn which specific strategies resonated with them and collected ideas on why some strategies were more successful than others. From students' perspectives, the most effective strategies for understanding social inequities as they related to law included: guest lectures, assigned readings featuring diverse authorship, first-person accounts, discussions on current events, lectures where space is given to discussion about social inequities, and assignments featuring critical thinking about the law as it relates to specific social inequity or reflective assignments on the topic.

Collecting data from many students across a variety of law classes provides students' perspectives on strategies to decolonize and/or include an explicit anti-racist lens in law-related courses. Our findings suggest that paying close attention to accurate representation of law, incorporating a diversity of perspectives, requiring students to think critically about the law and legal institutions as sites of colonization, and providing adequate support and professional development for instructors were all important components of successfully

DOI: 10.4324/9781003397885-20

meeting the objective. While each of these recommendations carries various challenges, the data suggest that students appreciate the efforts of their instructors and desire to see more effort to embed attention to anti-racism throughout their learning environments.

We wish to note that we undertook this project as a team comprised of two White, middle-class, able-bodied, heterosexual women, together with an Afro-Caribbean, middle-class, able-bodied, heterosexual woman. With two White researchers, we endeavor to avoid granting primacy to this discourse but realize that Whiteness will figure prominently in our analyses. While institutional data on the students in our courses does not include students' race, social class, or gender – we acknowledge that our students will experience course content differently depending on their social locations.

Truth, Reconciliation, and Post-secondary Education

Our departmental learning objective that all law courses have students learn about "social inequities as they relate to law" is a product of a broader societal awareness of Canada's racist history and the legacy of colonialism. Among many acts of colonial violence, for 116 years, the Canadian government tore Indigenous children from their families and forced them to live at what were called "residential schools" run by the church and the government whose purpose was to break the cultural link Indigenous children had with their communities. While in attendance, many children were also subjected to physical and sexual violence (TRC Commission, 2015a, 2015b, 1, 2). Survivors of the residential school system sued the Canadian government for the atrocities they experienced and subsequently settled their class action lawsuit in 2006. As part of the settlement, the Canadian government was required to create the Truth and Reconciliation Committee (TRC), whose mandate was to inform all Canadians about residential schools and find a path forward toward reconciliation (TRC, 2015, v).

After consulting with over 6,000 survivors of the residential school system, the TRC crafted calls to action for all aspects of public life in Canada. Legal education was singled out as a site for reconciliation, and schools were directed to teach about "the history and legacy of residential schools, the United Nations *Declaration on the Rights of Indigenous Peoples*, Treaties and Aboriginal rights, Indigenous law, and Aboriginal–Crown relations" along with "skills-based training in intercultural competency, conflict resolution, human rights, and antiracism" (TRC Calls to Action, 2015, 28). In response, post-secondary institutions in Canada have begun to integrate Indigenous knowledge systems and anti-racist literature into their curricula (McGuire & Murdoch, 2022).

While such a mandate can be seen as positive, some scholars criticize this kind of initiative as a "form of settler appropriation" (Tuck & Yang, 2012, 3), especially without critical examination of the structural racism and White privilege embedded within academic institutions (McGuire & Murdoch, 2022,

1, St Clair & Kishimoto, 2010). In the years since the TRC's report, little has actually been done to advance the calls to action – Canada and its institutions "remain complicit in the perpetuation of political and superficial rhetoric" (McGuire & Murdoch, 2022, 5). For better or worse, our mid-sized University's criminology department's effort to answer this call to action was to require all law courses to "teach about social inequities as they relate to law."

Our Study

How to implement this departmental – and societal – imperative was left to individual instructors. When we first approached our colleagues with the question of how they incorporated decolonial or anti-racist practices in their work, we did not define the key terms "decolonial," "decolonization," and "anti-racist." Different people would understand these terms differently (Adebisi, 2020, 473), and there is dispute as to whether they are even possible within institutions built on colonial and racist foundations (Moore, 2020; Tuck & Yang, 2012). To some, decolonization at the core is about land, power, and privilege (Rigney, 2020; Tuck & Yang, 2012, 21). Others see decolonization as an iterative process of opening ways to receive knowledge of all forms and avoid perpetuating colonial narratives that continue to "other" those considered to be non-hegemonic voices (McGuire & Murdoch, 2022, Matiluko, 2020, 552). Battiste (2013, 14, 124) suggests that decolonization in the classroom means questioning Eurocentric assumptions, approaches, and methodologies in our courses. Decolonial thought requires difficult conversations about the ways in which history has influenced what the law is, how law is taught, what law is taught, whom the law works for, and for whom the law does not work (Kishimoto, 2018). Taken together, extant scholarship suggests that decolonization – if it is even possible – involves overturning the Western–Eurocentric influence and re-casting education with Indigenous stories and pedagogies.

Verhaeghe, Przybylo, and Patel (2018) identify a distinction between decolonial and anti-racist pedagogy, while an anti-racist pedagogy seeks to "actively identify and dismantle racism in its multiple and insidious forms toward transformative social change"; in addition to doing the foregoing, a decolonial approach to pedagogy brings into focus Indigenous knowledge with a view to reframing educational practices so that they serve Indigenous peoples and their interests (Verhaeghe et al. 2018, 79). Anti-racist pedagogy is not about simply incorporating racial content into courses, curriculum, and disciplines (Suyemoto & Fox Tree, 2006). It is also about how one teaches, even in courses where race is not the subject matter (Kishimoto, 2018, 540). Ultimately, both seek to address and bring to the fore social inequities that exist – not only to seek inclusion but to also shift perceptions and power relations in real and effective ways. It is in this broader sense that we find our departmental objective to exist.

Criminology and law are both settler-colonial disciplines that have justified racism (Moore, 2020, 490), the settler-state (Rigney, 2020, 505), and the cultural genocide of Indigenous peoples in Canada (McLachlin, 2015, TRC, 1). At the same time, criminology graduates are placed to make positive changes from within these institutions when they work as police, in corrections, and courts – which makes a foundation in anti-racism and decolonization even more important (McGuire & Murdoch, 2022, 7). Moore (2020, 492) suggests decolonizing criminology may not be possible, but if it is, it requires an interrogation of concepts such as "law," "order," "justice," and "crime." Drawing on Agozino's (2003, 2018) scholarship, Moore (2020) concludes that decolonizing criminology would require exploring its history and links to colonization and racism, developing a theory of the state and structural racism, introducing non-Western epistemologies relating to harm and conflict resolution, and recognizing that "crime" is a legal construct that has been used as a tool of colonization (502).

Thus, the challenge for legal educators – especially those in criminology programs – is multifaceted. In addition to political resistance to challenging structures of institutions and untethering legal education from its colonial origins (Archer Alvaré 2018; Cartwright & Cartwright 2020; Jivraj 2020a), instructors who seek to incorporate anti-racist and decolonial pedagogies may face difficulty implementing these theoretical ideas, given the topics we teach. Given that both law and criminology are disciplines that continue to create and perpetuate colonialism and racism, we seek to intervene and critically reflect on how we can improve our educational practices to better challenge structural oppression and better prepare our students for their subsequent and related careers. Prior to moving forward though, we wanted to learn more about what was already happening in our department, how our colleagues were trying to meet the challenge of teaching about social inequities more broadly, and how students were experiencing their instructors' efforts.

Methods

First, to uncover the specific strategies our colleagues used to incorporate decolonial or anti-racist practices, we conducted semi-structured interviews with full-time faculty members in our Criminology department who taught undergraduate courses in law. Five different instructors (three White women – including two of the study's authors, and two White men) contributed to pedagogical strategies. These courses ranged from seminar-style classes (maximum 30 students) to lecture classes with over 200 students.

To understand students' perspectives of these strategies, we administered a short survey through the online course delivery platform to undergraduate law-related coursesand students in the criminology program more generally in April 2021 (N = 103).[2] Due to COVID-19, all courses in the Spring of 2021 were administered online, so the data reported here are largely students' experiences with courses delivered remotely. Participation was anonymous and voluntary with students receiving an opportunity to be entered into a draw for a gift card for participating. In these surveys, we asked students about their perspectives on whether their law courses helped them to understand social inequities related to law, the strategies adopted by their instructors, and the benefits or shortfalls of their instructors' methods.[3] We also administered a survey to graduate students who were teaching assistants (TAs) in the criminology program (N = 8). To be included, respondents had to have assisted with a law-related course within the previous three years (since 2018) at the time of the survey.

Findings

Overall, 73% of the student respondents (n = 75) indicated that their law courses helped them to understand social inequities as they relate to law. Only 9% (n = 10) of the students found that their law courses did not help them understand social inequities as they related to law, and 8% of students (n = 8) were unsure if their law courses had helped them to understand these realities. There was variability across the courses that likely reflected their core content: unsurprisingly, students found the electives related to critical criminology and human rights to meet the social inequities goals to a higher degree (100% and 91%, respectively) than did their introductory and breadth law-related courses, for whom responses show that between 60% and 80% of students felt that the introductory and breadth courses contributed to their understanding of social inequities.

Of those students who indicated that the course had helped them to understand social inequities as they related to law, the most common strategies used by instructors included textbook choices, including video clips and other media, through lectures, and by assigning academic articles. Course-specific data demonstrates that some courses include such strategies as guest speakers, or announcements, too, but others do not. Table 15.1 summarizes these findings.

Table 15.1 shows the strategies that are commonly used by instructors, but it does not highlight which of those strategies students found to be most effective at advancing those goals. Qualitative data from the open-ended survey questions, however, indicated that the most effective strategies included guest lectures, assigned readings featuring diverse authorship, first-person accounts, discussions on current events, lectures where space is given to discussion about social inequities, and assignments featuring critical thinking about the law as it relates to a specific social inequity or reflective assignments on the topic.

Textbooks and Academic Articles

In general, students found the textbooks did not often offer explicit information about social inequities and that faculty could consider course texts that provide more focus on social inequities or that otherwise reflect diverse

TABLE 15.1 Number of students exposed to the different strategies

Strategy	*Responses (N = 103)*	*Survey participants (%)*
Textbooks	56	41
Relating to current events	50	36
Lectures	48	35
Academic articles	44	32
Including different perspectives	40	29
Videos and other media	28	21
Guest speakers	19	14
Class announcements and discussions	4	4
Course structure	1	1

scholarship and perspectives. A student who identified the textbook as a challenge to learning about social inequities states:

> The textbook also didn't have anything about inequalities in the book, so it was difficult for the instructor to talk about it…

Textbooks can sustain inequity where they ignore or minimize social inequities or where they offer only one dominant perspective (White, male, colonial narrative). One student noted that while some instructors clearly make efforts to use inclusive texts, there remains considerable variability between instructors, writing: "Some instructors don't make much of an effort in the first place."

Video and Other Media

Students found supplementing course texts with other media (such as videos) reflecting more diverse authorship and providing information about current events are both effective practices. One student noted the impact of using videos featuring Indigenous experts:

> I think it was amazing … to watch an Indigenous speaker for our Indigenous law section. Hearing from an Indigenous speaker for that section really solidified their beliefs and ways since it was first-hand and informative and demonstrated the inequities in our society.

Likewise, participants found non-traditional materials, such as blog posts, websites, and podcasts, helpful in including diverse perspectives and in demonstrating how social inequities affect individuals:

> The professor included a number of articles, blog posts, videos, etc. from the perspective of former or current sex workers which I found very helpful as

> it allowed me to hear a voice that I'm often not exposed to in academic areas, and it gave me a better understanding of and compassion for people directly experiencing the effects of social inequities under the law.

Lectures and Course Structure

Lectures were seen as a key place where students received information about how the law applies inequitably and had opportunities to engage in discussion. Students mentioned some professors were adept at introducing and discussing such content, but others clearly struggled or were less confident. One student commented that a challenge in learning about social inequities as they relate to law was the instructor's struggle to "highlight the complexities of systemic inequality clearly and empathetically through lecture." Instructor comfort with the subject of social inequities, as well as instructor knowledge of current events, influences how students receive the information.

A core reality reflected in our findings is that any decolonial or anti-racist work must be approached with sincerity and create space(s) to have hard conversations that come with unlearning colonialism and systemic racism. According to Fanon (1967), colonization was a very violent process and therefore decolonization and/or any sort of framework being created to undo any of its effects should likewise be disruptive or even violent (cited in Xasan 2017). However, we are of the view that the use of violence that Fanon (1967) suggests serves to implicitly perpetuate the colonization experience because we continue to appropriate the "master's tools" (Matiluko, 2020). Indeed, in our survey, there were different ideas of instructor responsibilities regarding intervention in discussions where controversial, intolerant, or otherwise disagreeable perspectives were raised. One student observed challenges experienced by their instructor in raising issues with social inequities but also respecting the freedom of diverse opinions within the classroom setting when they wrote:

> I can imagine [the instructor] did face challenges as the topics we discussed are very 'touchy' and stigmatized so approaching those topics with grace and care is difficult. Also, I'd assume there are students who might take an opposing stance to many of the arguments made by the prof/the assigned materials which could create challenges.

Some students expressed disagreement about their instructors' responses, expecting greater intervention; others valued free and open discussion, even seeking to reach out to, or "play devil's advocate," to ensure a range of perspectives was represented. Students noted that some instructors clearly didn't want to offend but perhaps, due to their own lack of knowledge, ended up offending through language choices, glossing over topics, failing to conduct land acknowledgments, or otherwise incorporating sufficient attention to social inequities. Put succinctly by one respondent, a challenge with learning about social inequities in law is "being able to display social inequities correctly; not offending others."

Students found some courses center content relating to social inequities more than do others. In our department, courses such as Sex Work and the Law and Human Rights have more content related to inequities than the breadth courses in Criminal Procedure or Criminal Law, as reflected in student comments:

> Because much of this course is focused on the basic principles of law, there is not always opportunity to tie in inequity with the course material, such as going over parliament structure or looking at case law.
>
> With respect to criminal law, especially in a course with a focus of learning specific legal concepts and case precedents, I think it is quite a challenge to incorporate social inequities within the amount of material and concepts we have to cover relating to criminal law. … I just do not thing [sic] that this course is designed to cover topics of social inequity directly.
>
> I think that since this legal objective is not necessarily reflected in the curriculum that instructors are required to teach, instructors have difficulty finding the time to bring up the subject. On the one hand, it is important to delve into topics of social inequity in law classes. On the other hand, this subject is not usually tested, and since instructors don't want to overload students with additional work, they may feel pressure to only briefly go over the topic.

The degree of emphasis on social inequities was related to the focus of the course and the practical reality of the breadth of material covered in most of the law courses. The challenge then is finding a way to work in social inequity when there is already a breadth of substantive topics to cover in undergraduate law courses.

Regardless of the challenges, most faculty and students noted that opportunity to incorporate more content in these courses did exist and ought to be prioritized. The student participants demonstrated empathy toward most of their instructors' efforts but noted that not only could much more be done but that the onus did not solely rest on instructors:

> I think instructors do well in addressing the fact that social inequalities exist within the Justice system, but it's just left at that. I think that students should be motivated by instructors to challenge this notion as I'm finding most of my peers simply accept that this inequality exists but don't choose to do anything about it when actually on a career path.

Assignments

Scholarship on decolonization of courses centers the interrogation of key concepts and assumptions as a fundamental practice in decolonizing curriculum (Battiste 2013; Smith 1999). Assignments were a common strategy that allowed students to think critically about the law and legal institutions in their courses and understand social inequities as they related to law. For example, in an introductory law class students are asked on the final exam how the law was used as a tool for colonization and required students to provide specific examples. Another assignment required students to reflect on how certain legal defenses emerged from harmful stereotypes and myths about such matters as consent or provocation or to explain why some defendants have challenged institutional "color-blindness" in legal practices such as jury selection. One student commented:

> I enjoyed how this class emphasized having "critical" perspectives and analysis to how law affects people differently. In past law classes … I felt as if I was regurgitating textbook content and memorizing cases. In this class I felt I learned the skills of actually seeing how these laws affected people, and how to apply critical skills.

Another assignment in an introductory lecture-style course required students to make an artistic representation of any kind (e.g., photograph, song, poem, story) about the course content that demonstrates their opinion about how a legal concept occurs in their lives. In a similar manner, students are often asked to do some form of presentation or paper discussing judicial interpretations in specific cases and identifying critiques or concerns about the court decisions. While the students reported enjoying the creativity involved in these assignments, these kinds of analytical – and sometimes personal/political – assignments needed to be supported by clear grading rubrics so students know the basis on which they will be graded. TAs similarly raised the issues of sufficient training to feel confident grading critical and analytical content, as well as the need for clear rubrics. One TA noted:

> Grading guidelines should be clear when marking assignments related to this learning objective. I think students can learn a lot through their assignment feedback, so ensure TAs/TMs/etc. are equipped to provide that feedback.

Both TAs and students suggested that it is best to avoid heavy-handed tactics or requirements that students simply regurgitate the professor's opinions. One student wrote: "If possible, restrain the profs from testing us on their opinions. Social inequities can be tested on facts and concepts."

Both instructors and students also valued assignments related to – and encouragement of – self-reflection and learning how one's subjectivities and socio-political position would likely affect how we each view the law. Having students set out their positionality and existing knowledge about a topic at the outset and then providing them space to reflect on what they come to learn or to reconsider at the end of the term can be a particularly useful strategy.

> A very good job was done with this course. It caused me to reflect upon my preconceived notions and look at the issue from a different perspective.

One of the reasons why assignments were key to helping students understand social inequities as they related to law is because they required student participation. Research has shown that the experiences, perceptions, and knowledge of students matter and that inclusion in the production of knowledge can carry an "emancipatory potential" (Hubbard 1999). As academics, we become guides who recognize the value of each individual student voice, and our classrooms become communities where our students, as active participants in their educational journeys, feel a responsibility to contribute, thereby creating real knowledge and making education an exercise of liberation, or resistance, for both students and academics (Cartwright & Cartwright 2020, 536). Further, Jivraj (2020b, 12) finds that collaborating with students is a critical piece to creating change and developing them into co-producers of knowledge. Through assignments, students become active participants in the process rather than mere subjects on whom we impose our efforts.

Contextualizing Content

Students related that linking course materials to current events was a helpful way to ground learning of social inequities as they relate to law. One student wrote:

> Discussions on this topic are also super effective and really make us students think critically as well as engage with the material at a deeper level – for example, finding a media or news article that demonstrates the social inequity with the law being discussed.

Anchoring the study of social inequities as it relates to law helped provide specific examples of concepts rather than broad statements, which students appreciated. For example, learning how law was used as a tool of colonization via specific examples (reserve systems, residential schools, differential criminalization) was far more effective than simply stating that colonization happened and therefore Indigenous people are often discriminated against. Likewise, it is more effective to explain how the social, political, and legal forces contribute to the mass incarceration of racialized people in North American prisons rather than simply referencing statistics. Including current issues within course materials or providing students with evidence of social inequities, rather than simply opining about the topic, appears to be a particularly effective method of reaching student audiences. In this way, student comments reflected ideas raised by Archibald (2020), who suggests the best way to decolonize the classroom is to begin by learning the local colonial history. Once the local colonial history is established, educators should recognize the intergenerational impact of colonialism, engage in critical self-reflection, and use Indigenous perspectives and stories in teaching.

Guest Speakers and Including Diverse Perspectives

A major part of the decolonization project is practicing intellectual honesty in not only the material we present (e.g., including a truthful account of racist and colonial origins and uses of law) but also practicing intellectual honesty in how we present such material. According to Hall et al. (2021), a critical point raised in decolonizing discourse is a shared questioning of our positionality in relation to these issues, to venture beyond them. While it is important for White academics to acknowledge their privilege and/or address possible White-savior complexes, academics who have experienced forms of oppression must also do some unpacking because we sometimes come with mindsets that serve as barriers to the cause (Cartwright & Cartwright 2020, 535). Further, some time may need to be spent coming to terms with teaching in a predominately White space about the violence to which we are very close (Buenavista Hanna, 2019; Hinton & Ono-George 2019). As Cartwright and Cartwright (2020) assert, we are all called to first "decolonize" ourselves (532).

A strategy faculty members used to recognize our own Whiteness was to invite guest speakers with diverse backgrounds and experiences into classes. Where guests were invited, they were highly valued by students, especially where the guests could offer first-person accounts of how social inequity intersects with law, is sustained by law, or led to criminalization/incarceration. One student wrote:

> With law-related courses, it can be difficult for many of the students to see its effects and how it applies to people in the real world. As such, I do believe that bringing guest lecturers to share their experiences with us really helped us students to understand the magnitude of how these laws are applied.

Guest speakers relate their lived experiences to students and bring the law to life in ways that course readings or lectures from White instructors could not. A student observed:

> I feel like the professor didn't feel like it would be appropriate to teach about Indigenous inequalities because she herself has never experienced it.

Instructor self-consciousness presenting materials on social inequities from a position of privilege was also noted by another respondent, who wrote that their instructor was "not able to speak on behalf of some socially oppressed groups." Another student noted that there are sometimes matters of respect in terms of who can voice some Indigenous stories and knowledge or who ought to be voicing this type of content:

> I think maybe a challenge that could have been faced was the idea of incorporating many perspectives. With Indigenous peoples, it is important to not speak for them. So, what my instructor did was to direct us to links and additional articles that provided some Indigenous perspectives.

These comments highlight both the benefits of bringing in guest speakers and incorporating diverse perspectives but also that the need to include diverse perspectives highlighted the instructors' lack of lived experience in an area, including the instructors' privilege.

The absence of BIPOC faculty did not go un-noticed, as one student remarked, we should consider how the department's current, "…representation is reflective of power dynamics in society." This gap between policy and practice the student noted is well supported in the literature. Universities are typically characterized by colonial bureaucratic structures and feature some deeply entrenched ways of providing education (Jivraj 2020a, 552; Hall et al. 2021; Miller 2021). They too often pay "lip service" to anti-racist and decolonial projects without necessarily examining the processes by which they sustain inequities not only in terms of hiring and staffing but also in terms of grading policies, supports for students, the systems students need to navigate within the university, and so many other administrative components that heavily impact the student experience (Archer Alvaré 2018; Cartwright & Cartwright 2020; Miller 2021).

Decolonizing an institution or transforming the educational experience must be a whole school approach (Miller 2021), and guest speakers can be one way of side-stepping the University's own responsibilities to learn and grow and engage in critical self-reflection (Cartwright & Cartwright 2020; Miller 2021). While the literature is clear that ensuring diversity of voice and experience is necessary as a basic step toward inclusion and progress, tokenism can lead to harm because it unfairly burdens racialized faculty and students with the task of serving on committees and taking on supervisory roles, educating not only students but the education on undoing systemic oppression (Hall et al. 2021; Suyemoto & Fox Tree 2006).

Recommendations

Our data highlight key ideas on how to decolonize and/or include an explicit anti-racist/anti-oppression lens in law-related teaching practices. These strategies include paying close attention to accurate representation and diversity of voice, requiring students to develop critical thinking skills alongside their legal knowledge, and providing adequate support and professional development for instructors. While each of these recommendations carries various challenges, we find students appreciate the efforts of their instructors, even if the instructors make mistakes, or could have handled a situation with a little more empathy.

Representation and Voice

Post-secondary education relating to law can truly benefit from allowing guests to share space at the front of the room, especially those guests who have been impacted by social inequities and are willing to share their experiences. This is beneficial no matter the lived experience of the instructor, but it may be particularly beneficial for students when the instructor is White, cisgender, educated, socio-economically privileged, and able-bodied. Likewise, to introduce topics like Indigenous legal orders or ways of doing justice, invite Indigenous scholars or Elders, if you are not Indigenous. Not only is this respectful of protocols around who has the authority to share knowledge and in what manner, it is also political in the act of sharing space and relational in that we, as educators, ought to do the work among communities to develop relations with those who have much wisdom to share.

That said, there are limitations to using guest speakers in the classroom. Guest speakers ought to be compensated for sharing their expertise, but our department does not provide any funding for this purpose – remuneration must be provided by the instructor personally. Further, the ability to access guest speakers depends on an instructor's networks and personal relationships, which may be limited. Finally, there is the broader issue of how guest speakers provide a short-term solution for a more systemic issue of the absence of a more diverse faculty.

Our participants suggest that instructors should examine course materials through an intersectional lens to ensure that not only are equity issues discussed but that the materials also feature diverse perspectives and diverse authorship wherever possible. Again, this serves dual purposes of both the political act of supporting and disseminating authors and perspectives that are marginalized but also ensures more students see people like themselves represented as experts. Ideally, this will have the natural consequence of maintaining a focus on the socio-political context of law both in its role in creating and sustaining inequity but also in its ability to challenge and address inequity.

Critical Thinking, Self-reflection, and Student Engagement

A unifying recommendation across all participant groups was that assignments that allow students the space to reflect, think critically, and come to their own conclusions about a topic produced greater student engagement. Legal training typically includes some degree of applied demonstration of knowledge, but critical thinking skills require more than an ability to apply principles to a scenario. Our findings indicate that requiring students to think beyond an almost mathematical calculation to considering how and why principles might apply differently in different situations, or what implications flow from different possible applications of law can help students see how law is fluid and how it can play dual roles of reproducing and dismantling some forms of inequity. Further, students consistently share that when instructors work to incorporate current events, where students can address social issues that matter in their lives, or where they are able to reflect on their own social location and its role in determining how they view the world – and the law – students benefit in both academic and personal ways.

Professional Development and Support

None of the above is possible without adequate institutional support for instructors. Instructors who wish to succeed in these endeavors must be well-versed across not only their own domains of legal expertise but also in terms of anti-racist teaching pedagogies. For those in full-time and/or continuing roles, there are typically supports available for some degree of professional development. Too often though, these funds are used for instructors to disseminate knowledge about their own areas of expertise rather than to learn more about matters such as anti-oppression in the classroom. Our participants demonstrate the importance of this latter professional development; our teaching practices ought to be valued at least equally to our research or publication practices.

Conclusion

At the end of our first exploration into how to decolonize legal pedagogy, we are cautiously optimistic that while the goal of upending and restructuring a colonial and inherently capitalist system may be out of reach (for now), as individual instructors working within these structures, there is so much that we can – and must – do to bring a critical and anti-racist lens to our work as educators. This study adds to the existing body of knowledge about student experiences with courses incorporating an anti-racist/decolonial approach. We conclude that the design of such an anti-racist/decolonial curriculum should be dependent on the context, and it should feature attention to representation and voice, and the incorporation of critical thinking skills as equally as vital as knowledge of a particular domain of law. It is imperative to create learning spaces wherein students can have free exchange of ideas, thoughts, and experiences on the subject, under the guidance of instructors who have been supported to develop an anti-racist/decolonial approach. The objective ought not to be to create students who are committed anti-racist/decolonial *activists*. We are instead confident that, as Hinton and Ono-George (2019) assert, the experience they gain will put them in a better position to listen, question, and challenge racism in our communities.

Notes

1 We respectfully acknowledge the xʷməθkʷəy̓əm, Sḵwx̱wú7mesh, səl̓ilw̓ətaʔɬ, q̓íc̓əy̓, kʷikʷəƛ̓əm, qiqéyt, q'ʷa:n̓ƛ'ən̓, Səmyámə, and sc̓əwaθən Peoples, on whose unceded traditional territories Simon Fraser University's three campuses stand.
2 The courses on which these data were based include a first-year breadth course (Crim 135: Introduction to Canadian Legal Institutions), a second-year criminal law course (Crim 230: Criminal Law in Canada), and three third-year courses (Crim 317 (Sex, Work, and the Law), Crim 330 (Criminal Procedure and Evidence, and Crim 335 (Human Rights and Civil Liberties).
3 We obtained an exemption from the Research Ethics Board for this study because it involves program improvement/program evaluation within our institution.

References

Adebisi, F. (2020). Decolonising the law school: Presences, absences, silences… and hope. *The Law Teacher*, 54(4), 471–474.

Agozino, B. (2018). The withering away of the law: An Indigenous perspective on the decolonisation of the criminal justice system and criminology. *Journal of Global Indigeneity*, 3(1), Article 2.

Agozino, B. (2003). *Counter-Colonial Criminology: A Critique of Imperialist Reason.* Pluto Press.

Archer Alvaré, M. (2018). Addressing racial inequalities within schools: Exploring the potential of teacher education. *Sociology Compass*, *12*(10), doi: 10.1111/soc4.12628

Archibald, J. (2020, September 1). *A Conversation with Dr. Jo-ann Archibald Q'um Q'um Xiiem: The Many Facets of Decolonizing and Indigenizing the Academy* [Speech video recording]. https://www.youtube.com/watch?v=bYpSiCCdocM&feature=youtu.be

Battiste, M. (2013). *Decolonizing education: Nourishing the learning spirit*. Purich.

Buenavista Hanna, K. (2019). Pedagogies in the flesh: Building an anti- racist decolonized classroom. *Frontier. A Journal of Women Studies*, 40(1), 229–244.

Cartwright, N. & Cartwright, T. (2020). "Why is it my problem if they don't take part?" The (non)role of white academics in decolonising the law school. *Law Teacher*, 54(4), 532–546.

Evans-Winters, V. & Hines, D. (2020). Unmasking white fragility: How whiteness and white student resistance impacts anti-racist education. *Whiteness and Education*, 5(1), 1–16.

Hall, R., Ansley, L., Connolly, P., Loonat, S., Patel, K. & Whitham, B. (2021). Struggling for the anti-racist university: Learning from an institution-wide response to curriculum decolonization. *Teaching in Higher Education*, doi: 10.1080/13562517.2021.1911987

Hinton, M. & Ono-George, M. (2019). Teaching a history of "race" and anti-racist action in an academic classroom. *Royal Geographical Society*. doi: 10.1111/area.12536

Hollinrake, S., Hunt, G., Dix, H. & Wagner, A. (2019). Do we practice (or teach) what we preach? Developing a more inclusive learning environment to better prepare social work students for practice through improving the exploration of their different

ethnicities within teaching, learning and assessment opportunities. *Social Work Education*, 38(5), 582–603.
Hubbard, Phil. (1999). Researching female sex work: Reflections on geographical exclusion, critical methodologies and 'useful' knowledge. *Area*, 31(3), 229–237.
Jivraj, S. (2020a). Decolonizing the academy – Between a rock and a hard place. *Interventions (London, England)*, 22(4), 552–573.
Jivraj, S. (2020b). *Towards anti-racist legal pedagogy: A resource*. Socio-Legal Studies Association. https://research.kent.ac.uk/decolonising-law-schools/wp-content/uploads/sites/866/2020/09/Towards-Anti-racist-Legal-Pedagogy-A-Resource.pdf
Kishimoto, K. (2018). Anti-racist pedagogy: From faculty's self-reflection to organizing within and beyond the classroom, *Race Ethnicity and Education*, 21(4), 540–554.
Matiluko, O. (2020). Decolonising the master's house: How Black Feminist epistemologies can be and are used in decolonial strategy. *Law Teacher*, 54(4), 547–561. https://doi.org/10.1080/03069400.2020.1827839
McGuire, Michaela M. & Murdoch, Danielle J. (2022). "A Lot of my Day is Spent Looking at Injustice": Reflections on decolonizing teaching and relationship building across difference. *Journal of Criminal Justice Education*. https://doi.org/10.1080/10511253.2022.2121001
McLachlin, B. (2015, May 15). Reconciling unity and diversity in the modern era: Tolerance and intolerance [lecture]. Global Centre for Pluralism: Annual Lecture, Toronto, ON, Canada.
Miller, P. (2021). Anti-racist school leadership: Making 'race' count in leadership preparation and development. *Professional Development in Education*, 47(1), 7–21.
Moore, J. (2020) "Law", "order", "justice", "crime": disrupting key concepts in criminology through the study of colonial history. *The Law Teacher*, 54(4), 489–502. 10.1080/03069400.2020.1827787
Rigney, S. (2020). Creating the law school as a meeting place for epistemologies: Decolonising the teaching of jurisprudence and human rights. *The Law Teacher*, 54(4), 503–516.
Smith, L. (1999). *Decolonizing methodologies: Research and Indigenous Peoples*. Zed Books Ltd.
St. Clair, D. & Kishimoto, K. (2010). Decolonizing teaching: A cross-cultural and collaborative model about teaching race in the University. *Multicultural Education*, 18(1), 18–24.
Suyemoto, K. & Fox Tree, C. (2006). Building bridges across differences to meet social action goals: Being and creating allies among people of color. *American Journal Community Psychology*, 37, 237–246.
Tuck, E. & Yang, W. (2012). Decolonization is not a metaphor. *Decolonization, Indigeneity, and Society*, 1(1), 1–40.
Xasan, S. (2017). Race and racism in education: Seeking transformative change through an inclusive and anti-racist curriculum. In A. Abdulle & A. N. Obeyesekere (Eds.), *New Framings on Anti-Racism and Resistance: Volume 1 – Anti-Racism and Transgressive Pedagogies*, pp. 171–184.
Verhaeghe, A., Przybylo, E. & Patel, S. (2018). On the im/possibilities of anti-racist and decolonial publishing as pedagogical praxis. *Feminist Teacher*, 28(2–3), 79–90.

Reports

Truth and Reconciliation Commission of Canada. (2015a). *Calls to Action*. Truth and Reconciliation Commission.
Truth and Reconciliation Commission of Canada. (2015b). *Honoring the truth: Reconciling the future. A summary of the final report of the Truth and Reconciliation commission of Canada*. Truth and Reconciliation Commission.

Statutes

An Act for the better protection of the Lands and Property of the Indians in Lower Canada. 1850. (Can) online: https://bnald.lib.unb.ca/sites/default/files/UnC_1850_cap%2042_edited.pdf
The Indian Act. 1876. (Can) online: https://laws-lois.justice.gc.ca/eng/acts/i-5/

16

TROUBLING LAW'S TRADITIONAL CANON BY TEACHING LAW AND RACE

Foluke I Adebisi and Yvette Russell

Introduction

For law teachers in law schools, the ability to adopt antiracist pedagogy or anticolonial approaches is often limited not just by administrative and societal barriers but by the discipline within which these teaching methods are employed. Because the traditional instrumental approach to delivering the law curriculum says we should teach the 'neutral' foundations of the discipline first, before moving on to its critique, critical pedagogy is often more of an optional 'add-on' rather than a central component of the curriculum. As a result of this approach, legal scholars and students do not often engage with the complex ways in which the discipline of law is implicated in the societal problems it is called upon to combat, including racism and coloniality. The classification of human beings into uncertain hierarchies under the pseudo-scientific label of 'race' has functioned and continues to function as motivation and justification for oppressive social, cultural, economic, and political structures. This is evidenced by evolving histories that continue to the present of extractive colonisation, racialised enslavement, planetary exploitation, and endangerment, as well as persistent global racial inequalities that cut across all other categorisations of humanity. Law has a paradoxical relationship with these demarcations, being used in their creation, reproduction, and also in attempts at their subversion. Yet, the study of law in its traditional guise often ignores the entanglement between itself and these processes.

In 2017, we, the authors of this chapter, confronted these questions and more in the design and teaching of an optional final-year LLB unit at the University of Bristol Law School called 'Law and Race'.[1] In this chapter, we give an account of our experience of teaching the unit, as well as the impetus for

DOI: 10.4324/9781003397885-21

and our pedagogic goals in its delivery. We co-designed this unit with our students to engage in a critical exploration of the ways in which law has impacted upon and caused racial disparities, and how these factors are continuously embedded and reproduced within the operation of law. More than the substance of the unit, we also wanted to create a space for our students to have the conversations that they may have been unable to have so far in their law degrees. Student input was and continues to be vital to the content and delivery of the unit as we recognise that co-design, collaboration, and partnership encourage students to intellectually invest in the processes of constructing knowledge and also promote reciprocity in the learning process (Bryson 2016: 84–86). This collaboration was particularly important for 'Law and Race', which must of necessity touch on sensitive and traumatic material. Nevertheless, we remain committed with our students to sitting with the difficult feelings this material can bring up, knowing that in the face of racial injustice and planetary endangerment, discomfort is the least we can suffer for our own and each other's survival (hooks 2014: 42–43).

In what follows, we unpack both the personal and professional impetus for and aims that guided our design of 'Law and Race', including the anticolonial and antiracist framework the unit design relies upon. We detail our teaching methods and finally reflect on our experience of teaching this unit within a law school in the United Kingdom. We conclude that the inclusion of this unit, despite certain limitations, offers a compelling pedagogical advantage for students in its centring of antiracist and anticolonial perspectives and methods, and its conscious displacement of the ethos of the traditional law curriculum. Further, we argue that a unit like 'Law and Race' can provide those of us committed to thoroughgoing critical pedagogy with the tools and motivation to engage with decolonisation in the law curriculum more broadly.

Why did we develop 'Law and Race'?

I (Foluke) describe myself as Nigerian-British-Nigerian. In one sense, this describes the nations that I belong to, have been immersed in, and in whose similar jurisdictions I have studied and practised law. My first memories are British, of snow and mild summers. I have lived back and forth through each jurisdiction, and it is quite impossible to tell where the Nigerian in me ends and the British begins. In another sense, this allocation as Nigerian-British-Nigerian alludes to a much more conceptual point. It alludes to the fact that British adventures in Africa are integral to shaping the nature of the modern world. After the brutal trade in enslaved Africans that occasioned an incalculable population loss on Africa (Rawley and Behrendt 2005: 365), the next stage redrew the political, cultural, and legal lines of an already plundered continent. In a process that was ironically called 'Nation-Building', European countries destroyed pre-existing African nations and then drew borders around resource-rich areas. This created colonies that were administered for the purpose of plunder. It was these colonies that 'received independence', when the colonial officers departed from Africa's shores. What that means for my label of Nigerian-British-Nigerian is that Nigeria – its laws, its borders, and its epistemologies – is a British creation. To be Nigerian is to have a forever and fundamental link to this history out of which the present is born. Therefore, for me, a journey into decolonisation is a journey that seeks to answer the fundamental question of law – what does it mean to be human before the law? To put this another way, when does the African become human before the law? How do we, within our discipline's silence on these histories, account for the incalculable losses to the continent within a discipline that claims to strive for equality and justice? A decolonial and antiracist pedagogy offers a response, as yet incomplete, to these questions.

I (Yvette) was born in Aotearoa/New Zealand, which, similar to Nigeria, bears the marks of its legacy as a British colony. As someone whose familial history bears the intergenerational scars of colonial trauma (Waretini-Karena 2017), I have often struggled to think of myself both as a woman of indigenous descent from Aotearoa/New Zealand and as a British citizen. Trying to capture the dissonance of one's own identity is something several of our students resonated with in 'Law and Race', as well as trying to come to terms with the role that law plays in maintaining the categories and structures in which that dissonance plays out. I have always had a deep antipathy towards legal doctrine and discourse, which has manifested in my research as a thoroughgoing critical scepticism of law and its truth and knowledge claims. It was, therefore, both an intellectual drive to question that which we are told is true and is the natural order of things, and a personal quest for belonging and understanding that led me to think about what a unit on 'Law and Race' might look like, and how it might help us to trouble the law curriculum more broadly. Before these drivers crystallised, however, I was invited in April 2017 to speak at an event on Black Lives Matter and the criminal justice system, organised by two of our law students (who were soon to become key collaborators on 'Law and Race'), Kose Bamugemereire and Oluwaseun Matiluko. It occurred to me at this event, reflecting on the thoughtful and affecting discussion with panellists and students, that we simply did not have anywhere in our current law curriculum to talk about these issues together and to give them the time and care that they needed. The next day I emailed Foluke, and our collaboration started.

We were both of us then ready and able to do the work necessary to make 'Law and Race' a reality. We were joined in our agreement that a unit on 'Law and Race' was important and necessary for several interconnected reasons. We observed that it was the case that many of the racial aspects of current affairs and their intersection with law went unobserved in the traditional legal curriculum, which compounded our students' sense that their experiences and the experiences and perspectives of other racialised people were unconsidered and unimportant. We were acutely aware, in our law school at least, that there was very little mention of race in the core curriculum, even in units in which you might expect that it would be directly relevant (e.g. criminal law, jurisprudence, land law). Proceeding from these observations, we quickly agreed on principles for developing our unit going forward. Following Alana Lentin (2022), we resolved that for our unit to be antiracist, it must be overtly so. In other words, we were not interested in presenting a 'race perspective' as one among many and adopting a position of neutrality in our analysis of, for example, law and Empire. We wanted to centre race in our pedagogy, and to think through with our students, as a central motif, the ways in which law and race co-constitute one another in a seemingly continuous back and forth. Moreover, we wanted students to be empowered with the tools, not only to examine the nexus of race and law and its impact on their own lives but to embed decolonisation's logics in their own study. We were trying to encourage and model, therefore, a mode and ethos of critique which might enable students to reach outside the disciplinary silo in which law is traditionally taught and to contextualise their own personal experiences and their experience with and relationship to law. Part of this process involved unveiling and naming the invisible effects of racial demarcations both in everyday life but also in law through unpacking the historical constitution, for example, of legal positivism as a rationale and method in the context of British colonial expansion (Goldberg 2002). Central to developing and situating our critique and to this process of 'unveiling' was to challenge the notion of law as a perspective from nowhere (Crenshaw 1988; Williams 1991). This required us to delve into the history of law's constitution in our context, as well as furnishing ourselves with different theoretical frameworks through which we could understand and approach anew law's stories about itself.

Something that bears mentioning because it was also key to the success of 'Law and Race' is timing. When we set out to develop the unit in 2017, we had the impetus and energy, the right collaborators, access to a cultural and educational milieu and language that could make 'Law and Race' legible to our colleagues, and we benefitted from an institutional setting that welcomed our initiative at the University of Bristol Law School. In the parlance common in the neoliberal university, we had identified a gap in our provision that the school was incentivised to address, and thus we were provided with the support and freedom to craft our unit in the way we thought worked best. This was important because from the outset, we were clear that this unit would centre race and that it would engage with decolonisation substantively but also methodologically. That is to say that it would consciously seek to decolonise *not* diversify as one of its key pedagogic goals.

What does it mean for us to 'decolonise' and not 'diversify'?

We understand antiracist and decolonial pedagogy as distinct but overlapping approaches. These approaches are of specific interest to the teaching of law in particular, but also to legal knowledge in general. In other words, they are approaches that should extend beyond the curriculum into the law we research and practice. Therefore, it was vital to think beyond the boundaries of the increasingly common co-optation of 'decolonisation' within the neoliberal university. 'Decolonisation' in this context often refers to surface-level attempts at diversity or measures that equate decolonisation with superficial social justice work. For example, initiatives with a cursory focus on metrics-driven equality, diversity, representation, and inclusion but often without a material commitment to substantive and long-term change or to reckoning with the implications of the past (see further, Andreotti et al. 2015).

While these approaches can be well-meaning, they are often unable or unwilling to adequately speak to or 'sit-with' the umbilical relationship between race and law. They do not, in other words, seek to challenge in any fundamental or profound way the status quo. They rely on the presumption that people from marginalised communities are merely seeking to be included in the mainstream. Therefore, there is no attempt to unsettle the mainstream. As we hurtle towards the logical conclusion of this particular stage of capitalism, the paucity of strategies that prioritise diversity initiatives based on a crude form of identity politics becomes quickly apparent. In 2023 Britain, a Tory front bench including several prominent politicians of colour continue to enact oppressive and covertly, if not overtly, discriminatory policies disproportionately targeting those racialised as non-white. 'Soft-reform decolonisation', as Andreotti et al. (2015) call it, does not open up space, for example, for institutional divestment from unjust proceeds from racialised enslavement and dispossessive colonisation or seek to repair the harm caused by these.

Turning away from this soft-reform space of shallow decolonisation is especially significant in the context in which we teach, where the legacy of British imperialism is both urgently present and conspicuously absent. This is especially significant to us teaching in Bristol, which used to be a key port engaging in the triangle trade in kidnapped and enslaved Africans. Bristol ships were responsible for transporting at least one-fifth of the total Africans stolen from Africa and forced into cruel enslavement and dehumanisation (Otele 2012: 156). The entire enterprise, followed by the colonisation of most of the world by Euro-modern empires, required the complicity of Euro-modern legal architecture (Adébísí 2023: 38–64). These entanglements continue to have a profound effect on not just the social realities of racialised, colonised, and indigenous peoples but also on the nature of the law we teach and research, as well as the environmental, political, and economic conditions of the planet.

It was important to us that we engaged with the ways in which our discipline underwrote, legitimised, and reproduced harm in both overlapping periods of racialised enslavement and extractive colonisation. Thus, the design of the unit is quite keenly concerned with how the standard methods and concepts of legal knowledge may contribute to producing/reproducing the harms of the imperial project. To avoid a situation where we used our discipline to absolve itself, we relied on scholarly work from a broad range of disciplines outside of law and a wide range of jurisdictions beyond the UK. These include but are not limited to Tuck and Yang's (2012) thesis on the metaphorisation of decolonisation in higher education, writings on the global systemisation of racism as a politics from scholars such as Charles Mills (2014) and Grosfoguel (2016: 9–15; Grosfoguel et al. 2016), and writings on the effect on this systemisation on knowledge in higher education from scholars such as Bhambra and colleagues (Bhambra et al. 2018) and Maldonado-Torres (2007). These scholars invite us to first understand the ways in which our personal and intellectual commitments are thoroughly and completely infused by racist and colonial ideologies and challenge us to do the difficult work to undo or abandon these commitments. To do this, we and our students are called to unsettle our view of law's rationality and benevolence by resituating within our imaginary its role in shaping the modern colonial world.

As part of the process of epistemic decolonisation that this resituating of law involves, we include as many silenced, obscured, and denigrated legal epistemologies that can fit into the space we have. We also, within that same limitation, begin to (re)examine legal history to enable our students to understand why some legal epistemologies have been coded as natural and inevitable and left outside of history, while others are reduced to myth. For example, we examine how legal devices were needed to underwrite racial categorisation for enslavement and colonial dispossession. This allows us to, *inter alia*, unseat our inherited assumptions about legal knowledge and what it means to do justice for the present and the future. As the very meaning of 'race', 'racism', and even the colonial condition are all evolving, it is important to us to be flexible in what and how we teach, and to help our students to both learn and unlearn through the unit. To do this, relying on Rutazibwa, we focus on three main frames of knowledge (2018: 158–180). First, we place emphasis on what the discipline actually is, looking at it through the eyes of a global history of evolving modalities and ideologies of racialisation. Second, we consider various sources of knowledge about the discipline as well as counter knowledges – therefore, the unit is very interdisciplinary. In addition to this, we make use of non-traditional knowledge sources like poems, short stories, movies, documentaries, YouTube videos, and television programmes. Finally, through a series of specific case studies, we examine some ways in which change has been attempted or may be able to happen to move the world away from current cycles that produce racial harm.

How we teach 'Law and Race'

As designers of the unit, we had several goals, not all of which sat naturally with one another. Primarily, we needed to find a way to achieve the aim of the unit, that is, a critical exploration of how the law has impacted upon, caused, and reproduced racial disparities, and how these disparities are embedded within and reproduced by the operation of law. We also had to fit this within the pre-existing teaching structure prescribed by our law school – and later the structure developed to account for the effects of the global pandemic on teaching. In addition to this, we knew that we had to curate a limited body of scholarship about law and the British Empire, as well as find a way to convey difficult material in the classroom, most of which our students would have never encountered before, and much of which was outside the discipline. Our presumption was that most students would not be well versed in the imperial project and its operation, due to the absence of these types of discussions in the British school curriculum and in the law curriculum they would have encountered up until this point. We also had to consider the needs of our students, which would be varied depending on their personal and family background and story. Our ability to adequately account for our students' needs, as well as ensuring trust in the process, was helped by co-production with students as a method of unit design (Memon and Jivraj 2020: 475–488). Before we decided what should go into the design of the unit, we had a meeting with about five of our racialised students in the Law School, including Kose Bamugemereire and Oluwaseun Matiluko, mentioned above. This meeting helped us gauge their interest in introducing the unit – the interest was exceptionally high! The meeting also gave us a good idea about what they thought was missing from the curriculum and topics that they would find engaging to learn. We took the lead on developing the material and gave our students the opportunity to comment on the draft outline. We strongly believe that co-production of teaching with students does not grant us licence to abandon our own pedagogical responsibility and burden students with the unpaid labour of developing teaching material. We checked in with these students constantly during the pilot year. This process gave us adequate guidance as to what we needed to revise for the following year. We continue to use the formalised unit evaluation survey, as well as informal mechanisms, to provide us with feedback to continually update the unit.

The unit initially consisted of ten 1-hour lectures and ten 2-hour seminars. However, due to the effects of the global pandemic, all teaching in the law school was redesigned. The unit now consists of a mix of lectures, pre-recorded videos, seven 2-hour interactive seminars, and about twelve 1-hour lectures. Across the unit we cover various topics, starting with an examination of the history of the British Empire with a focus on how the relationship between law and race develops to the present day. We also examine a variety of theoretical frameworks of most relevance to our jurisdiction's discourse of law and race, for example: indigenous philosophies from Africa, Oceania, and the Americas; postcolonial theory; the Black radical tradition; and critical race theory, among others. Our focus here is to enable students to critically conceptualise and analyse the processes and outcomes of the British Empire and to appreciate the central role that law played historically as well as its continuation in the present. Equipped with these frameworks for understanding, we then examine and critique the traditional account of legal method and knowledge and unpack their limitations for addressing racial injustice. We examine law and literature as a response to these limitations but also to help us uncover the partial and selective stories law tells about itself. We then trace law's ontology using the theories and methods previously explored to examine the production/reproduction of race within case law and legislation. This includes a critical reflection on the nature of resistance and the role that law may or may not have in that process. We end with a discussion of decolonisation as a world-making strategy (Adébísí 2023: 148–157). Placing a discussion of decolonisation at the end of the unit allows us to pre-empt superficial engagement with decolonisation as a tool of diversity and allows us to dive deep into the possibilities it presents for re-imagining the law, in the context of the foregoing year-long discussion.

The decolonial and antiracist approaches that we adopt in our teaching require the reconstruction of knowledge scattered across manufactured disciplinary boundaries, as well as across our understanding of demarcated time and space (Bhambra 2014; Gordon 2014). This informs our use of interdisciplinarity in our seminars, as we adopt philosophical, sociological, literary, and historical analyses to explore and elucidate, in particular, the relationship between law and race. As such we teach using a variety of methods and mediums, including videos, literary critique, poetry, fiction, and non-fiction work. For example, we ask students to read a chapter from Octavia Butler's novel *Kindred* (1979). The objective is to get students to consider how law creates the conditions under which people who are differently racialised may experience time in different ways. We also use popular culture as a scaffolding technique to break down difficult academic principles and historical-legal processes. For example, students are invited to read an article which explains a complex and dense essay by Gayatri Spivak, 'Can the subaltern Speak?' (1988) through the Netflix series *Bridgerton* (Adébísí 2022: webpage). For us, using decolonial and antiracist pedagogy in this way ensures that student learning is not only inclusive and supportive but also deeply critical and rigorous as it gives them a clearer view of the world (Blake 2022: webpage). Furthermore, the variety of teaching methods and materials helps students in this process and facilitates active learning (Dewey 1997; Havelock 2013). Therefore, it is important to us that we ensure that there is a fundamental link and loop between learning objectives, learning activities, and assessment – centring students and inviting them to construct their own meaning in relationship with all aspects of the unit (Biggs and Tang 2010). To this end, the first lecture is dedicated to explaining to the students how the structure of the unit maps onto the learning outcomes so they might orientate themselves.

At the end of study on the unit, we expect that our students are able to demonstrate an understanding of how race and law are social products and how law enables the reproduction of racial hierarchy and its social outcomes. We also expect that our students should be able to articulate how racialisation produces and reproduces longstanding patterns of power, which continue to operate within the discipline. We especially want them to be able to appreciate and engage with the substantive role of law and legal institutions in enabling and supporting British imperial practices, especially as regards evolving processes and effects of racialisation that carry into the present. These can be evidenced by the plethora of racial disparities in employment, education, immigration, access to justice, policing, etc. It is also important that students can critically evaluate the paradoxical role of law and legal institutions in supporting and enabling racist practices whilst also being a site of antiracist praxis. Therefore, the tension in the law being both a tool for liberation and subjugation is fundamental to the unit.

As assessment for the unit, and to demonstrate the learning outcomes, students are expected to write a 3,000-word essay, that shows evidence of good research skills, knowledge, and comprehension of the unit, as well as good use of argumentation skills. The essay is written in response to three or four broad question sets that cut across the whole unit.

Feedback, reflections, and limitations

Feedback we have received from students on 'Law and Race' has been overwhelmingly positive. A student noted on Twitter, for example, how the 'atmosphere of the classroom was conducive to openness and vulnerability [which made it] really easy to talk about race and white supremacy'. We received the following email from another student to tell us how much they had enjoyed their reading that week:

> Having studied effectively [two] years of jurisprudential-focused modules … I particularly loved the Mills and Bouie readings. These readings helped me realise that so much of what I have been taught in my legal theory studies thus far, has essentially been, as the Bouie reading put it, 'hagiography to truth!' These readings in particular have really distorted - or corrected – that for me, and for that, I am so pleased. I am also now so interested to delve further into the paradox of the enlightenment, that I have seldom been taught! All in all, I feel as though I have gained a great deal already from just this week's required readings and I am really looking forward to the rest of the year studying this unit![2]

Notwithstanding this positive feedback, students also noted that they wanted *more*; more substance and more time to read and discuss. They continue to tell us that they wish that 'Law and Race' comes earlier in their degrees.

One of the key limitations we faced in designing and curating this unit is the fact that there is so little educational material available in our jurisdiction that focuses on the relationship between law and race. There are obviously pockets of scholarship in which this important work is being done (e.g. the relatively large body of work on race and criminal justice), but 'race and law' is not an area in which many scholars are researching and producing a large archive of work in the UK in the same way that there is in 'gender and law', for example. This required us to think carefully about how we would situate and help students with the interdisciplinary material we taught, as well as requiring us to borrow and adapt material from outside our jurisdiction, while trying to avoid overfocusing on the United States. Since we started 'Law and Race' in 2017, the movement to decolonise the curriculum has more concertedly penetrated some law schools in the UK, and several leading scholars have begun developing material and resources that address this gap as well and indicating areas for further work (Jivraj 2020; Adébísí 2023).

Another very real limitation to our unit and to critical pedagogy more broadly is the site in which it takes place. We are constrained by the context in which we work and the reality that is often ignored that universities are the sites, not only of commodification of education and its attendant deteriorating labour conditions but also of continuing racial violence (Arday and Mirza 2018; Wong et al. 2021; Ahmet 2020). In recognising this reality, we were careful to foster an environment in the classroom in which we agreed together the terms of the discussion as inclusive and respectful as a way to setting the right 'emotional climate' in which those conversations could take place (Wilson and Taylor 2001). It is traumatic and can be triggering for students to learn and think about the unceasing violence of racism, many of whom will themselves be facing that ongoing violence both inside and outside the institution. We have to be open and honest about facing what will be discomforting and difficult conversations for some, and traumatic for others, and of being able to provide the support necessary to students who need it.

One of our more ambitious aims with 'Law and Race' was to influence a broader decolonial reckoning with, in particular, the core of the law degree. While we generally had a lot of support for our work at Bristol, we did come across several instances of 'white fragility' while making the case initially for 'Law and Race' (DiAngelo 2018). While colleagues may be theoretically supportive of a unit that can be confined to an option for final-year students, a tone shift can come quite quickly when talk of decolonisation gets too close to their own unit, course, or module. Vigorous 'gatekeeping', therefore, can interact with and mobilise broader power structures that have an interest in maintaining the status quo. Notwithstanding these points, we think it is important to see a unit like 'Law and Race' as one strategy among many in which radical change is sought, in both the curriculum and towards social justice more broadly, and to take a 'long view' of the process of seeking that change as well as of measuring the indicia of progress. To this end, we took the view that one should not waste too much time with those who are unwilling to engage in a good faith dialogue about decolonial praxis, and rather one should work towards building a network of colleagues and allies with a view to empowering one another.

It is certainly true that a final-year optional unit like 'Law and Race' could languish in its own corner and have limited impact as a decolonial tool in the face of the broader curriculum that is so thoroughly in thrall to the colonial trappings of legal doctrine and discourse. However, our experience of teaching 'Law and Race' made us feel more optimistic about its potential. It took years of work for us to put together our teaching materials and to collaborate, pilot, and revise this unit, in an ongoing collaborative process with our students and reflecting on what works and does not. The knowledge and experience we have gained allow us to help other colleagues who want to shift their own practice and pedagogy, as well as having an archive of teaching materials that we can share. The high profile of this unit and the many invitations we receive to talk about 'Law and Race' showed us that there is an appetite and drive for decolonisation in the law curriculum which we can work towards together. These outcomes then are not fixed to our unit as a final-year option. The conversations we have and the archive of material and experience we have developed can and have spread throughout the law degree more broadly.

Conclusion

For those looking to 'decolonise their own curriculum', we have some powerful tools at our disposal. Working with and being allied to students was very important to the success of 'Law and Race'. In the neoliberal university, students possess an important power to make demands of university management and school leaders that staff may not. Harnessing that collaborative power can be very important, particularly so where we can mobilise the 'diversity and inclusion' rhetoric that is so common to neoliberal institutions nowadays to buttress our calls for change. We have noted the paucity of research in this area, while this is improving, we recognise that current moves to 'decolonise' need to be backed up with more research. This is particularly important as many law schools present themselves as engaging in teaching that is connected in some integral way with research, for example, 'research-led teaching'. However, our experience in designing 'Law and Race' makes it clear that effective decolonial and antiracist approaches in teaching can only happen on the back of in-depth, rigorous, and honest research that evidences a commitment to decolonisation in more than name only. Ultimately troubling the canon means giving ourselves and our students space to dream of new anticolonial worlds from within the law school – a world very different from this one, where we are all supported and empowered to move, breathe, and thrive.

Notes

1 'Law and Race' was taught for the first time in the 2018/2019 academic year.
2 The readings being referred to here are Mills 2014 and Bouie 2018.

References

Adébísí, Folúkẹ i. *Decolonisation and Legal Knowledge: Reflections on Power and Possibility*. Bristol University Press, 2023.
Adébísí, Folúkẹ i. 'Romance Is Not Our Way out of Hell: Of #Bridgerton, Representation & Imagining a World Beyond' | Foluke's African Skies' 2022. https://folukeafrica.com/romance-is-not-our-way-out-of-hell-of-bridgerton-representation-imagining-a-world-beyond/ [accessed 12 January 2023].
Ahmet, Akile. 'Who is worthy of a place on these walls? Postgraduate students, UK universities, and institutional racism.' *Area* 52, no. 4 (2020): 678–686.
Andreotti, Vanessa de Oliveira, Sharon Stein, Cash Ahenakew, and Dallas Hunt. 'Mapping Interpretations of Decolonization in the Context of Higher Education'. *Decolonization: Indigeneity, Education & Society* 4, no. 1 (2015).
Arday, Jason, and Heidi Safia Mirza, eds. *Dismantling race in higher education: Racism, whiteness and decolonising the academy*. Palgrave Macmillan, 2018.
Bhambra, Gurminder K. *Connected sociologies*. Bloomsbury Publishing, 2014.
Bhambra, Gurminder K., Dalia Gebrial, and Kerem Nişancıoğlu. *Decolonising the university*. Pluto Press, 2018.
Biggs, John, and Catherine Tang. 'Applying constructive alignment to outcomes-based teaching and learning.' In *Training material for "quality teaching for learning in higher education" workshop for master trainers*, Ministry of Higher Education, Kuala Lumpur, pp. 23–25. 2010.
Bouie, Jamelle. 'The Enlightenment's Dark Side'. *Slate*, 5 June 2018. https://slate.com/news-and-politics/2018/06/taking-the-enlightenment-seriously-requires-talking-about-race.html
Bryson, Colin. 'Engagement through Partnership: Students as Partners in Learning and Teaching in Higher Education'. *International Journal for Academic Development* 21, no. 1 (2016): 84–86.
Butler, Octavia E. *Kindred*. Doubleday, 1979.
Crenshaw, Kimberlé Williams. 'Toward a race-conscious pedagogy in legal education.' *National Black Law Journal* 11 (1988): 1–14.
Dewey, John. *How We Think*. Courier Corporation, 1997.
DiAngelo, Robyn. *White Fragility: Why It's So Hard for White People to Talk About Racism*. Penguin, 2018.
Goldberg, David T. *The Racial State*. Blackwell, 2002.
Gordon, Lewis R. 'Disciplinary Decadence and the Decolonisation of Knowledge' *Africa Development* 39, no. 1 (2014): 81–92.
Grosfoguel, Ramon. 'What is Racism?' *Journal of World-Systems Research* 22, no. 1 (2016): 9–15.
Grosfoguel, Ramon, Roberto Hernández, and Ernesto Rosen Velásquez, *Decolonizing the Westernized University: Interventions in Philosophy of Education from Within and Without* (Lexington Books, 2016).
Havelock, Rohan. 'Law studies and active learning: friends not foes?' *The Law Teacher* 47, no. 3 (2013): 382–403.

hooks, bell. *Teaching To Transgress*. Routledge, 2014.
Jivraj, Suhraiya. 'Towards Anti-racist Legal pedagogy: A resource.' University of Kent, 2020. doi: 10.22024/UniKent/01.02.82763
Lentin, Alana, 'Against Representation: Alana Lentin on Antoinette Lattouf' *Sydney Review of Books*. July 2022 https://sydneyreviewofbooks.com/review/lattouf-how-to-lose-friends-and-influence-white-people/
Maldonado-Torres, Nelson. 'On the Coloniality of Being', *Cultural Studies* 21, no. 2–3 (2007): 240–270.
Mills, Charles W. *The Racial Contract*. Cornell University Press, 2014.
Otele, Olivette. 'Bristol, Slavery and the Politics of Representation: The Slave Trade Gallery in the Bristol Museum'. *Social Semiotics* 22, no. 2 (2012): 155–172.
Memon, Ahmed R. and Suhraiya Jivraj. 'Trust, Courage and Silence: Carving out Decolonial Spaces in Higher Education through Student–Staff Partnerships'. *The Law Teacher* 54, no. 4 (2020): 475–488.
Rawley, James A., and Stephen D. Behrendt. *The Transatlantic Slave Trade: A History*. University of Nebraska Press, 2005.
Rutazibwa, Olivia U. 'On Babies and Bathwater: Decolonizing International Development Studies.' In Jong, Sara de, Rosalba Icaza, and Olivia U. Rutazibwa, (eds.) *Decolonization and Feminisms in Global Teaching and Learning*. 158–180. Routledge, 2018.
Spivak, Gayatri. 'Can the Subaltern Speak?' in Cary Nelson and Lawrence Grossberg (eds) *Marxism and the Interpretation of Culture*. 271–313. Macmillan, 1988.
Tuck, Eve, and K. Wayne Yang. 'Decolonization Is Not a Metaphor'. *Decolonization: Indigeneity, Education & Society* 1, no. 1 (2012). https://jps.library.utoronto.ca/index.php/des/article/view/18630
Waretini-Karena, Rawiri. 'Colonial Law, Dominant Discourses, and Intergenerational Trauma.' In: Deckert, Antje and Rick Sarre, (eds) *The Palgrave Handbook of Australian and New Zealand Criminology, Crime and Justice*. 697–709. Palgrave Macmillan, 2017.
Williams, Patricia J. *The Alchemy of Race and Rights*. Harvard University Press, 1991.
Wilson, Janie and Kelli Taylor. 'Professor immediacy as behaviors associated with liking students.' *Teaching of Psychology* 28 (2001): 136–138.
Wong, Billy, Reham Elmorally, Meggie Copsey-Blake, Ellie Highwood, and Joy Singarayer. 'Is race still relevant? Student perceptions and experiences of racism in higher education.' *Cambridge Journal of Education* 51, no. 3 (2021): 359–375.

INDEX

Pages in *italics* refer to figures, pages in **bold** refer to tables, and pages followed by "n" refer to notes.

For Product Safety Concerns and Information please contact our EU representative GPSR@taylorandfrancis.com
Taylor & Francis Verlag GmbH, Kaufingerstraße 24, 80331 München, Germany

www.ingramcontent.com/pod-product-compliance
Ingram Content Group UK Ltd.
Pitfield, Milton Keynes, MK11 3LW, UK
UKHW020151200926
475702UK00016B/2655
* 9 7 8 1 0 3 2 4 9 8 2 4 9 *